D1613555

# Current Topics in Human Intelligence

## Volume 1

### *Research Methodology*

# List of Contributors

Numbers in parentheses indicate the pages on which the authors' contributions begin.

Donna M. Bryant, Frank Porter Graham Child Development Center, University of North Carolina at Chapel Hill, Highway 54 Bypass West 071A, Chapel Hill, North Carolina 27514 (247)

Earl C. Butterfield, Office of Cognitive Studies, University of Washington, 322 Miller Hall DQ-12, Seattle, Washington 98195 (202)

John B. Carroll, Psychometrics Laboratory, Department of Psychology, University of North Carolina at Chapel Hill, Chapel Hill, North Carolina 27514 (25)

Jean P. Chapman, Department of Psychology, University of Wisconsin, 1202 West Johnson, Madison, Wisconsin 53706 (141)

Loren J. Chapman, Department of Psychology, 1202 West Johnson, Madison, Wisconsin 53706 (141)

Susan Embretson (Whitely), Department of Psychology, The University of Kansas, 426 Fraser Hall, Lawrence, Kansas 66045 (98)

Joseph F. Fagan III, Department of Psychology, Case Western Reserve University, Cleveland, Ohio 44106 (223)

Christopher Hertzog, Human Development, S-110, The Pennsylvania State University, University Park, Pennsylvania 16802 (59)

Lloyd G. Humphreys, Department of Psychology, University of Illinois at Urbana-Champaign, 603 East Daniel Street, Champaign, Illinois 61820 (3)

Earl Hunt, Department of Psychology, The University of Washington, Seattle, Washington 98195 (157)

Robert Plomin, Institute for Behavioral Genetics, University of Colorado, Box 447, Boulder, Colorado 80309 (297)

Craig T. Ramey, Frank Porter Graham Child Development Center, University of North Carolina at Chapel Hill, Highway 54 Bypass West 071A, Chapel Hill, North Carolina 27514 (247)

Robert J. Sternberg, Department of Psychology, Yale University, Box 11A Yale Station, New Haven, Connecticut 06520 (179)

Tanya M. Suarez, Frank Porter Graham Child Development Center, University of North Carolina at Chapel Hill, Highway 54 Bypass West 071A, Chapel Hill, North Carolina 27514 (247)

# Current Topics
## in
# Human Intelligence
## Volume 1
## Research Methodology

Editor

# Douglas K. Detterman
## Case Western Reserve University

**Ablex Publishing Corporation**
**Norwood, New Jersey**

Printed in the United States of America.

ISBN: 0-89391-173-9

ISSN: 8755-0040

Ablex Publishing Corporation
355 Chestnut Street
Norwood, New Jersey 07648

# Contents

## Section II: Research Approaches

## Current Topics in Human Intelligence
### Foreword to the Series

## Douglas K. Detterman, Editor

The purpose of this series is to focus on single issues of importance to the study of human intelligence. Unlike many edited volumes, this one is designed to be thematic. Each volume will present a detailed examination of some question relevant to human intelligence and, more generally, individual differences.

The reason for beginning this series is that a forum is needed for extensive discussions of pertinent questions. No such forum currently exists. A journal does not allow an author sufficient space or latitude to present fully elaborated ideas. Currently existing edited series are not thematic but, instead, offer researchers an opportunity to present an integrative summary of their own work. Both journals and edited, nonthematic monographs are essential to the advancement of the study of human intelligence. But they do not allow collective intelligence to be brought to bear on a single issue of importance.

Why is it important to examine specific issues in detail? The answer to this question depends on an appreciation of the historical development of the study of human intelligence. For at least 40 years, and perhaps longer, the study of human intelligence has been less than highly regarded as an academic pursuit. The reasons for this attitude are many and have been discussed elsewhere. Despite the reasons, the lack of academic sanction for the study of individual differences in human intelligence has produced a discipline without a unifying paradigm. When researchers study human intelligence, it is almost always from the perspective of training in a related, but different, discipline. Disciplines which have "sacrificed" researchers to human intelligence include: cognitive, developmental, and educational psychology, behavior genetics, psychometrics, mental retardation, neuropsychology, and even experimental psychology. Each of these researchers has brought a different set of assumptions and methods to the study of human intelligence.

That so many different points of view have been applied to a single subject area has, in my opinion, brought vitality to the endeavor, a vitality currently lacking in so many areas of the social sciences. But this vitality does not arise from the isolation and fractionation which can be the result of different points of view. On the contrary, it results from the juxtaposition of these different points of view, a juxtapositioning which has occurred with increasing frequency over the last 10 years.

Therefore, it is the purpose of this series to bring different points of view together on issues of importance to understanding human intelligence. The hope is that, at the very least, researchers will find more reason to give their primary allegiance to the study of human intelligence and, at the most, the series will contribute to the emergence of a unifying paradigm.

# Foreword to Volume 1:
# Research Methodology

The first volume in this series focuses on research methodology in the study of human intelligence. Research methodology seems particularly appropriate as a topic for the first volume. Although research methods suited to studying individual differences have received sporadic attention, there is no single source surveying the variety of statistical techniques used to study human intelligence and the variety of problems that are encountered in applying these techniques to specific, topical questions about human intelligence. This volume attempts to provide such a source.

Methods used in individual differences research, including human intelligence, are, without question, different from those used by nomothetic researchers. The aim of each kind of research is different, so it is not surprising that the methods used differ. In nomothetic research interest is in finding variables which affect group means, while in individual differences, or idiographic, research the purpose is to find variables which alter an individual's rank within the distribution. Nomothetic researchers quite obviously employ tests of differences between means while idiographic researchers use correlational techniques. Despite repeated calls for uniting these two approaches, they remain quite distinct enterprises.

There should be little question concerning the desirability of understanding individual differences in human populations. If there is one thing that makes humans a unique species, it is the wide variability in roles that are filled by individual members of the species. Understanding these differences is at least as important as understanding how all humans are alike.

Currently, nomothetic research techniques constitute the central corpus of "acceptable" methodology in psychology. Graduate education in research methods consists almost exclusively of presentation of nomothetic approaches.

Idiographic methods are given inadequate treatment, if mentioned at all. The degree of neglect suffered by individual differences methodology is apparent in the myths which have been learned and subsequently taught by otherwise well-trained researchers. Major among these myths is the obviously preposterous idea that correlation does not imply causation. This idea is superficially true. No statistic implies causation. The imputation of causation is an inferential process quite independent of the statistic employed. But this myth makes the more pernicious suggestion that research using correlation cannot establish causal relationships and, therefore, cannot be real science. If this were true, astronomy, a completely "correlational" science, would be in big trouble.

Besides providing an overview of research methods in human intelligence, it is hoped that this book will make a beginning at redressing the imbalance which currently exists between nomothetic and individual differences research methods. I believe that anyone who reads this book will be forced to conclude that doing individual differences research requires mastery of a set of techniques every bit as complex and powerful as those used in nomothetic research, but quite different from them. The book is divided into two parts. The first part presents statistical methods used frequently in individual differences research, while the second part is devoted to the methodological problems that arise within specific problem areas.

Chapters in the first section of the volume cover correlation (Humphreys), exploratory factor analysis (Carroll), confirmatory factor analysis (Hertzog), test theory models (Embretson), and problems with two-groups comparisons (Chapman and Chapman). Much of the material which is systematically presented here does not, unfortunately, appear in standard books on research methods. These chapters would be an excellent starting place for anyone wanting a sophisticated introduction to individual differences research methods. In fact, the material in these chapters applies equally well to nearly any area of individual differences research and is not limited to the study of human intelligence.

Chapters in the second section of the book survey research methods applied to the study of human intelligence within specific problem areas. These chapters include reviews of the empirical and theoretical foundations of the problem areas and the methodological approaches taken within each. Research methodology always becomes more complicted when data and theory become involved. Chapters in this section include the correlates approach (Hunt), componential analysis (Sternberg), instructional approaches (Butterfield), infancy (Fagan), intervention (Ramey), and behavioral genetics (Plomin). These chapters are a representative, though not exhaustive, sample of research approaches which have been used to attempt to understand human intelligence.

*Douglas K. Detterman*

# *STATISTICAL METHODS*

# CHAPTER 1

# Correlations in Psychological Research

*Lloyd G. Humphreys*

*University of Illinois, Urbana-Champaign*

## INTRODUCTION

**Centrality of Correlation.** An aim common to all empirical research is to establish relationships or correlations between variables. A difference between means of a dependent variable for groups distinguished by a difference in experimental treatments is as much a correlation, in the most general meaning of that term, as a product–moment correlation between two distributions of test scores. Unfortunately, one type of research is customarily called experimental and another type correlational. This terminology is unfortunate for several reasons. It has led to an overemphasis on simple hypothesis testing and to a preference among experimental psychologists to describe their relationships by $t$-ratios, $F$-ratios, and chi-squares only. These statistics of sampling stability are confounded by sample size. Most research requires in addition descriptions of the size of relationships by statistics that are independent of sample size.

The rejection of correlations as descriptive statistics for the relationship between an independent and a dependent variable has also been supported by over simplified interpretations of correlations. Every psychologist knows that a very large correlation (.866) is required to reduce the standard error of estimate, or the coefficient of alienation, to 50% of the standard deviation of the distribution of raw or standard scores, respectively, on the measure being estimated, but this interpretation is incomplete and, standing alone, highly misleading. The confusing terminology is responsible as well for inadequate experimental designs and incorrect analyses of data in studies in which some element of experimental control is lacking.

This is not to say that there are not real and important differences among the ways of obtaining correlations. Some are obtained under conditions of

3

experimental control. Others are obtained between variables in the absence of experimental control. *Experimental analyses* and *post hoc analyses* might be more suitable terms to describe the differences. And, of course, there are intermediate examples in which there is experimental control in certain aspects of the research, but important aspects are missing.

## Dimensions of Differences in Experimental Control

Following Underwood's analysis (1957) an experiment involves control and systematic variation of environmental, task, and subject variables. Variables likely to influence the dependent variable and not the focus of the research are controlled as environmental and task variables are systematically varied. The environmental and task variables are properly called "independent" because they can be manipulated by the experimenter. These independent variables are correlated with one or more dependent variables. The latter are evaluated in terms of reliability and of validity with respect to the hypothesis being tested.

Subject variables or individual differences are controlled by random assignment of the units of sampling, whether individuals, groups, or institutions, at random to the levels of environmental and task variables. Additional control of individual differences can be obtained by the use of covariates that are also reliable and valid. Subject variables cannot be true independent variables because they cannot be systematically and independently varied by the experimenter. It is not possible to assign subjects at random to treatments when the "treatments" are differences in sex, intelligence, manifest anxiety, etc. Furthermore, it is not possible to hold one subject variable constant or to systematically vary a subject variable without affecting all other subject variables with which the variable in question is correlated. The nonzero correlations among subject variables insure that groups separated on one, such as high and low intelligence, will also differ on every measure correlated with intelligence. When one subject variable is held constant, the variances of all measures correlated with it are reduced. Subject variables, whether covariates or dependent variables, are measures of individual differences. Treating them as if they were independent typically leads to inferior research designs and to misinterpretations of the data. Individual differences can be studied by experiment only when the independent variables are in the environmental or task categories.

The purest example of the absence of experimental control is a study of three or more measures obtained at the same point in time. It is not possible under these circumstances to distinguish independent and dependent variables and covariates. Sometimes by theory, sometimes by values or biases, an investigator assigns these designations to the measures available, but there are no objective operations that allow this. In certain post hoc research one variable may follow others in time. In a limited sense the later variable may be considered dependent, but a term like criterion carries less connotation of experimental control. If subject variables or covariates were consistently used for all measures of individual differences, whether they are found in experimental analyses or post hoc analyses, there would be less sloppy thinking about cause and effect in research outcomes.

Research at times may have all of the characteristics of an experiment except for one critical dimension. Objective, reliable measurement of the dependent variable and control of environmental and task variables does not constitute an experiment unless there has been random assignment of the units of sampling to treatments. If existing groups are assigned to different treatments, for example, one classroom to one level, a second classroom to a second level, the generic partial correlation methodology is an inadequate control of existing differences between the two groups. Completely adequate control requires that a covariate be measured without error and have a correlation of unity with true scores of the dependent variable within treatment groups. In the analysis of covariance, a partial correlation technique, independent and dependent variables can be designated without ambiguity, but the size of their correlation cannot be interpreted unambiguously in the absence of random assignment to treatments.

As the reliability and validity of the covariate increase, correcting for the inadequate control becomes less hazardous. A careful experimentalist who knows a good deal about his dependent variables and covariates psychometrically can still obtain useful results without initial random assignment. With inadequate covariates or none at all, however, the experimenter's control of independent variables provides little advantage over the analysis of experimentally uncontrolled measures. Partial experimental control frequently increases errors in interpretation of the data.

# THE BASIS FOR CORRELATIONS
# IN EXPERIMENTATION[1]

## Limitations of Hypothesis Testing

Most psychologists in their research, and most editors in evaluating that research, act as if a probability statement represents the culmination of the research enterprise. A conclusion that a mean difference or a correlation could occur less than 5 times in 100 as a sampling fluctuation from a population value of zero satisfies everyone concerned. Unfortunately, this information is rarely satisfying scientifically. It merely tells one that a modest degree of confidence can be placed in the *sign* of a relationship. Psychologists should instead be concerned with more precise measures of relationships. Sampling stability is important but insufficient. The accuracy with which dependent variables can be estimated from independent variables, described by a correlation, or the amount of change in the dependent variable that follows from a unit of change in the independent

---

[1] This section and a substantial part of following sections appeared in an unpublished manuscript of the author that was privately circulated in 1977.

variable, described by a regression weight, is the important finding for the advancement of the science.

The common null hypothesis is highly artificial. There are almost certainly no zero differences or correlations in nature. A perfectly controlled ESP experiment should produce a zero difference between experimental manipulations, but in stating this I assume that ESP is not a natural phenomenon *and* that perfect control is possible. Any degree of systematic error in combination with a large enough number of observations will produce a statistically significant difference. This principle holds for all natural phenomena: Inability to reject the null hypothesis in a well controlled experiment is due solely to lack of power in the experiment. Only the sign of the difference or correlation is unknown at the outset of the research when the aim is to do ordinary hypothesis testing. An interest in degree of relationship, however, provides for a much wider range of outcomes.

Simplistic hypothesis testing leads to little scientific advance when the findings are interpreted properly. Frequent misinterpretations of the tests conducted, on the other hand, have set back the science. After rejecting the null hypothesis, many experimenters interpret the relationship between the independent and dependent variables as if the correlation between the two were unity. This misinterpretation may stem from connotations concerning the meaning of "error" in the analysis of variance. When one finds evidence for the sampling stability of a difference in means of the dependent variable as a function of experimental treatments and when the only other component of variance is "error," the conclusion that the "real" correlation between the independent and the dependent variable is unity has a certain logic. Unfortunately, error in the analysis of variance is a very ambiguous concept. The error term in most analyses contains a very large component of the variance of true scores of the dependent variable of the subjects in the experiment. In a well designed and well controlled experiment the contribution of random measurement error may indeed be quite small, but the experimental treatments may make only a small contribution to the systematic, nonerror variance. Since the function of the experimental manipulation is to modify behavior, its effect should be discussed in terms of the degree to which modification has occurred. High confidence in the sign of an effect cannot be translated into a correlation of unity between independent and dependent variables.

Inability to reject the null hypothesis, on the other hand, is frequently discussed as if the correlation between independent and dependent variables were zero. This is a particularly flagrant abuse both of statistical logic and of the nature of psychological phenomena. Inability to reject the null hypothesis in any sample cannot logically be reinterpreted as acceptance of that hypothesis. There is, in addition, the consideration that there are no zero differences in nature. One can, however, redefine the problem in terms of degree of relationship and demonstrate that a difference or correlation is for all practical purposes zero. Potential differences or correlations can be categorized at the outset of the experiment as trivial or nontrivial in size. If the outcome in the sample is in the trivial region and if the confidence limits of the sample statistic also fall *entirely* within the trivial region, one is justified in concluding that the relationship between the independent and dependent variables is essentially zero. The requirement that the entire confidence interval fall within the trivial region requires small standard errors for sample statistics. Small standard errors can be obtained by use of large $N$ and effective covariates.

**Meehl's Paradox.** The fixation on hypothesis testing in psychology is responsible for Meehl's paradox (1967) while the alternative of predicting the degree of relationship is at least one solution to the paradox. Meehl pointed out that, as theory advances, disconfirmation of an hypothesis becomes easier in physics but more difficult in psychology. If an hypothesis predicts only the sign of a relationship, such predictions become more obvious as knowledge advances. The only mistake an experimenter can make is to misjudge the power of the experiment needed to obtain the required level of significance. This mistake can also be reworded as an error in evaluating the size of the relationship.

The hypothesis testing paradigm can be applied in a more precise fashion than commonly found in the journals. The paradigm does not require that the statistical hypothesis be a zero difference between means or a zero correlation. Hypotheses can be substituted for the ubiquitous zero that require more precise predictions of outcomes. An obtained difference in means can be compared with a nonzero difference, and an obtained correlation can be compared with a nonzero correlation. The null hypothesis is defined as a zero difference between an observed relationship and a hypothetical relationship of whatever size.

Frequently this desirable change in hypothesis testing becomes mandatory. To conclude that one difference in means or that one correlation is different from another, for example, in a replication of previous research, the sample statistics must be compared directly with each other (Humphreys, 1980). Ability to reject a zero relationship in one sample and inability to do so in a second sample does not constitute evidence for a difference in outcomes. Failure to compare the two relationships with each other is probably the most common logical-statistical error.

Reporting research outcomes in terms of correlations narrowly defined or correlations imbedded in regression weights constitutes yet another advance in response to Meehl's paradox. Ideally, also, the correlation should be accompanied by its confidence or credibility interval. These intervals, in effect, test an infinite number of hypotheses about population parameters. As confidence intervals become smaller through use of larger samples and effective covariates, experimentalists can make more nearly point predictions from hypotheses in place of the present gross predictions associated with hypothesis testing. Hypotheses become easier to disconfirm, and confirmed hypotheses create more confidence in the theory.

## Choice of Correlations

For a continuous dependent variable and two levels of an independent variable the familiar product–moment correlation, more commonly called the point biserial correlation in this situation, is the appropriate choice. For three or more levels $\eta$ is appropriate, or after conversion to dichotomous dummy variables (Cohen & Cohen, 1975) the appropriate statistic is the linear multiple correlation of the dummy variables with the independent variable. When there are $k$ levels of treatment, $k$-$1$ dummy variables are defined. Their intercorrelations are product-moment correlations, commonly called $\phi$ coefficients. These contain all of the information in the $k$ levels. Thus the linear multiple correlation equals the nonlinear correlation for the three or more levels. Because no sample statistic can be safely interpreted for theoretical purposes without knowledge of sampling stability, $F$-ratios are used to test null hypotheses.

Alternatively, regressions can be used to achieve the same goals as the use of correlations. Regressions are especially applicable when the units of measurement of the dependent variable are equal. One can only be certain that this assumption is met with physical scales of measurement. Psychological tests basically furnish rank-order information. A linear combination of items answered correctly does not produce an interval scale of measurement. When correlations alone are reported, information about the units of measurement of the dependent variable is lost. Regressions preserve that information, but the units of measurement in psychology are so frequently arbitrary that the preservation of information in regressions may promote misinterpretation.

## Information on Size of Correlations

Correlations are attenuated by measurement error and by restriction of range of talent, but this does not set them apart from $t$- and $F$-ratios. When neither variable is measured under experimental control, the degree of relationship is attenuated by random error in each. When an independent variable is under tight experimental control, the degree of relationship obtainable is affected only by random error in the dependent variable. An experimental psychologist randomly careless in the handling of independent variables loses an important advantage. Systematic error, on the other hand, voids research of any type. Cognitive psychologists at universities such as Harvard or Stanford have more difficulty in establishing relationships than their fellows in unselective institutions when their own undergraduates serve as subjects. Corrections for attenuation and restriction of range of talent are integral parts of measurement theory and should not be associated with test theory alone.

A regression coefficient can, under certain specified circumstances, correct or more properly compensate for differences in range of talent. When the regression is linear, arrays are homoscedastic, and the restriction is directly on $X$, the regression of $Y$ on $X$ is not affected. The reliabilities and variances of $X$ and $Y$, the correlation between them, and the regression of $X$ on $Y$ are all changed by the truncation on $X$. In experimentation, however, restriction of range occurs on $Y$, the dependent variable. Furthermore, the restriction on $Y$ is rarely explicit, but arises indirectly from restriction on some third variable or set of variables. Thus the use of regressions in place of correlations does not automatically correct for restriction in range of talent for the experimentalist.

Because the experimentalist fixes the levels of treatment, the size of any relationship obtained is frequently arbitrary. This makes the prediction of size of outcome from hypothesis difficult. Standardization of the levels of frequently used independent variables, either within a laboratory or between laboratories, would be helpful. The experience of an investigator working in a particular area of research should allow reasonably accurate prediction of the degree of relationship between independent and dependent variables. It should go without saying that the accuracy has to be evaluated in the light of random sampling error present.

## COMPUTING CORRELATIONS IN EXPERIMENTATION

### Computational Strategies

One can start an analysis of experimental data with the computation of correlations followed by tests of significance or one can compute the traditional $F$-ratios of the analyses of variance and convert to correlations for descriptive purposes as the last step. For the former the requisite formulas for zero-order correlations, both linear and nonlinear, and linear partial, semipartial, and multiple correlations are those in standard text books. One needs only to code categorical variables numerically to obtain sums, sums of squares, and sums of cross-products. In order to proceed in the second way $t$ and $F$-ratios can be transformed into correlations by very simple formulas. If the design is orthogonal, it is also easy to obtain higher-order correlations. When the design is not orthogonal, traditional ANOVA computational routines should be abandoned. There is no excuse for the use of rule-of-thumb procedures for unequal $N$ in analysis of variance designs. Correlations allow an unbiased treatment of the lack of orthogonality.

The question of whether to report sample correlations or population estimates is rather easily resolved. In making more nearly point predictions of outcomes, sample size will be sufficiently large that there will be a trivial difference between the sample statistic and the population estimate. On the other hand, when the sample is small relative to the needs of the research, population estimates are required. When random sampling error is large anyway, it is doubly unfortunate to add appreciable bias. Test of significance and confidence intervals require sample statistics as do the formulas for higher-order correlations in terms of the zero-order ones.

Although the relationships between significance ratios and correlations are simple and straightforward, they are not generally known. In the presentation that follows, $X$ is an independent variable, $Y$ a dependent, and $Z$ a covariate.

Sums of squares are represented by $SS$ and mean squares by $MS$ with subscripts $b$, $e$, and $t$ for between, error, and total. The Roman $e$ represents the nonlinear sample correlation in place of the Greek $\eta$, following the convention to use Greek letters for population parameters. This is parallel to the use of $r$ for the linear correlation. Multiple correlations are $R$ and $E$. For convenience all correlations are presented in terms of $F$ and are, therefore, squared. $N$ denotes sample size, $n$ the number of independent variables and interactions, and $k$ the number of treatments for a given independent variable.

*One Independent Variable.* The product–moment correlation between the independent and dependent variables when $k = 2$ can be written as a ratio of sums of squares or in terms of $F=MS_b/MS_e$ and the degrees of freedom for error. Here, also, $t^2=F$.

$$r^2_{yx}=SS_b/SS_t=F/(df_e+F) \tag{1}$$

When $k > 2$, the parallel formulas are for the nonlinear correlation.

$$e^2_{yx}=SS_b/SS_t = (k\text{-}1)F/[df_e+(k\text{-}1)F] \tag{2}$$

If the $k$ levels of treatment have been transformed into $k$-1 dummy variables, the correlation of each of these with the dependent variable is given by Equation 1. To reproduce with the dummy variables the nonlinear relationship described in Equation 2, the multiple correlation with the dependent variable is required. The dummy variables representing a given independent variable are not orthogonal with each other. They can reproduce the information in the $k$ treatments because their intercorrelations are largely negative. Whether the relationship is described by Equation 2 or by a multiple correlation, a population estimate is more often required than for the correlation in Equation 1. The expected value of $e^2$ in random data is $(k$-1$)/(N$-1$)$. This quantity doubles when $k$ changes from 2 to 3.

*Two or More Independent Variables.* Complex orthogonal designs represent an extension, with an important difference, of the one-variable design. The zero-order correlations for independent variables and interactions can be computed from the ratios of sums of squares as in Equations 1 and 2, but not from the same combination of $F$-ratios and $df_e$. This can be understood more readily in conjunction with a second difference between simple and complex designs. Hays (1963) presented population estimates for zero-order correlations, but in complex designs these are highly arbitrary and essentially meaningless population parameters in which no one should be interested. They are arbitrary because they are confounded by the number and choice of independent variables in the design, all of which are under the control of the experimenter. The partial correlation in which all independent variables and interactions, other than the one of immediate interest, are held constant in the variance of the dependent variable is the important statistic theoretically. The primacy of the partial correlation was recognized very early by Peters and Van Voorhis (1940).

When the design is orthogonal, the partial correlation is identical with one of the two possible semipartial correlations relating a given $X$ to $Y$. (The other of these two semipartial correlations among orthogonal variables is equal to the zero-order correlation.) The partial correlations describe the size of the relationship between a given independent variable or interaction and a dependent variable in a manner not confounded by the design. The population estimate of this correlation, in contrast to the usual $\omega^2$, is frequently useful.

As long as the design is orthogonal, formulas for the partial correlations require either ratios of sums of squares or combinations of $F$-ratios and $df_e$. For simplicity $x_j$ represents the set of independent variables and interactions that are being held constant. $F$ is again $MS_b/MS_e$.

$$r^2_{yx_i \cdot x_j} = SS_b/(SS_b + SS_e) = F/(df_e + F) \tag{3}$$

$$e^2_{yx_i \cdot x_j} = SS_b/(SS_b + SS_e) = (k-1)F/[df_e + (k-1)F] \tag{4}$$

Thus it is the partial correlation, the one that ought to be computed as an estimate of the size of the relationship between independent and dependent variables, that is represented by the standard $F$-ratio in a complex ANOVA.

In the same orthogonal design squared multiple correlations are obtained by a simple summation of sums of squares or of zero-order correlations.

$$R^2_{y \cdot x} = \sum_i^n SS_b / SS_t = \sum_i^n r^2_{yx} \tag{5}$$

$$E^2_{y \cdot x} = \sum_i^n SS_b / SS_t = \sum_i^n e^2_{y \cdot x} \tag{6}$$

The relationship of the several sums of squares in ANOVA to correlational statistics is also informative. The parallelism between $r^2$ and $e^2$ is so obvious that relationships involving the former are the only ones presented.

$$SS_{b_i} = r^2_{yx_i} SS_t \tag{7}$$

$$SS_e = (1 - R^2_{y \cdot x}) SS_t \tag{8}$$

These formulas make clear why it is not necessary to transform correlations into raw score regression statistics. The total sum of squares appears in both the numerator and the denominator of the ratio $MS_b/MS_e$. Use regressions if they are useful and informative, but do not be compulsive about it. Note also that $SS_e$ is not decreased by the addition of independent variables to a design, no matter how highly they are correlated with the dependent variable. The additional independent variables merely increase $SS_t$. The addition of valid covariates, however, does decrease $SS_e$ because they do not affect the variance of the dependent variable. Increasing sample size, on the other hand, has its effect on the power of the analysis by increasing $SS_b$.

## Nonorthogonal Designs

In nonorthogonal designs variances are not additive, and the equalities relating the two semipartial correlations to partial and zero-order correlations, respectively, disappear. Linear correlations allow the statistical manipulations required to orthogonalize the independent variables and interactions. Dummy coding of levels of treatments is required, therefore, when $k > 2$. From the complete matrix of product–moment correlations semipartial correlations are computed for each independent variable and interaction, holding constant the variance of all $x_j$ in the given $x_i$. These semipartial correlations orthogonalize the independent variables and interactions, and they are also the statistics that are usually tested for significance. They suffer, however, from the same defect as the zero-order correlations in a complex orthogonal design. Partial correlations in which the unwanted variance from all other variables is controlled in the dependent variable are the appropriate statistics for theoretical interpretation. Although the partial correlation is always larger than a given semipartial, the $F$-ratios for the two statistics are identical. A borderline $F$ cannot be increased in size by manipulation of these correlations. The partial correlations are merely more meaningful.

A convenient method for computing a semipartial correlation is derived from one of its definitions. If a given variable is one of a set of predictors in a first multiple, but is omitted from a second, all others remaining constant, the difference between the squares of the two multiple correlations is the square of the semipartial. It is written as follows:

$$r^2_{y(x_i \cdot x_j)} = R^2_1 - R^2_2 \tag{9}$$

To transform the semipartial to a partial correlation requires division by the variance error of estimate of $Y$ predicted from the remaining independent variables and interactions.

$$r^2_{yx_i \cdot x_j} = (R^2_1 - R^2_2) / (1 - R^2_{y \cdot x_j}) \tag{10}$$

When there are only two levels of treatment for an independent variable, there is only one $df$ for the difference between the multiples. When $k > 2$, the zero-order relationship for a given independent variable is a multiple correlation based on $k-1$ predictors. Now the $k-1$ variables are omitted from the second multiple and the difference, based on $k-1$ $df$, is the equivalent of a semipartial correlation. The $F$-ratios for both the partial and semipartial correlations are identical, but may not be obvious. A standard text is not sufficient reference.

$$F=(R_1^2-R_2^2)df_{e_1}/(1-R_1^2)(df_{e_1}-df_{e2} \tag{11}$$

## Covariate Analysis

The use of covariates in experimental designs is widely misunderstood. The primary objective is to reduce the size of the error term in the experiment, which, by definition, requires random assignment of the units of sampling to treatments. An incidental objective is to control to the extent possible the small random correlations between subject variables and treatments that are produced in samples by random assignment. One's assumption is that these correlations are zero in the population. The most desirable covariate is highly reliable and has a correlation of unity with the dependent variable when the correlation is corrected for attenuation and when both are administered without an intervening experimental treatment. Whenever possible, in other words, the covariate should be a parallel form of the dependent variable.

The use of covariate analysis to control statistically for the selection that determines the characteristics of existing groups used in research represents an extension of the primary objective. This extension is often based more on prayer than on a careful analysis of needs and possibilities. Selection may have taken place on several dimensions, but it is the correlation between one or more of those dimensions with a particular dependent variable that is the concern. Other dependent variables might be affected differently. Thus the need is to find a covariate, or composite of covariates, that meets the criteria specified in the preceding paragraph. When the need can be met, it is possible to evaluate with some degree of confidence the disturbing effects of a small amount of measurement error in the covariate on the outcome of the quasi-experiment.

Covariance analysis, as mentioned earlier, is a member of the family of partial correlations. For a single independent variable having two levels of treatment, the correlation describing the relationship between the independent and dependent variables is completely parallel to the right-hand term in Equation 1. The $F$ is the ratio of *adjusted* mean squares, and there is a loss of one *df* for the covariate.

$$r_{yx}^2=F/(df_e+F) \tag{12}$$

The translation of a relationship in an analysis of covariance to a correlation when $k > 2$ is seen most easily when dummy variables are substituted for the original independent variable. Equation 10 can be used to obtain the partial correlation, with the covariate $Z$ replacing the $X_j$ independent variables and interactions being held constant. The generalized error sum of squares, without regard to the complexity of the analysis, is the following:

$$SS_e = (1-R^2_{y \cdot xz})SS_t \qquad\qquad\qquad (13)$$

It is important to realize that the experimenter has a choice among correlations to describe the data. One can report the partial correlation between a given independent and the dependent variable with all other independent variables and interactions held constant, neglecting the influence of the covariate. For descriptive purposes it is not essential that the variance of the covariate be held constant in all variables. As a second step, it is defensible to remove the variance of the covariate from the independent variables only, thus controlling the random differences among treatment groups in the sample. The final step is to control in addition the variance of the covariate in the dependent variable, providing a measure of size of relationship between an independent variable and residual individual differences on the dependent variable.

## Interactions with Subject Variables

By definition an interaction is a product. Experimenters can enter products of continuous covariates and dichotomous independent variables, using dummy coding where necessary, and analyze the data by correlation–regression methods. This procedure has several advantages as compared to the common practice of creating two or more levels from a continuous distribution of individual differences. Categorizing continuous distributions loses information. By increasing the number of categories less information is lost, but there is a corresponding loss of degrees of freedom for error. In contrast the main effect of the covariate involves only one *df*, and all interactions also involve only the *df* of the independent variable.

It has also been a frequent practice to create levels for two or more subject variables and impose an orthogonal design on the combination of "treatments" created. Humphreys and Fleishman (1974) called such designs pseudo-orthogonal and recommended that they be avoided. When the subject variables are correlated to a nontrivial degree, the results from the ANOVA are not generalizeable to the population from which the sample was drawn. Main effects are distorted and spurious interactions can be created. It is permissible to create levels, insert the observed *N*s, and analyze the data in the appropriate fashion for nonorthogonal designs; but as described earlier the loss of information and, frequently, decrease in degrees of freedom for error reduce power in the statistical analysis.

Perhaps the most severe problem with the creation of levels of subject variables is more subtle. It is not intrinsic to the methodology, but experimenters who treat subject variables as if they were independent variables create for themselves an illusion of experimental control. *F*-ratios for main effects and interactions for subject variables are interpreted with the same confidence causally as those for environmental and task variables.

## When Categorization is Acceptable

Under certain limited circumstances it is acceptable to categorize the tails of continuous distributions for research purposes. One such circumstance is in preliminary research when one is merely looking for what goes with what. Another is when the dependent variable in the research planned is very expensive to obtain in time, money, or both. By forming groups from the tails of the less expensive covariate fewer subjects will be needed for the research without the loss in power that the smaller samples would otherwise produce. Maximum power is of course obtained when there has been no categorization and the full sample is used. In a normal distribution, once the decision has been made to categorize, maximum power is obtained with upper and lower 27% tails of the continuous distribution. If sample size for the covariate can be increased very cheaply, the investigator can compromise with maximum power by increasing the size of the basic sample and selecting ever more extreme tails.

The principal hazard in following the above procedure is that one can get much too excited by big differences between extreme groups. A very small correlation between two continuous distributions can be inflated dramatically when extreme groups are contrasted. It is possible, however, to estimate a continuous biserial correlation from information obtained from widespread classes. This is not a product-moment correlation but is instead an estimate of what the product-moment correlation would have been if both distributions had been continuously and normally distributed. The continuous biserial correlation is always larger than the product-moment correlations (point biserials) discussed heretofore by a factor of $\sqrt{pq}/h$ with $h$ being the ordinate of the normal curve at the point of separation of the two categories.


# INTERPRETATION OF CORRELATIONS

## Experimental Correlations

There is no doubt about the superiority of experimental methods in comparison to post hoc analysis of relationships. Philosophers of science may argue about the meaning of causation, but the working scientist is well aware that causation can be inferred from a well conducted experiment with considerable confidence. Systematic variation of the number of overlearning trials will, under controlled conditions, lead to consistent increases in retention. Number of hours spent studying for a final examination the last week of the course when correlated with the examination grade might for plausible reasons be negative. (These reasons do not necessarily include systematic errors in recording the hours. Care in measurement is important but not sufficient.) The quality of advice one gives a student on the basis of the two studies is clearly quite different.

Unfortunately, experimentation is not always possible. One reason is the constraint imposed by our ethical code. Babies cannot be taken away at birth from a random sample of mothers and assigned at random to foster parents just because the heritability of intelligence is considered an important problem. A second reason is the difficulty in translating important psychological problems as perceived in the environmental milieu into experimental manipulations. The experimental analogue of the problem is not infrequently a pale imitation of the real thing. Furthermore, the laboratory analogue is likely to be paler than an experiment in the field, but setting up a true experiment in the field is extraordinarily difficult. Finally, there are the mundane problems of time and money in experimentation. We frequently expect (hope) too much of treatments that can be continued over short time-periods only or that are applied to samples too small for the needs of the research.

Correlation analysis of uncontrolled variables can be justified when an adequate experiment is not possible or feasible, and such analyses can be especially justified when the problem is important psychologically and socially. The importance of the problem, however, is not justification for overinterpretation of the data. The investigator must carefully avoid being carried away by the problem's importance. Correlations as measures of size of relationships have the same interpretation in both experimentation and post hoc analysis, but going beyond description requires due regard for the limitations of the data.

## Interpretation of Zero-order Linear Correlations

The interpretation of $r$ as the percent of common variance between two variables is probably the most common statement encountered. It is represented by a simple equation.

$$S^2 = r^2 S^2 + (1-r^2)S^2 \tag{14}$$

The total variance of either variable is composed of the sum of common and unique variance. In terms of concrete operations, if one holds constant either $X$ or $Y$ at any specified level; and if the distribution is bivariate normal, the variance of the second variable will be reduced by $r^2 S^2$. Under the same condition of bivariate normality the unique variance is also the variance error of estimation. This is the variance of the observed scores about the estimated criterion score in each array of the predictor variable. Without homoscedasticity of the arrays $1-r^2$ is simply the variance of the discrepancies between observed and estimated scores accumulated over the entire distribution.

Variances, however, are only part of the story. Correlations, either explicitly or implicitly, appear in the regression equations that are used to make the estimates about which observed scores are distributed. When both variables are in standard score form, $r$ is the slope of both regressions. These slopes can vary from zero to unity. Thus $r$ unsquared is in this sense a percentage of a maximum relationship. When $r=.50$, for every unit of change on one variable there is a change of one-half unit on the other.

One way of describing the difference between $r$ and $r^2$ is that the former describes how much mean performance on one variable changes as level of performance changes on the other, while the latter describes how individual variability about the mean changes with variation in the size of the correlation. We psychologists can predict group trends in behavior much more accurately than we can predict the behavior of individuals. Small correlations can describe important group trends while, at the same time, individual prediction would be hazardous.

Experimental psychologists are typically concerned with group trends. When they have only two treatments or when their three or more treatments have been converted to dichotomous dummy variables, they have only two means of the dependent variable for each relationship. They do not need an equation to draw a straight line through two data points, but both the slope of that line and the variability of the observations around it in either raw score units or standard score units, or both, are important pieces of information. Experimental psychologists who embrace large $F$-ratios, but reject small correlations between subject variables, focus on $r$ in their own research and on $r^2$ when evaluating correlations between subject variables.

In the interpretation of post hoc correlations between subject variables I start from a behavioral point of view with respect to the determination of individual differences. A trait of physique such as astigmatism is caused in a relatively unitary manner by the physical characteristics of the cornea. There is a definite locus of the cause. In contrast there is no a priori reason to posit a unitary cause or a specific locus for psychological traits. The general principle is that one should not place an entity or unitary determinant inside the organism until forced to do so by the data. Traits are abstracted from behavior. Factors are mathematical dimensions that describe behavioral interrelationships. A factor is not necessarily a unitary thing or entity. Factors in psychological measurements can be produced by large numbers of overlapping causes or determinants.

The extent of the overlap of these multiple determinants is described by correlations. These can be interpreted causally to a degree. A nonzero correlation indicates overlap among the multiple determinants of individual differences measured by the two variables. The larger the correlation, the greater the amount of overlap. Correlations of trivial size indicate essentially zero overlap. Trivial correlations are a basis for the rejection of hypotheses concerning substantial overlap of causes, and nonzero correlations are at least a basis for searching for common causes. It is essential in interpreting correlations in this way that both the high and the trivial correlations have small confidence intervals. There is very little information in a correlation large enough in the sample to allow rejection of the hypothesis that the population value is zero but too small to allow rejection of .01.

The hypothesis that smoking cigarettes is linked causally to lung cancer is based on post hoc correlations. At one point in time I surveyed these data without going back to original sources and was impressed by the large number of correlations that "hung together." I do not remember a single one that would allow rejection of the hypothesis. The hypothesis that individual differences in intelligence as measured by a standard test are highly heritable is also based on post hoc correlations. As I view the literature, these correlations are not as consistent as those for smoking and lung cancer. There are also defects in the measurement operations proper in the intelligence literature that may or may not account for some of the inconsistency. Knowing something about medical research I realize that the cigarette smoking literature might reveal defects also if evaluated more carefully.

The causes of sex differences in psychological attributes are in dispute, because human data are post hoc correlational. One study resulted in relatively unambiguous results in my judgment. Humphreys, Lin, and Fleishman (1976) analyzed the correlations of the dichotomous variables of race (black/white), sex, high school grade level (lower/upper), area (south/nonsouth), and their interactions with each of 75 test variables from Project Talent as the criteria. Main effects and interactions were orthogonalized by means of partial correlations for each test variable. Then the intercorrelations of main effects and interactions were computed in the sample of 75 tests. The correlation between the sex main effect and the interactions with race and grade were almost .80. The correlation between the two interactions was of about the same size. The interaction of sex and area was also positively correlated with the sex main effect and the other two interactions, but these interactions were smaller and the correlations smaller as well. On the other hand, the correlations of each of the interactions of sex with race, grade, and area, respectively, were trivial in size. Thus there is a good deal of overlap among the determinants of sex differences and the interactions involving sex. These determinants are relatively independent of those for race and sectional differences and of the gains in scores during high school. We were not able to develop a genetic hypothesis for the sex differences on these tests that would account for all of the correlations. A successful hypothesis must explain both the communality among the determinants of sex differences and interactions and the near independence of the other main effects involved in the same interactions. Socialization pressures on boys and girls does seem to be a satisfactory hypothesis.

## Partial Correlations

The interpretation of partial correlations starts from a recognition that they are product–moment correlations between residual scores. The formula in effect subtracts an estimated $X$ from an observed $X$, does the same for $Y$, and computes the correlation between the residuals. Both $X$ and $Y$ are estimated from the same covariate, $Z$. It follows that the same complex of statistical interpretations as for zero-order correlations can be made. The only difference is the loss of 1 *df* for each variable controlled statistically. However, causal interpretations of partials in post hoc analysis are more hazardous. The most common error is the assumption that a specified trait has been held constant in a given relationship by means of partial correlation. A hypothetical trait cannot be held constant by a measure of the trait that is fallible in both reliability and validity.

The effect of measurement error on the partial correlation is made clear when the correlations involving the covariate are corrected for attenuation. The estimated true score of $Z$ is symbolized by $Z^*$.

$$r_{yx \cdot z*} = (r_{zz'}r_{xy} - r_{xy}r_{yz}) / \sqrt{r_{zz'} - r^2_{xz}} \sqrt{r^2_{zz'} - r^2_{yz}} \tag{15}$$

The difference between $r_{xy}$ and the product of the two correlations involving $Z$ in the numerator is a function of the reliability of $Z$. This is the only reliability, as a matter of fact, that affects the numerator. Full correction for attenuation requires the addition of the two remaining reliabilities in the denominator only.

$$r_{y*x* \cdot z*} = (r_{zz'}r_{xy} - r_{xy}r_{yz}) / \sqrt{r_{zz'} \cdot r_{xx} - r^2_{xz}} \sqrt{r^2_{zz'} \cdot r_{yy'} - r^2_{yz}} \tag{16}$$

Without correcting for attenuation it is readily possible to obtain a statistically significant partial correlation as a result of measurement error in the covariate. If the covariate is a parallel form of either $X$ or $Y$, for example, the expectation of the partial correlation is a positive nonzero value. High reliability of the covariate is necessary if spurious residual correlations are to be minimized, but this is not sufficient. The covariate is a measure of less than perfect validity in all cases other than the equation of true score with a very narrow trait. A significant partial correlation may reflect the lack of validity of the covariate in addition to the effect of measurement error.

The problems of fallible reliability and validity in interpretation of partial correlations are common to both experimental and post hoc analyses, but the experimentalist does avoid a third pitfall. The covariate in an experiment is administered prior to the experimental treatment. This third pitfall is well described by the phrase "throwing the baby out with the bath." When the definitions of covariate, independent, and dependent are arbitrary, covariates can be introduced that control the variance of the presumed independent variable.

In one sense this is merely an extension of the problem of validity and the difference between holding constant a trait and a fallible measure of the trait. The essential problem is the very human tendency to reify constructs from measurement operations. (Almost the sole valid criticism of psychometricians and of the construct of general intelligence in Gould, 1981, is his treatment of the error of reification.) At least some part of the baby is thrown out with the bath in the use of socioeconomic and intelligence measures in a variety of correlations with other measures. An environmentalist may obtain the partial correlation between intelligence and race with social status held constant. The partial correlation is interpreted as the residual correlation between intelligence and race with social privilege controlled. On the basis of present evidence, however, the status measure could be as highly heritable as intelligence. The partial correlation under these circumstances would discard genotypic variance. But hereditarians are as free to discard babies as environmentalists. When the partial correlation between socioeconomic status and race with intelligence held constant is essentially zero, an interpretation that the correlation between the status measure and race is genetic in origin is equally arbitrary. Based on current data, the intelligence test scores could be as valid a measure of privilege as the status measure.

For broad traits such as general intelligence, factor analysis is the only methodology available by which a trait can be held constant in relationships among fallible measures. Correlations among $X$, $Y$, and several other variables might be described accurately by loadings on two orthogonal factors, $A$ and $B$. If $X$ and $Y$ have substantial loadings on $A$, but if $X$ has a substantial and $Y$ a trivial loading on $B$, one can conclude that $X$ measures trait $B$ when trait $A$ is held constant in the relationship with $Y$. An example of this interpretation of factor loadings in exploratory analysis appears in Humphreys and Parsons (1977). Developments in confirmatory factor analysis methodology (Joreskog & Sorbom, 1978) provide a more objective basis for testing such hypotheses about traits. Confirmatory factor analysis is not, however, a methodology that can be applied intelligently by a novice after reading a description of the computer program.

## Multiple Correlations

Multiple correlations are also product–moment correlations in which the several components designed to predict a criterion score are assigned weights that minimize $SS_t(1-R^2_{yx})$ where $x$ represents two or more predictors. Multiple correlations can thus be interpreted statistically, subject to qualifications based on the relationship of $n$ to $N$, as other product–moment correlations.

Multiple correlations are said to *shrink*, but this term is used to describe two different effects. The first, which properly should not be called shrinkage, is the difference between a sample $R$ and its population estimate. The expected value of the squared sample multiple computed from the intercorrelations of random normal deviates is parallel to the expected value of the nonlinear correlation under similar circumstances, $(n-1)/(N-1)$ and $(k-1)/(N-1)$, respectively. This same relationship holds for a zero-order correlation, but the expected value of $R^2$ increases sharply with increases in $n$. Estimation of population multiples is important in most applications. In most texts the formula is described as the correction for shrinkage. It provides a population estimate that differs trivially from Hays' (1963)$\omega^2$.

The second effect is properly called shrinkage. When regression weights obtained in one sample are applied in a second sample, one expects the composite correlation in the latter sample to be smaller than the multiple correlation in either sample and the population estimate in either sample as well. Sample regression weights are not the unknown population regression weights that are responsible for the correlation in the population. This problem of shrinkage has traditionally been met by empirical cross-validation. Attempts have also been made to estimate this shrinkage statistically. A Monte Carlo investigation has been published by Drasgow, Dorans, and Tucker (1979).

## Multiple Regression Weights

Two basic procedures are commonly used: a stepwise procedure which ignores weights for variables beyond some pre-determined cutoff and computation of weights for the full set of $n$ predictors. One variant of the first procedure involves a rule-of-thumb ordering of predictors that is useful only for the selection of a subset of predictors for purposes of economical prediction. It is useless for theoretical purposes. Furthermore, it does not necessarily select an optimum subset. The other variant orders the predictors in accordance with statistical requirements or psychological theory. An example of a statistical requirement is placing an interaction third behind both of the components of the interaction. A psychological theory might place a measure of intelligence ahead of a measure of status, but a different theory might reverse the ordering. Clearly there are problems relating to reification present in this application as well as the problems associated with the interpretation of regression weights generally that are discussed below.

It is easy to interpret the regression weights for the full set of $n$ predictors correctly, but correct interpretations are of little use theoretically. On the other hand, it is all too easy to make errors in interpretations. First and foremost, the size of a regression weight does not indicate the importance or contribution of the predictor to the accuracy of the prediction of the criterion measure. The regression weight of a given variable is simply the weight that minimizes $SS_t(1-R^2_{y \cdot x})$ in a certain set of variables in a single sample from a defined population. Each qualification in this statement is essential.

Evaluation of the contribution of a predictor to the accuracy of prediction under the restraints listed above is made by computing the squared semipartial correlation for the $n$th predictor with each of the $n$ predictors being placed in the $n$th position in turn. One obtains $n$ sets of multiple regression weights and $n$ multiple correlations. From each of these multiples and the multiple in the full set, the squared semipartial correlations are computed by Equation 9. These are the measures of the unique contributions of the $n$ predictors. The sum of these squared semipartials will not equal $R^2$ and in many data sets the difference is huge. Most of the variance of the predicted scores is carried by the common variance among the predictors. To generalize the size of the semipartial to other samples from the same population, the ratio of $N$ to $n$ must be very large. It is not possible to generalize to other sets of predictors. Either the addition of one new predictor or the subtraction of one can change the size of both regression weights and semipartial correlations substantially and in that order of amount of change.

It is also possible to obtain information about standardized weights from the components of variance of the predicted criterion scores.

$$S^2_y \approx \sum_l^n b_i^2 + \sum_l^n \sum_{i \neq j}^n r_{ij} b_i b_j \tag{17}$$

The elements in the $n$ by $n$ matrix of squared regression weights and residual covariances over which the preceding summations take place can be inspected pair by pair. The contribution of each such pair consists of two squared regression weights plus twice the product of the respective weights and the correlation between the two variables. If both predictors have small positive weights, but the correlation between the two is quite large, the pair is making a larger contribution to variance than the combined size of their weights suggests. If both predictors have large weights of opposite sign, and the correlation between the two is again quite large, the pair is making a smaller contribution than the absolute size of their weights suggests.

Regression weights are completely determined by the correlations with the criterion of the predictors and by their intercorrelations. Measurement error affects regression weights more than the correlations from which the weights are derived. Restriction of range of talent may affect one dimension in the matrix of correlations more than others, and the weights of the variables loaded on this dimension will be affected disproportionately. Above all, regression weights are affected by the amount of redundancy in the information furnished by the $n$ predictors. When the estimated population value of the squared multiple correlation between one predictor and the remaining $n-1$ predictors approaches the reliability of that predictor, the regression weight becomes highly unstable. This is independent of whether the large multiple correlation is the result of the inclusion of a second predictor that is essentially a parallel form of the first, the classic example of collinearity, or whether the first merely has a great deal in common with the entire set of predictors.

## RECOMMENDATIONS

A central aim of all quantitative research is the establishment of relationships or correlations among variables. The common designations of experimental and correlational for research distinguished by the control, or lack thereof, exercized should be abandoned. Experimental analysis and post hoc analysis are more accurate terms to describe the types of quantitative research.

The fixation of experimental psychologists on reporting research outcomes in terms of tests of significance only should also be abandoned. The typical hypothesis tested involves only the sign of a relationship between two variables. Determination of degree of relationship is more important in the development of a science.

Degree of relationship requires a statistic that is independent of sample size. It is also convenient to have a statistic that is independent of the units of measurement and varies within standard limits. Linear and nonlinear correlations have these characteristics.

Sampling stability of the correlation is also important. This is best described by confidence intervals. These test an infinite number of hypotheses about population parameters in place of one, typically artificial, hypothesis. The artificial hypothesis is that the degree of relationship is zero.

The use of correlations and their confidence intervals allows investigators to make more precise predictions of research outcomes. This requires small standard errors. Confidence intervals can be kept small by the use of large samples and reliable, valid covariates.

Covariate or partial correlation analyses are interpretable with minimum ambiguity when experimental control is exercised. A core characteristic of such control is the assignment of subjects at random to experimental treatments. In the absence of random assignment, even when there is tight control of task and environmental variables, causal interpretation of the relationships observed is hazardous.

It is not accurate to define subject variables as independent because random assignment to treatments is not possible. Treating them as if they were independent leads frequently to misinterpretation of the obtained correlations. Categorizing measures of individual differences into levels represents an experimental design that can be justified only under highly restrictive circumstances. Categorizing two or more nonorthogonal measures of individual differences and imposing orthogonality in a factorial design distorts relationships. This also should be abandoned.

A limited amount of causal inference is legitimately obtained from post hoc zero-order correlations. Correlations of trivial size represent nearly complete independence of the determinants of the variables. Nontrivial correlations represent overlap of determinants, and the larger the correlation, the larger the amount of overlap. When the intercorrelations of $n$ variables are all in accordance with hypothesis, one's confidence in the hypothesis is increased. When the size of each correlation is also in line with hypothesis, support for the hypothesis is much stronger. This requires precisely stated hypotheses as well as the large samples and effective covariates mentioned earlier. If one is able to add that the correlations were obtained under conditions of experimental control, however, a substantial increase in confidence is justified.

# REFERENCES

Cohen, J., & Cohen, P. (1975). *Applied multiple regression/correlation analysis for the behavioral sciences.* Hillsdale, NJ: Lawrence Erlbaum Associates.

Drasgow, F., Dorans, N., & Tucker, L. (1979). Estimators of the squared cross-validity coefficient: A Monte Carlo study. *Applied Psychological Measurement, 3,* 387–399.

Gould, S. (1981). *The mismeasure of man.* New York: Norton.

Hays, W. (1963). *Statistics for psychologists.* New York: Holt, Rinehart and Winston.

Humphreys, L. (1980). The statistics of failure to replicate: A comment on Buriel's conclusions. *Journal of Educational Psychology, 72,* 71–75.

Humphreys, L. G. & Fleishman, A. (1974). Pseudo-orthogonal and other analysis of variance designs involving individual differences variables. *Journal of Educational Psychology 66,* 464–472.

Humphreys, L., Lin, P., & Fleishman, A. (1976). The sex by race interaction in cognitive measures. *Journal of Research in Personality, 10,* 42–58.

Humphreys, L., & Parsons, C. (1977). Partialing out intelligence: A methodological and substantive contribution. *Journal of Educational Psychology, 69,* 212–216.

Jöreskog, K., & Sörbom, D. (1978). *LISREL IV. A general computer program for the estimation of linear structural equation systems by maximum likelihood methods.* University of Uppsala, Sweden, Department of Statistics.

Meehl, P. (1967). Theory testing in psychology and phsyics: A methodological paradox. *Philosophy of Science, 34,* 103–115.

Peters, C. & Van Voorhis, W. (1940). *Statistical procedures and their mathematical bases.* New York: McGraw-Hill.

Underwood, B. (1957). *Psychological research.* New York: Appleton-Century-Crofts.

# CHAPTER 2

# Exploratory Factor Analysis: A Tutorial

*John B. Carroll*

*University of North Carolina at Chapel Hill*

## INTRODUCTION

As used in the study of intelligence and intellectual abilities, factor analysis (hereafter abbreviated as FA) has two major goals: (a) to identify a minimum number of latent variables or "factors" in a set of data that will most parsimoniously, and from the standpoint of psychological interpretation most intelligibly, account for covariation among the variables in the data, and (b) to determine the "structure" of these factors, that is, to reveal any hierarchical arrangement of the factors such that some factors are more general than others. Factors identified in this process are regarded as basic abilities, except that successive studies may suggest that an ability identified in a given study can better be regarded as a further analyzable composite.

Through achieving these goals, several subsidiary purposes can be served. Chief among these is the determination of the factorial composition of each variable in a set of data, that is, the specification of what common factors are present in a variable, and the weights that are to be assigned to the common factors in maximizing the prediction of scores on a variable from scores on those factors. Related to this is the determination of the *communality* of a variable, that is, the proportion of its variance that is accounted for by the common factors identified in the data set. The complement of the communality is the (squared) *uniqueness* of the variable. If the reliability of the variable is known or can be estimated (by commonly accepted techniques outside of factor analysis), the uniqueness can be divided into the variable's *specificity* and its *error variance*. These quantities, expressed as proportions, constitute information that is useful in further studies of the variables.

Another secondary goal of some factor analytic studies is the determination of *factor scores,* that is, estimated scores for individuals on the latent factors discovered in the analysis.

This chapter concerns what has come to be called *exploratory* FA, as opposed to *confirmatory* FA, treated in another chapter of this volume. Exploratory FA is the classical type of analysis that has been under development and in wide use for more than 50 years. Essentially, it seeks to let a data set "speak for itself" to indicate what its factors are and how they are structured. It does not directly permit the testing of statistical hypotheses, but it does permit the testing of *psychological* hypotheses about the nature of factors and the factorial compositions of variables. It has at least two advantages over confirmatory FA: (a) it does not call for the advance specification of any parameters or statistical hypotheses to be tested, and is thus unbiased by any such specifications (which are sometimes difficult to make in confirmatory FA); and (b) its computations are generally simpler and less expensive. If desired, the results of an exploratory FA can be submitted to confirmatory FA for testing of statistical hypotheses concerning the structure revealed by exploratory FA.

Although there is no strict demarcation between them, FA studies (either exploratory or confirmatory) can be classed into two types: (a) data reduction studies, and (b) more truly scientific studies in which the goal is to investigate psychological hypotheses about factors or underlying abilities.

Typically, data reduction studies undertake to analyze any arbitrary set of variables with the goal of finding the best way of summarizing these data in terms of a small number of factors or composites of variables. Often, the intention is to determine a set of factor scores for individuals. Examples are found among the literally dozens of FA studies of subscales of tests like the Wechsler Intelligence Scale for Children (WISC) or the Wechsler Adult Intelligence Scale (WAIS). Although such studies can provide useful and suggestive information about basic abilities, often the factors are complex, further analyzable in studies of the second type, in which more care is taken in the selection or construction of variables for purposes of FA. In this chapter, the discussion places emphasis on issues involved in conducting studies of this second type. At the same time, what is said about the technical procedures in computing FA studies applies to data reduction studies as well as to the more scientific types of study.

In the use of FA for scientific purposes, FA should be considered not only as a statistical technique but also as wide-ranging scientific enterprise. A given study can perhaps resolve some issues, but usually it will open up still others that need to be investigated in future studies.

In this brief chapter, space does not permit anything like a full treatment of FA techniques, about which there is an enormous literature. For the beginner, the introductory monographs of Kim and Mueller (1978a, 1978b) can be recommended, except that Kim and Mueller give the impression that factors are "causes" of variation; I would prefer to regard them more neutrally as "sources" of variance. Fuller introductory texts for the mathematically unsophisticated student are those of Cattell (1978), Comrey (1973), Cureton and D'Agostino (1983), Gorsuch (1983), and Rummel (1970), varying in style, difficulty and completeness. More advanced texts are those of Harman (1976) and Mulaik (1972). Nunnally's (1978) text on psychometric theory has good sections on FA but puts too much weight on principal component analysis as opposed to principal factor analysis (see discussion below).

These days, any respectable FA will be done by computer. Widely used statistical packages containing FA analysis programs for large-frame computers are those of Statistical Package for the Social Sciences (SPSS) (Nie, Hull, Jenkins, Steinbrenner, & Bent, 1975, and later editions) and Statistical Analysis System (SAS Institute, 1982). The manuals for these packages contain excellent introductions to exploratory FA. A more specialized FA program for large-frame computers is the "Big Jiffy" program developed by Gorsuch and Dreger (1979). The writer has found it possible and quite satisfactory to perform exploratory FA for problems with up to 30 or more variables with an Apple II Plus microcomputer, and has written and tested programs in compiled BASIC for this purpose (Carroll, in preparation). Computations for this chapter were performed with these programs.

## PROCEDURES IN A WELL DESIGNED FA STUDY

### The Domain of Variables

This discussion is limited to what Cattell (1978) has called $R$-technique, that is, the analytical procedure which starts with the correlations among a set of variables for which one set of measurements is available for a sample of individuals.

*Large Versus Small Domains.* The variables may be either from a large domain or a smaller, narrower domain of abilities. As summarized by French (1951), most of the classic studies in exploratory FA (e.g., Thurstone, 1938) selected variables from a large domain—the domain of all types of test items frequently found on individual and group intelligence tests, aptitude tests, and so forth. Other classic studies concentrated on abilities in narrower domains, for example, Carroll's (1941) study of verbal abilities, Coomb's (1941) study of numerical abilities, or Karlin's (1942) study of auditory and musical abilities. Studies of broad domains (e.g., Hakstian & Cattell's, 1978, study of 20 primary abilities) are still useful for helping better to define the higher-order structure of abilities, but the greater need now is for more studies of narrower domains, with careful construction and selection of variables, in order better to define factored abilities in such domains. Regardless of the size of the domain investigated, it is important to include in FA studies, as "markers" of known factors, variables that have been previously studied. The tests included in the Educational Testing Service (ETS)-sponsored kit of factor reference tests (Ekstrom, French, & Harman, 1976) are a useful source of such variables. It is recommended, however, that these tests be adapted, where necessary, to provide separate measurements of speed and accuracy of performance. It may also be useful to refine these and similar marker tests by standard test construction procedures in order to improve their factorial homogeneity and univocality.

A very small domain would be one covered by a single test item type, as exemplified in Corman and Budoff's (1974) study of items in Raven's Coloured Progressive Matrices test which appeared to yield three or more separate abilities in the performance of these items. Undoubtedly there are many other such small domains of tasks that are in need of detailed study.

*Types of Variables.* It is recommended that the variables included in a FA be exclusively those that can be considered as true *dependent* variables, in some way reflecting behavior or performance. Such variables include test or item scores, measurements of performance such as reaction times, and observations or ratings of performance. This recommendation is intended to exclude demographic variables like age, sex, socioeconomic or occupational status, and race, because such variables are better regarded as independent variables or sources of variance. If such variables are to be included at all in FA studies, they can be treated as "extension" variables (see below), or they may be studied in relation to factor scores derived from an analysis. With respect to demographic variables such as age and sex, consideration should be given to performing separate analyses for different groups—in the case of age, to reflect possible differential growth or decline characteristics of abilities, and in the case of sex, to investigate possible sex differences in factors or in factorial structure, such as have apparently been found in the spatial ability domain (Pellegrino & Kail, 1982).

*Scaling of Variables.* Ideally, variables should be scaled in equal units of measurement over a continuum. This ideal is difficult to approach in practice because, as is well known, we seldom know how to specify equal units in measuring abilities. Test scores obtained as "number correct" or the like are not necessarily on interval scales. For purposes of obtaining suitable estimates of underlying correlations among variables (Carroll, 1961), it is desirable that variables have approximately similar distribution shapes; generally some form of tranformation is to be recommended when distributions depart radically from normality (see Tukey, 1977). Reaction times and other speed measurements that are expressed as time per unit of performance are generally best converted to measurements expressed as amount of performance per unit of time, to produce more nearly normal distributions.

*Orientation of Variables.* It is desirable to scale variables in such a way that higher values represent "more" ability than low values; or even if this is not done, appropriate sign changes of correlations should be made before they are subjected to FA, so that it will be easier to evaluate the degree to which positive manifold (absence of salient negative loadings) is achieved in the FA.

*Selection of Variables.* Variables are selected on the basis of their anticipated or hypothesized factorial composition. In planning a well designed FA study, the investigator should specify what the factors are expected to be and draft a hypothesized factor pattern matrix indicating what variables are expected to load on each primary factor. Each primary factor should be represented by *at least* three variables expected to have high or "salient" loadings on it and no other factor. It is sometimes desirable, as well, to include variables that are expected to have salient loadings on two or more factors in order to test hypotheses about the factorial composition of the variables or the nature of the factors involved. A simple, small illustration is given in Table 2.1, for a study in which three factors are anticipated. Variables 4, 5, and 9 are indicated as expected to be complex. The reader may be reassured that the computational procedures of exploratory FA need not be in any way dependent on the structure of a hypothesized factor pattern. Computations can be conducted with no knowledge of, or attention to, such a table. Indeed, computations are best performed "blindly," with no knowledge of factor hypotheses or even of the identification of the variables.

**Table 2.1. A Hypothesized Factor Pattern**

| Variable | A | B | C |
|---|---|---|---|
| 1 | XX | ... | ... |
| 2 | XX | ... | ... |
| 3 | X | ... | ... |
| 4 | X | X | ... |
| 5 | X | ... | X |
| 6 | ... | XX | ... |
| 7 | ... | XX | ... |
| 8 | ... | X | ... |
| 9 | X | X | X |
| 10 | ... | ... | XX |
| 11 | ... | ... | XX |
| 12 | ... | ... | X |

Once a table of factor hypotheses has been constructed, the investigator should go about constructing or selecting variables which by his or her best knowledge, judgment and intuition will best produce the hypothesized pattern. This means that the continuum represented by each variable should reflect variation in whatever ability or abilities are hypothesized as having salient loadings on the variable.

Consider a variable designed to measure a single factor of ability. According to the Ability/Difficulty Interaction (A/DI) model that I have proposed elsewhere (Carroll, in press), an ability is to be defined in terms of relations between individual capabilities and the levels of task difficulty that the individuals are able to perform with a 50% chance of success (after correction for any guessing or "chance" success effects). Levels of task or item difficulty are to be defined in terms of the *intrinsic* properties of the task, parameterized as well as possible by objective measurements of those properties. For example, a test of tonal pitch discrimination ability would contain items of different difficulties as defined by the pitch differences between pairs of tones to be discriminated; a vocabulary test would have items such that the key vocabulary terms differ in familiarity or word-count frequency; a test of inductive ability would contain items differing in the complexity of the rules that need to be perceived to achieve solution, and so on. According to theory, each ability is related to a particular type of variation in task characteristics as parameterized in this way. A test variable that has salient loadings on two or more factors contains tasks that vary on two or more dimensions of characteristics. Such a theory, at least, can serve as a guide in developing and selecting variables for a FA study of abilities.

As indicated above, a requirement for a hypothesized factor pattern is that each factor be represented by at least three variables, preferably more. This is because FA is mainly concerned with analyzing covariation among variables. How can one develop or select two or more variables to reflect a factor without making them identical? It would be undesirable to make them identical or equivalent because the underlying common factor might then reflect also a specific factor in the variables, and the factor would be overdetermined. The solution is to include task variation, over the several variables, that is expected to be irrelevant to the definition of the ability. The variation might be, for example, over sense modalities—one vocabulary test could be a reading test, another a test of listening vocabulary. Or the variation could inhere in the types of responses required, one test being in a multiple-choice format, another being in a free-response format. Meeting the requirements of a hypothesized factor pattern is a challenge to the psychological knowledge and insight that the investigator can muster.

It appears that some abilities reflect variations in knowledge bases of individuals, while others reflect variations in cognitive capacities such an encoding of stimuli, handling temporary memory storage, and so on. One way of creating irrelevant task variation is the following: if an ability is hypothesized to concern cognitive capacities, irrelevant task variation can be introduced by varying required knowledge bases, whereas if the ability is hypothesized to reflect knowledge base variations, irrelevant task variation can be introduced by varying cognitive requirements. For suggestions as to types of knowledge bases and cognitive operations that might be involved in ability factors, see Carroll's (1976) analysis of a series of abilities included in the ETS factor reference kit.

With typical hypothesized factor patterns, the number of factors will be considerably less than half the number of variables *(n)*. The latter will rarely be less than about 10, and it can go as high as 50 or more. The number of extractable and readily interpretable common factors also appears to be related to sample size. A rule of thumb is that the sample size, $N$, needed to support the extraction of $m$ common and interpretable factors must be at least equal to $2m + 2^m$, or preferably much larger if $m$ is small.

Particularly to be avoided is any situation in which values of a given variable are exactly predictable from other variables or combinations thereof, for this will make the correlation matrix singular and more difficult to analyze. It may also create artifactual factors. For example, it would be undesirable to include variables defined as $(A + B)$ or $(A - B)$ where both $A$ and $B$ are already included in the variable set. As far as possible, also, variables should be experimentally independent. That is, caution should be observed in including two or more measures derived from the same task situation, for they may be somehow causally dependent on each other. Under some circumstances it is allowable to include two or more such variables if they are *logically* independent of each other, for example, a speed measurement and an accuracy variable derived from the same experimental setting, but even in this case a speed-accuracy tradeoff could introduce an undesirable perturbation in the analysis (see Carroll, 1978, for further discussion).

## Composition of the Sample

Samples should be selected so as to represent at least substantial variation in all the hypothesized abilities being investigated. Samples that are highly selected with respect to some ability or combination of abilities are to that degree suspect, although use of such samples is frequently observable in the literature. Sometimes it is convenient to select samples in such a way that they represent high and low portions of a distribution with respect to some ability or abilities, the middle portion being excluded; such samples are suspect to some extent, but acceptable if due account is taken of the possible inflating of correlations and factor loadings.

The bearing of sample size on factor structure has already been noted. Obviously, the larger the sample, the better, for reliability of results. In general, any sample size less than about 100 is suspect and may yield artifactual results that are due to chance covariation, the presence of "outliers" in bivariate distributions, and so forth.

Caution should be exercised in selecting a sample that is quite heterogeneous in age, since age variations may inflate correlations among variables that are subject to increases or declines with age. Discussions of this problem are to be found in a report by Carroll, Kohlberg, and DeVries (1984) and in an interchange between Guilford (1980) and Horn and Cattell (1982).

In studies of the operation of cognitive strategies, consideration should be given to the possibility of performing different analyses for portions of the sample that use different cognitive strategies—if sample sizes can still be adequately large. An interesting study in which this was attempted is that of French (1965).

## The Correlation Matrix

*Choice of Correlation Indices.* Normal FA theory is based on the assumption that the correlations are Pearsonian product-moment coefficients, and that the underlying relations are linear. Investigators should routinely check for linearity of relationships, either by inspection of bivariate scatterplots or by statistical tests for curvilinearity. Sometimes transformations of selected variables can remedy any curvilinearity that is noted; actually, curvilinearity that cannot be remedied by such transformations is rare in studies of ability. When some or all of the variables are dichotomous or measured in very broad categories, the Pearsonian coefficient is inappropriate since it may yield biased estimates of the underlying relationships (Carroll, 1961, 1983). Biserial or modified biserial correlations (Kraemer, 1981) may be appropriate in some cases, tetrachoric correlations in others, except that both have limitations in the presence of chance guessing effects (Carroll, 1945). The essential point is that the coefficient employed should be as nearly as possible an unbiased estimator of the linear relationship that would exist if the variables correlated could be measured on an unbiased continuum.

Investigators should assure themselves that the program used to compute whatever coefficient is selected is valid and accurate. Gorsuch (1983, p. 392) has pointed out a possible defect in some correlation programs.

*Missing Data.* FA theory assumes that the correlation matrix is based on complete data for all cases in the sample. This assumption is violated if the correlations are based on cases in which data are missing. Sporadic missing data points may not cause significant problems, but in general it is best to eliminate such cases completely unless sample size is thereby drastically reduced. The presence of missing data points can create artifactual results, particularly if the presence or absence of data points is correlated significantly with ability factors. FA studies in which there is a substantial missing data problem are to be held suspect; it is my belief that no missing data correlation routine adequately handles the problem.

## Factor Analysis: The Data Reduction Step

The first step in the FA procedure is data reduction to a factor matrix $\mathbf{F}$ with some relatively small number of factors that will satisfactorily account for the correlation matrix $\mathbf{R}$ through the matrix equation

$$\mathbf{R} = \mathbf{FF'} + \mathbf{U} + \mathbf{E} \tag{1}$$

where U is a diagonal matrix of squared uniqueness values, and E is a square matrix of residuals, the residual values being small and representing chance fluctuations in the correlations. In theory, the number of factors in $\mathbf{F}$ is the *rank* of the matrix $\mathbf{R}$. There is an infinity of matrices $\mathbf{F}$ that can satisfy the above equation, all being related by orthogonal transformation. What is required, however, is *some* matrix **F**, since further operations (rotations) can be performed to select or compute a factor matrix that is amenable to psychological interpretation.

An important first decision to be made is whether to follow the *principal component* (PC) model or the *common factor* (CF) model. The former analyzes *all* the variance of each variable, whereas the latter attempts to estimate and analyze only the common factor variance—in other words, that represented by the *communality* of the variable. It is now almost too easy (computationally) to follow the PC model. By computing the *m* principal components of the **R** matrix, one finds a matrix **F**, with *m* = *n* factors (where *n* is the number of variables), that (except for rare cases) will precisely satisfy the equation

$$\mathbf{R} = \mathbf{FF'} \tag{2}$$

Using only the first few (larger) factors of this matrix, a good approximation of Equation 1 can be achieved, except that factor loadings and communalities will generally be somewhat larger than those computed by a CF model. Because of its simplicity, and for other reasons, the principal component (PC) model has been used in numerous FA studies. Many authorities claim that the results achieved by the PC model are sufficiently similar to those computed by the CF model to prefer the former, and there is now some evidence to support this claim (Velicer, Peacock, & Jackson, 1982). The PC model also avoids various problems of indeterminacy and improper solutions that are encountered with the CF model.

Pending further research on this matter, however, I believe it is wise to prefer the CF model if only for the theoretical reason that it makes a necessary distinction between common and unique variance and permits a more accurate estimation of the latter. In my view, FA should be mainly concerned only with analyzing the covariation among variables, without the intrusion of the specific variance associated with particular variables (inevitably introduced by the PC model). I appeal to the principle of parsimony in claiming that the common factor model makes for cleaner recovery of the true factor structure of a set of data.

If one accepts the CF model, a number of computational methods are available in standard computer packages. Among these are image analysis, alpha factor analysis, *minres* analysis, and maximum likelihood analysis. The most popular and widely used, however, is *principal factor* (PF) *analysis with iteration for communalities,* and partly because of space limitations I restrict my further discussion to a consideration of the PF method. Many of the issues discussed apply also to other CF methods.

The reader should be clear on one point: The PF method uses exactly the same mathematical algorithm as is used by the PC method, the algorithm variously called the latent roots and vectors routine or the eigenvalues and eigenvectors routine. The major difference between the PC and PF methods is that the former operates on the correlation (**R**) matrix in its normal form, with unities in the diagonal, and obtains a solution immediately, whereas the latter operates on the **R** matrix with estimates of communalities placed in the diagonal, and obtains a final solution only after a series of iterations. The PF process starts with some set of initial estimates and iterates until a convergence criterion is met, that is, until communality estimates no longer change significantly. Normally the initial estimates are SMC values—squared multiple correlations of each variable as predicted by the other variables; these are lower bound estimates of the communalities, easily obtained from the inverse of the correlation matrix. If the **R** matrix is singular, the initial estimates can be the maximal off-diagonal values in the arrays.

Another difference between the PC and PF methods is that the former gives the same solution for any number of factors, up to the number of variables (though there is still a problem of how many factors to accept), while the latter runs into the "number of factors" problem more seriously because it produces different solutions given different numbers of factors to solve for. The issue in the PF method is, therefore, what is the "correct" number of factors? Or more precisely, how many common factors are there, that account satisfactorily for the off-diagonal values in the $R$ matrix? This issue arises for two reasons: (a) There is no way of exactly determining the "true" communalities of the variables; and (b) normally there is error variance in the data, that under certain conditions can masquerade as common factor variance. A particular correlation coefficient can be abnormally high, through chance error, and thus appear to support the existence of a common factor. Since the PF method is normally used without application of tests of significance, various rules of thumb, procedures, and judgment are used to decide on the appropriate number of common factors. (Statistical tests are available for evaluating the distribution of residuals, but these are infrequently used unless maximum likelihood factoring is employed.) I will comment on several guidelines commonly used. It should be emphasized, however, that no one method should be relied upon; a judgment based on several methods is probably soundest when criteria disagree (as they frequently do with real data sets).

*1. The Kaiser-Guttman Unity-eigenvalue Rule.* Use of this rule necessitates computation of the PC solution for at least $m = n/2$ factors. Based on work by Guttman, Kaiser (1960) proposed that the number of common factors be taken to be the number of eigenvalues that are greater than (or equal to) unity. Often this number corresponds approximately or exactly to the number suggested by other guidelines, but it can give too *low* a value if the factors are substantially correlated, and too *high* a value if the intercorrelations among the variables are generally low. Despite its simplicity, it must be used with extreme caution (Cattell, 1978, p. 62).

*2. The "Scree" Test.* The best statement of this rule is to be found in Cattell's text (1978, Chapter 5). Normally it is based on a plot of the successive eigenvalues in a PC solution, but the same principle can be applied to eigenvalues

computed at various stages of the PF solution (Gorsuch & Nelson, 1981), namely that the eigenvalues for the "true" common factors tend to form one more or
less straight line, while those for the error factors tend to form another more or
less straight line with a different, smaller slope (representing the "scree"—the
rubble at the foot of the mountain). Therefore, the number of common factors
is taken to be the number of eigenvalues encompassed by the line with the
higher slope, terminated by an "elbow" at the transition to the "scree" factor
line. Unfortunately, there are sometimes several such "elbows" and the scree test
is not a universally reliable guide, although Gorsuch and Nelson have sought to
provide an objective method of using it.

   *3. The Parallel Analysis Criterion.* Due to Montanelli and Humphreys (1976),
this criterion is based on a comparison of (a) the eigenvalues obtained from a PF
solution for SMC estimates of communalities with (b) eigenvalues estimated as
most likely to occur in a similar analysis of correlations for random data for the
given sample size. The number of common factors is taken to be $m$, that is, the
first $m$ SMC eigenvalues for the given data that are greater than the corresponding random data eigenvalues. Tucker (personal communication, October, 1979)
has provided a generalized algorithm for estimating the random data eigenvalues.
This guideline appears to work well in most cases, but sometimes the SMC eigenvalues are so close to the random data eigenvalues that a simple comparison may
not give valid results. (In fact, sometimes the plot lines for SMC and random
eigenvalues never cross, or cross more than once.) The Montanelli-Humphreys
rule therefore has to be evaluated relative to other guidelines and in the light of
other considerations. If the **R** matrix contains tetrachoric correlations, this
criterion is probably inapplicable since it assumes Pearsonian correlations.

   *4. Number of Iterations Required to Achieve Convergence.* Experience has
shown that when convergence requires an excessive number of iterations (say, 50
or more), overfactoring is likely to have occurred. Excessive iterations are also
likely to be associated with a "Heywood case" (see below).

   *5. Evaluation of the Pattern of a Varimax Rotation of the Converged Factor
Matrix.* Experience suggests that the best procedure for deciding on the number
of common factors in exploratory FA is to compute reasonably well converged
(iterated) factor matrices for several values of $m$ around those suggested by one
or more of the previous guidelines. Each such factor matrix is then rotated by
Kaiser's (1958) Varimax criterion (see below). In each rotated matrix, the highest factor loading for each variable is identified as a *salient* factor loading. The
number of common factors is then taken to be the largest value of $m$ such that
each factor contains at least two (or three) variables with salient factor loadings.
Even this rule must be used conservatively, however, for sometimes a factor with
only two salient loadings appears to arise only by chance; if the loadings are
relatively small, and the correlation on which the factor is based is of marginal
significance, it is generally wise to reject the factor.

   Algorithms in some statistical packages sometimes produce factor matrices
in which most or all of the values in some columns have negative signs. This is

solely due to an idiosyncrasy of certain eigenvalue-eigenvector routines. Since the orientation of a *factor* is arbitrary, it is recommended that any factor whose algebraic sum of loadings is negative be reversed in orientation. Actually, this is done automatically in some computer packages. (This recommendation also applies to rotated factor matrices.)

An important issue in PF computations is that of the handling of the iterative process. First of all, it is recommended that iterations *not* be governed by specification of a minimum eigenvalue, certainly not a minimum eigenvalue equal to 1.0 (which is the default parameter in certain packages), since this assumes the validity of the Kaiser–Guttman rule and in any case is inapplicable in PF computations. Any parameter that is used to limit the number of iterations should be liberal. Often the default parameter, such as 25 in the SPSS package, is too conservative since more iterations may be needed to achieve proper convergence. The best control of iterations is achieved by specification of the convergence criterion, that is, the value of the maximum allowable difference between two successive communality estimates for any variable at which iterations can be terminated. The default parameter for this in the SPSS package is .001 ("STOPFACT"); in the SAS package it is .005 (parameter "CONVERGE" for the PRINIT option). Generally, these parameters are too liberal; while a value of .005 may be acceptable for preliminary evaluations, it is recommended that a value of .0005 be specified for final computations. Using too liberal a value of the convergence parameter may fail to reveal the presence of a "Heywood case"—a variable whose communality estimate exceeds unity.

Of course, a Heywood case can occur even with a liberal convergence parameter like .01. What to do if such a case occurs? One option is to ignore it, and this is often done, without so much as a remark about it. A better option is either to reduce the number of factors by one or to drop the variable and recompute the analysis, later handling it as an extension variable (see below). Heywood cases often occur in association with variables that measure factors not well represented in the data set, or variables that are factorially highly complex. To avoid Heywood cases, and in fact as a standard procedure of factoring, Cureton and D'Agostino (1983, p. 140) recommend using initial communality values estimated as SMCs adjusted to make their sum equal to the sum of the highest absolute values of correlations in an array, followed by one additional iteration.

To illustrate various points throughout this discussion of FA procedures, I present the complete analysis of a small $R$ matrix. This matrix contains purely hypothetical data; it is generated, with some adjustments, by the hypothetical factor matrix shown in Table 2.2. In practice, of course, one would not have a hypothetical factor matrix; one would have only the observed **R** matrix. Table 2.2, however, has been designed to illustrate certain ideas. It is based largely on the hypothesized pattern matrix shown in Table 2.1, but it contains an extra factor that represents a "general" factor, with substantial loadings on all variables. This would be expected to produce correlations among the oblique factors that would eventually be produced in the subsequent factor rotation process.

**Table 2.2. Hypothetical Factor Matrix**

|    | g   | A   | B   | C   |
|----|-----|-----|-----|-----|
| 1  | .53 | .65 | ... | ... |
| 2  | .71 | .43 | ... | ... |
| 3  | .68 | .58 | ... | ... |
| 4  | .40 | ... | .51 | ... |
| 5  | .54 | .38 | ... | .58 |
| 6  | .57 | ... | .70 | ... |
| 7  | .62 | ... | .56 | ... |
| 8  | .53 | ... | .61 | ... |
| 9  | .71 | .32 | .40 | .53 |
| 10 | .42 | ... | ... | .68 |
| 11 | .57 | ... | ... | .75 |
| 12 | .59 | ... | ... | .53 |

The diagonal and lower triangle of Table 2.3 contain the values of the hypothetical **R** matrix reproduced from Table 2.2 by multiplying the matrix by its transpose, except that the diagonal values so produced have been replaced by unities (as would appear in a normal correlation matrix), and small positive and negative random values have been added to each off-diagonal reproduced *r* to simulate the effect of error variance for a sample size of about 100. We will assume that the communalities are unknown (as would be the case in practice). For the time being, the reader may ignore the values in the upper triangle of Table 2.3, and the last two rows of correlations (for extension variables Age and Sex).

The complete PC analysis of the **R** matrix contained in Table 2.3, with all eigenvalues, is shown in Table 2.4. The last column contains communalities, all unities because the complete variance has been analyzed. Note that 3 eigenvalues are greater than unity; according to the Kaiser-Guttman unity-eigenvalue rule, this suggests that there are 3 common factors in the **R** matrix. Also, a plot of the eigenvalues, included in Figure 2.1, suggests 3 common factors by the scree test. It is seen in the last row of the Table 2.4 that 3 components account for 79.6% of the total variance.

An initial PF analysis of the **R** matrix with SMC values in the diagonal is shown in Table 2.5. The SMC values that were used (obtained from the inverse of the **R** matrix) are in the last column. Solely for illustrative purposes, the number of factors was specified as 12 in order to maximize the number of eigenvalues computed. The rows at the bottom of the table show (a) the complete set of resulting eigenvalues, (b) random data eigenvalues by the Montanelli-Humphreys (Tucker) procedure, (c) percentages (raw and cumulative) of the

## Table 2.3. Illustrative Correlation Matrix[a]

| Variable | 1 | 2 | 3 | 4 | 5 | 6 | 7 | 8 | 9 | 10 | 11 | 12 |
|---|---|---|---|---|---|---|---|---|---|---|---|---|
| 1 | 1.000 | .708 | .741 | .177 | .549 | .252 | .296 | .231 | .598 | .231 | .301 | .346 |
| 2 | .713 | 1.000 | .702 | .270 | .560 | .393 | .419 | .358 | .684 | .305 | .398 | .419 |
| 3 | .745 | .690 | 1.000 | .286 | .593 | .417 | .444 | .380 | .725 | .328 | .428 | .448 |
| 4 | .161 | .306 | .262 | 1.000 | .194 | .553 | .523 | .523 | .466 | .139 | .222 | .227 |
| 5 | .551 | .554 | .601 | .218 | 1.000 | .305 | .329 | .258 | .752 | .600 | .715 | .647 |
| 6 | .266 | .389 | .399 | .552 | .308 | 1.000 | .765 | .749 | .699 | .235 | .360 | .359 |
| 7 | .237 | .444 | .507 | .501 | .296 | .762 | 1.000 | .708 | .696 | .242 | .363 | .364 |
| 8 | .289 | .308 | .358 | .533 | .269 | .757 | .705 | 1.000 | .628 | .187 | .299 | .306 |
| 9 | .592 | .708 | .673 | .512 | .819 | .691 | .686 | .626 | 1.000 | .626 | .790 | .734 |
| 10 | .271 | .283 | .297 | .119 | .610 | .244 | .252 | .195 | .649 | 1.000 | .770 | .649 |
| 11 | .281 | .385 | .471 | .230 | .710 | .337 | .334 | .335 | .735 | .772 | 1.000 | .773 |
| 12 | .329 | .466 | .422 | .220 | .643 | .377 | .400 | .252 | .728 | .646 | .772 | 1.000 |
| Age | .188 | .243 | .236 | .025 | .273 | .041 | .087 | .047 | .236 | .241 | .301 | .274 |
| Sex[b] | -.162 | -.107 | -.145 | .030 | .038 | -.012 | .040 | -.023 | .042 | .156 | .172 | .122 |

[a]Raw correlations in diagonal and lower triangle; correlations reproduced from final hierarchical factor matrix **H** (Table 2.10) in upper triangle.
[b]Biserial correlations.

## Table 2.4. Principal Component Solution for the Correlation Matrix of Table 2.3

| Variable | | | | | | Component | | | | | | | $h^2$ |
|---|---|---|---|---|---|---|---|---|---|---|---|---|---|
| | 1 | 2 | 3 | 4 | 5 | 6 | 7 | 8 | 9 | 10 | 11 | 12 | |
| 1 | .636 | -.181 | -.647 | -.003 | .218 | .157 | .054 | .152 | .146 | .103 | -.115 | .009 | 1.000 |
| 2 | .733 | -.075 | -.487 | .088 | -.270 | .237 | .048 | -.072 | -.248 | -.114 | .033 | .015 | 1.000 |
| 3 | .754 | -.079 | -.476 | -.105 | -.014 | -.383 | .102 | .075 | .068 | -.083 | .112 | -.006 | 1.000 |
| 4 | .511 | .535 | .115 | .649 | .001 | -.073 | .087 | .045 | .043 | .026 | .000 | .009 | 1.000 |
| 5 | .783 | -.413 | -.017 | .106 | .157 | -.098 | -.292 | -.283 | .012 | .066 | .012 | .034 | 1.000 |
| 6 | .697 | .561 | .144 | -.161 | -.008 | .141 | -.087 | -.057 | .241 | -.253 | -.006 | .013 | 1.000 |
| 7 | .706 | .519 | .089 | -.257 | -.234 | -.137 | .145 | -.143 | -.031 | .183 | -.098 | .017 | 1.000 |
| 8 | .640 | .590 | .122 | -.171 | .318 | .063 | -.101 | .163 | -.207 | .082 | .083 | .009 | 1.000 |
| 9 | .984 | -.009 | .053 | .033 | .025 | .061 | -.048 | -.110 | -.005 | .034 | -.011 | -.089 | 1.000 |
| 10 | .630 | -.467 | .431 | -.036 | .171 | .135 | .366 | -.090 | .047 | .015 | .071 | .014 | 1.000 |
| 11 | .752 | -.392 | .390 | .006 | .044 | -.158 | -.013 | .161 | -.157 | -.176 | -.140 | .004 | 1.000 |
| 12 | .741 | -.346 | .302 | -.012 | -.341 | .084 | -.154 | .239 | .118 | .134 | .063 | .007 | 1.000 |
| (Eigenvalues) Roots | 6.259 | 1.924 | 1.372 | .576 | .449 | .339 | .307 | .270 | .232 | .190 | .072 | .010 | 12.000 |
| % of Variance | 52.2 | 16.0 | 11.4 | 4.8 | 3.7 | 2.8 | 2.6 | 2.2 | 1.9 | 1.6 | .6 | .1 | |
| Cumulative % of Variance | 52.2 | 68.2 | 79.6 | 84.4 | 88.2 | 91.0 | 93.5 | 95.8 | 97.7 | 99.3 | 99.9 | 100.0 | |

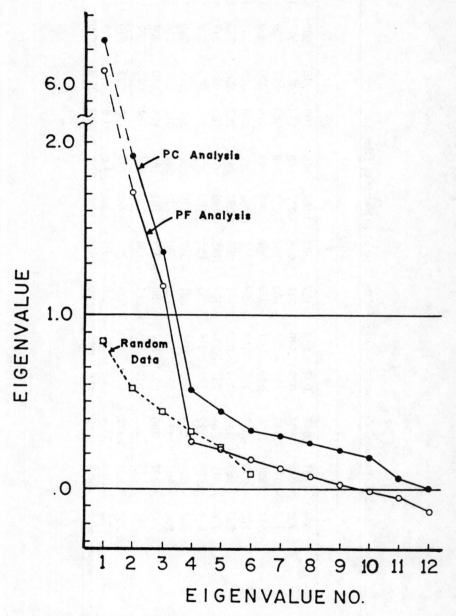

Figure 2.1. Scree plots for analyses of 12-variable correlation matrix.

total variance accounted for by successive roots, and (d) percentages (raw and cumulative) of the SMC variance. Scree plots of the observed and random data roots are included in Figure 2.1.

At this stage it appeared from both the scree test and the Montanelli–Humphreys criterion that 3 factors were significant, accounting for 74.7% of the total variance and 92.8% of the SMC variance. Accordingly, it was planned to perform PF analyses for 2, 3, and 4 factors, with a convergence parameter of .0005, to investigate other criteria for the number of factors. A 3-factor PF analysis of the 12-variable **R** matrix disclosed, however, that variable 9 was a Heywood case, and it was dropped from further PF analyses. The roots for 2-, 3-, and 4-factor converged PF solutions for the remaining 11 variables of the **R** matrix, with corresponding Varimax-rotated matrices, are shown in Table 2.6. The unrotated matrices, which are of no particular interest, are not shown, but the table includes the orthogonal transformation matrices producing the Varimax-rotated factor matrices. It should be pointed out that the columns of the rotated matrices are not ordered here as they were originally computed. Most Varimax routines arrange columns in the order of decreasing column sums of squares, but actually the order is arbitrary. Here the order was chosen so as to show correspondence with the hypothesized factor matrix of Table 2.1. My Varimax routine automatically orients column loadings so that their algebraic sums are positive.

Table 2.6 furnishes more evidence that three common factors—no more, no fewer—should be accepted for further analysis. The principal evidence is that 3 is the largest number of factors that yields a Varimax-rotated matrix such that each factor has at least 3 salient variables (indicated by asterisked loadings throughout the tables). Two factors are not sufficient, as indicated by the considerable increase from 2 to 3 factors in variance accounted for and the dramatic increases in communalities ($h^2$ values) for some variables. Note that in the case of the 4-factor solution, the transformation matrix shows that the fourth rotated factor is derived almost exclusively from the fourth unrotated factor (indicated by the value of $^-.999$ at the bottom of the last column). Such a phenomenon in a Varimax transformation matrix is often a useful sign of overfactoring.

This illustration is too simple to introduce all the types of complications that can arise in determining the "correct" number of factors for large, real data sets, but it should nevertheless serve to inform the reader about how to proceed with real data.

## Factor Analysis: Factor Rotation

We have already performed factor rotations, obtaining Varimax matrices in Table 2.6 to help decide on the correct number of factors to accept. It is now time to discuss the need for rotations, and rotational procedures, in greater detail.

Although to save space it was not shown in Table 2.6 (it is to be found in

Table 2.5. Initial (1st Iteration) PF Solution for the Correlation Matrix of Table 2.3 with SMC's in the Diagonal

| Variable | Factor | | | | | | | | | | | | SMCs |
|---|---|---|---|---|---|---|---|---|---|---|---|---|---|
| | 1 | 2 | 3 | 4 | 5 | 6 | 7 | 8 | 9 | 10[a] | 11 | 12 | |
| 1 | .625 | -.162 | -.602 | .061 | .140 | .149 | -.015 | -.025 | .030 | | | | .802 |
| 2 | .720 | -.060 | -.452 | -.095 | -.229 | .096 | -.057 | -.007 | -.064 | | | | .800 |
| 3 | .739 | -.061 | -.435 | -.125 | .110 | -.118 | .168 | .032 | .034 | | | | .787 |
| 4 | .482 | .441 | .089 | .229 | -.234 | .063 | .160 | .070 | .029 | | | | .575 |
| 5 | .786 | -.418 | -.022 | .257 | .007 | -.248 | -.090 | .012 | -.005 | | | | .925 |
| 6 | .683 | .542 | .141 | -.006 | .040 | .022 | -.100 | -.082 | .072 | | | | .800 |
| 7 | .697 | .521 | .095 | -.263 | .010 | -.132 | -.037 | .106 | -.018 | | | | .848 |
| 8 | .623 | .557 | .118 | .117 | .207 | .054 | .019 | -.075 | -.069 | | | | .767 |
| 9 | .995 | -.001 | .057 | .087 | -.056 | .015 | -.089 | .040 | -.008 | | | | .987 |
| 10 | .619 | -.438 | .393 | -.035 | .120 | .182 | -.039 | .148 | .014 | | | | .794 |
| 11 | .743 | -.375 | .367 | -.033 | .038 | .000 | .169 | -.071 | -.035 | | | | .833 |
| 12 | .720 | -.309 | .261 | -.161 | -.149 | .007 | -.016 | -.133 | .033 | | | | .736 |
| (Eigenvalues) Roots | 6.089 | 1.706 | 1.168 | .265 | .224 | .165 | .116 | .077 | .020 | -.012 | -.042 | -.123 | 9.653 |
| Random Data Roots | .767 | .566 | .439 | .335 | .233 | .091 | ... | ... | ... | ... | ... | ... | |
| % of Total Variance | 50.7 | 14.2 | 9.7 | 2.2 | 1.9 | 1.4 | 1.0 | .6 | .2 | | | | |
| Cumulative % of Total Variance | 50.7 | 65.0 | 74.7 | 76.9 | 78.8 | 80.1 | 81.1 | 81.7 | 81.9 | | | | |
| % of SMC Variance | 63.1 | 17.7 | 12.1 | 2.7 | 2.3 | 1.7 | 1.2 | .8 | .2 | | | | |
| Cumulative % of SMC Variance | 63.1 | 80.8 | 92.9 | 95.6 | 97.9 | 99.6 | 100.8 | 101.6 | 101.8 | | | | |

[a]Factors 10–12 not computed due to negative roots.

## Table 2.6. Eigenvalues for Converged PF Solutions for 11 Variables of the Correlation Matrix of Table 2.3, with Corresponding Varimax-Rotated Factor Matrices for 2, 3, and 4 Factors

|  | 2 Factors | | | 3 Factors | | | | 4 Factors | | | | |
|---|---|---|---|---|---|---|---|---|---|---|---|---|
|  | 1 | 2 | Sum | 1 | 2 | 3 | Sum | 1 | 2 | 3 | 4 | Sum |
| Roots | 4.904 | 1.568 | 6.472 | 5.022 | 1.622 | 1.124 | 7.767 | 5.055 | 1.669 | 1.177 | .262 | 8.164 |

### Varimax-Rotated Factor Matrices

| Variable | 1' | 2' | $h^2$ | 1' | 2' | 3' | $h^2$ | 1' | 2' | 3' | 4' | $h^2$ |
|---|---|---|---|---|---|---|---|---|---|---|---|---|
| 1 | .594ᵃ | .248 | .364 | .881ᵃ | .100 | .147 | .809 | .935ᵃ | .090 | .146 | -.192 | .940 |
| 2 | .583ᵃ | .369 | .476 | .733ᵃ | .270 | .243 | .669 | .729ᵃ | .268 | .247 | .179 | .696 |
| 3 | .616ᵃ | .389 | .531 | .764ᵃ | .288 | .266 | .737 | .742ᵃ | .289 | .277 | .093 | .719 |
| 4 | .126 | .599ᵃ | .375 | .118 | .597ᵃ | .091 | .379 | .120 | .585 | .095 | .025 | .367 |
| 5 | .855ᵃ | .147 | .753 | .499 | .126 | .662ᵃ | .703 | .486 | .127 | .668ᵃ | -.020 | .700 |
| 6 | .215 | .854ᵃ | .775 | .158 | .867ᵃ | .175 | .808 | .165 | .838ᵃ | .181 | .040 | .764 |
| 7 | .251 | .813ᵃ | .724 | .214 | .806ᵃ | .182 | .729 | .209 | .818ᵃ | .178 | .235 | .799 |
| 8 | .163 | .812ᵃ | .685 | .149 | .811ᵃ | .123 | .695 | .138 | .876ᵃ | .124 | -.311 | .898 |
| 10 | .707ᵃ | .051 | .502 | .120 | .087 | .800ᵃ | .662 | .116 | .085 | .801ᵃ | -.054 | .666 |
| 11 | .809ᵃ | .159 | .680 | .167 | .198 | .916ᵃ | .906 | .159 | .196 | .919ᵃ | -.036 | .909 |
| 12 | .756ᵃ | .191 | .608 | .242 | .218 | .752ᵃ | .671 | .234 | .212 | .759ᵃ | .174 | .706 |
| Column Sums of Squared Loadings | 3.630 | 2.842 | 6.472 | 2.355 | 2.692 | 2.720 | 7.767 | 2.390 | 2.750 | 2.758 | .266 | 8.164 |

### Varimax Transformation Matrices

|  | 1' | 2' | | 1' | 2' | 3' | | 1' | 2' | 3' | 4' |
|---|---|---|---|---|---|---|---|---|---|---|---|
| 1 | .786 | .618 | | .559 | .567 | .605 | | .555 | .570 | .606 | .024 |
| 2 | -.618 | .786 | | -.174 | .793 | -.584 | | -.201 | .799 | -.566 | -.020 |
| 3 |  |  | | -.811 | .221 | .542 | | -.807 | .192 | .557 | .022 |
| 4 |  |  | |  |  |  | | .000 | .002 | .038 | -.999 |

ᵃSalient loading for each variable

43

Table 2.10), the 3-factor orthogonal *PF* matrix that yielded the corresponding Varimax matrix is an "unrotated" factor matrix which is only one of an infinity of matrices that would reproduce the **R** matrix in exactly the same way; all these matrices are related to each other by orthogonal transformation. At this stage the problem is to find which transformed matrix would be most suitable for psychological interpretation. This problem is commonly described as that of rotation to simple structure. It is justified not only by the need for psychological interpretation but also on the basis of the principle of parsimony. We want the simplest possible description of each variable—ideally a description such that each variable has nonzero (or "nonvanishing") loadings on only one or a small number of factors.

The problem of rotation can also be viewed as one of recovering, as nearly as possible, a hypothesized pattern matrix, as this matrix normally represents a form of simple structure matrix. There is in fact a procedure (the Procrustean procedure discussed below) by which one could find the transformation of **F** that best fits, in a certain sense, a hypothesized pattern matrix, but such a procedure of fitting a preconceived pattern matrix could be criticized as "stacking the deck." We need procedures that can be used in the absence of any preconceived factor patterns.

Obviously, if a set of data can be satisfactorily accounted for by just one factor, there is no need for rotation.

*The Varimax Rotation.* By far the most popular and widely used rotational method is that due to Kaiser (1958); programs for this and various other methods discussed here are included in standard computer packages. It is an *orthogonal* rotation that maximizes the variance of *squared* factor loadings over factors. It can be applied in either its "raw" or its "normalized" form—usually the latter. The Varimax rotations shown in Table 2.6 were done using the normalized form.

Focusing attention on the 3-factor Varimax matrix, the three possible pairwise plots of factors are shown in Figure 2.2.

It is evident that the solution obtained for the present set of hypothetical data approximates a simple structure only very roughly. Few if any of the loadings are close to zero, as many of them should be if criteria of simple structure (Thurstone, 1947, p. 335) are to be attained. Of course, other data sets might give a better orthogonal simple structure. But a Varimax rotation should not be regarded as sacrosanct: It can be further adjusted, orthogonally, to improve the structure, even though this requires some judgment.

To attain a better simple structure in the case of our illustrative hypothetical data, it is necessary to perform an oblique rotation by one of the methods now to be discussed. The object would be to place oblique coordinates and primary vectors in such a way that a large number of loadings would be as close to zero as possible. Before oblique rotational methods are presented, it is necessary to distinguish three types of representation of oblique factors: the reference

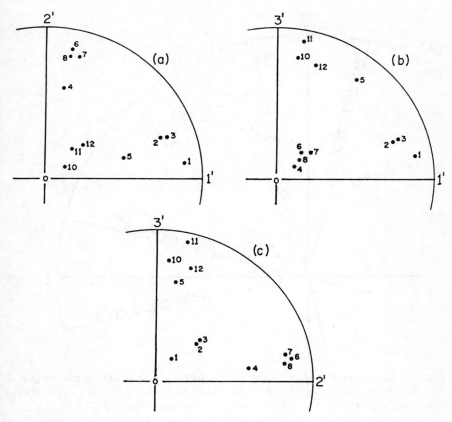

Figure 2.2. Pairwise plots of varimax factor loadings for (a) factors 1′ versus 2′; (b) factors 1′ versus 3′; (c) factors 2′ versus 3′.

vector matrix, the pattern matrix, and the structure matrix. These matrices differ in the manner in which loadings are measured with reference to oblique coordinates. To illustrate these differences, Figure 2.3 is a plot of factors 1 and 3′ of the 3-factor Varimax matrix of Table 2.6; thus, Figure 2.3 is essentially the same as Figure 2.2b, but material has been added.

The rotation desired would place hyperplanes through clusters of points such that a maximum number of points would have "vanishing" (close to zero) loadings on the respective factors. Two hyperplanes, labeled $A$ and $C$, are drawn through clusters of points by visual inspection. Now for convenience, consider only the measurement of loadings of point 5. According to the *reference vector* representation, its loadings are measured *from the respective hyperplanes,* parallel to the two "reference vectors," **A** and **C**, that are constructed perpendicular to the hyperplanes. These measurements are shown by two dotted lines ( . . . ).

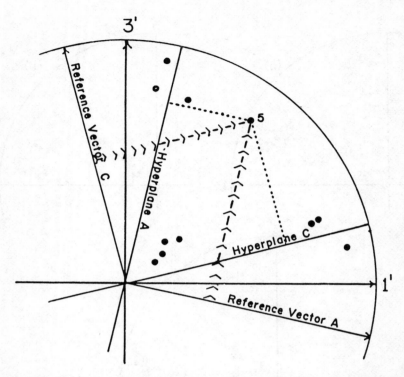

Figure 2.3. Illustration of reference vector, pattern, and structure matrix loading measurements (for Variable 5). Reference-vector measurements: . . . Pattern
matrix measurements: − − − Structure matrix measurements: $>>>$

According to the *pattern* matrix representation, the measurements are taken
from hyperplanes and parallel to primary vectors contained in hyperplanes.
(That is, hyperplane $A$ contains primary vector $C$, and hyperplane $C$ contains
primary vector $A$.) These measurements are shown as broken lines ( − − − ).
Finally, according to the *structure* matrix representation, the measurements are
taken *from the reference vectors* and parallel to the hyperplanes. These measurements are shown as arrowed lines ( $>>>$ ); over part of their extents, they
overlap with the pattern measurements.

I have dwelt on the differences between these matrices because authors use
different modes of representation of oblique factors, not always adequately
indicating which representation is used. Personally, I prefer the reference vector
representation over the pattern representation because the latter can contain
loadings greater than unity. Harman (1976) prefers the pattern representation
because it contains weights actually usable in predicting variables from factors.
From the standpoint of factor interpretation, however, it seems that either type
of representation is usable since they are proportional to each other, but one

must note that the magnitudes of the reference vector loadings are more conservative.

*Oblique Procrustes Rotation.* As mentioned above, a mathematical procedure is available for rotating an orthogonal matrix to an oblique matrix that best fits, in a least squares sense, any specified "target" matrix. Tucker's (1944) "semi-analytical" rotation is a useful form of this procedure. (There is also an orthogonally constrained Procrustes procedure [Cliff, 1966] that was much used by Guilford and Hoepfner, 1971, who disfavored oblique rotations.) The problem is: What target matrix should be used? One option is to use the hypothesized pattern matrix as the target, but this is arguably objectionable since it may bias the results towards confirming one's hypotheses. Horn and Knapp (1973) found that such Procrustean rotations can lead to artifactually confirming a wide range of theories. One alternative is to use an adaptation of the Varimax matrix in which only the salient loadings (as previously defined) are used, all other entries being zero. Still another alternative is to use all loadings in the Varimax matrix that are greater (in absolute magnitude) than some specified value, say .4. Table 2.7 shows Procrustes rotations, along with the corresponding matrices of correlations among factors, for these two alternatives; they are essentially similar, except for the factor correlations.

**Table 2.7. Two Oblique Procrustes Rotations of the 3-Factor Varimax Solution for 11 Variables (Reference-Vector Matrices)**

| | Using Only "Salient" Loadings | | | | Using All Loadings $\geqslant .4$ | | |
|---|---|---|---|---|---|---|---|
| | A | B | C | | A | B | C |
| 1 | .793 | -.103 | -.053 | 1 | .819 | -.103 | -.052 |
| 2 | .603 | .079 | .045 | 2 | .630 | .079 | .046 |
| 3 | .625 | .086 | .059 | 3 | .654 | .086 | .059 |
| 4 | .008 | .542 | -.023 | 4 | -.003 | .542 | -.023 |
| 5 | .293 | -.072 | .520 | 5 | .367 | -.072 | .521 |
| 6 | -.013 | .784 | .011 | 6 | -.024 | .784 | .010 |
| 7 | .048 | .712 | .014 | 7 | .040 | .712 | .014 |
| 8 | .000 | .738 | -.030 | 8 | -.015 | .738 | -.030 |
| 10 | -.099 | -.051 | .737 | 10 | -.015 | -.051 | .737 |
| 11 | -.099 | .030 | .823 | 11 | -.006 | .030 | .824 |
| 12 | .012 | .057 | .646 | 12 | .088 | .057 | .646 |

*Hyperplane Counts*

| | | | | Sum | | | | Sum |
|---|---|---|---|---|---|---|---|---|
| $\leqslant.05$ | 5 | 1 | 5 | 11 | 6 | 1 | 5 | 12 |
| $\leqslant.10$ | 5 | 6 | 7 | 18 | 7 | 6 | 7 | 20 |

*Factor Correlations*

| | | | | | | | |
|---|---|---|---|---|---|---|---|
| A | 1.000 | .445 | .526 | A | 1.000 | .458 | .435 |
| B | .445 | 1.000 | .413 | B | .458 | 1.000 | .387 |
| C | .526 | .413 | 1.000 | C | .435 | .387 | 1.000 |

*Oblique Promax Rotation.* This procedure, originated by Hendrickson and White (1964), can be viewed as a special form of Procrustean rotation. The target matrix is obtained by raising the entries of the Varimax matrix to a certain integer power $k$ (say, 3, 4, or 5), preserving the signs of the entries in any case. The higher the power, the greater is the relative influence of the high loadings in the Varimax matrix. Promax rotations for our 3-factor Varimax matrix for $k = 3$, 4, and 5 are shown in Table 2.8. Note that factor correlations are higher as $k$ increases. The reader may wish to make plots for these matrices, as well as those of Table 2.7, to judge the goodness of the structures.

**Table 2.8. Promax Rotations for $k$ = 3, 4, and 5**
**(Reference-Vector Matrices)**

|  | $k = 3$ | | | $k = 4$ | | | $k = 5$ | | |
|---|---|---|---|---|---|---|---|---|---|
|  | A | B | C | A | B | C | A | B | C |
| 1 | .804 | -.086 | -.079 | .794 | -.099 | -.105 | .788 | -.105 | -.121 |
| 2 | .614 | .095 | .027 | .602 | .082 | .006 | .594 | .078 | -.007 |
| 3 | .636 | .103 | .040 | .623 | .091 | .018 | .615 | .086 | .004 |
| 4 | .000 | .547 | -.014 | -.006 | .544 | -.015 | -.010 | .542 | -.014 |
| 5 | .323 | -.058 | .505 | .304 | -.067 | .486 | .292 | -.069 | .475 |
| 6 | -.022 | .792 | .024 | -.032 | .787 | .022 | -.038 | .785 | .024 |
| 7 | .041 | .721 | .024 | .031 | .715 | .021 | .024 | .713 | .021 |
| 8 | -.010 | .746 | -.017 | -.019 | .741 | -.019 | -.024 | .739 | -.017 |
| 10 | -.065 | -.043 | .732 | -.085 | -.046 | .723 | -.097 | -.046 | .718 |
| 11 | -.062 | .041 | .819 | -.085 | .036 | .809 | -.099 | .036 | .802 |
| 12 | .042 | .068 | .640 | .022 | .062 | .629 | .010 | .061 | .622 |

*Hyperplane Counts*

|  |  |  |  | Sum |  |  |  | Sum |  |  |  | Sum |
|---|---|---|---|---|---|---|---|---|---|---|---|---|
| ⩽ .05 | 5 | 2 | 6 | 13 | 5 | 2 | 6 | 13 | 5 | 2 | 6 | 13 |
| ⩽ .10 | 7 | 6 | 7 | 20 | 7 | 7 | 6 | 20 | 7 | 6 | 6 | 19 |

*Factor Correlations*

|  | A | B | C | A | B | C | A | B | C |
|---|---|---|---|---|---|---|---|---|---|
| A | 1.000 | .436 | .506 | 1.000 | .467 | .557 | 1.000 | .481 | .585 |
| B | .436 | 1.000 | .379 | .467 | 1.000 | .400 | .481 | 1.000 | .408 |
| C | .506 | .379 | 1.000 | .557 | .400 | 1.000 | .585 | .408 | 1.000 |

*Hyperplane Counts.* We now have a number of slightly different oblique rotations of the same set of data. (There are perhaps a dozen more rotational procedures that could have been used; the ones shown here are the more popular and widely used.) Which is best? One criterion, recommended by Cattell (1978), is the maximization of hyperplane counts, that is, the number of loadings (either separately by factors, or over the whole factor matrix) that in absolute magnitude are less than a prespecified quantity, that is, within a specified distance from a hyperplane. The hyperplane count parameter can be set at, say, .05 or .10 depending on how conservative or liberal the investigator chooses to be. Either reference vector or pattern matrix loadings can be evaluated by this criterion, although which of these are used can make some difference because pattern matrix loadings are generally larger than reference vector loadings. (I prefer to use reference vector loadings.) Tables 2.7 and 2.8 show hyperplane counts for parameters of .05 and .10. Using these parameters, it appears that Promax rotations for either $k = 3$ or 4 are somewhat superior to the others shown.

*Visual Inspection and Graphical Rotations.* Although we now get farther into the realm of subjective judgment (already inevitably involved in the choice of rotational method!), it is not unreasonable to believe that improved results can be obtained by visual inspection of pairwise plots of factor loadings and further rotations based on visual inspection. Sometimes hyperplane counts can be improved in this way, although one need not be a slave to hyperplane counts since other considerations sometimes apply. (For example, one might wish to avoid having a substantial negative loading.) Table 2.9 and Figure 2.4 show a graphical rotation of our hypothetical data, and corresponding factor plots *on oblique axes,* that appears to me to be at least a slight improvement over any of those produced by more objective methods. Points are slightly closer to hyper-

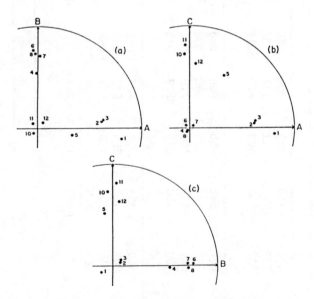

Figure 2.4. Pairwise plots of oblique reference-vector loadings for (a) factors *A* versus *B*; (b) factors *A* versus *C*; (c) factors *B* versus *C*. The coordinate axes are oblique.

**Table 2.9. Final Solutions (with Variables Reordered): F: Unrotated (Orthogonal) Principal Factor Matrix; V: Graphically Rotated Oblique Reference–Vector Matrix; H: Hierarchical (Orthogonalized) Factor Matrix**

| | PF Matrix (F) | | | | Reference–Vector Matrix (V) | | | Hierarchical Factor Matrix (H) | | | | |
|---|---|---|---|---|---|---|---|---|---|---|---|---|
| | 1 | 2 | 3 | $h^2$ | A | B | C | g | a | b | c | $h^2$ |
| | | | | | Factor A | | | | Factor a | | | |
| 1 | .638 | -.159 | -.613 | .809 | .805 | -.109 | -.065 | .627 | .634 | -.099 | -.058 | .808 |
| 3 | .751 | -.059 | -.412 | .737 | .635 | .082 | .051 | .692 | .500 | .075 | .046 | .737 |
| 2 | .709 | -.055 | -.403 | .669 | .612 | .075 | .038 | .656 | .482 | .068 | .034 | .668 |
| | | | | | Factor B | | | | Factor b | | | |
| 6 | .687 | .558 | .158 | .808 | -.040 | .783 | .019 | .547 | -.031 | .713 | .017 | .809 |
| 8 | .618 | .546 | .125 | .695 | -.028 | .738 | -.022 | .494 | -.022 | .671 | -.020 | .695 |
| 7 | .687 | .496 | .102 | .729 | .025 | .711 | .021 | .556 | .019 | .647 | .019 | .728 |
| 4 | .460 | .400 | .045 | .379 | -.013 | .541 | -.017 | .368 | -.010 | .493 | -.016 | .379 |
| | | | | | Factor C | | | | Factor c | | | |
| 11 | .760 | -.407 | .404 | .906 | -.045 | .035 | .822 | .591 | -.036 | .032 | .745 | .907 |
| 10 | .601 | -.418 | .355 | .662 | -.049 | -.047 | .735 | .463 | -.039 | -.043 | .666 | .661 |
| 12 | .714 | -.308 | .258 | .671 | .054 | .060 | .644 | .571 | .043 | .054 | .584 | .672 |
| 5 | .751 | -.373 | -.018 | .703 | .336 | -.072 | .514 | .642 | .264 | -.065 | .466 | .703 |
| Roots | 5.022 | 1.622 | 1.124 | 7.767 | | | | 3.591 | .961 | 1.651 | 1.565 | 7.767 |

Column Sum Squares: 3.591

*Hyperplane Counts*

| | A | B | C | Sum | g | a | b | c | Sum |
|---|---|---|---|---|---|---|---|---|---|
| <.05 | 6 | 2 | 5 | 13 | 0 | 7 | 2 | 6 | 15 |
| <.10 | 7 | 6 | 7 | 20 | 0 | 7 | 7 | 7 | 21 |

## PF Matrix (F)

|  | 1 | 2 | 3 |
|---|---|---|---|
| g | 1.003 | -.001 | .068 |
| Age | .273 | -.225 | -.012 |
| Sex | .014 | -.083 | .320 |

## Reference-Vector Matrix (V)

Extension Variables

|  | A | B | C |
|---|---|---|---|
| g | .260 | .373 | .434 |
| Age | .146 | -.107 | .239 |
| Sex | -.274 | .032 | .273 |

## Hierarchical Factor Matrix (H)

|  | g | a | b | c |
|---|---|---|---|---|
| g | .836 | .205 | .339 | .393 |
| Age | .236 | .115 | -.097 | .217 |
| Sex | -.032 | -.216 | .029 | .247 |

## Transformation Matrix

|  | A | B | C |
|---|---|---|---|
| 1 | .322 | .351 | .387 |
| 2 | -.206 | .882 | -.632 |
| 3 | -.924 | .313 | .672 |

## Factor Correlations[a]

|  | A | B | C | g |
|---|---|---|---|---|
| A | .585 | .477 | .487 | .765 |
| B | .478 | .389 | .394 | .624 |
| C | .484 | .394 | .399 | .632 |

[a]Values reproduced from the g loadings are shown in the diagonal and upper triangle.

51

planes, although the total hyperplane counts are not improved. The moral is not that this particular rotation is the best, but that there is no one rotational procedure that is defensibly the best. Such is the state of affairs in factor analysis. Nevertheless, it should be evident that the general pattern of results is generally the same regardless of the rotational procedure, and factor interpretations are not radically affected by different rotations if they are carefully done. (See Tucker & Finkbeiner, 1981, for a recently proposed rotational method claimed to yield generally superior results.)

Pattern and structure matrices corresponding to the oblique reference vector matrix $V$ of Table 2.9 are given in Table 2.10. Note that reference–vector and pattern loadings differ only by proportionality factors. Structure matrix loadings, on the other hand, represent correlations of variables with oblique factors.

### Table 2.10. Pattern and Structure Matrices Corresponding to the Oblique Reference-Vector Matrix V of Table 2.9

| | Pattern Matrix | | | | Structure Matrix | | |
|---|---|---|---|---|---|---|---|
| | A | B | C | | A | B | C |
| | Factor A | | | | Factor A | | |
| 1 | .985 | -.127 | -.075 | 1 | .888 | .315 | .352 |
| 3 | .777 | .096 | .060 | 3 | .852 | .491 | .474 |
| 2 | .749 | .098 | .044 | 2 | .812 | .463 | .441 |
| | Factor B | | | | Factor B | | |
| 6 | -.049 | .913 | .022 | 6 | .399 | .898 | .358 |
| 8 | -.035 | .859 | -.025 | 8 | .364 | .833 | .296 |
| 7 | .030 | .828 | .025 | 7 | .438 | .853 | .366 |
| 4 | -.016 | .630 | -.020 | 4 | .276 | .615 | .220 |
| | Factor C | | | | Factor C | | |
| 11 | -.056 | .040 | .962 | 11 | .429 | .393 | .951 |
| 10 | -.060 | -.055 | .860 | 10 | .330 | .255 | .809 |
| 12 | .066 | .070 | .753 | 12 | .465 | .398 | .813 |
| 5 | .411 | -.083 | .601 | 5 | .662 | .350 | .767 |
| | Extension Variables | | | | Extension Variables | | |
| 9 | .319 | .434 | .507 | 9 | .772 | .787 | .833 |
| Age | .178 | -.124 | .280 | Age | .255 | .071 | .317 |
| Sex | -.336 | .038 | .319 | Sex | -.163 | .003 | .171 |

## Hierarchical Analysis

The graphically rotated oblique reference-vector factor matrix **V** in Table 2.9 has loadings for 11 variables on three *correlated* "primary" factors. For purposes of examining the overall structure of the data, it is desirable to develop a solution that will reveal any second-order factors present. This can be done by the hierarchical analysis developed by Schmid and Leiman (1957), which "orthogonalizes" the primary factors and generates one or more factors at the second-order level. In effect, the covariance of the primary factors is reapportioned among orthogonalized primary factors and any second-order factors. The procedure involves a factoring of the matrix of correlations among first-order factors. In our case, it turned out that a single factor, labeled $g$, accounted very satisfactorily for the correlations among primary factors. The "$g$" factor loadings of the primary factors are shown alongside the matrix of their correlations, middle bottom of Table 2.9. By the Schmid-Leiman procedure, the orthogonalized factor matrix $H$ at the right of Table 2.9 was computed. All variables have substantial loadings on the $g$ factor, and the hyperplane counts for the orthogonalized primary factors $a$, $b$, and $c$ are improved over those of the reference-vector matrix. This orthogonalized factor matrix is useful in conceiving the four factors it contains as representing independent sources of variance in the variables, in the sense that the *factors* can be independent in the population even though the rank of the matrix $F$ containing their loadings has a rank of only three. The orthogonalized hierarchical factor matrix is also useful because it can make unnecessary the reporting of separate reference-vector pattern, or structure matrices for correlated factors. An orthogonal matrix is at once a reference-vector, pattern, and structure matrix.

The present illustration is only a simple application of the Schmid-Leiman technique. More generally, if multiple second-order factors are rotated in such a way that they are correlated, a still higher order of orthogonal factors can be generated by redistributing the variance from second-order factors, and in theory this process can be repeated indefinitely. In practice it is rare that it would go beyond the third order unless one is dealing with a very large number of variables.

## Reproduced Correlations

The final analyses shown in Table 2.9 take us full circle to the approximate recovery of the hypothesized factor matrices of Tables 2.1 and 2.2. The hierarchical factor matrix $H$ is very similar to the matrix of Table 2.2, and its pattern is generally similar to that of Table 2.1. By multiplying $H$ by its transpose, we can compute a reproduced correlation matrix; the values are shown in the upper triangle of Table 2.3, which the reader was earlier urged to ignore. It will be seen that these reproduced values are quite similar to the corresponding "observed" values. The residuals (differences between "observed" and reproduced $r$) are distributed around zero and are not greater than .067 in absolute magnitude.

Comparing factors $a$, $b$, and $c$ of matrix $H$ with factors $A$, $B$, and $C$ of Table 2.1, we see that the only major difference appears in the loadings of variable 4 on factors $A$ versus $a$. If these were real data, we would be inclined to conclude that our supposition about variable 4, whatever it might be, is not confirmed by the analysis.

## Extension Analysis

The reader will recall the recommendation that variables like age and sex be excluded from a factor analysis because they are not true dependent variables. Also, it was noted that one variable in the analysis, variable 9, proved to be a Heywood case, and was dropped from the final analysis. Through a procedure often known as Dwyer's extension (Dwyer, 1937; Gorsuch, 1983, p. 236), the loadings of such variables as projected on the space defined by the factor analysis can be computed. This can be done for any type of factor matrix. The extension loadings for age, sex, and variable 9 in our hypothetical data set are included in Table 2.9.

## Factor Scores

Factor scores are usually computed only in data reduction studies; they are generally of little use in scientific studies of abilities. Several different procedures, based on somewhat different assumptions and yielding results with somewhat different characteristics, are available for computing factor scores (Harman, 1976, pp. 363-387). However, for PF analysis, most standard computer packages utilize only one of these, the regression method.

## Interpretation and Presentation of Results

The report of a FA investigation should contain all or most of the data that would allow a reader to re-do at least the FA itself, if not recompute the correlations. This recommendation means that the report (or auxiliary documentation) should contain the correlation matrix, the criteria used to decide on the number of factors, an unrotated factor matrix, and the rotated factor matrix (labeled as to its type). If the rotated factors are correlated, their correlations should be reported. A hierarchical analysis, if performed, would of course be reported.

It is recommended that the order of variables and factors in final matrices be organized so as to group and order variables according to their salient loadings on factors; this will facilitate readers' understanding and interpretation of the data. The organization of Table 2.9 exemplifies this recommendation.

Many authors follow somewhat unfortunate practices in reporting tables of results: Either values less than a certain quantity are completely omitted (to the frustration of a reader who might like to examine them or use them in making complete factor plots), or all values are reported to more decimals than are necessary. Probably two decimals would have been sufficient for reporting the computations in the present article; three decimals are reported for readers who might like to check the computations or use the data in other ways.

Factors are interpreted by comparing the task characteristics of variables with high or substantial loadings with the task characteristics of variables with vanishing loadings, that is, variables near the factor hyperplanes. According to the A/DI model mentioned earlier, an ability—as indicated by a factor—is to be defined by noting how the ability is related to variations in task difficulty. High ability individuals are thought to have a high probability of successfully performing the more difficult tasks; low ability individuals can successfully perform only tasks of low difficulty. The several variables loading on a given factor should, therefore, contain highly similar task difficulty continua. That is, their task difficulty continua should vary in similar ways as a function of variations in such task characteristics as type of stimulus, stimulus complexity, unfamiliarity, and so on. These considerations may be borne in mind in attempts to interpret factors. (See Carroll, in press, for further discussion of this model, particularly as it relates to the problem of interpreting the composition of variables that are factorially complex.)

## FINAL COMMENT

Although FA has often been viewed as a difficult and arcane procedure, fraught with many technical problems and requiring many subjective and arbitrary decisions, many of the difficulties are minimized, or disappear entirely, in carefully designed studies that are executed according to intelligently applied procedures. Well trained, technically informed, and experienced investigators can arrive at generally acceptable and replicable results. If technical sophistication in factor analysis is combined with an equivalent amount of sophistication about the nature of abilities and ways of measuring them, factor analysis will continue for some time to be a method of choice in the study of cognitive abilities. Because exploratory FA is in many ways simpler, less demanding, and less consuming of time, effort, and resources than confirmatory FA, investigators will continue to turn to it, at least as a preliminary procedure, in their quest for knowledge about the nature of intelligent behavior.

## REFERENCES

Carroll, J. B. (1941). A factor analysis of verbal abilities. *Psychometrika, 6,* 279–307.

Carroll, J. B. (1945). The effect of difficulty and chance success on correlations between items or between tests. *Psychometrika, 10,* 1–19.

Carroll, J. B. (1961). The nature of the data, or how to choose a correlation coefficient. *Psychometrika, 26,* 347–372.

Carroll, J. B. (1976). Psychometric tests as cognitive tasks: A new "Structure of Intellect." In L. Resnick (Ed.), *The nature of intelligence.* Hillsdale, NJ: Lawrence Erlbaum Associates, 27–56.

Carroll, J. B. (1978). How shall we study individual differences in cognitive abilities?—Methodological and theoretical perspectives. *Intelligence, 2,* 87–115.

Carroll, J. B. (1983a). The difficulty of a test and its factor composition revisited. In H. Wainer & S. Messick (Eds.), *Principals of modern psychological measurement: A Festschrift for Frederic M. Lord.* Hillsdale, NJ: Lawrence Erlbaum Associates. 257–282.

Carroll, J. B. (in press). Intellectual abilities and aptitudes. In R. Glaser & A. M. Lesgold (Eds.), *Handbook of psychology and education.* Hillsdale, NJ: Lawrence Erlbaum Associates.

Carroll, J. B. (in preparation). Factor analysis programs for the Apple II Plus.

Carroll, J. B., Kohlberg, L., & DeVries, R. (1984). Psychometric and Piagetian intelligences: Toward resolution of controversy. *Intelligence, 8,* 67–91.

Cattell, R. B. (1978). *The scientific use of factor analysis in behavioral and life sciences.* New York: Plenum.

Cliff, N. (1966). Orthogonal rotation to congruence. *Psychometrika, 31,* 33–42.

Comrey, A. L. (1973). *A first course in factor analysis.* New York: Academic.

Coombs, C. H. (1941). A factorial study of number ability. *Psychometrika, 6,* 161–189.

Corman, L., & Budoff, M. (1974). Factor structures of retarded and nonretarded children on Raven's Progressive Matrices. *Educational & Psychological Measurement, 34,* 407–412.

Cureton, E. E., & D'Agostino, R. B. (1983). *Factor analysis: An applied approach.* Hillsdale, NJ: Lawrence Erlbaum Associates.

Dwyer, P. S. (1937). The determination of the factor loadings of a given test from the known factor loadings of other tests. *Psychometrika, 2,* 173–178.

Ekstrom, R. B., French, J. W., & Harman, H. H. (1976). *Manual for kit of factor-referenced cognitive tests, 1976.* Princeton, NJ: Educational Testing Service.

French, J. W. (1951). The description of aptitude and achievement tests in terms of rotated factors. *Psychometric Monographs,* (5).

French, J. W. (1965). The relationship of problem-solving styles to the factor composition of tests. *Educational & Psychological Measurement, 25,* 9–28.

Gorsuch, R. L. (1983). *Factor analysis,* (2nd ed.). Hillsdale, NJ: Lawrence Erlbaum Associates.

Gorsuch, R. L., & Dreger, R. M. (1979). "Big Jiffy": A more sophisticated factor analysis and rotation program. *Educational & Psychological Measurement, 39,* 209–214.

Gorsuch, R. L., & Nelson, J. (1981, November). CNG scree test: An objective procedure for determining the number of factors. Paper presented at the meeting of the Society for Multivariate Experimental Psychology, Vancouver, British Columbia, Canada.

Guilford, J. P. (1980). Fluid and crystallized intelligences: Two fanciful concepts. *Psychological Bulletin, 88,* 406–412.

Guilford, J. P., & Hoepfner, R. (1971). *The analysis of intelligence.* New York: McGraw-Hill.

Hakstian, A. R., & Cattell, R. B. (1978). Higher-stratum ability structures on a basis of twenty primary abilities. *Journal of Educational Psychology, 70,* 657–669.

Harman, H. H. (1976). *Modern factor analysis,* Third edition revised. Chicago, IL: University of Chicago Press.

Hendrickson, A. E., & White, P. O. (1964). PROMAX: A quick method for rotation to oblique simple structure. *British Journal of Statistical Psychology, 17,* 65–70.

Horn, J. L., & Cattell, R. B. (1982). Whimsy and misunderstandings of Gf-Gc theory: A comment on Guilford. *Psychological Bulletin, 91,* 623–633.

Horn, J. L., & Knapp, J. R. (1973). On the subjective character of the empirical base of Guilford's Structure-of-Intellect model. *Psychological Bulletin, 80,* 33–43.

Kaiser, H. F. (1958). The varimax criterion for analytic rotation in factor analysis. *Psychometrika, 23,* 187–200.

Kaiser, H. F. (1960). The application of electronic computers to factor analysis. *Educational & Psychological Measurement, 20,* 141–151.

Karlin, J. E. (1942). A factorial study of auditory function. *Psychometrika, 7,* 251–279.

Kim, J-O., & Mueller, C. W. (1978a). *Factor analysis: Statistical methods and practical issues.* Beverly Hills, CA: Sage Publications.

Kim, J-O., & Mueller, C. W. (1978b). *Introduction to factor analysis: What it is and how to do it.* Beverly Hills, CA: Sage Publications.

Kraemer, H. C. (1981). Modified biserial correlation coefficients. *Psychometrika, 46,* 275–282.

Montanelli, R. C., Jr., & Humphreys, L. G. (1976). Latent roots of random data correlation matrices with squared multiple correlations on the diagonal: A Monte Carlo study. *Psychometrika, 41,* 341–348.

Mulaik, S. A. (1972). *The foundations of factor analysis.* New York: McGraw-Hill.

Nie, N. H., Hull, C. H., Jenkins, J. G., Steinbrenner, K., & Bent, D. H. (1975). *Statistical package for the social sciences (SPSS).* (2nd ed.) New York: McGraw-Hill.

Nunnally, J. C. (1978). *Psychometric theory.* (2nd ed.) New York: McGraw-Hill.

Pellegrino, J. W., & Kail, R., Jr. (1982). Process analyses of spatial aptitude. In R. J. Sternberg (Ed.), *Advances in the psychology of intelligence, 1.* Hillsdale, NJ: Lawrence Erlbaum Associates, 311–365.

Rummel, R. J. (1970). *Applied factor analysis,* 2nd edition. Evanston, IL: Northwestern University Press.

SAS Institute Inc. (1982). *SAS user's guide: Statistics.* Cary, NC: SAS Institute Inc.

Schmid, J., & Leiman, J. M. (1957). The development of hierarchical factor solutions. *Psychometrika, 22,* 53–61.

Thurstone, L. L. (1938). Primary mental abilities. *Psychometric Monographs,* (1).

Thurstone, L. L. (1949). *Multiple factor analysis: A development and expansion of* The Vectors of Mind. Chicago, IL: University of Chicago Press.

Tucker, L. R. (1944). A semi-analytical method of factorial rotation to simple structure. *Psychometrika, 9,* 43–68.

Tucker, L. R., & Finkbeiner, C. T. (1981, December). Transformation of factors by artificial personal probability functions. Princeton, NJ: Educational Testing Service Research Report RR-81-58.

Tukey, J. W. (1977). *Exploratory data analysis.* Reading, MA: Addison-Wesley.

Velicer, W. F., Peacock, A. C., & Jackson, D. N. (1982). A comparison of component and factor patterns: A Monte Carlo approach. *Multivariate Behavioral Research, 17,* 371–388.

# CHAPTER 3

# Applications of Confirmatory Factor Analysis to the Study of Intelligence

*Christopher Hertzog*

*Individual and Family Studies*
*College of Human Development*
*The Pennsylvania State University*

## INTRODUCTION

The study of intelligence has undergone profound theoretical and methodological changes over the past two decades, as the chapters in this volume readily illustrate. The changes have included a veritable revolution in mathematical models for psychometric assumptions deriving from classical test theory, and the development of covariance structures modeling as a general approach to multivariate analysis of psychometric batteries measuring intelligence and related constructs. One of the critical problems in the field, however, is that specialized methodological skills are becoming more critical in addressing certain types of research questions, while at the same time the methods to be mastered are increasing geometrically in complexity. Thus it appears that the recipe for a properly trained psychologist who studies intelligent behavior is one-third experimental cognitive psychologist, one-third psychometrician, and one-third mathematical statistician, with dashes of physiological psychology and artificial intelligence thrown in for seasoning. In any event, one difficult problem in learning methods such as covariance structures modeling is that most of the theoretical papers and applications prevalent in the literature have been written for statisticians or others with strong quantitative backgrounds. Simple, conceptually oriented treatments of such techniques are relatively rare. There are several reasons for this—some of them more justifiable than others. Certainly one good reason is that it is difficult to explain complex methods and their proper application without introducing a fair measure of mathematical complexity in the process.

This chapter is an attempt to bridge the gap between the psychologist interested in using covariance-structures modeling, particularly confirmatory factor analysis, to study intelligence and the mathematically oriented presentations of those methods available in the original writings of Karl Jöreskog and others. I have three specific goals in mind: (a) to provide a basic discussion of the principles of covariance structures modeling and its use in confirmatory factor analysis; (b) to outline aspects of these methods most relevant to issues in research on psychometric intelligence; and (c) to cite selected covariance structures applications which can be read as illustrations of the techniques as well as for their substantive contributions. Space limitations prevent a full discussion of many important nuances in restricted factor analysis techniques; wherever possible the text provides the additional references needed.

## CONFIRMATORY FACTOR ANALYSIS: BASIC CONCEPTS

I shall assume that the reader is familiar with basic treatments of traditional factor analysis, as represented in texts by Harman (1967) or Mulaik (1972) (see also Carroll, Chapter 2 of this volume). The discussion will therefore concentrate on the differences between traditional exploratory factor analysis and the confirmatory approach. The interested reader is referred to excellent discussions of these distinctions by Mulaik (1972, 1975). Briefly, traditional factor analysis may be generally considered to be exploratory in nature: One attempts to discover the nature of a set of underlying constructs by an inductive examination of the factor structure of a set of observed measures. In contrast, confirmatory factor analysis is a hypothesis testing approach in which one uses theoretical conceptions regarding the nature of the constructs and their relations to observed variables to specify (a priori) a model predicting the factor structure of a set of measures. The conceptions might be based upon previous empirical research, a well defined set of theoretical notions, or some combination of the two. The idea is that one collects data in an attempt to disconfirm or falsify a particular model or set of models generated from theory by showing that the empirically obtained correlation matrix is not consistent with the proposed model. A related but quite different distinction is that of restricted versus unrestricted factor analysis. The exploratory/confirmatory distinction entails methods for using factor analysis to make inferences from empirical data. The restricted/unrestricted distinction refers essentially to the type of factor analytic algorithm used to estimate a factor analysis model's parameters. The utility in distinguishing confirmatory factor analysis from restricted factor analysis derives from the following: Jöreskog's restricted factor analysis methods (e.g., Jöreskog, 1969; Jöreskog and Sörbom, 1979) are often used in studies which can only be characterized as being exploratory in nature. Conversely, some of the steps involved in confirmatory factor analysis (e.g., careful selection of empirical variables to obtain a content valid representation of factorial domains of interest, given a set of hypotheses about the nature of the underlying factor structure) were fully discussed and emphasized in the literature well before the advent of restricted factor analytic methods (e.g., Thurstone, 1947). The reason this presentation (and others) emphasizes the use of restricted factor analysis methods is that they are uniquely suited to confirmatory factor analytic investigations, and make available a powerful set of tools for statistical inference that are not available in more traditional unrestricted methods. Nevertheless, some of the more critical aspects of sound confirmatory factor analytic technique have little or nothing to do with restricted factor analysis methods per se, and use of COFAMM, LISREL, or similar programs is certainly not sufficient to produce sound confirmatory factor analysis.

## The Common Factor Model

Restricted and unrestricted factor analysis both operate on the basis of the same common factor model. Assume a model relating $p$ observed (or manifest) variables to $m$ unobserved common factors. The usual representation[1] is:

$$Y_1 = \lambda_{1,1}\eta_1 + \lambda_{3,2}\eta_2 + ... + \lambda_{1,m}\eta_m + \epsilon_1$$
$$Y_2 = \lambda_{2,1}\eta_1 + \lambda_{2,2}\eta_2 + ... + \lambda_{2,m}\eta_m + \epsilon_2 \tag{1}$$
$$Y_p = \lambda_{p;1}\eta_1 + \lambda_{p,2}\eta_2 + ... + \lambda_{p,m}\eta_m + \epsilon_p$$

which shows each observed variable to be a linear combination of the factors, denoted $\eta_1$, $\eta_2$, and so forth, and a residual component, $\epsilon_p$. The factor pattern coefficients (loadings), the $\lambda_{p,m}$, are regressions of the observed variables on the factors. In matrix notation, Equation 1 is represented as

$$Y = \Lambda\eta + \epsilon \tag{2}$$

where there are $p$ observed variables in $Y$, $m$ factors in $\eta$, $p$ unique components in $\epsilon$, and $\Lambda$ is a $p \times m$ matrix of regressions coefficients regressing $Y$ on $\eta$. Equation 2 may be used to derive the expectation of the covariance matrix of $Y$, $\Sigma$, assuming $\eta$ and $\epsilon$ to be uncorrelated, which is the usual representation of regression residuals. The common factor model represents $\Sigma$ as

$$\Sigma = \Lambda\Psi\Lambda' + \Theta_\epsilon \tag{3}$$

where $\Lambda$ is as before, $\Psi$ is the covariance matrix of the factors, and $\Theta_\epsilon$ is the covariance matrix of the unique components. In other words, the diagonal elements

---

[1] I have used LISREL notation in this chapter to minimize the difficulty in translating notation from this paper to actual use of LISREL. The factor models are specified on LISREL's $Y$-side because this is necessary if factor means are to be incorporated. The reader should be aware that the $\Psi$ matrix is a regression residual matrix in the general LISREL model; it can be used as a factor covariance matrix if only the $Y$-side measurement model is used.

of $\Theta_\epsilon$ are the unique variances (variance not explained by the common factors) while the off-diagonal elements are covariances among the unique components. Similarly, the diagonal elements of $\Psi$ are the variances of the factors, while the off-diagonal elements are the covariances among the factors.

The model in Equation 3 has been extended to a model for the simultaneous analysis of multiple groups (Jöreskog, 1971b; Sörbom, 1974; Jöreskog and Sörbom, 1981). In terms of Equation 3, one simply adds a superscript $g$ to indicate the factor analysis specification in the $g$th group:

$$\Sigma^{(g)} = \Lambda^{(g)}\Psi^{(g)}\Lambda^{(g)'} + \Theta_\epsilon^{(g)} \tag{4}$$

The single group model of Equation 3 can be seen to be a special case of Equation 4 with one group.

## Unrestricted versus Restricted Factor Solutions

The major difference between unrestricted and restricted factor analysis involves the way in which these methods seek to estimate parameters from Equation 4. Given that the factors in $\eta$ and the residuals in $\epsilon$ are unobserved, there are an infinite number of solutions for Equation 4 in terms of parameters in $\Lambda$, $\Psi$, and $\Theta_\epsilon$ which will reproduce the covariance matrix $\Sigma$. The unrestricted approach places no restrictions on the common factor part of Equation 4–$\Lambda\Psi\Lambda'$. Instead it specifies $\Theta_\epsilon$ to be a diagonal matrix of unique variances (i.e., it assumes no correlations among the unique components) and (temporarily) specifies $\Psi$ to be an identity matrix, with factor variances standardized to 1 and factor correlations fixed to zero. Then, given a specification of the number of factors, one of a set of familiar methods is used to estimate the unrestricted factor pattern matrix (Carroll, Chapter 2 of this volume; Jöreskog, 1967; Mulaik, 1972). This factor pattern matrix is also not unique and may be subjected to any arbitrary transformation (rotation) to arrive at a "final" solution.

The restricted approach is quite different (Jöreskog, 1967; 1969). At first all parameters in the three parameter matrices $\Lambda$, $\Psi$, and $\Theta_\epsilon$ are included in the model. One proceeds by specifying a model for the factor structure of the observed variables in $Y$ by (a) hypothesizing the number of factors a priori, and (b) by restricting the values of a sufficient number of the parameters in the three parameter matrices to enable an estimation of the remaining unknown parameters. There are two types of restrictions: parameters are (a) fixed to some specific value in advance (by hypothesis) or (b) some set of unknown parameters are constrained to an equal value. For example, if we hypothesized that a variable is not determined (at least in part) by a certain factor, we would fix the regression of that variable on the factor to zero. If we hypothesized that two variables had exactly the same magnitude of (a nonzero) relationship to a given factor, we would represent that hypothesis by constraining the associated factor loadings to be equal. Provided that a sufficient set of fixed and constrained restrictions have been placed upon the model to provide a unique solution, the remaining parameters may be estimated.

The restricted approach is so named because it does place restrictions on the common factor space (Jöreskog, 1969; Mulaik, 1975); it is necessary to place a sufficient number of restrictions on the parameters in $\Lambda$ and $\Psi$ to uniquely identify the remaining unknowns. Thus the validity of the restricted model's parameter estimates is contingent upon the validity of the restrictions placed upon the model. Is it really the case that the loading of variable 1 on factor 2 should be fixed to zero, given our hypotheses about the properties of the factor? One of the implications of the restricted approach is that the observed variables must be carefully selected for factor analysis so that a meaningful factor model may be specified in advance (see below). In the following section we outline the salient features of restricted factor analysis models as they relate to the process of confirmatory factor analysis.

## Stages of Confirmatory Factor Analysis

### Operational Definitions of Hypotheses

Without question the most critical phase of confirmatory factor analysis is the first one: a clear statement of the hypotheses to be tested and their impact upon the subsequent factor analysis design. No amount of "mathemagic" can convert correlations from a poorly selected test battery or from an inappropriate subpopulation into information which may be used to address the hypothesis of interest. The rationale for confirmatory factor analysis is founded upon the assumption that one cannot in fact inductively discover the "true" structure of intelligence (or anything else) by exploratory analysis of haphazardly selected tests; instead, one is required to specify in advance a hypothesis about the factor structure of a carefully selected set of tests, given a factorial theory about the ways in which individual differences in the test will be determined. The logic of inference in confirmatory analysis is essentially proof by falsification. We can never show a factor model to be true, but we can infer that a model is false if it cannot account for the data at hand. However, there are several reasons why a model might not fit a set of data, including the statistical properties of the observed variables and the construct validity of the variables selected. These alternatives limit the generality of the falsification of theoretical models, and require careful attention to the factor analytic design in order to protect the validity of the theoretical inferences (Meehl, 1978). If we are to insure that the results of a confirmatory factor analysis can in fact be used for the purposes of hypothesis testing, we must insure a valid linkage between the hypothesis regarding the nature of the constructs to be studied (i.e., regarding the factor structure of some domain of observed variables) and the actual design of the factorial study. In other words, we must rule out rival explanations for the failure of a model to fit the sample data other than the primary explanation we wish to assert:

namely, that the hypothesis regarding the factor structure generated by the theory in question is incorrect.

Issues to be considered in this regard include

1. selection of the subset of variables actually measured from the larger domain of observed variables measuring the factor;
2. consideration of the properties of the observed variables as they define a factor space. This consideration includes sufficient sampling of domains to enable (a) representation of the meaningful covariances among tests in the common factor space by sufficient sampling of observed variables from the domain and (b) identification of the differences among domains by insuring sufficient hyperplane counts (see Cattell, 1978);
3. careful decisions regarding the target population defined by the research question; and
4. sampling from that population in a way which insures the statistical viability of the confirmatory analysis as well as the external validity of the results.

Let us say, for example, that we wish to test a hypothesis which argues that the cognitive style factor of Field Independence (Vernon, 1972) is in reality nothing more than a reinterpretation of the perceptual factor Flexibility of Closure, as measured in the Educational Testing Service (ETS) Reference Factors (Ekstrom, French, Harman & Dermen, 1976). This issue was considered by Widiger, Knudsen, and Rorer (1980), who attempted to address the issue by using exploratory factor analysis. Alternatively, it can be shown that the hypothesis may be translated into a confirmatory factor model for both Field Independence and Flexibility of Closure in which the correlation between the two factors is hypothesized to equal 1 (Jöreskog, 1974; MacLeod[2]). The methods described below may be used to obtain a likelihood ratio $\chi^2$ test of this hypothesis. However, it must be clearly understood that the statistical test calculated is nothing more than a test of the empirical relations among the variables selected to represent the two factors. Before the data is collected we would need to carefully consider whether Field Independence should be measured by the Embedded Figures Test, the Rod and Frame Test, or other measures. The validity of the design will depend upon the ramifications (expected and unexpected) of the selection of variables. What kinds of additional sources of variance are present in each test? For example, does the speeded nature of the ETS tests measuring Flexibility of Closure introduce a method-specific component which would prevent a perfect correlation between the two factors, even if the hypothesis that the two constructs are the same is actually correct? How broadly or narrowly should Field Independence be defined, given the theoretical position of Witkin and

---

[2] Colin MacLeod reported to me that he had in fact collected data on multiple indicators of Flexibility of Closure and Field Independence. He was not able to reject the hypothesis that the factor correlation was equal to 1 in a covariance structures model.

others (Witkin, Dyk, Faterson, Goodenough & Karp, 1962), and what are the implications of choosing observed variables other than the Embedded Figures Test? These and other questions must be addressed prior to the selection of variables and the collection of the data. Make no mistake—after the data is collected the analysis is determined! One of the major advantages of confirmatory factor analysis is that it forces us to work through such issues prior to the collection of the data, precisely because answers to such questions are necessary to determine the model to be tested, and hence, the design to be executed.

Before proceeding to discuss some of the technical nuances of model specification, which also bear upon the issue of selection of variables, let us return briefly to the concept of proof by falsification. To some this point must seem somewhat strange, since the technique is labeled "confirmatory" rather than "disconfirmatory" factor analysis. Let me emphasize, however, that there is no empirical method for proving a factor model to be true—to confirm it in the logical sense of the word. We can only show that competing models are disconfirmed by the data, or that one model fits better than a different set of models. Furthermore, certain classes of factor models cannot be distinguished from one another by empirical falsification. For example, a primary factor model with correlated factors can account for the correlations among a set of intelligence subtests, but so can the "British" model of a general intelligence factor with specific factors which are uncorrelated with $g$ (Jöreskog, 1969). Selection of one or the other is determined by the theoretical predilection of the researcher, not by comparison of the empirical results from estimating each model.

The term *confirmation* derives in part from a rather different connotation. Before we seriously entertain a factor model as being a useful representation of the factor structure of a set of tests, we wish to demonstrate that the empirical solution is replicable across different samples from the same population. However, assume that we replicate the results. We have confirmed that the model produces consistent patterns of parameter estimates, but we have not shown that the theory which produced the model is correct. In short, we must recognize that confirmation in this limited sense refers to empirical consistency and not to the validity of the theory which produced the model. In principle the restricted factor analysis method both enables the assessment of empirical consistency across independent samples and provides the means for statistical hypothesis testing.

## Model Specification in Restricted Factor Analysis

Some of the important considerations in the selection of variables for confirmatory factor analysis involve the nature of the model specification procedure in restricted factor analysis, particularly with respect to the issue of identification. That is, the set of observed variables must not only be selected to measure adequately the factorial domains of interest, they must also be selected so as to insure the estimability of the factor analytic parameters not fixed a priori to specific values. In this section we briefly consider the issues involved in model specification. The interested reader is referred to additional technical material in Jöreskog and Sörbom (1979) and Algina (1980). Anderson and Rubin (1956) provide an interesting early discussion of some of the issues involved. Excellent path analytic orientations to the issues may be found in Long (1976) and Kenny (1979).

The major goals in model specification are (a) representation of the hypotheses regarding the factor structure in the model, and (b) identification of all unknown parameters through a specification which places a sufficient number of restrictions on the model to enable estimation of the remaining unknown parameters. Identification of the unknown parameters is achieved if, and only if, the model specification reduces the number of unknowns to the point that no other factor-pattern matrix and factor-covariance matrix could be specified that would produce the same hypothesized population covariance matrix. This condition is often stated in terms of the familiar rotational equation: We say that a model is unique if, for any hypothesized matrix, $\Sigma$, there is no nonsingular transformation matrix T such that

$$\Sigma = \Sigma^* = (\Lambda T^{-1}) T \Psi T (T^{-1} \Lambda') + \Theta_\epsilon \tag{5}$$

The answer to the obvious question, "but where does this hypothesized $\Sigma$ come from?" derives from a better understanding of the nature of the restricted factor model. Equations 3 and 4 showed that the model for the restricted factor-analysis model represents the population–covariance matrix, $\Sigma$, as a combination of the factor-parameter matrices. Thus every model specification for the factor-parameter matrices implicitly generates a hypothesized $\Sigma$ expressed in terms of the factor-model parameters. The process of identification really represents reducing the number of parameters which are used to generate the hypothesized $\Sigma$ so that the remaining unknowns may be solved, using the logic of solving simultaneous equations. A minimum criterion is that we must have fewer remaining unknown parameters than the number of unique parameters in the covariance matrix (with $p$ observed variables, there are $p(p+1)/2$ unique parameters: $p$ variances and $p(p-1)/2$ covariances). This is a necessary but not sufficient condition for identification. We must also achieve what is called *local identification*, so that, loosely speaking, each subset of related parameters are also identified.

Jöreskog (1969, 1979) has discussed some general rules for identification of restricted factor models when the restrictions take the form of fixed-zero factor loadings in $\Lambda$. Assume that we have decided that we are interested in studying a domain of variables containing $m$ common factors. Then we must select measures for these factors with the idea that we will place $m^2$ restrictions on the common factor space, including at least $m-1$ fixed-zero factor loadings in each column of $\Lambda$. This translates into $m^2-m$ restrictions on the factor loadings and $m$ restrictions to identify the metric of the factors (which is arbitrary and undefined without appropriate restrictions, see below). More restrictions may be necessary if the restrictions to be placed include fixed-nonzero factor loadings.

An abstract example may help to illustrate the concept. Figure 3.1a shows a matrix specification for a single group common factor model, in which two factors producing the covariances among six observed variables. With no restrictions on the model, we can express each element of $\Sigma$ as a rather complex combination of the parameters in $\Lambda$, $\Psi$, and $\Theta_\epsilon$ by simply multiplying through the right-hand side of Equation 3. In general, the factor parameter equivalent of each element is quite complex; for example, the first diagonal element, $\sigma_{11}$, is

$$\sigma_{11} = \lambda_1{}^2 \psi_{11} + 2(\lambda_1 \psi_{21} \lambda_2) + \lambda_2{}^2 \psi_{22} + \theta_{11}$$

while the first off-diagonal element, $\sigma_{21}$, is

$$\sigma_{21} = \lambda_1 \lambda_3 \psi_{11} + (\lambda_3 \lambda_4 + \lambda_1 \lambda_2)\psi_{21} + \lambda_2 \lambda_4 \psi_{22} + \theta_{21}$$

(a).
$$\begin{bmatrix} y_1 \\ y_2 \\ y_3 \\ y_4 \\ y_5 \\ y_6 \end{bmatrix} = \begin{bmatrix} \lambda_1 & \lambda_2 \\ \lambda_3 & \lambda_4 \\ \lambda_5 & \lambda_6 \\ \lambda_7 & \lambda_8 \\ \lambda_9 & \lambda_{10} \\ \lambda_{11} & \lambda_{12} \end{bmatrix} \cdot \begin{bmatrix} \eta_1 \\ \eta_2 \end{bmatrix} + \begin{bmatrix} \epsilon_1 \\ \epsilon_2 \\ \epsilon_3 \\ \epsilon_4 \\ \epsilon_5 \\ \epsilon_6 \end{bmatrix}$$

(b).
$$\begin{bmatrix} y_1 \\ y_2 \\ y_3 \\ y_4 \\ y_5 \\ y_6 \end{bmatrix} = \begin{bmatrix} \lambda_1 & 0 \\ \lambda_2 & 0 \\ \lambda_3 & 0 \\ 0 & \lambda_4 \\ 0 & \lambda_5 \\ 0 & \lambda_6 \end{bmatrix} \cdot \begin{bmatrix} \eta_1 \\ \eta_2 \end{bmatrix} + \begin{bmatrix} \epsilon_1 \\ \epsilon_2 \\ \epsilon_3 \\ \epsilon_4 \\ \epsilon_5 \\ \epsilon_6 \end{bmatrix}$$

Figure 3.1. (a) General model for 6 variables and 2 factors. (b) Model assuming $y_1 - y_3$ to load only on $\eta_1$ and $y_4 - y_6$ only on $\eta_2$. The additional assumption of $\Theta_\epsilon$ to be a diagonal matrix produces the $\Sigma$ shown in Figure 2a.

Now let us assume that we have selected the variables in advance so that the first three variables are determined only by $\eta_1$, and the second three observed variables are determined only by $\eta_2$. For the sake of simplicity, we assume also that the residual elements are uncorrelated, so that $\Theta_\epsilon$ is a diagonal matrix of unique variances. The specification shown in Figure 3.1b generates the hypothesized covariance matrix shown in Figure 3.2a. It is evident that the restrictions of zero residual covariances and zero factor loadings has greatly reduced the complexity of the hypothesized form of $\Sigma$ (in terms of the factor analytic parameters). In fact, there are now only 6 factor loadings, 3 elements in the factor covariance matrix $\Psi$, and 6 unique variances in $\Theta$, for a total of 15 unknown parameters. Since there are 21 unique elements in $\Sigma$, we satisfy the minimum condition for identification given above.

(a).

$$\Sigma = \begin{bmatrix}
\lambda_1^2 \psi_{11} + \theta_1 \\
\lambda_2 \psi_{11} \lambda_1 & \lambda_2^2 \psi_{11} + \theta_2 \\
\lambda_3 \psi_{11} \lambda_1 & \lambda_3 \psi_{11} \lambda_2 & \lambda_3^2 \psi_{11} + \theta_3 \\
\lambda_4 \psi_{21} \lambda_1 & \lambda_4 \psi_{21} \lambda_2 & \lambda_4 \psi_{21} \lambda_3 & \lambda_4^2 \psi_{22} + \theta_4 \\
\lambda_5 \psi_{21} \lambda_1 & \lambda_5 \psi_{21} \lambda_2 & \lambda_5 \psi_{21} \lambda_3 & \lambda_5 \psi_{22} \lambda_4 & \lambda_5^2 \psi_{22} + \theta_5 \\
\lambda_6 \psi_{21} \lambda_1 & \lambda_6 \psi_{21} \lambda_2 & \lambda_6 \psi_{21} \lambda_3 & \lambda_6 \psi_{22} \lambda_4 & \lambda_6 \psi_{22} \lambda_5 & \lambda_6 \psi_{22} + \theta_6
\end{bmatrix}$$

(b).

$$\Sigma = \begin{bmatrix}
\psi_{11} + \theta_1 \\
\lambda_2 \psi_{11} & \lambda_2^2 \psi_{11} + \theta_2 \\
\lambda_3 \psi_{11} & \lambda_3 \psi_{11} \lambda_2 & \lambda_3^2 \psi_{11} + \theta_3 \\
\psi_{21} & \psi_{21} \lambda_2 & \psi_{21} \lambda_3 & \psi_{22} + \theta_4 \\
\lambda_5 \psi_{21} & \lambda_5 \psi_{21} \lambda_2 & \lambda_5 \psi_{21} \lambda_3 & \lambda_5 \psi_{22} & \lambda_5^2 \psi_{22} + \theta_5 \\
\lambda_6 \psi_{21} & \lambda_6 \psi_{21} \lambda_2 & \lambda_6 \psi_{21} \lambda_3 & \lambda_6 \psi_{22} & \lambda_6 \psi_{22} \lambda_5 & \lambda_6^2 \psi_{22} + \theta_6
\end{bmatrix}$$

Figure 3.2. (a) Model in Figure 1b generates the hypothesized population covariance matrix shown above. The expressions for the elements are greatly simplified, but the model is still not identified (see text). (b) Assuming $\lambda_1 = \lambda_4 = 1$ identifies the metric of the factors, and generates the covariance structure shown above. Note the reduced complexity of terms associates with columns 1 and 4 of $\Sigma$. In particular, $\sigma_{41}$ is now seen to be the covariance of the two factors ($\Psi_{21}$).

Actually, the model is still not identified. There are two types of identification required: (a) identification of the relative location of the variables in the common factor space, and (b) identification of the units of measurement in that space. We have not yet determined the scale units of the factors. The maximum likelihood solution used in the Jöreskog programs (e.g., Jöreskog and Sörbom, 1981) is generally scale-free, so that the unit of measurement is actually arbitrary (see, however, Swaminathan & Algina, 1978). Assuming, for the moment, a factor model in a single group, it does not matter, for example, if the analysis is done in covariance metric or in standardized metric. Nevertheless, some solution for the metric of the factors must be imposed. The easiest method is to specify a standardized solution, fixing the diagonal elements of $\Psi$ to 1, and thereby forcing the factors to be in standard score form. An alternative method is to choose arbitrarily one of the nonzero factor loadings in each column of $\Lambda$ and fix it to any constant (conveniently, 1). The fixed loading implicitly defines the factor metric as a function of the variance of the observed variables. This method results in an analysis in covariance metric, in which the factor structure coefficients are no longer constrained to lie inbetween $-1$ and $1$, and the factor covariance matrix is unstandardized.

Given the fact that the solutions are generally scale-free, why would one not routinely take the first method, analyze a correlation matrix, and fix the factor variances to 1 in order to obtain the more interpretable standardized parameter estimates? In fact, this is a reasonable approach in most single group analyses. However, this approach is not acceptable if the covariance-structures approach is used to analyze simultaneously the data from several groups; separate standardization of each group's sample covariance matrix may have the undesirable effect of obscuring group similarities in factor structure (see below). It is also not appropriate to standardize in longitudinal factor analysis, where the longitudinal changes in observed and factor variances are meaningful information which would be lost if a correlation matrix were analyzed.

Perhaps one of the more difficult aspects of confirmatory factor applications is the use of fixed factor loadings to identify the factor metric, because most of us have been trained to think in standardized metric when performing factor analysis. Thus it is hard to accept the idea that fixing a single factor loading for each factor does not place any restrictions upon the relative magnitude of the factor loadings to each other (so long as the factor variance is treated as an unknown parameter to be estimated). It is not the case, for example, that fixing a factor loading to 1 in an orthogonal solution implies that all the variance in the observed variable is accounted for by the factor—even though it would have that implication in a standardized analysis. Standardized logic does not apply in covariance metric solutions! Let us illustrate how the fixed factor loading helps to define the factor variances. In the example presented in Figure 3.2b, the assumption is made that the loadings of variable 1 on factor 1 and variable 4 on factor

2 are fixed to 1, which further simplifies the representation of $\Sigma$. It is easy to show that the elements of $\Sigma$ are identified by demonstrating that a unique algebraic solution exists for each of the parameters in $\Lambda$, $\Psi$, and $\Theta_\epsilon$ in terms of the elements in $\Sigma$. In this case it is obvious that $\psi_{21}$ is identified, since it is equal to $\sigma_{41}$. If $\psi_{21}$ is identified, $\lambda_{21}$, $\lambda_3$, $\lambda_5$, and $\lambda_6$ are identified in $\sigma_{42}$, $\sigma_{43}$, $\sigma_{51}$, and $\sigma_{61}$ respectively (and so on).

The model in Figure 3.2b is actually overidentified–that is, there are more restrictions placed upon the model than are actually necessary to identify the unknowns. Recall our rule of $m-1$ fixed-zero loadings in each column of $\Lambda$; we actually have $m+1$ such restrictions. One way of observing this overidentification is to note that there are more than one algebraic expression for many of the parameters. For example, the matrix in Figure 3.2b gives two independent expressions for $\lambda_2$:

$$\lambda_2 = \sigma_{42}/\sigma_{41} = \lambda_2 \psi_{21}/\psi_{21}$$

$$\lambda_2 = \sigma_{32}/\sigma_{31} = \lambda_3 \psi_{11} \lambda_2 / \lambda_3 \psi_{11}$$

The overidentifying restrictions play an important role in the statistical hypothesis testing procedures involved in restricted factor analysis. For the moment, suffice it to say that the model may be considered to have 8 overidentifying restrictions, since there are only 13 factor analytic parameters and 21 available elements in $\Sigma$; this means that the model shown in Figure 3.2b actually has 8 degrees of freedom in its simultaneous equations. Even further restrictions are possible, provided that they are theoretically justified (or that one wishes to test the hypothesis that these restrictions fit the data). For example, assume that the factor loadings for each factor are equal as indicated in Figure 3.3a; this generates the hypothesized $\Sigma$ shown in Figure 3.3b. As can be seen from the figure, the specification of constrained factor loadings forces a symmetric structure on $\Sigma$, which is highlighted by the lines partitioning the matrix into three parts. All correlations among variables loading on the same factor are equal to one another, while all "cross-correlations" between variables loading on different factors are also equal. Thus there are only three unique covariance elements in $\Sigma$, given that the factor model is true.

Naturally the restricted covariance structure of Figure 3.3b will not be manifest in a given sample covariance matrix from the population, given sampling variability around the population coefficients. The purpose of confirmatory factor analysis is to evaluate the likelihood that such a structure could in fact hold in the population, given the sample data at hand. In order to test the hypothesis that the population-covariance matrix takes the form specified by the hypothesis, we must estimate the unknown parameters and then compare the predicted population covariance matrix to the sample covariance matrix.

(a).

$$
\begin{bmatrix} y_1 \\ y_2 \\ y_3 \\ y_4 \\ y_5 \\ y_6 \end{bmatrix}
=
\begin{bmatrix} \lambda_1 & 0 \\ \lambda_1 & 0 \\ \lambda_1 & 0 \\ 0 & \lambda_2 \\ 0 & \lambda_2 \\ 0 & \lambda_2 \end{bmatrix}
\cdot
\begin{bmatrix} \eta_1 \\ \eta_2 \end{bmatrix}
+
\begin{bmatrix} \epsilon_1 \\ \epsilon_2 \\ \epsilon_3 \\ \epsilon_4 \\ \epsilon_5 \\ \epsilon_6 \end{bmatrix}
$$

diagonal $(\Psi) = 1$

(b).

$$
\Sigma =
\begin{bmatrix}
\lambda_1^2 + \theta_1 & & & & & \\
\lambda_1^2 & \lambda_1^2 + \theta_2 & & & & \\
\lambda_1^2 & \lambda_1^2 & \lambda_1^2 + \theta_3 & & & \\
\lambda_1\lambda_2\Psi_{21} & \lambda_1\lambda_2\Psi_{21} & \lambda_1\lambda_2\Psi_{21} & \lambda_2^2 + \theta_4 & & \\
\lambda_1\lambda_2\Psi_{21} & \lambda_1\lambda_2\Psi_{21} & \lambda_1\lambda_2\Psi_{21} & \lambda_2^2 & \lambda_2^2 + \theta_5 & \\
\lambda_1\lambda_2\Psi_{21} & \lambda_1\lambda_2\Psi_{21} & \lambda_1\lambda_2\Psi_{21} & \lambda_2^2 & \lambda_2^2 & \lambda_2^2 + \theta_6
\end{bmatrix}
$$

Figure 3.3. (a) Model with factor loadings on each factor constrained equal and $\Psi$ a correlation matrix (diagonal elements fixed to 1. (b) Covariance structure generated by model in (a). Note the symmetry of the offdiagonal elements. For example, the $3 \times 3$ submatrix of "cross correlations" between variables loading on different factors contains only one parameter $(\lambda_1\lambda_2\Psi_{21})$. This model has 9 parameters and 12 $df$.

## Model Estimation

The process of parameter estimation in covariance structures algorithms is too complex to be treated in any detail here. The maximum likelihood method used by LISREL is by no means the only estimation procedure available, although we shall restrict our discussion to a brief description of the conceptual aspects of this method (see McArdle & McDonald, 1981; Bentler, 1980; Bentler & Weeks, 1979; and McDonald, 1978, for a fuller discussion of alternatives to the Jöreskog approach). Under the assumption of multivariate normality, Wishart's theorem is used to give an equation for the distribution of elements of a sample covariance matrix, $S$, given a population covariance matrix $(\Sigma)$ of known form (see Anderson, 1958). The Wishart distribution may be used to establish a log likelihood equation relating $S$ to $\Sigma$; Jöreskog (1969; 1971b) showed that maximizing the log likelihood was equivalent to minimizing a fitting function (F) which is a function of the unknown parameters in the three parameter matrices. Expressions for the first and second partial derivatives of F with respect to the elements of the three parameter matrices (Bock & Bargmann, 1966; Jöreskog, 1966, 1969) are then used to find those values of the unknown parameters which minimize F by setting the first derivatives of the unknowns to zero and iteratively estimating the parameters.

The maximum likelihood algorithm used by the Jöreskog programs is the Fletcher-Powell method (Fletcher & Powell, 1963) which has been criticized for being very slow to converge to a final solution (Bentler, 1976) and for being unnecessarily prone to estimates of negative unique variances (Heywood cases) and other improper solutions (van Driel, 1978). Unfortunately, programs using alternative algorithms and models have not achieved widespread distribution.

There are two problems with the procedure which should be mentioned here. First, there is no guarantee that the converged solution found by the program is in fact the absolute minimum of the fitting function. If F has several minima due to empirical underidentification or other properties of the data set, then one may have only found a *local minimum* for F. This can be checked by providing the program with widely different sets of starting values. However, this can be a rather costly check, given the slow convergence of the Fletcher/Powell algorithm. The user should also be aware of a very common problem in LISREL model testing: Badly misspecified or otherwise illogical models are often not detected by the program, and the program will often iterate to the time limit only to be unable to converge on a final solution. This failure to converge may be due to an underidentified model or to a misspecification (e.g., fixing a factor loading to a positive value to scale the factor when it has a near zero relationship to other variables loading on the factor). Thus it is often a sound, if conservative, procedure to set a very short time limit on iterations in a first run of a new problem in order to ascertain that the model has been correctly specified in the program. The program can detect most kinds of underidentification, and its report of model specification may be checked to determine that the desired model has in fact been correctly specified. Provided that the initial check of the specification is passed, the model may then be estimated.

## Evaluation and Testing

One of the more useful features of covariance-structures modeling is that the fitting function F is used to calculate a likelihood ratio "goodness-of-fit" statistic which may be used to evaluate the ability of an overidentified model to account for $S$. Under the assumptions of multivariate normality and asymptotic estimates of the population-covariance matrices, then $N-1(F)$ is asymptotically distributed as a $\chi^2$ variable with $(p*(p-1))/2 - t$ degrees of freedom, which is the number of independent elements in $\Sigma$ less $t$—the total number of unknown parameters estimated. The null hypothesis being tested is that the sample covariance matrix is in fact drawn from a $\Sigma$ of the restricted form specified by the common factor model. In essence, one is asking for the likelihood that $S$ could have been randomly drawn from a $\Sigma$ having the form specified by the model.

Because $\chi^2$ variates are additively distributed as $\chi^2$, the $\chi^2$ test statistics have additional utility for hypothesis testing. Given two factor analysis models, one can evaluate the statistical significance of the improvement in fit from one model to the other, providing that the two models are nested—that is, that the restrictions of the model with the fewest restrictions are matched exactly in the more restricted model. That is, given a basis set of restrictions on the model (fixed-zero loadings, factor covariances, etc.) R1 for model M1, we say that model M1 is nested within model M2 if, and only if, for the set of restrictions R2 of M2,

$$R_1 \cap R_2 = R_1 \text{ and } R_1 \cup R_3 = R_2 : R_3 \neq \emptyset \tag{6}$$

that is, that the intersection of R1 and R2 is R1, and the nonintersecting restrictions in R2, R3, is not an empty set. In this case, we may consider a null hypothesis

$H_0 : R_3$ true

which implies that relaxing the restrictions R3 by adopting the less restrictive model M1 does not produce an improvement of fit of the model to $S$. This hypothesis may be statistically tested by taking the difference in $\chi^2$ between M2 and M1, which will be asymptotically distributed as $\chi^2$ with $(df2 - df1)$ $df$ (the number of restrictions relaxed in M1).

This additive property of the $\chi^2$ statistics allows us to specify in advance a set of models which could be estimated in order to test a set of a priori hypotheses regarding the nature of the factor model in the population. If we were interested in testing the restricted model of constrained equal factor loadings shown in Figure 3.3, then we would calculate the difference in $\chi^2$ for the two models in Figure 3.2b and Figure 3.3b, evaluate its significance against the 4 $df$ created by the constrained loadings at a specified Type I error rate. A significant $\chi^2$ would cause rejection of the null hypothesis that the constrained loadings were in fact equal in the population, conditional upon the validity of the basis specification in M1. This qualification regarding the conditional nature of the hypothesis test is critically important for the validity of $\chi^2$ relative to the null hypothesis being tested. If in fact the model M1 is not the "true" common factor model for the population, then the difference in $\chi^2$ may be affected by the misspecified basis model. It might be possible, for example, that the model without equality constraints would provide a statistically better fit to the data, not because the loadings of those variables on the factors of interest are not equal, but because the model has omitted a third factor or a set of residual correlations, thus enabling the model without the constrained equal loadings to do a slightly better job of accounting for the covariances among all observed variables, but for the "wrong" reasons.

The evaluation and testing procedures apply equally well to any number of groups (subpopulations). The assumption in simultaneous analysis is that the information from the groups are conditionally independent, so that it is possible to add the $\chi^2$ from each group to calculate the overall $\chi^2$ test statistic. The assumption does not imply that one must assume the parameters from different groups to be uncorrelated; rather, one simply assumes that the observations are independent units so that, in principle, the null hypothesis of bivariate conditional independence could hold in the population. Using data from the same individuals in two different groups would, for example, violate the assumption. The principles of $\chi^2$ testing in multiple groups models is exactly the same as described above. One of the important applications of simultaneous factor analysis in multiple groups is to test a series of hypotheses regarding the equivalence of factor model parameters between the multiple groups. This is easily accomplished in covariance structures modeling by computing two models, one imposing between groups equality restrictions on a set of parameters of interest, the other specifying the same model with the equality constraints relaxed. One then evaluates the statistical significance of the change in $\chi^2$ as a test of the null hypothesis that the parameters may in fact be considered equal between the two subpopulations.

One of the features with the use of $\chi^2$ is that, like other statistics, its power increases with increasing sample size. This becomes an apparent problem because the significance testing procedures in covariance-structures model fitting are inverted in logic—a nonsignificant $\chi^2$ is an indication of a good fit of the model to the data, and is hence considered desirable. In part this apparent problem stems from a failure to understand that significance testing is part of the falsification process; we should look to reject models rather than to accept them. Thus with extremely large sample sizes, relatively small deviations of sample covariance matrix from predicted population covariance matrix will be statistically reliable. Nevertheless, we might not be willing to reject as useless a model which we are attempting to falsify if the rejection implies an extremely small root mean square deviation of sample covariances from estimated population covariances. Conversely, with small sample sizes relatively large discrepancies between sample and population might not be detected as statistically reliable. The same problem holds true for differences in $\chi^2$, since it follows from our definition that the difference in $\chi^2$ is equal to

$$\chi_1^2 - \chi_2^2 = N\,(F_1 - F_2) \tag{7}$$

that is, the difference in fitting function values weighted by the number of observations. Since the degrees of freedom depend upon the number of free parameters in the model (which is independent of sample size), it is easy to see that the probability of rejecting the null hypothesis increases for differences in $\chi^2$ as well. Thus given large sample sizes, we may reject the hypothesis of group equivalence in factor loadings even when the differences in estimated factor loadings between the groups are extremely small. Obviously we need a way of assessing the degree of fit of the model other than $\chi^2$ alone.

There are several ways of evaluating the fit of the model other than simply relying on absolute $\chi^2$; there are also alternative indices of improved fit between models other than the simple difference in $\chi^2$. The absolute fit of the model may be examined by inspection of residuals, calculation of a root mean square residual, and so on. However, an alternative approach is to estimate the fit of the model relative to a range of possible levels of fit given what is known about the data. Bentler and Bonett (1980) provide an excellent discussion of the issues involved, as well as some reasonable suggestions for methods of evaluating the degree of fit of the model to the data. Their proposal is based upon the logic involved in the Tucker-Lewis reliability coefficient in exploratory factor analysis (Tucker & Lewis, 1973). First, one defines a null model, $M_0$, which is relevant to the specific model being evaluated. For most factor analysis models, the null model used by Tucker and Lewis (1973) of zero common factors is appropriate. This assumption is equivalent to the assumption of no association in the covariance matrix (Anderson, 1958) which has been used as an omnibus multivariate test of zero correlation (Larzelere & Mulaik, 1977). The null hypothesis is that all covariance elements in $\Sigma$ are zero—that is, that $\Sigma$ is a diagonal matrix of variances. If the null model were true, then there would be no point in attempting to account for the sample covariances, because they would properly be considered sampling fluctuations around population parameters of zero. Thus the null model of no association is a useful preliminary test prior to factor-analytic model testing. It is also useful, however, in that it establishes an *upper bound* for the fitting function F in terms of a model which accounts for none of the covariance in $S$. The theoretical lower bound of F in usual factor analysis models is zero, which would be achieved by any just-identified model (with zero $df$) or any other model which perfectly fit the data. A just-identified model may be considered to be the saturated model, call it $M_s$. In practice the F value for an identified model will lie somewhere in between the F for $M_0$ and the F for $M_s$. In that case it is reasonable to ask, how far have we come from $M_0$ toward $M_s$? The restricted factor analysis analog to the Tucker-Lewis coefficient, (in Bentler and Bonett's (1980) terms, the nonnormed fit index) examines the distance traversed between the null model and any model in which the null hypothesis may be considered true, using the equation:

$$\rho_{TL} = (\chi_0^2/df_0) - (\chi_1^2/df_1) / (\chi_0^2/df_0) - 1 \qquad (8)$$

The expected value of $\chi^2$, given the null hypothesis to be true, equals the degrees of freedom. It is reasonable to interpret this coefficient as a relative fit index showing the amount of covariance accounted for by the model in question, although it is possible in practice to achieve a $\chi^2$ less than its expected value of the *df,* this nonnormed index does not have an upper bound of 1. A normed fit index:

$$\rho_N = (F_0 - F_1) / F_0 \tag{9}$$

would have a value between 0 and 1. Either of these descriptive statistics may be used to assess relative increments in fit as well.

These statistics are analogous to proportion of variance statistics in ANOVA applications. One does not merely ask whether the improvement in fit is statistically reliable; one also measures the magnitude of such an improvement, calculated in terms of the relative fit from the null to the saturated model. One unaddressed problem with this approach is that the fitting function F may not represent a valid ratio scale of fit—given a .2 decrease in F from the null value of 2.5, is this equivalent to a .2 decrease from an F value of .5?

Goodness-of-fit statistics refer to the overall fit of the model. We may also be interested in whether individual parameter estimates may be considered to be salient. With respect to factor loadings or factor covariances, it is often useful to ask whether the parameter estimates are statistically different from a null value of zero, and whether they are of sufficient magnitude to warrant retention in the model. The restricted factor analysis algorithm permits the calculation of standard errors of estimate for each parameter. These may be used to construct confidence intervals around the parameter estimates, and thus may be used to determine whether the confidence interval at a given Type I error rate includes zero as a test of statistical significance (see Jöreskog & Sörbom, 1981).

## Model Modification

Although the most elegant uses for restricted factor analysis lie in attempting to falsify a set of alternative models for the factor structure of a given set of variables, the method is often used in analyses which are more exploratory in nature. Indeed, the hypothesis testing procedures are often used to explore a limited number of prespecified alternatives regarding group equivalence in factor structure, and so forth, which strictly speaking is more of an exploratory than a confirmatory application of the method. It is also often the case that the investigator is able to make a sufficient set of predictions regarding the nature of the factor structure of the data without being certain that his predictions exhaust the nature of the structure being investigated. The hypothesis might be relatively general, incomplete, or otherwise inaccurate. Moreover, given that a model is disconfirmed on the basis of a poor fit to the sample data, the investigator may well be interested in pursuing the analysis further by determining whether modifications to the model might result in a sufficiently improved fit to warrant retention of some of the characteristics of the model which was falsified. Again, it is in this sense that the restricted factor analysis approach may be truly exploratory in nature.

The factor analysis programs such as LISREL in fact provide a set of descriptive statistics regarding the model which may be used as a basis for data guided rather than theory guided model modifications. Before describing them, the point must be emphasized that such data-dependent alterations in the model specified vitiate, at least in part, one of the primary advantages of restricted factor analysis; namely, that the analysis relies on a theoretical specification of the factor structure and is therefore relatively more immune to vagaries of sampling fluctuation and limited and specific relationships among certain variables in determining the factor structure estimated. Once we allow the degree of fit to the sample data to determine the subsequent modifications—in order to search for a better fit to the sample data—we run the real risk that any modifications introduced will be capitalizing on chance fluctuations in the data rather than producing an improved fit due to the discovery of population characteristics.

There is only one adequate protection against this risk: confirmation of the model modification by replication of the results in an independent sample drawn from the same population. It is only when a set of results are replicated independently across samples that we may have any confidence in the validity of the results as descriptions of the population factor structure. Thus, whenever a "partially" exploratory approach is planned in advance, the best design is one of split-half validation, in which a sufficiently large sample is collected to enable random assignment of subjects to an exploratory and a confirmatory half-sample. Model modifications may then be examined in the exploratory sample, with the proviso that only if these modifications replicate in the confirmatory sample will they be considered as potentially indicative of population factor structure characteristics. In any case, replication in independent samples is the only way to insure the validity of data dependent model modifications.

There are essentially two different types of program indicators for sources of poor fit: indicators based upon the residuals (differences between $\hat{\Sigma}$ and $S$) and indicators based upon the first derivatives of fixed and constrained parameters. One can inspect the residuals to determine which elements of the sample covariance matrix are poorly accounted for by the model; LISREL V has the additional advantage of computing normalized residuals, which express the residuals in z-score form, showing which residuals are significantly different from a perfect match of zero. One problem with inspecting residuals, normalized or not, is that a misspecified model may have wide ranging effects which are not obviously translated into missing residuals (Costner & Schoenberg, 1973). The advantage of using the derivative based indicators is that they indicate directly those fixed and constrained parameters which, if left as unknown parameters to be estimated, would be most likely to improve the fit of the model (Sörbom, 1975). First derivatives of unknown parameters were set to zero in order to estimate the solution. First derivatives of fixed and free parameters will deviate from zero if the restriction configures the parameter space in a way which does not fit the sample data. Thus one can search for large first derivatives as indicators of poor fit. The problem, however, is that the derivatives are of relative magnitude, depending upon the metric of the associated parameters and the constraint that the first derivatives of a given parameter matrix must sum to zero. Thus one is not sure whether a derivative of a given magnitude indicates a major or a minor source of problems for fit. LISREL V assists the modification process by rescaling the first derivatives to the "modification indices," which estimate the expected reduction in $\chi^2$ if the particular restriction was relaxed.

Two caveats are in order with respect to use of residuals or modification indices. First, since a change in the parameter specification can affect many of the elements in $\Sigma$, both because of the equations relating $\Sigma$ to the parameters in $\Lambda$, $\Psi$, and $\Theta_\epsilon$, and because the estimation method simultaneously fits all elements of $\Sigma$, the investigator is best advised to change one or, at most, a few related parameter specifications at a time. More important, one must keep in mind that the modification indices merely point to the sources of poor fit that can be identified, given the basis specification. If an additional factor should be added, splitting one factor with many salient loadings into two correlated factors, the program's modification indices cannot directly indicate such a major modification. Instead, such a modification might be indicated by large modification indices for residual correlations among variables loading on the same factor (indicating additional covariance among variables not accounted for by single factor). Thus the paradox of model modification is that a badly misspecified model may provide the worst clues as to the ways in which it should be modified to improve fit. Thus, in exploratory situations, the investigator ought to either have (a) good a priori justification for specifying a given number of factors, as well as a set of reference variables loading on those factors, or (b) empirical data on the number of factors (e.g., a scree test, goodness-of-fit tests from unrestricted solutions (Horn & Engstrom, 1978) before assuming that "minor" modifications of the model based upon the modification indices will be sufficient.

Finally, modification is also called for when a model appears to be "overfit," that is, when too many factors have been fit to the data. An overfit model may be indicated by an extremely low $\chi^2$, high intercorrelations between factors, or large numbers of nonsignificant or marginally significant factor loadings. Restricted factor models are just as prone as unrestricted models to invalidity due to overestimating the number of factors. Ultimately, the modification of a restricted model should be based not upon any indication of poor fit or overfit as it is upon the theoretical parsimony of the parameters being added. Does it make any theoretical sense to posit a residual correlation between variables $x$ and $y$, given either the nature of the constructs being measured or the measurement properties of the two variables?

## ADVANCED ISSUES IN INTELLIGENCE RESEARCH
## AS RESTRICTED FACTOR MODELS

In this section the basic methods of confirmatory factor analysis are discussed with respect to a set of important applications in research on intelligence. We consider six domains of relevant applications:

1. confirmatory tests of hypothetical factor models with new samples;
2. models testing invariance of common factor models across multiple populations;
3. models testing invariance of factor domains under selection of measures;
4. models involving simultaneous estimation of factor means and factor structure;
5. models for assessing measurement properties and construct validity of psychometric tests; and
6. longitudinal factor analysis models.

### Confirmation of Factorial Models of Intelligence

One obvious application of confirmatory factor analysis is the estimation of the fit of a model derived in an exploratory sample in a second, independent sample from the same population (as discussed above). One of the more critical issues to consider is whether small factor loadings obtained in an exploratory analysis should be considered "hyperplane stuff" (Cattell, 1978)—that is, zero or near zero loadings which define the factor hyperplane. In essence, this decision involves the validity of inferring that the small, near zero loading is a sampling fluctuation about a population parameter of zero. The validity of such an inference is of course strengthened if the battery were originally designed with such a hyperplane definition in mind. If we are justified in inferring that the empirically obtained loading in an unrestricted factor analysis is a sample estimate of a population parameter of zero, then we may use this inference to fix the loading of the variable on the factor to zero for confirmatory model specification. If, on the other hand, the loading is thought to represent a small but nonzero population factor loading, then fixing the loading to zero in the confirmatory model is a specification error which will in principle adversely affect the validity of the other parameters being estimated. The distinction between the population parameter and the sample based estimate of that parameter is certainly obscured by the exploratory analysis procedure; confirmatory factor analysis's emphasis on models for population parameters helps bring this crucial distinction into focus.

Given that we are either interested in (a) confirming a model derived from an exploratory sample, or (b) testing a model developed directly from theory, one proceeds in the manner discussed above. The model to be tested is specified, estimated, and its fit to the sample data evaluated. One of the best examples of this approach is the paper by Bechtoldt (1974) examining the fit of Thurstone's primary ability factor model to a set of tests designed specifically to measure six primary mental abilities in a sample of 425 Chicago area students (Thurstone & Thurstone, 1941). Bechtoldt (1974) reanalyzed the data testing a restricted model in which each variable loaded only on its specific primary ability factor. This model was rejected by a significant $\chi^2$; however, all parameter estimates were judged to be significant relative to their standard errors. Bechtoldt then entertained hypotheses of small nonzero loadings other than the restricted primary ability configuration to achieve a better fit. Judging from the small magnitude of the additional loadings that proved statistically reliable, as well as the salience of the loadings specified a priori, Bechtoldt (1974) concluded that the "goal of an isolated cluster configuration was missed but not by much." (p. 325) This indeed seemed to be the case, and given the sample size, it would be useful to examine a relative fit index to see if the model accounted for most of the correlations in the data. Bechtoldt (1974) then proceeded to show that a random split of the sample into two groups, followed by a simultaneous two-group analysis, resulted in a model with invariant factor pattern matrices between the two half-samples, but different factor-covariance matrices and unique variances. This pattern is of critical interest, as discussed in the following section; Bechtoldt (1974) interpreted it as evidence for an invariant factor solution affected by sampling fluctuations in variability at the levels of the observed subtests and the primary ability factors.

## Factorial Invariance in Multiple Populations

Bechtoldt's (1974) analysis tested whether random samples from the same population could be shown to have invariant ability factor structures. This question is distinct from the question of whether the factor structure of some set of intellectual abilities is invariant across different populations. These populations could represent socially homogeneous groups, such as geographically and/or culturally distinct populations, groups defined by individual differences on other "status" variables (such as sex, age, or ethnicity), or alternatively, groups defined by dimensions hypothesized to differ in some aspect of psychological or physiological functioning that may be related to psychometric intelligence (such as mental retardation, cognitive style, or level of acculturation within a society). A lack of factorial invariance in different subgroups might indicate group differences in the underlying determinants of intelligent thought processes, the psychometric properties of the tests, or both (Mulaik, 1972; Thurstone, 1947). In developmental psychology, it has been argued that age-group differences in factor structure may indicate developmental changes in the way cognitive resources are applied to solve complex problems (Anastasi, 1970; Reinert, 1970).

One of the difficult issues in multiple-group factor analysis involves the determination of criteria for assessing factorial invariance. When may we conclude that the factor structure is not invariant across a selected set of populations? This problem involves both the determination of the possible forms invariance might take in the population and the potential utility of model estimation techniques for producing empirical evidence which enable inferences regarding the degree of invariance. As pointed out by Reinert (1970; see also Olsson & Bergman, 1977) the plethora of criteria for invariance used in the literature on age-related factorial invariance, combined with the wide variation of factor analytic methods, has led to a rather confused picture. The confusion stems from the fact that seemingly contradictory evidence from exploratory factor-analytic studies exist which are, upon close inspection, not amenable to direct comparison and evaluation. In fact, several studies which used different methods and emphasized different criteria for invariance came to widely different conclusions on factorial invariance of the Wechsler Adult Intelligence Scale (WAIS) standardization data across age groups, even though the same data were analyzed by all investigators (see Cunningham, 1978).

What should be the criteria for inferring factorial invariance across multiple populations? Meredith (1964) presented a useful line of argument on this question, building upon earlier work by Lawley (1943) and Ahmavaara (1954) on the problem of selection from a single population. The basic idea is as follows: Assume that we have defined a population for which a single common factor model describes the factor structure for all individuals in the population. If groups are selected from this population according to some nonrandom set of selection variables, what is the possible range of factor structures that would emerge? We must know the answer to this question before we can determine criteria for arguing that any two groups are in fact not merely selected from a parent population in which a single common factor model holds.

If groups are selected into subpopulations differing in mean levels on the factors, then Meredith's (1964) work showed that group selection will produce group differences in the covariance matrices of both variables and factors. Furthermore, only the raw score (unstandardized) regressions of variables on factors (factor loadings) may be expected to be invariant over groups. Thus an unstandardized factor analysis of the groups's covariance matrices is necessary for a meaningful assessment of the hypothesis of structural invariance. The correlation matrices for the groups would involve scaling by different standard deviations in each group, which could introduce artifactual differences in factor loadings and correlations. Meredith's (1964) results also suggest that one must reject the hypothesis of invariant raw score factor-pattern matrices in order to be able to falsify the hypothesis that the group differences are not merely a function of selection from a population with an invariant common factor model. In other words, many of the potential group differences in factor correlations, and so forth would not be unequivocal evidence of different factor structures between subpopulations (see also Bloxom, 1972; Mulaik, 1972).

Given this background on selection, it is easier to understand why the restricted factor analysis techniques are so ideally suited to tests of factorial invariance in multiple populations. The covariance structures models allow for the required unstandardized factor analysis while permitting the specification of varying levels of factorial invariance as a priori models which can be tested by the likelihood ratio hypothesis tests described above. The alternative models involve the specification of equality constraints on corresponding model parameters across the groups; one specifies the same factor model in all groups and also require an appropriate subset of model parameters to be constrained equal over the groups. Indeed, Jöreskog (1971b; see also Alwin & Jackson, 1981) has outlined a series of models which may be used to test alternative hypotheses regarding factorial invariance in multiple groups, including the critical test of equality of raw score factor pattern matrices. The levels of invariance to be tested include (a) the hypothesis that the groups have the same number of common factors; (b) that the same basic common factor model applies to all groups; (c) that the factor-pattern matrices are invariant over groups; (d) that the factor-covariance matrices are invariant over groups; and (e) that the residual covariance matrices are invariant over groups. In order for the tests of hypotheses (c)-(e) to be meaningful, hypotheses (a) and (b) must be true; otherwise one could reject a hypothesis of invariance in the factor-pattern matrices because these matrices were based upon a misspecified common factor model. Jöreskog (1971b) suggested testing the hypotheses in a strictly ascending series of level of invariance, starting with the hypothesis of the same number of common factors and then testing factor-pattern invariance, residual covariance-matrix invariance, and factor covariance-matrix invariance only after the preceding invariance hypotheses could not be rejected (see Alwin & Jackson, 1981, for a rationale for a different ordering of hypothesis tests).

As discussed above, these tests are calculated as likelihood ratio $\chi^2$, taking the difference in $\chi^2$ between the two competing models representing the restrictions to be tested. For example, the test of invariant factor pattern matrices is obtained by estimating a model with identical common factor models across all groups, but with no between groups equality constraints on the factor loadings. The alternative model constraining all corresponding factor pattern coefficients equal across groups is then estimated, with the $\chi^2$ difference a test of the null hypothesis that the sample covariance matrices are drawn from a population in which the additional restriction of invariant factor loadings is true. Rejection of the hypothesis would imply group differences in factor-pattern matrices, which would not be consistent with the selection hypothesis discussed above. Using this method, McGaw and Jöreskog (1971) found evidence of factorial invariance, in terms of invariant raw score factor-pattern matrices, in four groups defined by dichotomous "high-low" partitions on socioeconomic status (SES) and intelligence.

Several studies have used confirmatory factor analysis to examine the hypothesis of factorial invariance in psychometric intelligence across age or sex groups (e.g., Cunningham, 1980, 1981; Hertzog & Carter, 1982; Hertzog & Schaie, 1984; Hyde, Geiringer & Yen, 1975). The studies by Cunningham present an interesting contrast to some of the earlier factor analytic work which suggested dedifferentiation of a primary ability factor structure in old age. While Cunningham's results pointed to an increase in the primary ability factor correlations across age groups, the hypothesis of equal numbers of factors and invariant factor-pattern matrices was considered tenable. Thus the hypothesis of selection from a parent population cannot be rejected on the basis of Cunningham's work (similar results from a longitudinal factor analysis were found by Hertzog & Schaie, 1984). The interesting question remains: Are the increased correlations a reflection of some developmental change in psychometric performance or merely an artifact of late life decline in level of performance, which is tantamount to selection into a subgroup where the distribution of scores is weighted toward the lower tails of the overall population distribution? Certainly the failure to reject the hypothesis of invariant factor-pattern matrices limits the nature of the developmental hypotheses which might be considered in this regard.

Some caveats are in order regarding the use of the Jöreskog (1971b) hypothesis testing procedures to evaluate factorial invariance in multiple groups. Given the possibility for model misspecification (namely, that the base factor model specified is incorrect) and the sensitivity of the $\chi^2$-difference test to sample size, the hypothesis testing procedures should not be used in a rote method of hypothesis evaluation. Thus it would be incorrect to characterize the confirmatory factor analysis procedure as providing an "objective" method for evaluating the hypothesis of invariance, since the interpretive skill (and hence the subjective bias) of the investigator inevitably come into play. For example, Hertzog and Carter (1982) found that the omnibus hypothesis of invariant factor-pattern matrices across male and female groups was rejected according to the statistical test but concluded, on the basis of the apparent invariance of a subset of critical factor loadings and other aspects of the estimated parameters, that there was no major qualitative gender difference in the structure of their broadly defined spatial and verbal intelligence factors. The problem is that this conclusion neither excludes specific alternative hypotheses regarding variance in some aspects of the factor structure nor tests the alternative hypotheses invoked by the authors as reasons for the rejected omnibus test, under the assumption of underlying invariance. A simple replication of the results in independent samples would be welcome but could not address the issue of selecting among alternative hypotheses. What would be necessary is the use of strong inference (Platt, 1964) to generate specific models for the underlying factor structure which derive from the alternative hypotheses. For example, Hertzog and Carter (1982) suggested that the use of factorially complex subtests and broadly defined second-order factors may have obscured factorial invariance at the primary ability factor level. This interpretation leads to the hypothesis that a primary ability factor structure, defined in part by the same variables used in the study, would produce an invariant (primary ability) factor-pattern matrix. In general, the purpose of such inferences is to shape the design of new studies which test models attempting to falsify the alternative hypotheses. In the example, rejection of the hypothesis of invariance at the primary factor level would be one step toward falsifying the hypothesis that there was factorial invariance in spite of the initial rejection of the omnibus hypothesis of invariant factor-pattern matrices.

## Factorial Invariance in Ability Domains

The other major form of invariance of concern to researchers on intelligence involves the invariance of factors with respect to selection of observed variables (particular intelligence subtests). The debate on this issue has a long and illustrious (if apparently inconclusive) history (Mulaik, 1972; Schönemann & Steiger, 1976). Recently, Mulaik and McDonald (1978; McDonald & Mulaik, 1979) provided a useful perspective which makes it possible to develop confirmatory factor-analytic models examining factorial invariance with respect to selection of variables. Their argument involves the assumption that a core set of observed variables have been selected on a priori grounds from a universe or domain of observed variables hypothesized to measure a given factor. Mulaik and McDonald (1978) then proceeded to show that the concept of invariance with respect to the core variables implies that the core variables have invariant factor-pattern matrices when factored separately or with any other arbitrarily selected set of variables from the domain outside the core set (under the assumption that these other variables are actually drawn from the domain defined by the factor). The action of including additional variables may result in specific variance within the core being redefined as the common factor variance, but this redefinition should not affect the factor loadings defined by the relationships among the core set of variables.

Their treatment suggests a confirmatory factor-analysis design to test the hypothesis of invariance with respect to selection of variables. First define a core set of variables from the domain, and then an alternative set of variables outside the core also drawn from that domain. Administer the full battery under the same conditions to two random samples from the same population. Arbitrarily assign one sample to the core model, the other to the core plus other variables model. Then the hypothesis of invariance specifies that the factor-pattern coefficients of the core variables should be invariant between samples, which may be tested in a simultaneous two group analysis by constraining the appropriate loadings equal. The major additional advantage of the confirmatory factor model in this application is that it may be used to specify correlated specific components between subtests within the core or within the extra-core set of variables. If the hypothesis of invariance is rejected, then the results call into question the assumption that the variables are drawn from a well defined factor domain which will estimate the same factor irrespective of the observed variables selected to represent the factor. As coherently discussed by McDonald and Mulaik (1979), a lack of invariance would have unhappy consequences for definition of factors, since it would raise the possibility that individuals could start with the same set of *marker variables* and yet end up defining and (mis)interpreting quite different factors.

## Models with Factor Means

An important development in covariance structures modeling is the inclusion of a vector of observed means, so that the observed means of the population may be structured as a function of the means of the latent variables (factors) identified by the common factor model. This approach provides a method for assessing hypotheses of subpopulation differences in mean factor scores while avoiding the nasty problem of indeterminacy of factor score estimation. From a strictly factor-analytic perspective, the model is only useful when subpopulations are being compared or alternatively, when longitudinal changes in factor means over time are to be estimated. Sörbom (1974) presented the first extension of the multiple group covariance structures factor model to incorporate structured means; his model served as the basis for the COFAMM program (Sörbom & Jöreskog, 1976). Basically, the approach extends the common factor model specified in Equations 1–4 by adding a representation of the vector of observed means, $\mu^{(g)}$, in Equation 2:

$$Y^{(g)} = \mu^{(g)} + \Lambda^{(g)}\eta^{(g)} + \epsilon^{(g)} \tag{10}$$

and representing the observed means in terms of the factor means:

$$\mu^{(g)} = \nu^{(g)} + \Lambda^{(g)} \alpha^{(g)} \tag{11}$$

Actually, Sörbom (1974) only discussed one of the potential models available in COFAMM (Model A2), which assumes that one has specified an invariant vector of observed *location parameters*, $\nu$, for each group:

$$\mu^{(g)} = \nu + \Lambda^{(g)} \alpha^{(g)} \tag{12}$$

(notice the lack of the $g$ superscript on $\nu$). The vector of invariant location parameters is sometimes (but not always) equivalent to the vector of grand means for the observed variables. Sörbom's (1974) model then represents population deviations around this invariant mean vector $\nu$ in terms of group differences in the factor means in $\alpha$, as seen in the preceding equation. The model is not identified; estimating the location parameters for the population has the consequence that only the relative group differences in factor means, not the absolute differences, are identified.[3] The solution is to arbitrarily fix one group's factor means to zero, redefining the vector of location parameters relative to

---

[3] If the population grand means were known, the values could be fixed in a LISREL model for the mean structure (Sörbom, 1981), in which case all group means would be expressed as deviations from the known grand means. This would be appropriate, for example, if the data had been scaled to $T$-scores (mean of 50) on the basis of large sample norms. Then the grand means could be fixed at 50 and the group means expressed as deviations from the overall population means.

that group, and therefore defining the remaining factor means as deviation contrasts (in the ANOVA sense) about the factor means fixed to zero. One advantage of this approach is that the standard errors of the mean parameters may be used to test the meaningful null hypothesis that the estimated factor mean is significantly different from the group mean fixed at zero.

A problem is that the status of the other two models in COFAMM is poorly understood and, in principle, may lead to mistaken inferences about model comparisons. Model A3 in COFAMM is exactly equivalent to the model of Equations 1–4 because the mean vectors of the groups are allowed to vary freely, while the factor means are fixed to zero. This model therefore places no structure on the vector of population means and provides a perfect (yet trivial) fit to the sample means. It is not the case that a COFAMM model using Model A2 may be compared to a COFAMM model using model A3 to test the null hypothesis that all the factor means are equal to zero. This may superficially seem to be the case, since Model A3 specifies the factor means as zero, but the lack of restrictions on the vector of location parameters renders this comparison meaningless with respect to the null hypothesis that the factor means are equal in the groups. The correct specification is to use Model A2 and fix all factor means to zero; the difference in $\chi^2$ between this model and the less restricted model described above is a likelihood ratio $\chi^2$ test of the hypothesis that all factor means are equal across groups.

It is also possible to specify factor means in the LISREL V program (Sörbom, 1981). The advantage of using LISREL V is that the investigator is afforded a set of model options not available in COFAMM, but at the price of increased complexity in specification.

A final note about the models with factor means: Implicit in Equation 11 is the assumption that $\Sigma(\alpha) = 0$—that is, the means of the unique components in the population are zero. This may be problematic for many factor models in which the residual components include specific but reliable sources of variance which will in principle not have equal mean levels across subpopulations. For example, if one were estimating a second-order factor and its mean differences across groups, it is unlikely that there would not also be group differences in first-order factor means. Whether or not these differences may be represented solely at the level of the second-order factor means seems to be a matter of theory (and a hypothesis to be tested empirically). The assumption that all residuals have means of zero is not justifiable in the general case. This problem is easily handled, however, by representing the unique components in the common factor part of the model through models similar to Jöreskog's (1970) early covariance structures models. All one needs to do is to define a "factor" with a fixed loading of 1 on the observed variable and fixed loadings of zero on all other variables, fix the corresponding residual in $\Theta_\epsilon$ to zero, and freely estimate the "factor" variance—actually, the unique variance. Then the mean of the residual components may be incorporated into $\alpha^{(g)}$. This specification allows us to treat the Sörbom (1974) model with all residuals in $\Theta_\epsilon$ as a restricted hypothesis that the population differences in observed means are solely a function of population differences in factor means. This hypothesis may then be tested against more general alternatives (provided that the residual means are in fact identified).

Sörbom (1974, 1981) provided useful examples of factor models with means. Hertzog and Carter (1982) used the LISREL model to examine sex differences in factor means. Horn and McArdle (1980) have an interesting discussion on variants of models for structured means, as well as many of the issues in structural modeling considered in this chapter.

## Confirmatory Factor Analysis and Assessment of Psychometric Measures

One of the chief advantages of the confirmatory factor model is its utility in addressing the validity of alternative models for the psychometric properties of intelligence tests, including both (a) the assessment of components of true- and error-score variance as related to the issue of reliability and measurement equivalence across multiple groups and (b) the assessment of the construct validity of tests through the use of confirmatory-factor analytic designs to assess (i) convergent and discriminant validity and (ii) trait- and method-variance components.

### Assessment of Psychometric Properties of Intelligence Tests

Confirmatory-factor analytic models are well suited to the specification and testing of alternative models of psychometric tests specified in classical test theory (Lord & Novick, 1968). Jöreskog (1971a, 1974) showed that models of ($\tau$) tau-equivalence and parallelism implied different factor-analytic models for the covariance structure of alternate forms of psychometric tests. The assumption of ($\tau$) tau-equivalence specifies that alternate forms have equal true-score variances but different error variances (and hence different observed variances). Jöreskog (1971a) showed that this assumption translated into a one-factor model for the alternate forms in which the factor loadings could be constrained equal. The more restrictive assumption of parallelism involves the assumption of equal true-score variances and equal error-score variances. The parallelism assumption specifies a model in which both factor loadings and unique variances for the alternate forms are constrained equal. Both these models may be contrasted against the weaker assumption of congenerism, which assumes that alternate forms measure the same sources of variances without specifying the relationship of true- and error-score components across forms.

An important extension of the confirmatory-factor analysis model for psychometric properties is the examination of measurement equivalence in multiple groups. Often inferences about population differences in intelligence are made without direct attention to the nagging issue of the equivalence of measurement properties across the groups. Strictly speaking, one cannot make unambiguous comparisons of observed score means between populations if the populations have different reliabilities. Rock, Werts, and Flaugher (1978) provided a useful summary of their work with Jöreskog on models for evaluating measurement properties between groups. They showed that there are a series of models one may test to examine the issues of group equivalence in measurement properties. These tests take the same form as the tests described by Jöreskog (1971b) for examining factorial invariance, except that the use of a factor-analytic design with alternative forms lends special interpretation to the meaning of the tests of between-groups equivalence. Assuming a set of alternate forms hypothesized to measure a given construct, Rock, et al., (1978) discuss the interpretation of the hypothesis of equal factor loadings, factor variance, and unique variance. Given that a single factor model fits the covariance structure of the observed variables, the critical test is the equality of the factor loadings across groups. Equivalent factor loadings imply equal scaling units (assuming an unstandardized analysis). If this hypothesis is rejected there can be no meaningful group comparisons of levels of test scores. Requiring equivalence in $\Lambda$ and constraining equal the factor variance in $\Psi$ implies equal true-score variances across groups; adding the assumption of equal $\Theta_\epsilon$ corresponds to the assumption of equal reliabilities.

Perhaps the most critical feature of this approach is that one empirically tests the psychometric assumptions of the tests and is therefore in a strong position to state explicitly the nature of population equivalence in psychometric properties. The advantage of this approach is that it is possible to use models incorporating factor means to estimate group differences in mean levels of the latent variables under less restrictive assumptions than are necessary to compare population mean differences on the observed variables themselves (see Rock, et al., 1978).

*Confirmatory-factor Models for Construct Validity.* While the issue of measurement equivalence is certainly of critical importance, it in no way supercedes the issue of what we might term *construct equivalence* of the measures. Even if it can be shown that a scale has similar patterns of systematic and error variance across multiple groups, we cannot assume that the measure has equivalent construct validity with respect to the underlying determinants of that variability. Measures can be highly reliable and completely invalid with respect to the measurement of a construct of interest; similarly, measures can have similar measurement properties but differential validity. Assessing the validity of a given measure is certainly not an easy task (Cronbach, 1970). Often the best that can be done is to show that a *nomological net* (Cronbach & Meehl, 1955) of evidence may be gathered, which, as a whole, makes it highly plausible that the measure in fact does tap the construct of interest. The nomological net consists of attempts to make inferences about the expected pattern of covariance of the measure with other measures, conditional upon the assumption of construct validity, and then to determine whether the predicted pattern of associations may be empirically observed. Thus one often seeks to use indices of concurrent or predictive validity—that is, covariances of a measure with an independently derived criterion that is related to the construct in a known or hypothesized manner—as the basis for arguing for the construct validity of a measure.

The focus of the analysis is demonstrating that one can obtain convergent and discriminant validity for the measure with other measures (Campbell & Fiske, 1959; Cronbach, 1970). Convergent validity refers to the empirical result that measures of the same or closely related constructs should converge together; that is, they should show high covariances with one another. Discriminant validity refers to the empirical result that measures of conceptually distinct constructs have weak relationships with one another (in the form of low covariances). Taken together, convergent and discriminant validity imply that measures of the same or closely related constructs should covary more highly with each other than with measures of poorly related constructs. Convergent and discriminant validity, as discussed by Campbell and Fiske (1959), thus involves the empirical hypothesis that the highest elements of a correlation matrix should involve convergent relationships, and the lowest elements should be associated with those hypothesized to be discriminant.

It is possible to translate the notions of convergent and discriminant validity into a latent variable model, which may be tested in LISREL. First, we need to define the nature of convergent validity. In the strictest sense, convergence involves the covariance among formally different measures that tap the same construct (as opposed to alternate forms of the same measure). For example, the Duncan Socioeconomic Index (cf. Duncan, Haller & Portes, 1971) and the ratio of rooms in a dwelling to the number of inhabitants may be argued to be different measures of the same construct—SES. A consequence of convergence on a construct by multiple measures is that one should be able to show that the measures may, in fact, be modeled as being determined by a latent variable or factor in LISREL. Depending, in part, upon the sources of variance in each measure other than the construct of interest, one should therefore be able to show (a) that the multiple indicators have statistically significant regressions on a common latent variable, and (b) that the latent variable model reasonably accounts for the covariances among the measures. On the other hand, it should also be possible to show that multiple indicators of a different construct form a latent variable that is not isomorphic with other constructs that are being measured (i.e., one should be able to show that the correlation between different latent variables is less than unity) and in fact, that the covariances between theoretically divergent constructs are small (possibly, not significantly greater than zero). Further, given that a weaker form of convergence is predicted—namely, that two constructs are conceptually distinct but strongly correlated—then it should be possible to show that the correlations among latent variables measuring such related constructs are greater than the correlations among latent variables measuring divergent constructs.

The latent variable approach to convergent and discriminant validity has two advantages:

1. the explicit formulation of strong convergence in terms of the viability of a latent variable model for multiple indicators.
2. the fact that the parameters most critical to the assessment of discriminant validity, the factor covariances, will be unaffected by measurement error.

It is well known from the test theory literature that validity coefficients (and, indeed, all simple correlation coefficients) have an upper bound of less than 1.0 or $-1.0$ because of the influence of measurement error, because only the reliable (true-score) components of a measure may covary with the true-score components of another measure. One of the problems with assessing a correlation matrix of observed variables for convergent and discriminant validity is that the coefficients may be affected by differential reliabilities among the measures. The LISREL approach, which separates error variance and specific variance from common variance, estimates covariances among the latent variables, which are in theory disattenuated for measurement error. Use of the LISREL model to examine convergent and discriminant validity in multiple age or cohort groups has an additional advantage: One can examine the issue of construct equivalence in the convergent measures by testing the hypothesis of invariant factor loadings between the groups.

A nagging problem in measurement is the fact that the true-score components of a measure may in fact be determined by multiple sources of variance, yet often only one source of variance is of interest. While this problem may be limited to some extent by careful design of instruments, one class of influences is not easily removed—variance produced by the measurement method itself. For example, some of the reliable differences between individuals found on laboratory reaction time tasks may be familiarity with experimental equipment, individual differences in movement time (which is generally not the construct of interest in reaction time experiments), or in individual response characteristics, such as the willingness to trade speed of response for accuracy of response. The only way to evaluate the importance of such method-specific factors in the determination of individual differences on a given measure is to design a study in which the method variance may be isolated from other sources of variance in the measure—by assessing the same constructs with multiple measurement methods. Moreover, in order to isolate the variance attributable to a particular construct, it is necessary also to vary the constructs assessed by the different measurement methods. Hence the derivation of the multitrait–multimethod matrix. The goal of a multitrait–multimethod study is to islate "trait" or attribute factors and method factors.[4] The goal of a developmentally oriented study would be to de-termine the relative contribution of such trait and method factors in determining variation in the measures employed. The question is, to what extent does a measure lack construct equivalence across developmental levels (etc.) because of shifts in the relative contribution of method variance to total variance in the measure?

Analysis of multitrait–multimethod matrices with exploratory factor-analysis techniques is highly problematic; it is straightforwardly performed by using the LISREL model. It is necessary to specify trait and method factors which may be correlated with other trait and method factors; however, trait and method fac-tors must often be specified to be uncorrelated in order to achieve identification and/or convergence to a final solution. Using the covariance structures approach, a minimum of three trait and two method factors must be measured in order to identify the model without resorting to specification of extra (and possibly implausible) equality constraints on the trait and method factor loadings (see Althauser, Heberlein & Scott, 1971). Jöreskog (1974) illustrated the covariance structure approach to the problem by reanalyzing Lord's (1956) data on the relative contributions of speed and power components to intellectual test per-formance. A different example and a useful introductory discussion are given by Kenny (1979).

## Longitudinal Factor Analysis

One of the major advantages of restricted factor analysis as represented in the LISREL model is their application to the unique problems of longitudinal factor analysis. When multiple indicators of a set of factors are measured at mul-tiple longitudinal occasions, it is often the case that the covariance matrix of these observed variables will have the highest level of association represented in the covariances of variables with themselves at other occasions. Thus the covari-ance matrix might be said to be dominated by the *test-specific* covariances. A consequence of this pattern is that traditional exploratory factor analysis of this data matrix will tend to uncover test-specific factors which collapse over the occasions of measurement. Although such an analysis has interesting properties, its parameters are not optimally suited for representing the process of change over time. Several methodologists have developed longitudinal factor-analysis models which better represent the nature of the developmental process (e.g., Bentler 1973; Corballis, 1973; Corballis & Traub, 1970). It can be shown that the models of Corballis and Traub (1970) and Corballis (1973) may be considered special cases of a more general LISREL model for longitudinal factor analysis

---

[4] The term trait should be taken in its weakest sense here, since it is possible to measure attributes as factors which are not enduring characteristics of the individuals but are rather factors which cut across measurement methods at a given point in time.

developed by Jöreskog and Sörbom (1977). The general approach is to specify an *occasion-specific* factor model in which the factor model, which characterizes the structure of a single longitudinal occasion, is extended or replicated at all longitudinal occasions. The unique feature of the Jöreskog and Sörbom approach is that it treats the problem in unstandardized (covariance) metric and uses restricted factor-analysis methods to estimate the parameters and to test hypotheses about factorial invariance across occasions. The Corballis (1973) model is highly similar to the Jöreskog–Sörbom model, but it requires standardization of the observed variables and the factors, and postulates orthogonal factors at each occasion.

The Jöreskog–Sörbom model has several features that are of special importance for examining the consequences of interindividual differences in intraindividual change in latent variables. First, factorial invariance in terms of the regressions of variables on factors may be assessed by testing the hypothesis that the raw score factor-pattern elements may be constrained equal across the different longitudinal occasions (as described for the model examining measurement equivalence in multiple populations). As was the case for simultaneous multiple group analysis, changes in the magnitude of individual differences over time would make it inadvisable to standardize the data prior to the analysis; under conditions of changing variance over time, only the raw score regression coefficients in $\Lambda$ could be expected to be invariant over occasions. Second, parameters of the factor covariance matrix are relevant with regard to the hypothesis of interindividual differences in intraindividual change (Baltes & Nesselroade, 1973). Longitudinal changes in factor variances (the diagonal elements of $\Psi$) would indicate time-related changes in the magnitude of interindividual differences, which could only occur if the individuals differed in the magnitude of change over time. The magnitude of the covariances between isomorphic factors at different occasions indicates the stability of interindividual differences, since high covariances represent little shift in interindividual differences as a function of developmental change. When rescaled to correlations, these parameter estimates should approach 1.0 as individuals approach exact maintenance of their distribution about the factor mean over time. Conversely, low levels of covariance would indicate substantial "crossing over" of the change functions over time, which could be indicative of differential patterns of development. Note that these measures of individual differences are taken at the level of the latent variables or factors, and not at the level of observed variables. This aspect of the model is critically important, since it assures that the stability over time, as reflected in the factor covariances will be unaffected by measurement error. Moreover, it guarantees that patterns of individual differences will be generalizable over a set of variables measuring a common construct, rather than specific to an isolated empirical variable, which increases the construct validity of the observed changes.

An important additional feature of the Jöreskog–Sörbom model is that one can model covariances between residual (unique) components in $\Theta_\epsilon$. Since, as discussed above, the unique components in such factor models contain reliable but specific components other than stochastic measurement error, it is usually the case that the components for replicated observed variables will covary across occasions. As noted by Corballis (1973), Sörbom (1975), and others, failure to specify and estimate such "autocorrelated residuals" will perturb other parameter estimates of the model. For example, Hertzog and Schaie (1984) found estimated factor correlations exceeding 1.0 in a longitudinal factor-analysis model when $\Theta_\epsilon$ was specified as a diagonal matrix of unique variances. Fitting residual covariances for replicated measures across different occasions substantially improved the fit of the model and resulted in more parsimonious estimates of factor covariances.

Jöreskog and Sörbom (1977) discuss more complex variants of the longitudinal factor model which incorporate occasion-specific and test-specific common factors. The model can also easily be extended to the analysis of cohort-sequential data matrices, where multiple cohorts are measured longitudinally (Jöreskog & Sörbom, 1980). The model can also be expanded to include the simultaneous analysis of factor means as well as factor structure (Jöreskog & Sörbom, 1980). This feature is especially useful, because the model then represents an operational method for implementing the suggestion of Baltes and Nesselroade (1973) that hypotheses about changes in developmental level simultaneously consider the issue of qualitative invariance in the factor structure. Developmentally oriented applications of the model may be found in Olsson and Bergman (1977) and Hertzog and Schaie (1984). The latter paper also illustrates the simultaneous analysis of factor means and factor structure in sequential data.

## CONCLUDING COMMENTS

The preceding sections have reviewed a series of potential applications for confirmatory factor analysis to the study of intelligence. Hopefully, one theme that has emerged is that confirmatory factor analysis is in no way a replacement for exploratory factor analysis. Instead, it should be viewed as a valuable complement. Confirmatory analysis will often follow an exploratory factor analysis which has provided a useful first attempt at understanding the structure of a set of ability variables. The importance of confirmatory approaches stems both from its emphasis on theory-based hypothesis testing and upon the flexibility of model specification available in the restricted factor-analysis model. As discussed above, a series of critically important issues in factor analytic research (e.g., longitudinal factor analysis, multitrait–multimethod models) are best treated as restricted covariance-structures models. Unrestricted factor analysis cannot hope to provide a method for evaluating the most interesting hypotheses in these models. The next decade in psychometric research should see a continued evolution in our understanding of the utility of confirmatory factor analytic methods to address fundamental but difficult issues in intelligence research.

# REFERENCES

Ahmavaara, Y. (1954). The mathematical theory of factorial invariance under selection. *Psychometrika, 19,* 27–38.

Algina, J. (1980). A note on identification in the oblique and orthogonal factor analysis models. *Psychometrika, 45,* 393–396.

Althauser, R. P., Heberlein, T. A., & Scott, R. A. (1971). A causal assessment of validity: The augmented multitrait-multimethod matrix. In H. M. Blalock (Ed.), *Causal Models in the Social Sciences.* Chicago, IL: Aldine.

Alwin, D. F., & Jackson, D. J. (1981). Applications of simultaneous factor analysis to issues of factorial invariance. In D. J. Jackson & E. F. Borgatta (Eds.), *Factor analysis and measurement.* London, England: Sage.

Anastasi, A. (1970). On the formation of psychological traits. *American Psychologist, 25,* 899–910.

Anderson, T. W. (1958). *An introduction to multivariate statistical analysis.* New York: Wiley.

Anderson, T. W., & Rubin, H. (1956). Statistical inference in factor analysis. In J. Heyman (Ed.), *Proceedings of the Third Berkeley Symposium on Mathematical Statistics and Probability,* (Vol. 5). Berkeley, CA: University of California Press, 111–150.

Baltes, P. B., & Nesselroade, J. R. (1973). The developmental analysis of individual differences on multiple measures. In J. R. Nesselroade & H. W. Reese (Eds.), *Life-span developmental psychology: Methodological issues.* New York: Academic Press.

Bechtoldt, H. P. (1974). A confirmatory analysis of the factor stability hypothesis. *Psychometrika, 39,* 319–326.

Bentler, P. M. (1973). Assessment of developmental factor change at the individual and group level. In J. R. Nesselroade & H. W. Reese (Eds.), *Life-span developmental psychology: Methodological issues.* New York: Academic Press.

Bentler, P. M. (1976). Multistructure statistical model applied to factor analysis. *Multivariate Behavior Research, 11,* 3–25.

Bentler, P. M. (1980). Multivariate analysis with latent variables: Causal modeling. *Annual Review of Psychology, 31,* 419–456.

Bentler, P. M., & Bonett, D. G. (1980). Significance tests and goodness of fit in the analysis of covariance structures. *Psychological Bulletin, 88,* 588–606.

Bentler, P. M., & Weeks, D. G. (1979). Interrelations among models for the analysis of moment structures. *Multivariate Behavioral Research, 14,* 169–185.

Bloxom, B. (1972). Alternative approaches to factorial invariance. *Psychometrika, 37,* 425–440.

Bock, R. D., & Bargmann, R. E. (1966). Analysis of covariance structures. *Psychometrika, 31,* 507–534.

Campbell, D. T., & Fiske, D. W. (1959). Convergent and discriminant validation by the multitrait–multimethod matrix. *Psychological Bulletin, 56,* 81–105.

Cattell, R. B. (1978). *The scientific use of factor analysis in behavioral and life sciences.* New York: Plenum.

Corballis, M. C. (1973). A factor model for analyzing change. *British Journal of Mathematical and Statistical Psychology, 26,* 90–97.

Corballis, M. C., & Traub, R. E. (1970). Longitudinal factor analysis. *Psychometrika, 35,* 79–98.

Costner, H. L., & Schoenberg, R. (1973). Diagnosing indicator ills in multiple indicator models. In A. S. Goldberger & O. D. Duncan (Eds.), *Structural equations models in the social sciences.* New York: Seminar Press.

Cronbach, L. J. (1970). *The essentials of psychological testing* (3rd. ed.). New York: Harper and Row.

Cronbach, L. J., & Meehl, P. E. (1955). Construct validity in psychological tests. *Psychological Bulletin, 52,* 281–302.

Cunningham, W. R. (1978). Principles for identifying structural differences: Some methodological issues related to comparative factor analysis. *Journal of Gerontology, 33,* 82–86.

Cunningham, W. R. (1980). Age comparative factor analysis of ability variables in adulthood and old age. *Intelligence, 4,* 133–149.

Cunningham, W. R. (1981). Ability factor structure differences in adulthood and old age. *Multivariate Behavioral Research, 16,* 3–22.

Duncan, O. D., Haller, A. O., & Portes, A. (1971). Peer influences on aspirations: A reinterpretation. In H. M. Blalock (Ed.), *Causal models in the social sciences.* Chicago, IL: Aldine.

Ekstrom, R. B., French, J. W., Harman, H. H., & Dermen, D. (1976). *Manual for kit of factor-referenced cognitive tests.* Princeton, NJ: Educational Testing Service.

Fletcher, R. & Powell, M. J. D. (1963). A rapidly convergent descent method for minimization. *The Computer Journal, 6,* 163–168.

Harman, H. H. (1967). *Modern factor analysis* (2nd ed.). Chicago, IL: University of Chicago Press.

Hertzog, C., & Carter, L. (1982). Sex differences in the structure of intelligence: A confirmatory factor analysis. *Intelligence, 6,* 287–303.

Hertzog, C., & Schaie, K. W. (1984). Age changes in intellectual structure: A structural equations analysis. Unpublished manuscript.

Horn, J. L., & Engstrom, R. (1979). Cattell's scree test in relation to Bartlett's chi-square test and other observations on the number of factors problem. *Multivariate Behavioral Research, 14,* 283–300.

Horn, J. L., & McArdle, J. J. (1980). Perspectives on mathematical/statistical model building (MASMOB) in research on aging. In L. W. Poon (Ed.), *Aging in the 1980's: Psychological issues.* Washington, DC: American Psychological Association.

Hyde, J. S., Geiringer, E. R., & Yen, W. M. (1975). The empirical relation between spatial ability and sex differences in other aspects of cognitive performance. *Multivariate Behavioral Research, 10,* 289–310.

Jöreskog, K. G. (1966). Testing a simple structure hypothesis in factor analysis. *Psychometrika, 31,* 165–178.

Jöreskog, K. G. (1967). Some contributions to maximum likelihood factor analysis. *Psychometrika, 32,* 443–482.

Jöreskog, K. G. (1969). A general approach to confirmatory maximum likelihood factor analysis. *Psychometrika, 34,* 183–220.

Jöreskog, K. G. (1971a). Statistical analysis of sets of congeneric tests. *Psychometrika, 36,* 109–133.

Jöreskog, K. G. (1971b). Simultaneous factor analysis in several populations. *Psychometrika, 36,* 409–426.

Jöreskog, K. G. (1974). Analyzing psychological data by structural analysis of covariance matrices. In D. H. Krautz, R. C. Atkinson, R. D. Luce, & P. Suppes (Eds.), *Contemporary developments in mathematical psychology* (Vol. 2). San Francisco, CA: W. H. Freeman.

Jöreskog, K. G. (1979). Author's addendum. In K. G. Jöreskog & D. Sörbom, *Advances in factor analysis and structural equations models.* Cambridge, MA: Abt Associates.

Jöreskog, K. G., & Sörbom, D. (1977). Statistical models and methods for analyses of longitudinal data. In D. S. Aigner & A. S. Goldberger (Eds.), *Latent variables in socio-economic models.* Amsterdam, The Netherlands: North Holland.

Jöreskog, K. G., & Sörbom, D. (1979). *Advances in factor analysis and structural equation models.* Cambridge, MA: Abt Associates.

Jöreskog, K. G., & Sörbom, D. (1980). Simultaneous analysis of longitudinal data from several cohorts. Technical Report 80-5, Department of Statistics, University of Uppsala, Sweden.

Jöreskog, K. G., & Sörbom, D. (1981). *LISREL V Users Guide.* Chicago, IL: National Educational Resources.

Kenny, D. A. (1979). *Correlation and causality.* New York: Wiley.

Larzelere, R. E., & Mulaik, S. A. (1977). Single-sample tests for many correlations. *Psychological Bulletin, 84,* 557–569.

Lawley, D. N. (1943). A note on Karl Pearson's selection formulae. *Proceedings of the Royal Society of Edinburgh, 2,* 28–30.

Long, J. S. (1976). Estimation and hypothesis testing in linear models containing measurement error. *Sociological Methods and Research, 5,* 157–206.

Lord, F. M. (1956). A study of speed factors in tests and academic grades. *Psychometrika, 21,* 31–50.

Lord, F. M., & Novick, M. R. (1968). *Statistical theories of mental test scores.* Reading, MA: Addison-Wesley.

McArdle, J. J., & McDonald, R. P. (1981). A simple algebraic representation of structural equations models. Unpublished manuscript.

McDonald, R. P. (1978). A simple comprehensive model for the analysis of covariance structures. *British Journal of Mathematical and Statistical Psychology, 31,* 59–72.

McDonald, R. P., & Mulaik, S. A. (1979). Determinacy of common factors: A nontechnical review. *Psychological Bulletin, 86,* 297–306.

McGaw, B., & Jöreskog, K. G. (1971). Factorial invariance of ability measures in groups differing in intelligence and socioeconomic status. *British Journal of Mathematical and Statistical Psychology, 24,* 154–168.

Meehl, P. E. (1978). Theoretical risks and tabular asterisks: Sir Karl, Sir Ronald, and the slow progress of soft psychology. *Journal of Consulting and Clinical Psychology, 46,* 806–834.

Meredith, W. (1964). Notes on factorial invariance. *Psychometrika, 29,* 177–185.
Mulaik, S. A. (1972). *The foundation of factor analysis.* New York: McGraw-Hill.
Mulaik, S. A. (1975). Confirmatory factor analysis. In O. J. Amick & H. J. Walberg (Eds.), *Introduction: Multivariate analysis.* Berkeley, CA: McCutchan.
Mulaik, S. A., & McDonald, R. P. (1978). The effect of additional variables on factor indeterminancy models with a single common factor. *Psychometrika, 43,* 177–192.
Olsson, V., & Bergman, L. R. (1977). A longitudinal factor model for studying change in ability structure. *Multivariate Behavioral Research, 12,* 221–241.
Platt, J. R. (1964). Strong inference. *Science, 146,* 347–353.
Reinert, G. (1970). Comparative factor analytic studies of intelligence throughout the human lifespan. In L. R. Goulet & P. B. Baltes (Eds.), *Life-span development: Research and theory.* New York: Academic Press.
Rock, D. A., Werts, C. E., & Flaugher, R. L. (1978). The use of analysis of covariance structures for comparing the psychometric properties of multiple variables across populations. *Multivariate Behavioral Research, 13,* 403–418.
Schönemann, P. H., & Steiger, J. H. (1976). Regression component analysis. *British Journal of Mathematical and Statistical Psychology, 29,* 175–189.
Sörbom, D. (1974). A general method for studying differences in factor means and factor structure between groups. *British Journal of Mathematical and Statistical Psychology, 27,* 229–239.
Sörbom, D. (1975). Detection of correlated errors in longitudinal data. *British Journal of Mathematical and Statistical Psychology, 28,* 138–151.
Sörbom, D. (1981). Structural equations models with structured means. In K. G. Jöreskog & H. Wold (Eds.), *Systems under indirect observation: Causality-structure-prediction.* Amsterdam, The Netherlands: North Holland.
Sörbom, D. & Jöreskog, K. G. (1976). *COFAMM: Confirmatory factor analysis with model modification (User's Guide).* Chicago, IL: National Educational Resources.
Swaminathan, H., & Algina, J. (1978). Scale freeness in factor analysis. *Psychometrika, 43,* 581–583.
Thurstone, L. L. (1947). *Multiple factor analysis.* Chicago, IL: University of Chicago Press.
Thurstone, L. L., & Thurstone, T. G. (1941). Factorial studies of intelligence. *Psychometric Monographs,* (No. 2). Chicago, IL: University of Chicago Press.
Tucker, L. R. & Lewis, C. (1973). A reliability coefficient for maximum likelihood factor analysis. *Psychometrika, 38,* 1–10.
van Driel, O. P. (1978). On various causes of improper solutions in maximum likelihood factor analysis. *Psychometrika, 43,* 225–243.
Vernon, P. E. (1972). The distinctiveness of field independence. *Journal of Personality, 40,* 366–391.
Widiger, T. A., Knudson, R. M., & Rorer, L. G. (1980). Convergent and discriminant validity of measures of cognitive styles and abilities. *Journal of Personality and Social Psychology, 39,* 116–129.
Witkin, H. A., Dyk, R. B., Faterson, H. F., Goodenough, D. R., & Karp, S. A. (1962). *Psychological differentiation.* New York: Wiley.

# CHAPTER 4

# Studying Intelligence
# with Test Theory Models

*Susan Embretson (Whitely)*

*University of Kansas*

## INTRODUCTION

It is impossible to imagine a scientific discipline of human intelligence without methods to measure individual differences. Historically, substantive research on intelligence and psychometric methods have been inextricably linked. Jenkins and Paterson (1961, p. vi), in their history of psychological research on intelligence, noted that scientific study was not possible until three conditions were met: "(1) a breaking down of the fixed belief that the 'mind' was beyond measurement, followed by methods of measurement; (2) a concern with individuals, as distinct from the search for 'general laws'; (3) the invention of statistical tools for describing, relating, and interpreting measurements, once they were obtained."

Galton (1869, 1888) is often credited for originating the scientific study of intelligence, embodying all three of the above qualities. No less significant, however, are Spearman's (1904, 1910, 1913, 1923, 1927) early contributions that also spanned substantive theory, statistics and psychometric methods. Thus, the early intelligence theorists were also the first psychometricians.

Contemporary psychometric methods seem quite removed from the study of intelligence. The trend toward specialization in psychology seemingly precludes the breadth and depth of contribution that was made by Galton and Spearman. An original contribution of modern psychometric methods, such as latent trait models, typically requires knowledge of mathematical statistics. Consequently, many test theorists have had little opportunity or interest in developing expertise in psychological theory. Conversely, intelligence theorists are often highly specialized in (experimental) methods to test hypotheses and typically do not contribute to psychometric methods.

Even though intelligence research and psychometric methods have become highly specialized, developments in the two areas are interdependent. Psychometric methods define the construct of intelligence by providing principles for measuring individual differences. These principles not only determine how to evaluate a measure (i.e., reliability and validity) but also determine which tasks are selected and how task performance is scored to measure intelligence. Thus, psychometric methods have direct impact on the nature of "intelligent" performance. Substantive research, on the other hand, is germane not only to understanding what is measured by current intelligence tests but also to providing an external perspective on the theoretical adequacy of the tests.

Academic specialization has adversely influenced the interdependency of psychometric methods and substantive theories of intelligence. Although both psychometric methods and intelligence research have changed dramatically in the last decade, only occasionally are contemporary developments in both areas reflected in research. Often substantive research employs measures of intelligence that were developed by classical test theory principles rather than latent trait models. For example, cognitive component analysis (Pellegrino & Glaser, 1979; Sternberg, 1977a, 1977b) and cognitive correlate analysis (Hunt, Lunneborg, & Lewis, 1975) seek to understand individual differences in intelligence from underlying information processing abilities. However, the results of these studies depend subtly, but intimately, on the test theory principles that are embedded in the intelligence measures that are studied. Typically these intelligence tests are based on classical test theory principles.

Similarly, developments in psychometric methods often are not linked to modern conceptualizations of intelligence. Many psychometric developments are linked to the trait and factor conceptualization of intelligence that originated with Spearman (1927). For example, research on factor scores is relevant to the measurement of traits. Modern intelligence research, in contrast, emphasizes underlying information processes that determine responses rather than traits. It is not clear that the psychometric methods applicable to traits can be extended directly to information processing variables.

The purpose of this chapter is to examine classical test theory and contemporary latent trait theory as principles that define the construct of intelligence. Recent research has attempted to extend both classical and contemporary test theory to new conceptualizations of intelligence. These developments will be presented and explored for potential.

The chapter contains three main sections. The first section briefly examines an important new direction in intelligence research—cognitive component analysis. The cognitive component approach is illustrated with the series completion task and is contrasted to traditional intelligence research on the task. The second section examines classical test theory as a set of principles for measuring intelligence. Within this section, it is shown that controlling the distribution of scores and maximizing internal consistency are the two major principles that have guided cognitive test development. Then, classical test theory is examined with respect to current emphases in intelligence. Finally, a development that extends classical test theory to contemporary theory (Calfee, 1976) is presented.

The third section examines latent trait models as providing principles for measuring intelligence. It is shown that modeling performance replaces internal consistency as a principle. Extensions of latent trait theory to cognitive component analysis—component latent trait models (Embretson, in press; Fischer, 1973; Whitely, 1980)—are then presented.

## Individual Differences in Intelligence: Contemporary Research

Contemporary research on individual differences in intelligence has been strongly influenced by cognitive psychology, particularly information processing theory. Carroll and Maxwell (1979) suggest that cognitive psychology offers new potential for theoretical research. Pellegrino and Glaser (1979) define two separate approaches to cognitive research on intelligence, cognitive component analysis and cognitive correlate analysis. Of these two approaches, the cognitive component approach has generated the most research. Sternberg's (1977a, 1977b) thesis on the componential analysis of intelligence has been highly influential in the cognitive component approach.

Cognitive component analysis seeks to decompose the processes that underlie performance on "intelligent" tasks. For example, when applied to intelligence test items, item difficulty is modeled from the complexity of the task stimuli or subtasks that represent the processing components. Interestingly, it is not the focus on modeling *per se* that differentiates contemporary research from traditional research on intelligence. Rather, the type of data has changed. Earlier research on intelligence modeled task intercorrelations, while contemporary research models task difficulty.

The current section examines the mathematical-modeling approach of cognitive component analysis. The method is illustrated by some recent research on the series-completion task. The series-completion task provides an excellent example because the task not only has been important in contemporary intelligence research (Butterfield, in press; Holzman, Pellegrino & Glaser, in press) but also has been studied by the trait-and-factor approach (Guilford, 1959; Thurstone, 1941) as well as cognitive psychology (Klahr & Wallace, 1970; Simon & Kotovsky, 1963).

### Mathematical Modeling of Test Items

Mathematical models are used to operationalize theories about the cognitive components that underlie responses to test items. A theory of information processing can be evaluated, in part, by goodness of fit for a mathematical model that contains the operationalized constructs of a theory as independent variables. A wide variety of task features are used in mathematical models, including (a) task content, such as a stimulus complexity type or semantic features, (b) task presentation conditions, such as rate or stimulus clarity and (c) task completeness, which is varied by presenting partial tasks or precues before the full task. Task difficulty is measured by either response time or accuracy, or both, depending on the task and the goals of the study. Often a specific rationale, such as additive or subtractive factor modeling, accompanies the modeling method.

The parameters of a mathematical model represent the effects of the theoretical variables that underlie performance. Alternative theories about the underlying variables often leads to models with different methods to identify or combine the independent variables, or different independent variables. To the extent that the models operationalize the theories, comparing the models compares the theories.

**Table 4.1. Thurstone and Thurstone's (1941) Letter-Series Problems, in Which Subjects are Asked to Continue One or More Letters**

```
 1. C  D  C  D  C  D  —
 2. A  A  A  B  B  B  C  C  C  D  D  —
 3. A  B  M  C  D  M  E  F  M  G  H  M  —
 4. A  T  B  A  T  A  A  T  B  A  T  —
 5. Q  X  A  P  X  B  Q  X  A  —
 6. M  A  B  M  B  C  M  C  D  M  —
 7. A  B  Y  A  B  X  A  B  W  A  B  —
 8. U  R  T  U  S  T  U  T  T  U  —
 9. W  X  A  X  Y  B  Y  Z  C  Z  A  D  A  B  —
10. R  S  C  D  S  T  D  E  T  U  E  F  —
11. J  K  Q  R  K  L  R  S  L  M  S  T  —
12. N  P  A  O  Q  A  P  R  A  Q  S  A  —
13. D  E  F  G  E  F  G  H  G  H  I  —
14. A  D  U  A  C  U  A  E  U  A  B  U  A  F  —
15. P  O  N  O  N  M  N  M  L  M  L  K  —
```

Recent research on the series completion task illustrates some basic features of mathematical modeling. Table 4.1 presents some series completion problems that appear in Thurstone and Thurstone's (1941) Primary Mental Abilities Test. Recently, Butterfield (in press) compared his model of the task with several others that had been proposed. Butterfield postulated two factors to account for task difficulty, number of operations (Op) and level of knowledge (Kn). Table 4.2 and Table 4.3 show how Kn and Op are scored for series completion items. For Kn knowledge levels are determined by both type of relationship and complexity of the letter string structures. The lowest level requires knowledge only of identity relationships, while the highest level requires knowledge of string structure as well as the relationships included in all previous levels. For

**Table 4.2. Levels of Encoding Knowledge and Sample Series Represented by Each**

1. Identical letters go together
   1. O E I O E I O E I        2. K K T K K T K K T

2. Groups of adjacent identical letters between which a moving relation holds go together.
   1. E E U F F U G G U        2. V V V W W W X X X

3. An individual letter and a group of identical letters between which a moving relation holds go together.
   1. V V W W W X X X Y        2. S T T U V V W X X

4. Individual letters between which a moving relation holds go together.
   1. M S S N R R O Q Q        2. F R N G S M H T L

5. Groups of nonadjacent identical letters between which a moving relation holds go together.
   1. R M R S L S T K T        2. T S B S R C R Q D

6. A string structure is continuable only when all strings in the structure have the same period, and when each string connects the same relative positions within and across periods. When application of the first five rules creates a string structure that does not meet these two criteria, an alternative structure that does meet these criteria is created, by using rules 1 to 5 in conjunction with rule 6.
   1. I H G H G F G F E        2. J K L K L M L M N
   3. I M U J L U K K U        4. Q N P O M N M L L

**Table 4.3. Conventions for Calculating the Number of Operations to be Sequenced to Generate P Letters from the Rule Describing a Given Letter Series**

1. A letter series is continued by performing the I, N, or B operations specified in the rule describing the series. Duplicating a letter with an I relation requires no memory operations. Generating one letter from another with an N relation requires one working memory operation, and with a B relation it requires two working memory operations.
2. The operations are performed left-to-right in the order of their appearance in the rule, regardless of the rule's string structure.
3. The letter upon which an operation is to be performed is found by searching backward through the series to the last letter on the string specified by the rule for that operation.
4. Searching through a series for a letter on an I string is accomplished perceptually without (place keeping by) counting, but searching for a letter on a moving string requires counting unless that letter is identical to one just generated on the same moving string.
5. When counting back to locate a letter on a moving string, adjacent identical letters on the same string are counted as only one letter. Adjacent spurious identities are counted as separate letters.

Op, each operation is determined by the relationships between letters. The three possible relationships between letters are identity (I), next up the alphabet (N) and back on down the alphabet (B). Butterfield constructed a set of items in which Kn and Op were counterbalanced in a 4 × 5 design.

In one of eight experiments, Butterfield (in press) evaluated the fit of his model for series completion data from 112 children in Grades 2 to 6. Butterfield regressed item accuracy on the two independent variables in his model, using multiple regression. To demonstrate Butterfield's modeling method here, 40 items were sampled from his design. Both Kn and Op were significant predictors ($p < .01$) with a squared-multiple correlation of .92. These results are comparable to those obtained by Butterfield in the full data set.

Butterfield's two-factor model was compared to several other models on the PMA series completion task. Simon and Kotovsky's (1963) model predicts task difficulty from the computer time required by their program to solve the item, while Klahr and Wallace's (1970) model predicts difficulty from the number of operations required by their computer model to represent the item. Butterfield (in press) also proposed a single factor model that combines Kn and Op. These four models, respectively, yielded squared multiple correlations of .92, .34, .10 and .84, respectively. Thus, Butterfield's two factor model provides better fit, relative to alternative theories of the task.

*Relationship to Psychometrics.* Mathematical modeling of intelligence test items, such as Butterfield's modeling of the series completion task, contributes to substantive theory by explaining performance on tasks that have established importance as indicators of intelligence. As noted elsewhere (Embretson, 1983b), mathematical modeling also contributes to psychometrics by allowing two types of construct validation research to be separated, *nomothetic span* and *construct representation*. Traditionally, construct validation research examines the correlations of individual differences on an intelligence test with other measures. This type of construct validation research concerns nomothetic span because it assesses the importance of the test as a measure of individual differences. Mathematical modeling of task difficulty, in contrast, studies the construct representation of the task by identifying the constructs that account for performance.

However, it should be noted that mathematical modeling of test items is not sufficient to assess construct validity. Although a construct may be involved in task performance, it may not be an important measure of individual differences. For example, scanning the answer sheet to find the response alternative that was selected in the test booklet is clearly a cognitive process (i.e., matching to target), yet this process is unimportant in determining individual differences on intelligence tests.

Furthermore, the parameters that can be estimated by fitting mathematical models to individual subjects do not substitute for psychometric indices. As noted elsewhere (Embretson, 1983b), the parameters from individual mathematical models are confounded with other aspects of individual differences, and hence they have limited value as psychometric indices.

# CLASSICAL TEST THEORY

Test theory is a set of principles that guide test construction. As such, they influence how an individual's behavior is translated into an ability score. Although textbooks on classical test theory are readily available, they do not examine test-theory principles for their impact on the nature of what is measured by intelligence tests. The principles that determine how an individual's behavior is translated into a measure of intelligence will be examined in three general categories in this section. First, the conceptualizations of the basic methodological issues may be examined for how they formally define the goals for test theory methods. Second, the methods for selecting test content may be examined for how they determine, in practice, the tasks that are selected as indicators of ability. Third, the methods for translating behavior into ability scores can be examined for how they determine which aspects of task performance are indicators of ability.

The purpose of this section is to determine how the major test theory principles influence the relationship between behavior and ability. Test theory will be traced historically because many developments were available quite early in psychology and have influenced testing practice from the beginning of the testing movement. Then, the three categories of principles will be elaborated and then compared to contemporary concerns in intelligence research.

## The Development of Classical Test Theory

Gulliksen's (1950) book is the major reference for classical test theory. It contains detailed, theoretical derivations and procedures for test construction. However, classical test theory was actually developed and widely implemented much earlier. Many basic ideas that underlie test theory, such as normal distributions of abilities. the covariance statistic and the notion of equivalent measures can be traced to Galton (1869, 1888). However, Spearman perhaps can be regarded as the father of classical test theory. Gulliksen (1950, p. 1) notes that Spearman's early papers (prior to 1913) contain nearly all the basic formulas for classical test theory. Interestingly, Spearman (1923, 1927) also can be credited for the first psychological theory of intelligence. Spearman postulated that intelligence ("g") was a general trait. Certain patterns of correlations between tasks (i.e., tetrad differences) were expected if "g" accounted for the consistency of individual differences across tasks. Thus, the fundamental developments for test theory were closely linked to early theory on intelligence.

Although Binet (1911) strongly influenced psychological testing, his work often is given only passing reference in textbooks on test theory. Perhaps the major reason for the scant treatment of Binet's impact on testing is that his mathematical formulation of ability as the ratio IQ was replaced by developments based on the normal distribution and the correlation coefficient. Kelley notes that (1927, p. 4) Binet's conceptualization of intelligence as a composite of psychological functions appears to have been his most important contribution.

## Principles in Classical Test Theory

*Basic Issues for Test Theory.* As noted by Gulliksen (1950, p. 4), "The estimation of the error in a set of test scores and the differentiation between 'error' and 'true' scores are central problems in mental measurement." "True and error score theory," as Gulliksen's (1950) developments have become known, contains derivations for estimating reliability, error variance and so on, from the basic assumption that error is random and uncorrelated with true score.

Spearman (1904) laid the foundation for true and error score theory in his description of "accidental errors" of measurement and their attenuating effect on correlations. Spearman (1904, 1907) suggests that product–moment correlations can be applied to similar measures to assess reliability, which then can be used to disattenuate the correlations between separate mental measurements. Gulliksen (1950) noted that these early developments for test theory essentially assumed that the "similar" measures are parallel forms. Parallel forms are basic to Gulliksen's derivations for true and error score theory.

However, Gulliksen recognized that estimates of measurement error depend on the experimental conditions under which the measurements are observed. Classifications of the various experimental conditions and their corresponding assessment of errors, appear in many popular textbooks on measurement (e.g., Magnuson, 1967) and testing (Anastasi, 1982). A formal test theory to link measurement errors to experimental conditions, popularly known as generalizability theory, was proposed by Cronbach, Gleser, Nanda and Rajaratnam (1972).

It is interesting how validity seemingly gets short shrift in most books on test theory (Gulliksen, 1950; Magnusson, 1967; Nunnally, 1978). Typically, only a chapter or two is devoted to validity. Historically, it is obvious that reliability has been regarded as the more fundamental issue for test theory. The notion that reliability precedes validity is implicit even in very early developments. Spearman (1904) showed how accidental measurement errors attenuate the correlations between mental measurements. Similarly, Gulliksen (1950) postulates that the conceptualization of score accuracy is the most fundamental problem in the test development process because it influences all other aspects of test development. The test theory derivation that shows that the maximum validity coefficient is the square root of the reliability coefficient (see Gulliksen, 1950) is often cited to support the focus on reliability.

The central concept that emerges from these conceptualizations of classical test theory is that observations must be replicable over some specified conditions. These conditions include parallel forms, and retesting intervals and items, which lead to different reliability coefficients (i.e., coefficients of equivalence, stability and internal consistency, respectively).

Interestingly, the conditions for reliability do not have equal importance in either classical test theory or test development practice. The major mathematical derivations for classical test theory are built around the coefficient of equivalence while, as shown below, test development practice is influenced mainly by the coefficient of internal consistency.

*Test Content.* Test content has been heavily influenced by Binet's concept of intelligence as a composite of psychological functions. Binet's (1911) scale consisted of tasks that required complex judgments and reasoning to solve. Since then, both individual and group tests of general intelligence typically include several item types that require complex cognitive processing.

Classical test theory became influential in determining test content shortly after World War I. Sophisticated textbooks on correlational research methods for mental measurements appeared at this time (Brown & Thomson, 1925; Kelley, 1923). For example, Freeman's (1926) book on mental tests presents two chapters on test development—which include the types of tasks for measuring intelligence and the selection and organization of test items. However, in both modern and older texts on test theory, the principles for designing and constructing items either are treated as an auxiliary topic or are omitted entirely (Guilford, 1954; Gulliksen, 1950; Kelley, 1927).

Classical test theory rigorously develops only three principles for selecting test content. These principles are item difficulty, item reliability and item validity (Guilford, 1954; Gulliksen, 1950; Magnusson, 1967). Item validity, the correlation of an item with an external criterion, clearly has had a lesser role for two reasons. First, in theory, intelligence is regarded as a general quality so that no single external criterion can define ability adequately, such as may be possible for a test designed for specific predictive validity. Second, in practice, adequate validity indices, such as the correlations of items with achievement, typically are not available for item analysis.

In contrast, item difficulty and item reliability have had major impact on test development. Item difficulty predates item reliability as a principle for item selection. The basic goal is to match item difficulty to the population. As early as the late 1920's, Symonds (1929) presents ogives that show the relationship of ability (in standard score units) to item accuracy. Symonds presents several propositions about the relationship of item difficulty to accuracy in estimating ability at various levels. These propositions show that the optimum item for an individual has a probability of .50 of being passed.

By 1936, a second principle of item selection had become widely prevalent. As noted by Richardson (1936, p. 69), "the development of the procedures of item analysis has consisted chiefly of the invention of various forms of an association between the test item and the total test score." At that time, at least ten different indices had been proposed. Richardson (1936) shows that for items of equal difficulty, the item/total score correlation is proportional to the average correlation of that item with the other items in the test. Furthermore, he shows that if the average item intercorrelation is used to estimate reliability, the Spearman–Brown prophesy formula shows that test reliability can be increased by eliminating items with low correlations with total score. Thus, Richardson provides the basic rationale for item analysis by item relationship with total score. This rationale became more formalized by deriving an internal consistency formula based on item covariances and total score variances (Kuder & Richardson, 1937).

## Scoring Behavior

Translating test behavior into ability scores involves at least three stages: (a) determining the aspect of behavior that is to be scored, (b) combining performance on items into test scores, and (c) converting test scores into ability. All three stages contribute to the nature of ability that is measured by the test.

Traditionally, even with many of Galton's (1869) tasks, the aspect of behavior that has been scored is accuracy, rather than response time or process. However, it should be noted that accuracy scores do not necessarily represent response quality or power. They represent response speed if testing time is sufficiently brief. Speed versus power was an issue even for the beginnings of large scale, group testing with the Army Alpha (Yerkes, 1921). Scores on most aptitude tests represent some combination of speed and power. However, power is usually favored because classical test theory does not apply as well to speeded test scores. Although many aspects of performance other than accuracy could be scored, it should be noted that accuracy corresponds well to early theories of intelligence as "good responses" or "response power" (Spearman, 1927).

Performance on items is typically translated into aptitude test scores as the unweighted sum of accuracy over items. Sometimes scores are corrected for guessing to accommodate the multiple choice format. However, raw unweighted scores are the basic test score.

Interestingly, the methods for translating test behavior into ability scores also developed relatively early. One of Galton's major contributions was the notion that the variability of human mental abilities could be described by the normal distribution. Significant developments for norm-referenced individual scores were available quite early (e.g., Kelley, 1914) and the use of standard scores was fully advocated by the late 1920s (Kelley, 1927). It is interesting that although score $z$ scores locate an individual precisely with respect to a population, the relative distance between scores is not affected because standard score (such as a $z$ score) is a linear transformation of the test score. Thus, the intervals defined by the raw test-score are implicitly assumed to define adequately the relative distances between individuals.

These observations on scoring behavior into ability lead to an interesting point. Items are regarded as essentially equivalent in classical test theory, as no weights to reflect differences in item quality enter into raw scores. Thus, each item is assumed to contain equally valid information about ability, so that the tasks defined by the items are essentially substitutable. Furthermore, increases in ability are proportional to increases in accuracy for the task set.

## Summary

.The basic issue for classical test theory is the separation of true score from error score by replicating measurements over some specified conditions. Interestingly, the type of replications varies between theory and practice. Although replication over parallel forms is the major condition for classical test theory, replication over test items has primary importance in test development. Thus, testing practice favors the development of internally consistent tests in which the items are highly intercorrelated.

Test content has been influenced primarily by two criteria. Internal consistency appears to have become the major principle for test development because (a) derivations in test theory (e.g., Gulliksen, 1950) clearly show that item parameters determine internal consistency reliability, and (b) items are treated as if they are equivalent. Matching item difficulty to the target population is also an important principle for determining the tasks that are selected for an intelligence test. The maximum information for estimating an ability is obtained when the probability of passing is .50. Thus, items with moderate difficulties are favored.

Several principles are involved in scoring test behavior in classical test theory. Task accuracy is the aspect of behavior that is scored and tasks are usually combined as unweighted sums over items. Scores are anchored to norms, for interpretation, because raw scores depend on the specific characteristics of the test. However, raw scores are linearly related to normative scores, so that the interval between abilities is proportional to raw score differences.

## Classical Test Theory and Contemporary Research

The basic issue for classical test theory constrasts sharply with the focus of contemporary research on the cognitive components of aptitude. The major focus of classical test theory is the assessment and minimization of measurement error. High correlations between tasks indicate that reliability has been achieved. Test content is selected to assure that high correlations are achieved. In contrast, under the cognitive component approach, tasks are selected (or constructed) to maximize their potential to test psychological theory. Various factors are counterbalanced to allow the most powerful hypothesis-testing procedures to be employed. However, this procedure does not necessarily lead to high correlations among tasks.

Classical test theory is linked to the trait and factor conceptualization of intelligence as across-task consistency, which may be traced to Spearman. In this conceptualization of intelligence, correlations between measurements are attenuated by error, so that error must be minimized. In contrast, cognitive component analysis emphasizes the explanation of relative task difficulty, which could involve several processing abilities. Hence, a task set may not be highly intercorrelated and yet still be considered as indicating intelligence.

In classical test theory, item selection by maximizing internal consistency means that the initial specifications are quite important in determining the content of the test. That is, items that are most highly correlated with others in the set are retained. Unfortunately, as noted elsewhere (Embretson, in press c), specifications for intelligence tests are very imprecise as compared to the mathematical modeler's rigorous specification of theoretical factors to be embedded in the items. Test specifications usually consist of general guides to content and some rules of thumb. It is assumed that aberrant items will be detected by their failure to correlate with others in the set. Thus, specification failure is assumed to be compensated by correlational analysis.

Thus, classical test theory principles make little contact with contemporary research on intelligence tests. The item statistics that influence test content, item difficulty, and correlation with total score do not assess the features that lead to item difficulty or the processes that underlie performance.

A limitation of classical test theory is that the ability estimates are dependent on the items that appear on the test. That is, the score that is obtained (total score or a linear transformation) depends on the difficulty of the items. Scores on one test are not easily translated into scores on another highly similar form, even by using equating methods (such as equipercentile equating).

Similarly, the indices obtained for the items are dependent on the population. An item may appear easy in one population and difficult in another, depending on the ability of the populations. Extreme populations present special difficulties. Since ability is not linearly related to the probability of passing an individual item (i.e, ogives describe this relationship), the intervals between items will vary across populations. For example, differences in accuracy will be negligible for items that are much too easy for a population. However, the intervals will be larger in a less extreme population. This is problematic not only for assessing the relative difficulty of items, but mathematical modeling based on these accuracy levels will not be general.

## Extensions of Classical Test Theory

Classical test theory can be extended to meet some of the limitations noted above. A new method, cognitive contrast analysis (Calfee, 1976; Calfee & Hedges, 1980) has some promise to link classical test theory to mathematical modeling. However, before this development can be considered, it is necessary to examine the meaning of internal consistency in a way that is more related to relative task difficulties.

*Internal Consistency and Mathematical Modeling.* As noted above, a major index of the psychometric quality of a test in classical test theory is internal consistency. Both the Kuder-Richardson (1937) Formula 21 (KR-21) and Cronbach's (1951) $\alpha$, assess the consistency of an item set for measuring an attribute of persons. Mathematical modelers have rarely used internal consistency as an index since they are not particularly interested in measuring attributes.

However, internal consistency has a secondary meaning that has rarely been emphasized by psychometricians. That is, it indicates the uniformity of task relationships over persons. Hoyt's (1941) analysis of variance (ANOVA) approach to internal consistency most clearly shows this relationship.

**Table 4.4. Basic Data Matrix for Hoyt's ANOVA Approach to Internal Consistency**

| Items | Person 1 | 2 | 3 | 4 | 5 | 6 | 7 | 8 | 9 | 10 | $X_i$ |
|---|---|---|---|---|---|---|---|---|---|---|---|
| 1 | 1 | 1 | 1 | 1 | 1 | 1 | 1 | 1 | 1 | 1 | 10 |
| 2 | 0 | 1 | 1 | 1 | 1 | 1 | 1 | 1 | 1 | 1 | 9 |
| 3 | 1 | 1 | 1 | 0 | 1 | 1 | 1 | 1 | 1 | 1 | 9 |
| 4 | 0 | 0 | 1 | 1 | 1 | 1 | 1 | 1 | 1 | 1 | 8 |
| 5 | 0 | 0 | 0 | 1 | 1 | 1 | 1 | 0 | 1 | 1 | 6 |
| 6 | 0 | 1 | 0 | 0 | 0 | 1 | 1 | 0 | 1 | 1 | 5 |
| 7 | 0 | 0 | 0 | 0 | 0 | 1 | 1 | 1 | 1 | 1 | 5 |
| 8 | 0 | 0 | 0 | 1 | 0 | 0 | 0 | 1 | 1 | 1 | 4 |
| 9 | 0 | 0 | 0 | 0 | 0 | 0 | 1 | 1 | 1 | 1 | 4 |
| 10 | 0 | 0 | 0 | 0 | 0 | 0 | 0 | 1 | 1 | 1 | 3 |
| 11 | 0 | 0 | 0 | 0 | 0 | 0 | 0 | 0 | 1 | 1 | 2 |
| 12 | 0 | 0 | 0 | 0 | 0 | 0 | 0 | 0 | 0 | 1 | 1 |
| $X_j$ | 2 | 4 | 4 | 5 | 5 | 7 | 8 | 8 | 11 | 12 | 66 |

| Source | SS | df | MS |
|---|---|---|---|
| Persons | 7.70 | 9 | .856 |
| Items | 9.500 | 11 | .863 |
| $I \times P$ | 12.500 | 99 | .126 |

$$\alpha = \frac{MS_P - MS_{I \times P}}{MS_P} = .852$$

Table 4.4 presents an item by person data matrix. In Hoyt's (1941) development, these data are treated as a Person $\times$ Item factorial ANOVA with one observation per cell. The interaction mean square, $MS_{I \times P}$, indicates the extent to which the person and item marginals fail to reproduce the response patterns. The interaction becomes large when the same relative pattern of item difficulty does not hold for all subjects. Internal consistency is given by the following formula, which refers to the mean squares presented in Table 4.2.

$$\alpha = \frac{MS_P - MS_{I \times P}}{MS_P} \tag{1}$$

Equation 1 shows that Hoyt's internal consistency index decreases when the person $\times$ item interaction mean square is large relative to the person mean square, $MS_P$. This relationship also applies to other internal consistency indices in classical test theory because it can be shown that Hoyt's index is algebraically equivalent to KR-21 and Cronbach's $\alpha$ (Guilford, 1954). Thus, it can be seen that internal consistency, in general, is highest when the same pattern of task difficulties hold over individuals.

Consistent task difficulty patterns over persons is a prerequisite for a general mathematical model of the data. That is, if the task orders are different, then the same model will not fit all persons.

Although Hoyt's development makes classical test theory seemingly more relevant to mathematical modeling, it does not directly address the issue of model generality. Although consistent task performance patterns over persons would be a prerequisite, the generality of mathematical models for the task is not considered in this development.

## Cognitive Contrast Analysis

A new development by Calfee and collaborators (Calfee, 1976; Calfee & Hedges, 1980) has some promise in extending classical test theory to mathematical modeling. Contrast analysis uses the same data design as Hoyt's internal consistency formulation. The major difference is that contrasts replace the one-way ANOVA design for items. The contrasts represent theoretical constructs.

Table 4.5 presents a contrast coding system for the 12 items presented on Table 4.4. In the design matrix, contrasts were formed to represent two ortho-gonal factors and their interaction. The first factor has two levels, while the second factor has three levels, such that one and two contrasts, respectively, are needed to represent the factors. In the series completion task, for example, the first factor hypothetically could represent response format (verification (V) versus completion (C) while the second factor could represent period length (two, three, or four letters). Or, Butterfield's (in press) level of knowledge and number of operations could be represented as design factors. As a set, the contrasts are a mathematical model of task difficulty.

Each contrast can be evaluated for generality across persons by computing a consistency index similar to the Hoyt index. The following formula evaluates the generality of the first factor:

**Table 4.5. Design Matrix for Cognitive Contrast Analysis**

(a)

| Item | Factor 1 C1 | Factor 2 C2 | C3 | Factor 1 × Factor 2 C4 | C5 | Item Type | Period Length |
|---|---|---|---|---|---|---|---|
| 1 | 1 | 2 | 0 | 2 | 0 | V | 2 |
| 2 | 1 | 2 | 0 | 2 | 0 | V | 2 |
| 3 | 1 | −1 | 1 | −1 | 1 | V | 3 |
| 4 | 1 | −1 | 1 | −1 | 1 | V | 3 |
| 5 | 1 | −1 | −1 | −1 | −1 | V | 4 |
| 6 | 1 | −1 | −1 | −1 | −1 | V | 4 |
| 7 | −1 | 2 | 0 | −2 | 0 | V | 2 |
| 8 | −1 | 2 | 0 | −2 | 0 | C | 2 |
| 9 | −1 | −1 | 1 | 1 | −1 | C | 3 |
| 10 | −1 | −1 | 1 | 1 | −1 | C | 3 |
| 11 | −1 | −1 | 1 | 1 | 1 | C | 4 |
| 12 | −1 | −1 | 1 | 1 | 1 | C | 4 |

V = verification
C = completion

(b)

| Source | SS | df | ms |
|---|---|---|---|
| Persons | 7.700 | 9 | .856 |
| Items | 9.500 | 11 | .863 |
|   Factor 1 | | 1 | |
|   Factor 2 | | 2 | |
|   Interaction | | 2 | |
|   Residual | | 6 | |
| I × P | 12.50 | 99 | .126 |
|   Factor 1 | | 9 | |
|   Factor 2 | | 18 | |
|   Residual | | 72 | |

$$\alpha_{FI} = \frac{MS_{FI} - MS_{FI \times P}}{MS_{FI}} \tag{2}$$

The index in Equation 2 shows the relative consistency of the first factor differences over persons. Thus, in the current example, it evaluates the consistency of differences between the completion and verification formats across persons.

### Evaluation

Cognitive contrast analysis, in conjunction with Hoyt's proof of the relationship of ANOVA to internal consistency, makes classical test theory relevant to mathematical modeling. The contrasts can represent mathematical models and the consistency indices assess the generality of the contrast variable across persons. Thus, theory testing about test items is possible in cognitive contrast analysis.

However, further developments are needed to extend cognitive contrast analysis to classical test theory. First, negative indices for $\alpha$ can readily be obtained so that the statistic does not range from 0 to 1. Second, Equation 2 does not link the items to person variance, as in Hoyt's development. If such a development were given by the subtraction of the person by contrast interactions from the person variance, then it could be seen that contrast uniformity across persons would lead to a highly consistent item set. Thus, internal consistency would still be favored as a principle.

Another limitation is the dependence of classical test theory item and person parameters on the specific item set and population, as in classical test theory. Thus, the variance among items and persons will influence the degree of consistency that is obtained. This is an undesirable quality if the research goal is to make a more general statement about a model to explain performance.

# LATENT TRAIT THEORY

## Unidimensional Latent Trait Models

Latent trait models developed in a rather different context than classical test theory. Instead of developing in conjunction with theories of intelligence, like classical test theory, latent trait theory developed in the context of technical problems in test development and mathematical statistics. Two rather separate lines of development must be noted because they employ different latent trait models and conceptualizations of the issues for test theory.

George Rasch, a Danish mathematician, developed what has become known as the Rasch (1960) model among latent trait theorists. Rasch became interested in the problem of objective mental measurement in 1945 when he standardized a group intelligence test for the Danish Department of Defense. This model has had major impact in European psychometrics, but somewhat less impact in the United States. In the United States, Lord and Novick's (1968) book on contemporary test theory marks the beginning of influence for latent trait models. Particularly significant is Birnbaum's (Lord & Novick, 1968) contribution of statistical theory for latent trait models.

Latent trait theory differs substantially from classical test theory in that the developments apply to individual response probabilities rather than variance relationships. Latent trait theory can explain variance relationships, however, so it must be considered as a more basic development.

Several unidimensional latent trait models (ULTM) have been proposed. These models vary in two ways. First, the item response model may be either a logistic ogive or a normal ogive. The former is typically preferred due to the simplicity of the models and estimators. Second, the number of item parameters may vary. A one parameter latent trait model (e.g., the Rasch model) contains only parameters for item difficulty; a two parameter model contains both item difficulty and item discrimination; a three parameter model contains item difficulty, item discrimination and guessing.

## The Rasch Model

For the purpose of exposition, the Rasch model will be used since it is not only the simplest model, but it also achieves the most complete separation of persons and items. The following equation presents the Rasch model:

$$P(X_{ij} = 1) = \frac{e^{(\theta_j - \xi_i)}}{1 + e^{(\theta_j - \xi_i)}} \tag{3}$$

Where
$\theta_j$ = ability for person $j$
$\xi_i$ = difficulty for item $i$
$X_{ij}$ = response of person $j$ to item $i$

Several features of the Rasch model can be readily understood by an inspection of Equation 3. First, it should be noted that $X_{ij}$ is a dichotomous variable for item accuracy. Second, the prediction $X_{ij}$ is given for the individual person $j$ encountering a specified item $i$. Thus, we see the model describes exactly how the individual's ability determines his respone to the item, as noted by Lord (1980) to be a major desideratum for test theory. Third, person ability and task difficulty combine additively in the exponent to determine the response likelihood. Thus, persons and items are scaled in comparable metrics on the same latent continuum. Ability and difficulty combine additively to determine the effective response potential for the encounter. It should be noted that $X_{ij}$ is a dichotomous variable for item accuracy.

## Estimation and the Basic Data Matrix

An intuitive understanding of how the person and item parameters are estimated from test data can be gained by studying the basic data matrix that is presented on Table 4.6. The rows are defined by items and the columns by persons with the same total score. Total score is a sufficient statistic for estimating ability in the Rasch model. It should be noted that persons who fail all the items or pass all the items are omitted from the table. No estimate of ability for these persons can be obtained from the item set.

Each cell of the matrix contains indices based on the probability that a person in score group $j$ will pass item $i$. However, the values shown in the cell are

**Table 4.6. Basic Data Matrix of Item by Score Group Likelihood Ratios**

| Item | *Person–Score Groups* | | | |
|---|---|---|---|---|
| | *1* | *j* | *J* | |
| 1 | $ln \dfrac{P_{11}}{1-P_{11}}$ | $ln \dfrac{P_{1j}}{1-P_{1j}}$ | $ln \dfrac{P_{1J}}{1-P_{1J}}$ | $\xi_1$ |
| 2 | $ln \dfrac{P_{21}}{1-P_{21}}$ | $ln \dfrac{P_{2j}}{1-P_{2j}}$ | $ln \dfrac{P_{2J}}{1-P_{2J}}$ | $\xi_2$ |
| o | o | o | o | o |
| o | o | o | o | o |
| o | o | o | o | o |
| i | $ln \dfrac{P_{i1}}{1-P_{i1}}$ | $ln \dfrac{P_{ij}}{1-P_{ij}}$ | $ln \dfrac{P_{iJ}}{1-P_{iJ}}$ | |
| o | o | o | o | o |
| o | o | o | o | o |
| o | o | o | o | o |
| I | $ln \dfrac{P_{I1}}{1-P_{I1}}$ | $ln \dfrac{P_{Ij}}{1-P_{Ij}}$ | $ln \dfrac{P_{IJ}}{1-P_{IJ}}$ | |
| | $\theta_1$ | $\theta_j$ | $\theta_J$ | |

Rasch Model Prediction:
$$ln \frac{P_{ij}}{1-P_{ij}} = \theta_j - \xi_i$$

the log odds for the score group, $ln(P_{ij}/1-P_{ij})$, rather than the probablility, $P_{ij}$. This transformation is required because the Rasch model ability parameters predict log odds for the cells as the simple difference between ability and item difficulty as follows:

$$ln(P_{ij}/1-P_{ij}) = \theta_j - \xi_i \qquad (4)$$

If the data fit the model, the values reproduced by the Rasch model parameters correspond closely to the actual values in the data matrix.

Rasch (1960) presented least squares estimators for the parameters of his model. Although his least squares estimators do not have the desirable properties of maximum likelihood estimators (Andersen, 1972), such as relationship to a statistical distribution, they do provide an intuitive understanding of the parameters. Furthermore, the least squares estimators are often good approximations of the maximum likelihood estimators. In Rasch (1960), item difficulty is estimated as follows:

$$\hat{\xi}i = -((1/J) \sum_j ln(P_{ij}/1-P_{ij}) - (1/IJ) \sum_i \sum_j ln(P_{ij}/1-P_{ij}) + q)$$  (5)

Thus, the cell log odds are averaged over score groups for an item, corrected for the grand mean log odds. In Equation 5, $q$ is a normalization constant to anchor the item set difficulties to some specified level.

It should be noted that calculating the item parameters by conditioning on score groups eliminates the influence of ability level and variance on the item parameters. That is, the score groups have equal weights in estimating the log odds for the item.

Least squares estimates may be obtained for ability as follows:

$$\hat{\theta}_j = (1/J) \sum_i ln(P_{ij}/1-P_{ij}) - (1/IJ) \sum_i \sum_j ln(P_{ij}/1-P_{ij}) + h$$  (6)

Thus, ability is the mean log odds for a score group across the items, corrected for log odds in the whole set. In Equation 6, $h$ is a scaling constant.

### Specific Objectivity

If the data fit the model, then comparable estimates of item parameters may be obtained from any group, even if their performance levels vary widely. The item parameter, $i$, will have the same location and the same metric measurement. This is not true of the response probabilities from classical test theory, which vary in both location and metric measurement over score groups.

**Table 4.7. Population Ability Effects on Mathematical Model Parameters**

| Item | Group 1 ($\theta_j = 0.00$) | | Group 2 ($\theta_j = 3.50$) | | Item Difficulty |
|------|------------|-----------|------------|-----------|------------|
|      | $P_{ij}$   | $\xi_{i1}$ | $P_{i2}$  | $\xi_{i2}$ | $\xi_{i2}$ |
| 1    | .37        | .50       | .96        | -3.00     | .50        |
| 2    | .73        | -1.00     | .99        | -4.50     | -1.00      |
| 3    | .62        | -.50      | .98        | -4.00     | -.50       |
| 4    | .50        | .00       | .97        | -3.50     | .00        |
| 5    | .27        | 1.00      | .92        | -2.50     | 1.00       |

$\xi_i = -ln \dfrac{P_{ij}}{1-P_{ij}}$

To give an example of specific objectivity, consider the data that is presented in Table 4.7. Item difficulties are presented for five items. Also presented on Table 4.7 are the response probabilities for the five items in two different score groups, assuming that the Rasch model fits the data. Group 1 has average ability with respect to the items ($\theta_j = .00$) while Group 2 has very high ability ($\theta_j = 3.50$). It can be seen on Table 4.7 that the response probabilities are very different within the two groups. The items have different locations, as shown by the mean level of $P_i$ which is high in Group 2 and moderate in Group 1. The items also have different metrics because the intervals between the probabilities are different between Group 1 and Group 2. These response probabilities are equivalent to the item parameters for accuracy in classical test theory.

However, if the log odds transformation of $-ln(P_i/1-P_i)$ is applied, values for $\hat{\xi}_i$ can be obtained. Note that these values differ only in location, which is exactly equal to the ability difference between score groups. The interval between the item parameters are equal between the groups. If the mean item difficulties are anchored to a common value in the groups, such as is typical for applications of the Rasch model, comparable estimates could be expected from the two groups.

## Principles in Latent Trait Theory

*Basic Issues for Test Theory.* The basic issue for latent trait theory in American psychometrics has been the estimation of persons and items on a latent continuum. Lord (1980, p. 11) summarizes the goal of test theory as follows: "In most testing work, our main task is to infer the examinee's ability level or skill. In order to do this, we must know something about how his ability or skill determines his response."

Since accurate estimation of ability (and items) is the goal, the standard error of the parameter estimates is the important source of measurement error. The standard errors are linked to the specific latent trait model and estimation method. In general, the standard error depends on the match between the ability of the population and items in the set. The standard error given above is the reciprocal of the second partial derivative of the likelihood function with respect to $\xi_j$.

Thus, in latent trait theory, the standard error of measurement for an ability is the precision of statistical estimation of the ability level from the item set. Extreme abilities, with respect to the items, receive larger standard errors because relatively less information is available from the items.

The development of better estimators or more efficient algorithms (Andersen, 1972; Bock & Aitken, 1981; Bock & Lieberman, 1970; Gustafsson, 1980b) and the theoretical properties of estimators (Fischer, 1981) has been a major focus in latent trait model research. Another area of research has been to compare estimation error across models (Thissen & Wainer, 1982) and sample sizes (Lord, 1979). The "robustness" of the various models with respect to violations of assumptions has also been examined in several studies (Hambleton & Traub, 1973; Reckase, 1979; Wainer & Wright, 1980). This research is highly related to the debate about the number of item parameters to be estimated in the model since it concerns the contribution of the item discrimination and guessing parameters.

A rather heated debate has emerged in American psychometrics over the number of item parameters that should be estimated. Lord (1980), who prefers the three parameter logistic model, has been highly influential in testing practice due to both his role in developing latent trait theory and his affiliation with the Educational Testing Service. Wright (1968), in contrast, prefers the Rasch model and has influenced educational testing as well since he made a program for the Rasch model widely available in the United States (Wright & Panchapakasen, 1969). Estimation research, such as mentioned above, has seemingly limited relevance to substantive research on intelligence. Although inaccurate estimates of an aptitude can attenuate correlations of the measure with other variables, estimation research ignores substantive issues about what is measured.

In contrast, Rasch (1960) emphasized the achievement of specific objectivity as the goal for measurement. That is, comparisons of persons on the latent continuum must be free of the specific items given to the persons, and comparisons between items must be free of the specific population used to calibrate the items. In European psychometrics, specific objectivity is regarded so highly that it is often described as an *epistemological principle* (Fischer, 1978). Specific objectivity can be understood only after a description of latent trait models and the estimation of their parameters.

Hypothesis-testing has also been emphasized in European psychometrics especially in conjunction with the Rasch model. The assessment of model fit has received increasing attention (Andersen, 1973; Gustafsson, 1980a; Waller, 1981; Wollenberg, 1982; Yen, 1981). Model fit is relevant to estimation because, technically, the estimates are not meaningful if the latent trait model does not fit the data. However, model fit is also relevant to intelligence if the specific test of fit reflects substantive issues. For example, model generality (over groups) can be examined by Andersen's (1973) likelihood ratio goodness of fit test for the Rasch model.

Andersen's test of fit for the Rasch model compares item parameter estimates from different score groups. If the model fits the data, according to the property of population-free estimates, then comparable estimates should be achieved. Andersen's likelihood ratio test can be used to evaluate goodness of fit, using conditional maximum likelihood estimators. First, the item parameters are estimated in the whole group. The likelihood of the data, given the model, is obtained. Then, the item parameters are separately estimated in two or more score groups. The likelihoods for the data, given the model, are obtained and summed across groups. Andersen (1973) shows that -2 times the log likelihood difference between the whole group and separate groups is asymptotically distributed as chi square. If chi square is not significant, then the model fits at the individual level, since increased fit is not achieved by separating individuals into groups.

The far right column of Table 4.8 gives an example of Andersen's (1973) test of fit on Butterfield's (in press) series completion data. The sample was divided into two groups, high and low ability. Likelihoods from the high and low ability groups are presented and summed. Also, the likelihood from the total

Table 4.8. Fit of Models to Individual Data

| | Model Item Parameters | | Log Likelihood | |
|---|---|---|---|---|
| | $\eta_i$ | $SE\eta_i$ | Complexity Factor | Rasch |
| *Low Ability (N = 43)* | | | | |
| Kn | .30** | .04 | −540.19 ⎤ | −494.56 ⎤ |
| Op | .23* | .09 | | |
| | | | −1726.67 | −1530.37 |
| *High Ability (N = 69)* | | | | |
| Kn | .37** | .02 | −1186.48 ⎦ | −1035.81 ⎦ |
| Op | .23** | .01 | | |
| *Total (N = 112)* | | | | |
| Kn | .31** | .02 | −1732.44 | −1536.22 |
| Op | .25** | .01 | − | |
| *Difference* | | | −5.77 | −5.95 |
| $\chi^2$ | | | 11.70 | 11.54 |

* $p < .05$
** $p < .01$

sample is presented. Chi square is −2 times the difference between the likelihoods. With 39 degrees of freedom, the difference in number of parameters estimated from separated versus total group, the chi square of 11.54 is not significant. Thus, the test indicates that the series completion data fit the Rasch model.

*Test Content.* Thus far, unidimensional latent trait models have yielded little basic change in test content over classical test theory. Latent trait models are often applied to existing tests to provide efficient scoring and equating. Such applications have no influence on test content.

However, it is expected that some major aptitude tests will employ latent trait models in the near future (e.g., the Armed Forces Vocational Aptitude Battery and the Scholastic Aptitude Test). Computerized adaptive testing fully utilizes the test equating potential of latent trait models. In computerized adaptive testing, items are banked by their parameters, such as difficulty, discrimination, and guessing. Items are then selected for an individual to provide the most information about his or her ability. In general, items which have a probability of .50 of being passed are optimal.

Computerized adaptive testing has potential to change test content. Ideally, items are selected for inclusion in the item bank according to their goodness of fit to a latent trait model. Then, items that provide the most information about ability are selected for an individual that is tested. Thus, using latent trait models for computerized adaptive testing influences item content by (a) providing a goodness of fit criterion for inclusion in the item bank and (b) differentially selecting items to efficiently measure ability in the target population.

The goodness of fit for items depends on how well the data meet the assumptions of the latent trait model. The latent trait models that have been applied thus far have two general assumptions, unidimensionality and local independence. Unidimensionality means that a single ability accounts for individual differences in item solving. Data that would yield two or more factors in a factor analysis on the items would violate unidimensionality. Local independence, on the other hand, means that no relationship exists among the items after accounting for parameters of the latent trait model. Contingencies in solving items, practice effects, set effects and so on, would yield data that violate local independence. In combination, these two general criteria for fit favor item sets that measure a single factor and have no interactive effects among the items.

Further constraint on goodness of fit depend on the specific latent trait model. The two or three parameter latent trait models allow items to vary in discriminations. This is roughly analogous to items that have unequal loadings on the single common factor in the data. The Rasch model, however, provides a more stringent criterion for fit, since items are assumed to have equal discriminations. This is comparable to an item set in which factor loadings are equal. Thus, fitting the Rasch model will yield a more narrow set of items than two or three parameter latent trait models.

Like classical test theory, fitting latent trait models tends to select internally consistent item sets. However, since latent trait models make stronger assumptions about the data (unidimensionality, local independence, and sometimes, item equivalence), selecting items to fit the model narrows the content of the items as compared to classical test theory.

Selecting items from the bank for individualized tests influences primarily the difficulty level of the items. Efficient measurement criteria adaptive testing generally selects items that an individual has a probability of .50 to solve. If ability in the target population is normally distributed, then items that are moderately difficult will be selected most often. For two or three parameter models, however, items with high discriminations are also favored because they provide more information about ability. Thus, although items in the bank will have unequal difficulties, the items that are selected for the individualized tests will have high relationships to total score.

## Scoring Behavior

Unlike classical test theory, ability scores in latent trait models are not linearly related to total score. Scoring behavior into ability requires that item parameters (e.g., item difficulty) have been calibrated for the test. Then, ability for an individual typically is estimated to maximize the likelihood of his observed responses to the test items, given their parameters.

For the Rasch model, ability scores are monotonically related to total score, regardless of the specific items that are passed on the test. Total score is a sufficient statistic for ability in the Rasch model because the items are assumed to vary only in difficulty. For two and three parameter latent trait models, however, items also vary in discrimination, so that total score is not a sufficient statistic. Thus, item responses are differentially weighted in determining the abilities, so that the value of the "composite" score depends on saturation with the major factor.

When calibrated by latent trait models, ability does not depend on the difficulty of the specific items that appear on the test. Items are calibrated in advance, so that their difficulty is anchored to a (possibly) larger set. The individual's ability is the log odds in the larger set.

The latent trait method of scoring behavior into ability has at least two advantages. First, comparable ability estimates may be obtained from any subset of items. Unlike classical test theory, comparable estimates can be obtained from tests that differed in average item difficulty or the spread of item difficulties. Second, latent trait abilities have potential for domain-referenced interpretations. In classical test theory, scores are norm-referenced because raw scores are meaningless with respect to an item domain, due to differences in means and standard deviations. For latent trait models, the abilities have precise meaning about the person's skill in solving items in some set. If the set has been well specified, the scores may be interpreted with respect to an item domain. Ability is the log odds of solving items in a specified domain. This feature leads to an interesting potential for latent trait abilities, although item specification for aptitude tests typically do not specify the item domain sufficiently to allow domain-referenced interpretations (see Whitely & Davis, 1974).

## Summary and Evaluation

The basic issue for measurement in latent trait model is different than for classical test theory. The issue is estimation accuracy rather than separating true score from error. Accurate estimation of ability results from choosing the optimal items for a person.

Thus far, the major effect of latent trait theory has been on scoring behavior rather than determining test content. Latent trait models are often applied to existing tests that have been developed according to classical test theory principles. In the future, however, tests will probably be built specifically to fit a latent trait model when computerized adaptive testing is implemented. Fitting latent trait models or efficiently estimating ability leads to narrowing test content as compared to classical test theory. That is, both internal consistency and medium task difficulty have more stringent meanings in latent trait models.

Thus, it can be concluded that ULTMs narrow the construct of intelligence as compared to classical test theory. Intelligence will still be scored as a composite over tasks, but either the task content will be selected more narrowly (as for the Rasch model) or items will be differentially weighted according to saturation with the common factor (as for two or three parameter models).

Narrowing the construct of intelligence is at odds with the contemporary trend in theoretical research on intelligence. The cognitive component approach, for example, has emphasized multiple components, knowledge stores, and strategies that are involved in performance. These approaches would suggest that performance on tests involves multiple abilities and the development of strategy algorithms for solving items with test experience. These conditions violate both the unidimensionality and local independence assumptions of ULTM.

The modeling of item responses by latent trait models creates potential for significant change, however. Ability can possibly have a domain-referenced interpretation if sufficiently precise item specifications are developed. Perhaps most importantly, the focus on item response models creates the possibility of more complex models that are linked to cognitive theory. The next section examines some extensions of latent trait models that have this property.

## Extensions of Latent Trait Models

Three extensions of latent trait models have been proposed to link latent trait models to more modern issues about intelligence. Specifically, these models have parameters that reflect theoretical variables, such as information complexity or processing difficulty. The models are (a) the linear logistic latent trait model (Fischer, 1973), and (b) the multicomponent latent trait model (Whitely, 1980), and (c) the general component latent trait model (Embretson, in press a), which is a generalization that includes the other two models as special cases. The linear logistic model (LLTM) will be presented first because it is the most appropriate model for Butterfield's (in press) theory of the series completion task, as described above. The LLTM requires stimulus complexity data for the items to represent theoretical variables. In contrast, the multicomponent latent trait model (MLTM) requires process outcome data, as could be obtained from item subtasks. The general component latent trait model (GLTM) requires both subtask and stimulus complexity data. GLTM is beyond the scope of this chapter, but a more detailed presentation is available elsewhere (Embretson, in press a).

Multidimensional latent trait models (e.g., Samejima, 1974) are other extensions that may have potential to link test theory to substantive issues about intelligence because they contain multiple items or ability parameters. However, these models have not yet been sufficiently developed to be directly relevant to current theoretical issues.

## Linear Logistic Latent Trait Model

### The Model

LLTM contains both a mathematical model that relates item difficulty to the information complexity of the item stimuli and a psychometric model that relates item difficulty and ability to responses. The following equation presents the mathematical model for LLTM:

$$\xi_i = \sum_m \eta_m q_{im} + d \tag{8}$$

Where

$\xi_i$ = difficulty of item $i$

$q_{im}$ = the complexity of factor $m$ in item $i$

$\eta_m$ = the impact of complexity factor $m$ on item difficulty

$d$ = a normalization constant

On the series completion task, Butterfield's two complexity factors, $Kn$ and $Op$, would lead to the following mathematical model of item difficulty:

$$\xi_i' = \eta_1 Kn + \eta_2 Op + d \tag{9}$$

However, the item difficulty that is predicted is not accuracy level, as in Butterfield's study. The dependent variable in LLTM is the log odds for the item, as scaled in the Rasch model.

LLTM combines the mathematical model with the Rasch model, as follows, to give a psychometric model of the response potential of person $j$ on item $i$:

$$P(X_{ij} = 1) = \frac{e^s}{1 + e^s} \tag{10}$$

Where $s = \theta_j - \sum_m q_{im}\eta_m + d$

Compared to the Rasch model in Equation 3, it can be seen that item difficulty is replaced by the mathematical model that is given in Equation 8. Table 4.8 also shows the parameter estimates that were obtained for Butterfield's series completion data. Similar to the regression model used by Butterfield (in press), it can be seen that both factors are highly significant on the total data. However, unlike Butterfield's method of treating these data, Equation 10 makes predictions about the response potential of a specified person.

*An Application.* A major issue for research that applies LLTM is to evaluate the quality of the mathematical model. Several studies have applied LLTM to test hypotheses about the influence of information structure on item difficulty (see Fischer, 1978). However, few studies are available in English (Whitely & Schneider, 1981, is an exception). LLTM has been influential in European psychometrics, but until recently was virtually unknown in American psychometrics.

Butterfield's (in press) research on the series completion task provides an illustration of hypothesis testing with LLTM. Three general types of hypotheses are important in the context of LLTM. First, the fit of LLTM as a psychometric model may be evaluated. Second, the overall quality of the LLTM mathematical model may be evaluated. Third, under certain conditions, alternative mathematical' models may be compared. All three concerns will be illustrated by applying LLTM to Butterfield's data.

LLTM may be evaluated as a psychometric model by extending Andersen's (1973) test of fit for the Rasch model, as described above, to LLTM. Table 4.8 also shows the likelihoods obtained for the high ability, low ability and total groups for LLTM on the series-completion task, with Butterfield's (in press) two-factor model as the mathematical model. Table 4.8 shows that the likelihoods for the LLTM models are always smaller than for the Rasch (1960) model. Compared to the Rasch model, LLTM is a restricted model of item difficulty because it contains fewer parameters. Each item gets a separate parameter in the Rasch model, while item difficulty is predicted in LLTM from only a few parameters.

Comparison of the summed separate group likelihood to the total group likelihood by the Andersen (1973) test yields a significant difference ($\chi^2_3 = 11.70$, $p < .01$). Thus LLTM varies somewhat between high and low ability subjects. It should be recalled that the ability groups were not significantly different with the Rasch model comparison. Thus, it must be concluded that the Butterfield (in press) two-factor model falls short as a psychometric model.

Evaluating the overall quality of a model for the series completion task requires several alternative indices. Embretson (1983a) notes that two different types of significance tests are generally needed to evaluate a mathematical model in LLTM: (a) comparison to a null model to determine if significant predictions are made, and (b) comparison to a saturated model to determine if significant information remains to be modeled. Embretson (1983a) has elaborated both an appropriate null and saturated model for LLTM mathematical models.

The null model specifies that all item differences are due to random error. Thus, no significant information can be modeled by any LLTM mathematical model. Such a null model would specify that the true item difficulties are all equal, as follows:

$$\xi_i = d \qquad\qquad\qquad (11)$$

The significance test for the model is made by comparing the goodness of fit for the restricted model to the goodness of fit for the null model, as follows:

$$\chi^2 = \chi^2_{restricted} - \chi^2_{null} \qquad\qquad\qquad (12)$$

The null model comparison test was applied to the Butterfield (in press) two factor model on the same data as on Table 4.8. Table 4.9 shows that the mathematical model is highly significant compared to the null model. The null model comparison test is similar to testing the significance of the squared multiple correlation in the Butterfield study. The null model comparison test on Table 4.9 has two degrees of freedom which is computed from the difference in number of parameters estimated in the two models.

**Table 4.9. Butterfield's (in press) Model of Series Completion Difficulty**

| | $\eta_i$ | $SE\eta_i$ | Fit $[\chi^2/df]$ Rasch | Fit $[\chi^2/df]$ Null | $\Delta$ | $R^2$ |
|---|---|---|---|---|---|---|
| Kn | .31*** | .02 | | | | |
| | | | 11.24*** | 223.47*** | .53 | .52 |
| Op | .22*** | .01 | (df = 36) | (df = 2) | | |

$\xi_i = \eta_1 Kn + \eta_2 Op + a$

$$\Delta = \text{Incremental Fix Index} = \frac{L_{null\ model} - L_{restricted\ model}}{L_{null\ model} - L_{Rasch\ model}}$$

*** $p < .01$

The second statistical test needed to evaluate overall quality of the restricted model is to compare the mathematical model with a saturated model that accurately reproduces the data. The Rasch (1960) model is a saturated model of item difficulty because it contains one parameter for every item. Thus, to determine if no significant loss of information is obtained by using the restricted model the following test can be given:

$$\chi^2 = \chi^2_{restricted} - \chi^2_{Rasch} \tag{13}$$

Table 4.9 shows that this value is also significant for the series completion data, so that the model does not yield full prediction of item difficulty.

Likelihood ratio tests need to be supplemented to evaluate a given model. The goodness of fit test is highly sensitive to sample size so that a study with a large sample is quite likely to find significant departures of fit from the saturated model. Embretson (1983a) proposed an incremental fit index needed to locate a target model on the continuum of the null model to the saturated model. This principle can be applied to testing fit for LLTM by the following index of fit, based on the model likelihoods:

$$\Delta = \frac{L_{\text{null}} - L_{\text{math}}}{L_{\text{null}} - L_{\text{Rasch}}} \tag{14}$$

This index ranges from 0 to 1. Loosely speaking, it represents the proportion of available information that is accounted for by the mathematical model of task difficulty. Table 4.9 shows that moderate level of fit was achieved by the target model since $\Delta$ is only .53.

Comparing theoretical models is also important in LLTM. Butterfield (in press) compared his model to several other models on the 15 series completions from the Primary Mental Abilities Test. The goodness of fit tests available in LLTM make possible direct comparisons of theoretical models if they are hierarchially nested; that is, the larger models contain all the parameters of the more restricted model. The difference between log likelihoods for the models, multiplied by –2, is distributed as *chi* square, with degrees of freedom equal to the number of additional parameters contained by the larger model. Unfortunately, the series completion models are not hierarchially nested (i.e., one model is a subset of another), so that the direct statistical comparison is not appropriate. However, the significance of prediction, loss of information and incremental fit may still be evaluated separately for each model and then compared informally.

Table 4.10 shows the incremental fit index for each model as well as the comparison to the null model and the saturated Rasch (1960) model. It can be seen that, although all models provide significant prediction and have significant loss of information, the incremental fit for the Butterfield (in press) models is clearly better. Interestingly, the incremental fit values are quite close to the squared multiple correlation of the predicted values from the model with the Rasch item difficulties.

## Test Theory Principles in LLTM

*Basic Issues.* Significant differences in measurement can result with LLTM as compared to ULTM. First, unlike ULTM, the basic issue for LLTM has been hypothesis-testing rather than estimation accuracy. Although hypothesis-testing is an issue for ULTM, only the goodness of fit as a psychometric model is evaluated. Thus, the meaning of these tests for theories of intelligence is quite limited because they indicate only if the measure is unidimensional.

In contrast, LLTM can be linked directly to theories about the processes that underlie task performance because the mathematical model in LLTM is specified by a theory. As noted elsewhere (Embretson, 1983b), hypothesis testing about item components leads to a new type of construct validation research, assessing construct representation. That is, the processing components, strategies, and knowledge stores that underlie item responses can be assessed.

Estimation, however, is not entirely a forgotten issue for LLTM. Statistically optimal estimators of the item parameters are available, since Fischer (1973)

**Table 4.10. Fit of Mathematical Models of Thurstone's PMA Series Completion Tasks**

| Model | Null Model | | Saturated Model | | Fit Index | |
|---|---|---|---|---|---|---|
| | df | $\chi^2/df$ | df | $\chi^2/df$ | $\Delta$ | $r^2$ |
| Butterfield—2 | 2 | 239.13** | 12 | 5.22** | .88 | .92 |
| Simon & Kotovsky | 1 | 160.36** | 13 | 29.27** | .30 | .34 |
| Butterfield—1 | 1 | 431.84** | 13 | 8.39** | .80 | .84 |
| Klahr & Wallace | 1 | 33.42** | 13 | 39.04** | .06 | .10 |

** $p < .01$

derives conditional maximum likelihood estimators for LLTM. Numerically, however, the available methods, such as Fischer and Formann's (1972) program and LINLOG (Whitely & Nieh, 1981), are slow and can handle only a few items. Thus, developments in estimation are needed to make LLTM available for routine application.

*Test Content.* As yet, test content has not been influenced by LLTM. LLTM has not yet been applied to develop a major test. However, the model has real potential to influence test design. Since LLTM can assess the influence of specified stimulus factors on item difficulty, it is possible to design test items with known sources of difficulty by controlling the stimulus factors. Currently, research is in progress (Embretson & Wetzel, 1984) to explore the potential of LLTM for the design of the Armed Services Vocational Aptitude Battery and the Scholastic Aptitude Test items.

*Scoring Behavior.* LLTM leads to relatively minimal changes in scoring behavior. In ULTM, only one ability is postulated to underlie responses. Like the Rasch (1960) model, ability is estimated after the item parameters are calibrated. If the mathematical model completely describes item difficulty, then the LLTM ability will be the same as the Rasch ability because the item parameters will be the same. If the model does not fit well, then inaccuracy in reproducing item difficulty will lead to poor estimates of ability. Thus, no new aspects of individual differences are measured with LLTM.

## Multicomponent Latent Trait Model

### The Model

The multicomponent latent trait model (MLTM) is a family of models that relate component process outcomes to the total task. In contrast to LLTM, MLTM requires subtask data to estimate the component parameters. It contains parameters for both items and persons on underlying processing components and hence MLTM is a multidimensional model.

Similar to LLTM, it is convenient to separate the mathematical model of MLTM from the psychometric model. The least complex mathematical model in the MLTM family of models gives the item probability as the product of the probabilities for solving each component subtask, as follows:

$$P(X_{ijT}) = \prod_{k} P(X_{ijk}) \tag{15}$$

Where

$P(X_{ijT})$ = probability that the total item $i$ is solved by person $j$

$P(X_{ijk})$ = probability that component $k$ on item $i$ is solved by person $j$

It is assumed that the component outcomes are measured by responses to subtasks for each item.

To give an example, solving a series completion item may require two separate component outcomes: (a) correctly representing the relationships in the series (e.g., number of moving strings, types of relationships), and (b) generating one or more letters to complete the series, according to the relationships. The first component, $X_{ij1}$, could be assessed by a subtask that asked a person to represent the relationships diagrammatically, such as indicated in the following example, using Butterfield's (in press) notation for relationship type:

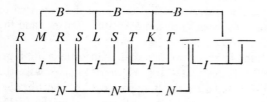

Where

$B$ = back down the alphabet

$N$ = next up the alphabet

$I$ = identity

Then, the second component, $X_{ij2}$, could be assessed independently from the first component by presenting the correct structure and asking the person to generate letters to complete the series. The following equation shows the corresponding mathematical model for MLTM:

$$P(X_{ijT}) = P(X_{ij1})P(X_{ij2})$$

It should be noted in this example that problems are not necessarily equally difficult on the components. Some problems may be difficult to represent while other problems may be more difficult to generate the responses. Furthermore, a person may have different abilities to perform the two components. Thus, the relative difficulty of the components depends on the person.

Assuming that the components represent the task completely, the full task will be solved only if both components are correct. As shown in Equation 15, the mathematical model expresses the probability of solving the full task as the joint probability of solving the components.

The multicomponent latent trait model is given by the following equation:

$$P(X_{ijT} = 1) = \prod_{k} \frac{e^{(\theta_{jk} - \xi_{ik})}}{1 + e^{(\theta_{jk} - \xi_{ik})}} \tag{16}$$

Where

$\theta_{ik}$ = the difficulty of item $i$ on component $k$

$\xi_{jk}$ = the ability of person $j$ on component $k$

MLTM combines the mathematical model of the component probabilities, as given in Equation 15, with a psychometric model. The psychometric model for MLTM is the Rasch (1960) model, as for LLTM. However, in MLTM, the Rasch model is given for each component. Thus, persons can vary in component abilities and items can vary in component difficulty.

Table 4.11. Component Item Difficulties and Person Abilities for a Hypothetical Data Set

| | Component | | | |
|---|---|---|---|---|
| | 1 | 2 | 3 | 4 |
| Item | | | | |
| 1 | −3 | −1 | −3 | −1 |
| 2 | −1 | −3 | −1 | −3 |
| 3 | 0 | −2 | 0 | −2 |
| 4 | −3 | −1 | 0 | 0 |
| 5 | 0 | −2 | −6 | 0 |
| 6 | −6 | −2 | 0 | 0 |
| Person | | | | |
| 1 | 1 | 1 | 1 | 1 |
| 2 | 2 | 2 | −1 | 1 |
| 3 | −2 | 2 | 3 | 1 |
| 4 | 3 | 2 | −2 | 1 |
| 5 | 0 | 0 | 0 | 0 |

To illustrate the model, Table 4.11 presents some hypothetical abilities and difficulties for four components. As for any latent trait model, MLTM expresses the probability that a particular person will solve a specified item. However, MLTM also provides detailed predictions for each component on the items. For example, the probability that Person 3 will solve Component 2 on Item 2 is given as follows:

$$P(X_{232}) = \frac{e^{2-(-3)}}{1 + e^{2-(-3)}}$$

$$= .99.$$

Similarly, predictions could be given for the other components on Item 2 for Person 3, which are .27, .98 and .98 for Components 1, 3 and 4, respectively. These predictions are combined as the simple product, according to Equation 15 to give the probability for solving the full task, as follows:

$$P(X_{23T}) = (.27)(.99)(.98)(.98)$$

$$= .26.$$

Two important features of MLTM can be observed from these calculations. First, person ability and item difficulty within each component are measured on the same scale. They combine additively in the exponent to determine the response potential. Ability and item difficulty have a compensatory relationship

Table 4.12. Item Correlations in Two Slightly Different Sets

| Item | 1 | 2 | 3 | 4 | 6 |
|---|---|---|---|---|---|
| | | | Set I | | |
| 1 | 1.00 | | | | |
| 2 | .45 | 1.00 | | | |
| 3 | .59 | .97 | 1.00 | | |
| 4 | .34 | .32 | .44 | 1.00 | |
| 6 | .20 | .15 | .26 | .98 | 1.00 |
| | | | Set II | | |
| 1 | 1.00 | | | | |
| 2 | .45 | 1.00 | | | |
| 3 | .59 | .97 | 1.00 | | |
| 5 | .56 | .19 | .24 | 1.00 | |
| 6 | .20 | .15 | .26 | −.66 | 1.00 |

because a high response potential can be observed for a difficult task if a person has sufficient ability to compensate for the task difficulty level.

Second, the relationship between components is noncompensatory. If a person has a low probability of solving one component, then he has a low probability for solving the task because all information is required for solution. In the example above, the task probability is low ($P = .26$) because Person 3 has a low probability of solving Component 1 ($P = .27$) on Item 2. Although the probabilities of solving the other components are high, they do not compensate for the information that is required from Component 1.

### An Application

Likelihood ratio, goodness of fit tests can evaluate alternative mathematical models for the data, as for LLTM. The mathematical models vary in the number of components or strategies that are applied to task solution. Embretson (in press b) examined two strategies for solving verbal analogy items with MLTM. Hypothesis testing about strategy contributions to performance is possible if additional subtasks are generated to provide indices for each strategy.

Table 4.13 shows the subtasks used by Embretson (in press b) to separate a rule strategy from an association strategy in solving verbal analogies. The rule strategy consisted of the rule construction subtask and the response evaluation subtask, C1 and C2, respectively. In these subtasks, the subject first generates a rule that the answer must fulfill and then chooses an alternative to fit the *correct* rule (see example on Table 4.13) that was presented with the item. The association strategy consisted of a single subtask in which the subject selected the alternative that was most highly associated with the unmatched term in the stem. By using a more complex mathematical model for MLTM, it was possible to separate the probability of correctly executing a strategy from the probability of applying the strategy. The latter variable represents metacomponents in processing theory.

#### Table 4.13. Subtask Set

| | |
|---|---|
| Association Subtask | Dog<br>a) Lion  b) Wolf  c) Bark  d) Puppy  e) Horse |
| Total Item | Cat : Tiger : : Dog : ____<br>a) Lion  b) Wolf  c) Bark  d) Puppy  e) Horse |
| Rule (Image)<br>  Construction | Cat : Tiger : : Dog : ____<br>Rule __?__ |
| Response Evaluation | Cat : Tiger : : Dog : ____<br>a) Lion  b) Wolf  c) Bark  d) Puppy  e) Horse<br>Rule: A large or wild canine |

MLTM predicts the joint response patterns to the subtasks and full task for each item. The probability of each possible response pattern is obtained by MLTM. The likelihood of the observed data can be expressed by multiplying the probability of the observed responses across subjects and items.

In Embretson's (in press b) study on analogical reasoning, it is assumed that the association strategy is attempted only if the rule strategy fails. A two-strategy mathematical model for MLTM is given as follows:

$$P(X_T = 1) = a_k P_k + c P_A (1 - {}_k P_k) + g(1 - P_A)(1 - {}_k P_k) \qquad (17)$$

Where

$P_k = P(X_{ijk})$ as in Equation 16 for MLTM

$\overset{\bullet}{P}_A = P(X_{ijA})$, the probability that person $j$ solves the association subtask on item $i$

$a$ = conditional probability of applying the rule strategy

$c$ = conditional probability of applying the association strategy

$g$ = the probability of successful guessing when no other strategy is available

For a given individual, the likelihood of his responses are multiplied to give the likelihood of his data, and then these likelihoods can be multiplied over the full sample. Alternative models can be compared by likelihood of the data, as in LLTM comparisons that were presented above.

In the analogy data, the influence of association as an alternative strategy was determined by the incremental fit of the data when it is added to the rule strategy in MLTM. The appropriate comparison model would not allow the association strategy to contribute to the toal item (i.e., $c = 0$ in Equation 17). Embretson (in press b) presents several tests of hypothesis about alternative strategies for solving analogies.

## Test Theory Principles in MLTM

*Basic Issues.* Like LLTM, hypothesis testing has been a major focus in research that uses MLTM. In MLTM research, constructs are identified by their contributions in a mathematical model of the task. As summarized elsewhere (Embretson, 1983b), a basic concern for construct validation research is to identify the constructs that are involved in responding to the test items.

Test design is also an important issue in research with MLTM. It is possible to control the abilities that are measured by an item type by selecting test content according to the MLTM item parameters. The implications for test design will be more fully elaborated below.

*Test Content.* Like LLTM, MLTM influences test content. However, MLTM permits greater flexibility in test design than LLTM because internal consistency is no longer a guiding principle for model fit. MLTM is a multidimensional model that postulates that performance depends on correctly executing parameters of MLTM and can be used to assess and control the abilities that are important in individual differences in item solving.

The relative component difficulties is directly related to the abilities that are reflected in item solving. The regression of item response probabilities on one component ability, depends on the response potential on the other components. For example, solving a two component item may be either strongly or weakly related to one component, depending on the relative difficulty of the other component for the target persons. If the response potential of the second component is high, so that the component in the item is relatively easy for a target person's ability level, then the probability of solving the whole item strongly depends on individual differences in the first component ability. In contrast if the response potential on the second component is low, then the item responses are not as strongly related to the first component. In this case, the item does not measure the first component very well since increases in ability are not strongly related to item solving. Whitely (1981) presents ogives to show how component difficulties influence the regression of item probabilities on ability.

An intuitive understanding of how component difficulties influence what component is measured may be gained by comparing Item 5 with Item 6 on Table 4.11. These items have different patterns of component difficulties. Item 5 is easy on Component 2 and Component 3, while Item 6 is easy on Component 1 and Component 2. The easy components have little impact on task probabilities because even a person of low ability will have a high probability of solving the component. For example, Person 4 has low ability on Component 3. However, his probability of solving the Component 3 on Item 5 is quite high, as shown below:

$$P(X_{543}) = \frac{e^{-2-(-6)}}{1 + e^{-2-(-6)}}$$

$$= .98.$$

Individual differences on Component 3 have little impact on the probability of solving Item 5 because the probability is near 1.00 even for a low ability person. Thus, individual differences in solving Item 5 will be due to their abilities on the more difficult components. In contrast, Item 6 will depend on Component 3 abilities, since it has a medium difficulty on the component. Thus, solving Item 6 depends on different abilities than solving Item 5.

If an item type is truly multicomponent, the MLTM relationships of components to the full task are interesting in at least two ways. First, as indicated above, test design becomes feasible for aptitude tests because items may be explicitly selected to measure specified abilities by controlling component difficulties. Whitely (1981) shows how items can be selected to measure predominantly one or the other component by considering their location on a scattergram of item difficulties.

Relative component difficulties are sometimes used informally in test development to control what is measured. For example, the verbal analogies on the Scholastic Aptitude Test measure mostly the encoding component, since they are difficult on vocabulary, but they are easy on the relational inference components. In contrast, analogies on the Cognitive Abilities Test measure mostly relational inference ability, as the encoding component is relatively easy for the target populations. MLTM permits these factors to be formalized for use in item selection by providing quantitative indices of relative component difficulties.

Second, the influence of other test theory methods (i.e., methods that favor internal consistency) on test content may be understood by MLTM relationships between components and total item probability. To provide a small illustration, total response probabilities for the six items on Table 4.11 were generated using MLTM for the five persons. These response probabilities were then correlated between the items. The resulting correlations are higher than the test data because item probabilities, rather than dichotomous accuracy responses, were used.

The quality of Item 6 was examined in two slightly different sets of items. The sets consist of five items each, with only one item differing between the sets. In the first set, Item 6 appears to be a moderately good item. Although it has only small correlations with Item 1, Item 2 and Item 3, it correlates highly with Item 4. In the second set, Item 6 appears to be a poor item. It has the same low correlations with Item 1, Item 2 and Item 3, but it has a negative correlation with Item 5. Item 6 would probably be eliminated from this set.

Table 4.11 shows that although Item 6 has an extreme pattern of component difficulty, Item 4 has this same extreme pattern. Varying the inclusion of Item 4 in the item analysis set creates some apprently different diagnostics on Item 6.

The effects of context differences on the large item sets that are typical in test development will not depend on the effects of a single item. However, the general context effect will probably be at least as pronounced if the set contains clusters of items with different patterns of component difficulties. The relative representation of the cluster in the whole set will determine the apparent quality of any given item.

*Scoring Behavior.* Scoring behavior into ability is different on MLTM from the other latent trait models that were examined. If the subtasks are administered, it is possible to measure a person's ability on each component on the item. Within components, however, MLTM scores behavior in the same manner as the Rasch (1960) model, using total score on the subtask as a sufficient statistic for component ability. Thus, component abilities have the same properties and advantages of the Rasch model, as elaborated above.

## CONCLUSION

This chapter has traced the influence of psychometric methods on the intelligence construct. It was shown that psychometric methods determine (a) the basic goal for test development, (b) which tasks are selected for intelligence tests, and (c) which aspects of task behavior are scored as indicators of intelligence. Since intelligence theory has changed in the past decade, this chapter examined the principles of classical test theory, latent-trait theory and some proposed extensions with respect to contemporary paradigms for intelligence research.

A major concern of contemporary research on intelligence has been to identify the cognitive components that underlie item solving. The basic issue for such research is to test hypotheses about processing from mathematical models of task response, time and accuracy. The tasks that are selected for study typically are determined by the demands of theory-testing. Thus, item content is specified by a structure that is counterbalanced for the various facets of the theories that are to be tested. Since the intercorrelations of items are used to select the task to be studied, the item set most likely is not unidimensional with respect to ability.

The aspects of behavior that indicate intelligence are unclear in contemporary intelligence research. Response time is a somewhat more popular, basic-task measure than accuracy. However, response time is most meaningful on correctly completed tasks, so that easy items are selected for study. Individual scores are sometimes derived as the parameters in an individual mathematical model. However, these parameters do not have desirable psychometric properties.

The principles of classical test theory shape the construct of intelligence quite differently from contemporary research. The basic issue for classical test theory is the separation of true score from error by replication over some conditions. Test content has been influenced by two major principles (a) maximizing internal consistency from item/total score correlations, and (b) maximizing ability information with moderately difficult items. The aspect of task behavior that indicates ability is task accuracy, which is summed over items and then linearly transformed to a norm-referenced ability score.

The classical test theory principles obviously contrast sharply with modern intelligence research. They differ in basic issues, optimal test content, and which aspects of behavior are indicators of ability. In fact, classical test theory actually complements Spearman's (1927) concept of "g," which postulated a single ability factor that accounted for task consistency. This is not surprising, as the basic derivations for classical test theory can also be traced to Spearman.

The principles of latent trait theory also shape the construct of intelligence differently than contemporary research. The basic issue for American research on latent trait models has been obtaining optimal estimates of ability. Because latent trait models are item response models (i.e., they model the encounter of the person with the item), ability estimates do not depend on the specific items. As latent trait models become routinely implemented for item banking, test content becomes narrowed over the test content selected by classical test theory.

That is, test content becomes more rigorously unidimensional, and items with contingency effects (practice effects, context effect, etc.) are eliminated. The same aspect of behavior indicates ability, namely accuracy, but the raw score metric is not linearly related to ability. Interpretations of ability as item-solving likelihood in the task domain are possible if the task domain is well specified.

Latent trait theory does not bring psychometric concepts closer to contemporary intelligence research, although it offers some valuable potentials. That is, modeling respones (i.e., item responses) are a major focus, which is similar to individual mathematical modeling in contemporary intelligence research. Furthermore, the potential for domain-referenced interpretations of ability scores has at least general potential for the domain-specifications from contemporary research. Recent extensions of both classical test theory and latent trait theory models define different basic issues for psychometrics. Both cognitive contrast analysis (Calfee, 1976) and component latent trait models (Embretson, in press a; Fischer, 1973; Whitely, 1980) emphasize hypothesis testing concerning the theoretical factors that underlie task difficulty. Cognitive contrast analysis corresponds to classical test theory and tests hypotheses concerning the stimulus content of items. However, it is not a complete test theory development when it is not directly related to person variance. Further, cognitive contrast analysis has limited use for test design because, like classical test theory, it is not useful for item banking.

Component latent trait models are useful for test design, however, because they have the same properties of other latent trait models. Both the linear logistic latent trait model (Fischer, 1973) and the multicomponent latent trait model (Whitely, 1980) permit item banking by the cognitive characteristics of the items. Hence, both models influence test content. However, the multicomponent latent trait model has greater flexibility for test design because it is a multidimensional model. MLTM can be used to select items that reflect specified cognitive abilities.

Interestingly, none of the extensions that were reviewed in this chapter score different aspects of task behavior as ability indicators than do contemporary latent-trait models. That is, task accuracy, summed over items, is still the essence of ability. Contemporary research on intelligence, in contrast, emphasizes task-response time and also the strategies that a person employs to solve the task.

Perhaps a future need for test theory models is to explore these aspects of task behavior as indicators of ability. Two new latent trait models are developments in this direction, although neither has yet been applied extensively. Scheibelchner's (in press) model combines response time and accuracy data. Embretson (in press b) scores strategy application as an individual differences variable.

## REFERENCES

Anastasi, A. (1982). *Psychological Testing.* (5th ed.). New York: Macmillan & Company.

Andersen, E. B. (1973). A goodness of fit test for the Pasch model. *Psychometria,* *38,* 123–140.

Andersen, E. B. (1972). The numerical solution to a set of conditional estimation equations. *Journal of the Royal Statistical Society,* (Series B), *34,* 42–54.

Binet, A. (1911). Nouvelles recherches sur la mesure du niveau intellectual chez les infants d'ecole. *L'Annee Psychologique, 17,* 145–201.

Bock, R. D. & Lieberman, B. (1970). Fitting a response model for dichotomously scored items. *Psychometrika, 35,* 179–197.

Bock, R. D., & Aitken, M. (1981). Marginal maximum likelihood estimation of item parameters: An application of an EM algorithm. *Psychometrika, 46,* 443–459.

Brown, W., & Thomson, G. H. (1925). *The essentials of mental measurement* (3rd ed.). London, England: Cambridge University Press.

Butterfield, E. C. (in press). A model that predicts series continuation accuracy. In S. Embretson (Ed.), *Test design: Directions in psychology and psychometrics.* New York: Academic Press.

Calfee, R. C. (1976). Sources of dependency on cognitive processes. In D. Klahr (Ed.), *Cognition and instruction.* Hillsdale, NJ: Lawrence Erlbaum Assoc.

Calfee, R. C. & Hedges, L. V. (1980). Independent process analyses of aptitude. In R. E. Snow, P. A. Federico, & W. E. Montague (Eds.), *Aptitude, learning and instruction.* Hillsdale, NJ: Lawrence Erlbaum Assoc.

Carroll, J., & Maxwell, S. (1979). Individual differences in ability. *Annual Review of Psychology, 30,* 603–634.

Cronbach, L. J. (1951). Coefficient alpha and the internal structure of tests. *Psychometria, 16,* 297–334.

Cronbach, L. J., Gleser, G. C., Narda, H., & Rajaratnam, N. (1972). *The dependability of behavioral measurements: Theory of generalizability for scores and profiles.* New York: John Wiley & Sons.

Embretson, S. (1983a, June). An incremental fit index for the linear logistic latent trait model. Paper presented at the annual meeting of the Psychometric Society, Los Angeles, CA.

Embretson, S. E. (1983b). Construct validity: Construct representation versus nomothetic span. *Psychological Bulletin, 93,* 179–197.

Embretson, S. (in press a). A general latent trait model for response processes. *Psychometrika.*

Embretson, S. (in press b). Latent trial models for analyzing and assessing individual differences. In R. J. Sternberg (Ed.), *Advances in the psychology of human intelligence.* Hillsdale, NJ: Lawrence Erlbaum Assoc.

Embretson, S. (in press c). *Test design: Directions in psychology and psychometrics.* New York: Academic Press.

Embretson, S. E. & Wetzel, D. (1984). Latent trait models for cognitive components. Paper presented at the annual meeting of the American Educational Research Association. (April). New Orleans, LA.

Fischer, G. (1973). Linear logistic test model as an instrument in educational research. *Acta Psychologica, 37,* 359–374.

Fischer, G. (1978). Probabilistic test models and their applications. *German Journal of Psychology, 2,* 298–319.

Fischer, G. H. (1981). On the existence and uniqueness of maximum-likelihood estimates in the Rasch model. *Psychometrika, 46*, 59–77.

Fischer, G. H., & Formann, A. K. (1972, October). An algorithm and a FORTRAN program for estimating the item parameters of the linear logistic test model. *Research Bulletin No. 11, Psychologisches Institut der Universitat Vien, Vienna, Austria.*

Freeman, F. (1926). *Mental tests.* Boston, MA: Houghton Mifflin Company.

Galton, F. (1869). *Hereditary genius: An inquiry into its laws and consequences.* London, England: D. Appleton & Company.

Galton, F. (1888). Correlations and their measurement, chiefly from anthropometric data. *Proceedings of the Royal Society of London, XLU*, 135–145.

Guilford, J. P. (1954). *Psychometric methods.* New York: McGraw-Hill.

Guilford, J. P. (1959). Three faces of intellect. *American Psychologist, 14,* 469–479.

Gulliksen, H. (1950). *Theory of mental tests.* New York: John Wiley & Sons.

Gustafsson, J. E. (1980a). Testing and obtaining fit of data to the Rasch model. *British Journal of Mathematical and Statistical Psychology, 33,* 205–233.

Gustafsson, J. E. (1980b). A solution of the conditional estimation problem for long tests in the Rasch model for dichotomous items. *Educational and Psychological Measurement, 40,* 377–385.

Hambleton, R. K., & Traub, R. E. (1973). Analysis of empirical data using two logistic latent trait models. *British Journal of Mathematical and Statistical Psychology, 26,* 195–211.

Heller, J. I. (1979). Cognitive processing in verbal analogy solution. Unpublished doctoral dissertation, University of Pittsburg.

Holzman, T. G., Pellegrino, J. W., & Glaser, R. (in press). Cognitive variables in series completion. *Journal of Educational Psychology.*

Hoyt, C. (1941). Test reliability obtained by analysis of variance. *Psychometrika, 6,* 153–160.

Hunt, E. B., Lunneborg, C., & Lewis, J. (1975). What does it mean to be high verbal? *Cognitive Psychology, 7,* 194–227.

Jenkins, J. J., & Paterson, D. G. (1961). *Studies in individual differences: The search for intelligence.* New York: Appleton-Century-Crofts.

Kelley, T. L. (1914). Comparable measures. *Journal of Educational Psychology, 6,* 314–328.

Kelley, T. L. (1923). *Statistical method.* New York: Macmillan Company.

Kelley, T. L. (1927). *Interpretation of educational measurements.* Yonkers-in-Hudson, NY: World Book Company.

Klahr, D., & Wallace, J. G. (1970). The development of serial completion strategies: An information processing analysis. *British Journal of Psychology, 61,* 243–257.

Kuder, G. F., & Richardson, M. W. (1937). The theory of estimation of test reliability. *Psychometrika, 2,* 151–160.

Lord, F. M. (1980). *Applications of item response theory to practical testing problems.* Hillsdale, NJ: Lawrence Erlbaum Assoc.

Lord, F. N. (1979, June). Small N justifies Rasch methods. *Proceedings of the 1979 Computerized Adaptive Testing Conference.* D. K. Weiss (Ed.), Minneapolis, MN: West Publishing Company.

Lord, F. N., & Novick, M. R. (1968). *Statistical theories of mental test scores.* Reading, MA: Addison-Wesley.

Magnusson, D. (1967). *Test theory.* Reading, MA: Addison-Wesley.

Nunnally, J. C. (1978). *Psychometric theory.* New York: McGraw-Hill.

Pellegrino, J. W., & Glaser, R. (1979). Cognitive correlates and components in the analysis of individual differences. *Intelligence, 3,* 187–214.

Pellegrino, J. W., & Lyon, D. R. (1979). The components of a componential analysis. *Intelligence, 3,* 169–186.

Rasch, G. (1960). *Probabilistic models for some intelligence and achievement tests.* Copenhagen, Denmark: Nielsen and Lydiche.

Reckase, M. D. (1979). Unifactor latent trait models applied to multifactor tests: Results and implications. *Journal of Educational Statistics, 4,* 207–230.

Richardson, M. W. (1936). Notes on the rationale of item analysis. *Psychometrika, 1,* 61–76.

Samejima, F. (1974). Normal ogive model on the continuous response level in the multi-dimensional latent space. *Psychometrika, 39,* 111–121.

Scheiblechner, H. (in press). Psychometric models for speeded test construction: The linear exponential model. In S. Embretson (Ed.), *Test design: Directions in psychology and psychometrics.* New York: Academic Press.

Simon, H. A., & Kotovsky, K. (1963). Human acquisition of concepts for sequential patterns. *Psychological Review, 70,* 534–546.

Spearman, C. (1904). The proof and measurement of association between two things. *American Journal of Psychology, 15,* 72–101.

Spearman, C. (1907). Demonstration of formulae for true measurement of correlation. *American Journal of Psychology, 18,* 161–169.

Spearman, C. (1910). Correlation calculated with faculty data. *British Journal of Psychology, 3,* 271–295.

Spearman, C. (1913). Correlations of sums and differences. *British Journal of Psychology, 5,* 417–426.

Spearman, C. (1923). *The nature of intelligence and the principles of cognition.* London, England: Macmillan & Company, Ltd.

Spearman, C. (1927). *The abilities of man.* New York: Macmillan.

Sternberg, R. J. (1977a). Component processes in analogical reasoning. *Psychological Review, 31,* 356–378.

Sternberg, R. J. (1977b). *Intelligence, information processing and analogical reasoning.* Hillsdale, NJ: Lawrence Erlbaum, Publishers.

Symonds, P. M. (1929). Choice of items for a test on the basis of difficulty. *Journal of Educational Psychology, 7,* 481–493.

Thissen, D., & Wainer, H. (1982). Some standard errors in item response theory. *Psychometrika, 47,* 397–412.

Thurstone, L. L. (1938). Primary mental abilities. *Psychometric Monographs* (Whole #1).

Thurstone, L. L., & Thurstone, T. G. (1941). Factorial studies of intelligence. *Psychometric Monographs* (Whole #2).

Waller, M. (1981). A procedure for comparing logistic latent trait models. *Journal of Educational Measurement, 18,* 119–125.

Wollenberg, A. L. van den. (1982). Two new test statistics for the Rasch model. *Psychometrika, 47,* 123–140.

Wainer, H., & Wright, R. D. (1980). Robust estimation of ability in the Rasch model. *45*, 373–391.

Whitely, S. E. (1980). Multicomponent latent trait models for ability tests, *Psychometrika, 45*, 479–494.

Whitely, S. E. (1981). Measuring aptitude processes with multicomponent latent trait models. *Journal of Educational Measurement, 18*, 67–84.

Whitely, S. E., & Davis, R. B. (1974). The nature of the objectivity with the Rasch model. *Journal of Educational Measurement, 11*, 163–178.

Whitely, S. E., & Nieh, K. (1981, August). Program MULTICOMP. Unpublished manuscript, University of Kansas, Lawrence, KS.

Whitely, S. E., & Schneider, L. M. (1981). Information structure on geometric analogies: A test theory approach. *Applied Psychological Measurement, 5*, 383–397.

Wright, B. (1968). Sample-free test calibration and person measurement. *Proceedings of the 1967 Invitational Conference on Testing Problems.* Princeton, NJ: Educational Testing Service, 84–101.

Wright, B., & Panchapakesan, N. (1969). A procedure for sample-free item analysis. *Educational and Psychological Measurement, 29*, 23–48.

Yen, W. M. (1981). Using simulation results to choose a latent trait model. *Applied Psychological Measurement, 5*, 245–262.

Yerkes, R. M. (1921). *Psychological examining in the United States Army, 15*, National Academy of Sciences.

# CHAPTER 5

# Methodological Problems in the Study of Differential Deficits in Retarded Groups

*Loren J. Chapman*

*and*

*Jean P. Chapman*

University of Wisconsin–Madison

## INTRODUCTION

Several writers have discussed the problems that result from ceiling and floor effects in studies of the performance of retarded and nonretarded subjects who are equal on chronological age (Baumeister, 1967; Belmont & Butterfield, 1969; Berkson & Cantor, 1962; Ellis, 1969; Winters, 1972). All of these writers have pointed out that a difference in performance on two tasks may be observed in retarded subjects but not in nonretarded subjects if tasks are so easy that non-retarded subjects are near a ceiling of perfect scores. Conversely, these writers point out, a difference in performance may be observed in nonretarded but not in retarded subjects if both tasks are so difficult that retarded subjects are near a floor of no correct responses. Hence, the relative shapes of the two groups' performance curves may depend largely upon task difficulty and may say very little about the groups' possible underlying psychological differences.

This paper discusses a similar phenomenon that operates throughout the entire range of task difficulty, not just when one of the groups is near a floor or ceiling on errors. We contend that when an investigator uses two or more tasks which differ on relevant psychometric characteristics, poorer performance by retarded subjects than by nonretarded subjects makes it difficult to interpret any observed differences in performance among the tasks. One cannot interpret a difference in performance on two or more such tasks as indicating a greater deficit in one ability than in a second ability. This problem usually occurs in comparisons of retarded subjects with nonretarded subjects of the same chronological age but often also in comparisons with nonretarded subjects of the same mental age. The retarded subjects may score lower than controls on the kind of tasks being studied despite matching with controls on mental age, and if the tasks differ on relevant psychometric characteristics, one cannot infer a greater deficit in the ability measured by one task than on the ability measured by another task.

The central problem is that a differential deficit in performance does not necessarily indicate a differential deficit in ability. It may, instead, merely reflect the retarded subjects' generalized performance deficit coupled with the fact that one of the two tasks is affected more by generalized deficit than the other. If retarded subjects do not perform as well as control subjects, they will show a greater performance deficit on the one of the two tasks that yields the greater dispersion of scores. It follows, that to measure differential deficit, one must match tasks on psychometric characteristics which affect the dispersion of scores among the more able and the less able subjects. Two such psychometric characteristics are reliability and difficulty.

## RELIABILITY, DIFFICULTY, AND MEAN DIFFERENCE BETWEEN GROUPS

In a typical differential-deficit study comparing retarded and control subjects, the investigator administers two or more tasks that differ in a way hypothesized to affect the accuracy of retarded subjects more than that of nonretarded subjects. For example, he might manipulate degree of spacing of practice in a learning task, with the hypothesis that massing of practice impairs retarded subjects' performance more than control subjects' performance. Any change in the difference between retarded and control subjects' performance depends, however, not only on their response to the variable, per se, but also on the tasks's psychometric characteristics which may have little to do with what is being measured. Especially important characteristics are difficulty level and task reliability. Tests are often described in terms of their "discriminating power," which refers to the effectiveness with which the score on a test differentiates the more able from the less able subjects. In psychometric theory, reliability is conventionally viewed as an index of discriminating power. This follows from the fact that the square root of the reliability coefficient is the correlation of obtained scores with error-free true scores. As discussed below, test reliability is only one of the test characteristics that influence the size of the mean difference between groups. However, with groups of roughly the same size, with difficulty held constant, and with the same ability being measured by both tests, the more reliable test will yield the larger mean difference between groups of more able and less able subjects. If retarded subjects are as inferior to nonretarded subjects in the ability measured by one test as in the ability measured by a second test, but one test is more reliable than the other, a greater performance deficit is likely to be found for retarded subjects on the more reliable test.

Test reliability is determined in part by difficulty level. Other things being equal, items that are at a 50% level of difficulty for the entire group tested are most reliable on a dichotomously scored free-response test on which subjects can seldom use sheer guessing to obtain a correct answer (Lord, 1952b). On multiple-choice tests, the highest reliability is expected for accuracy levels somewhat higher than midway between chance and 100% accuracy (Lord, 1952a).

In addition to the effect of its contribution to test reliability, item difficulty affects the difference between the more able and less able subjects in other ways as well. Tests that differ on difficulty but are equal on reliability will tend not to yield the same difference in mean score between subgroups of high-scoring and low-scoring subjects. Other things being equal, item difficulties in the middle range yield higher test variance for the total group. Assuming equivalent reliabilities, the test with the larger variance will yield the larger mean difference between such subgroups.

This is *not* just a ceiling or a floor effect. One cannot avoid the effects of difficulty on the difference in mean score of groups by limiting one's manipulation of a variable to the middle range of difficulty, using, for example, tasks that produce an error rate between 25% and 75%. Differences in difficulty within this middle range have a substantial effect on the difference between the more able and the less able subjects. Lord and Novick (1968, p. 329) show how the variance of observed scores may be computed from the item difficulties. For a free-response test of uniform inter-item correlation of .25, the test variance is approximately 309 for a 100-item test with uniform item difficulty of .50, but the variance drops to approximately 198 for a uniform item difficulty of .80. The smaller variance for the .80 level of difficulty will result in a smaller difference in mean scores between the higher-scoring and lower-scoring groups of subjects. In practice, however, the difference in variance will be even larger than indicated by these values because the middle range of item difficulty will also yield a higher reliability which, in turn, affects the observed test variance.

## An Illustrative Example

The effect of item difficulty on differential performance of groups of differing ability can be illustrated by some data on comparative performance of groups of mildly retarded and average subjects on vocabulary items that differ in difficulty. These vocabulary items were those of the Wechsler Adult Intelligence Scale. Figure 5.1 shows the percentage accuracy of a group of 40 mildly retarded adult prison inmates and a group of 40 prison inmates of average intelligence. Their intelligence level was estimated from their scores on a second vocabulary test, that of the Stanford–Binet Intelligence Scale. The mildly retarded subjects earned a mean score of 15.15 ($SD$ = 2.86), which corresponds to an MA of 12, and the average subjects earned a mean score of 19.88 ($SD$ = 2.80), which corresponds to an MA of Average Adult. The abscissa of Figure 5.1 presents five sequential groups of vocabulary items, gradated by level of difficulty (as measured by percentage accuracy for retarded and average subjects combined). Thus, each point of the abscissa represents several vocabulary items in a given range of difficulty. Against this abscissa are plotted curves for the percentage of retarded subjects and percentage of average subjects passing each set of items. (If the two groups were combined, the resulting curve would represent a variable plotted against itself.) The curves for the two groups tend to join at the extreme ends of the dimension of difficulty, and they attain greatest vertical separation for items at about the 50% level of difficulty for the two groups combined. Figure 5.1 clearly demonstrates that the powerful effect of difficulty level on degree of separation of retarded and average subjects exists throughout the entire range of difficulty.

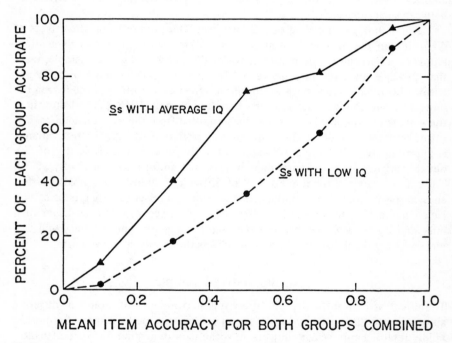

Figure 5.1. Accuracy of subjects (Ss) with low IQ on Wechsler Adult Intelligence Scale items of gradated difficulty.

## DIFFERENCE BETWEEN GROUPS AND
## THE MANIPULATION OF A VARIABLE

If an investigator manipulates a variable that affects accuracy, but all of the items are more difficult than the level of maximal differentiation of groups, the performance curves of retarded and nonretarded subjects will usually diverge with increased levels of the independent variable. This divergence corresponds to the left-hand half of Figure 5.1. If, on the other hand, all of the tasks are less difficult than the difficulty level of maximal differentiation of groups, the performance curves for retarded and nonretarded subjects will usually converge with increased levels of the independent variable. This convergence corresponds to the right-hand half of Figure 5.1. These are powerful effects that may mask other kinds of differential response of the two groups to the variable being manipulated.

In Figure 5.1, the direction of the effects of the probable artifact is very clear because the five sets of items differ in difficulty for the average subjects. In many studies, the direction of the effect of the probable artifact is not clear because the study uses two tasks that are so easy that most members of the more able group make almost no errors on either task. Still other studies use tasks for which adequacy of performance is defined by criteria other than the number of errors, such as by speed of response—as in reaction-time tasks—or trials to criterion, as in verbal-learning tasks. If such tasks differ on difficulty and reliability, artifactual findings are very likely to occur, even though the direction of the probable artifact is ambiguous.

The effects of both reliability and difficulty on the spread of scores of the more able and less able subjects are subsumed in a single index, the true-score variance. The true-score variance is the product of the reliability and the observed-score variance. To explicate the logic of its use, we must consider some of the principles of classic psychometric theory.

## Some Principles of Psychometric Theory

When parallel tests are given on successive occasions, any given subject will usually not earn identical scores on the two testings. He will score differently even when he does not change in his knowledge of the material and shows no practice effects as a result of his taking the earlier test. These fluctuations in test score are attributable to changes in such variables as the subject's motivation, fatigue, emotional state, alertness, luck in guessing, and to changes in conditions of testing. Fluctuations in test score that occur for such reasons are random and are usually described as reflecting errors of measurement.

It is customary to divide test scores into two components, true score and error of measurement.

$$X_o = X_t + X_e \tag{1}$$

Where

$X_o$ = observed score

$X_t$ = true score

$X_e$ = errors of measurement

Errors of measurement are as often positive as negative. If a series of parallel tests were to be administered, the series of test scores for a single subject would be expected to form a normal distribution. The mean of this normal distribution would be the subject's true score, and the difference between the subject's observed score on a given testing and his true score would be attributable to the errors of measurement for the individual on that testing.

The term *true score* may be misleading. It does not refer to the validity of the test as a measure of a specific named ability. Instead, it refers to the portion of the score which is replicable, that is, reliable.

It is assumed that true score and errors of measurement are uncorrelated. It follows that the variance of observed scores is the sum of the variances of true scores and of errors of measurement.

$$S_o^2 = S_t^2 + S_e^2 \qquad\qquad (2)$$

Where

$S_o^2$ = variance of observed scores

$S_t^2$ = variance of true scores

$S_e^2$ = variance of errors of measurement

This means that when we observe the distribution of scores of a sample of subjects, the distribution reflects two component distributions, one being the distribution of true scores and the other the distribution of errors of measurement. Thus, the variance of true scores is smaller than the variance of observed scores (except in the unrealistic case of a perfectly reliable test). The relationship of the variance of observed scores and the variance of true scores is expressed as follows:

$$S_t^2 = rS_o^2 \qquad\qquad (3)$$

Where

$S_t^2$ = variance of true scores

$r$ = reliability of the test

$S_o^2$ = variance of observed scores

## Some Implications of These Principles

Let us consider the problem of inferring differential deficit in ability from performance on two 30-item tests which differ on true-score variance. We will call these Test 1 and Test 2. Figure 5.2 presents hypothetical frequency distributions of true scores for subjects who have taken both tests.

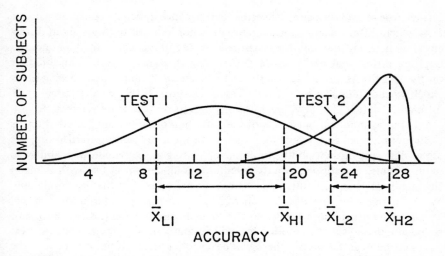

Figure 5.2. Hypothetical distributions of true scores on two 30-item tests, one of medium difficulty and one of low difficulty.

Figure 5.2 is drawn so as to make the difference between the tests in true-score variance a very large one. Test 1 has the larger true-score variance. In the particular case represented here, the variance of Test 2 is small because of the use of very easy items. Now, consider the result if one compares the mean score of the more able subjects with the mean score of the less able subjects on each of these two tests. For example, one might compare for each test the mean of the high-scoring half of the subjects with the mean of the low-scoring half of the subjects. Test 1 yields a relatively large mean difference in true score between subjects of high ability and subjects of low ability $(\overline{X}_{H1}-\overline{X}_{L1})$. For Test 2, the comparable mean difference $(\overline{X}_{H2}-\overline{X}_{L2})$ is smaller. Test 1 is intended, of course, as a measure of Ability 1, and Test 2 is intended as a measure of Ability 2. However, the larger difference in true score for Test 1 does not mean that the more able and less able subjects differ more on Ability 1 than on Ability 2, but instead, reflects only the fact that the test items were chosen so that Test 1 has a greater true-score variance than Test 2. The differential deficit in performance merely reflects the particular choice of items for the two tests. In many comparisons of retarded and nonretarded subjects, the situation is very much like the example represented in Figure 5.2. The retarded subjects are the lower scoring subjects and the nonretarded subjects are the higher scoring subjects, except, of course, that the two groups may sometimes overlap somewhat in their accuracy scores. The mean of the true scores for retarded subjects or for non-retarded subjects is expected to be identical to the mean of their observed scores. It follows that the retarded subjects will show a greater performance deficit on a test which, like Test 1, has a greater true-score variance than on a test with a smaller true-score variance. Differential performance deficit obtained on pairs of tests which differ on true-score variance does not indicate anything about differential deficit in the abilities measured by the tests. One could obtain the opposite differential performance deficit, that is, a greater performance deficit on the test for Ability 2 than on the test for Ability 1, simply by choosing items which yield differing true-score variances for the tests. It follows that, to measure differential deficit in ability, one must match tests on true-score variance.

Let us assume that one test is of the definition of nouns and the other test is of the definition of adjectives and, unknown to the investigator, retarded subjects are as deficient in their ability to define adjectives as they are in their ability to define nouns. Investigator A puts together a noun-definition test with items in the middle range of difficulty and an adjective-definition test that is considerably easier. In this case, the distribution of scores for the noun-definition test will resemble the distribution labeled as Test 1 in Figure 5.2 and the distribution of scores for the adjective-definition test will resemble the distribution labeled Test 2. As in the example above, there will be a greater mean difference between the more able (nonretarded) and the less able (retarded) subjects on the test with the greater true-score variance—in this case, the noun-definition test. So Investigator A concludes that retarded subjects show a greater deficit (as judged by comparison with nonretarded subjects) in defining nouns than in defining adjectives. Now Investigator B sets out to replicate this finding except that he or she chooses adjectives that are in the middle range of difficulty (say about .50) and chooses nouns that are easier (say about .75 accuracy). This time the distribution of test scores for defining nouns will look like Test 2 and the distribution of scores for defining adjectives will look like Test 1. The finding will be a greater mean difference between retarded and nonretarded in defining adjectives than in defining nouns. Investigator B might conclude that retarded subjects show a greater deficit in the ability to define adjectives than in the ability to define nouns. Obviously, both investigators cannot be correct. Both findings may be artifacts of the difference in true-score variance on the tests which the investigator chose to test the hypothesis.

But, one might ask, why not consider observed-score variance of tests instead of true-score variance? The answer is that observed-score variance includes variance due to errors of measurement, that is, variance which is not replicable. A less reliable test will not reflect the effects of generalized incompetence as well does a more reliable test. One might match two tests of differing reliability on observed-score variance and then give the tests to retarded subjects and to control subjects. The retarded subjects would be expected to show less deficit on the less reliable test than on the more reliable test even if the retarded have equal deficit in the two abilities. This principle is most intuitively obvious in the extreme case of a test with a reliability of zero. An example is the task of obtaining "heads" in coin tossing. If each of a group of subjects tosses 10 coins and is given a score of number of heads obtained, the resultant distribution of obtained scores has a variance just as any other distribution of scores. The reliability, however, is zero and, therefore, the true-score variance is also zero. If this task were to be paired with a second task that has the same obtained-score variance but has a nonzero reliability, only the second task could distinguish groups that differ on generalized competence.

## An Example from the Literature

A recent research report from the American Journal of Mental Deficiency will serve to illustrate the difficulties involved in using designs of unmatched tasks. We choose an example of an especially sophisticated piece of research. Mosley (1981) attempted to demonstrate a deficit in iconic memory in retarded individuals. Mildly retarded and nonretarded subjects matched for MA and CA were presented a series of arrays of letters that differed on the number of letters in the array. The letter arrays were presented tachistoscopically. The stimuli were presented for a very short exposure time (20 msec.) and were followed by a visual mask. The time between stimulus and mask onset was systematically varied from 0 to 200 msec. Thus, two variables were being studied: number of letters in the array and time between the stimulus and the mask.

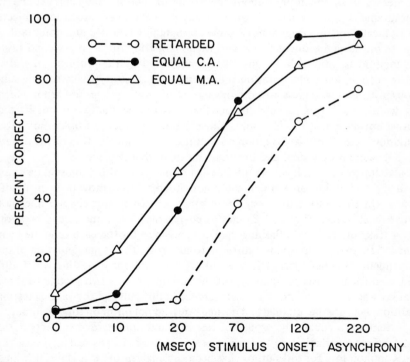

Figure 5.3. Mean percent correct reports by three groups presented with three-letter arrays with six stimulus-onset asynchronies (intervals between letters and mask). (Adapted from Mosley, 1981).

Figure 5.3 presents illustrative data extracted from his paper, specifically, the mean percentage of correct responses on the three-letter arrays for retarded and the two control groups. We choose Mosley's (1981) three-letter array because all subjects responded to the variable of stimulus-mask interval with few errors for no mask and with nearly all errors for immediate presentation of mask. Figure 5.3 shows that the groups were maximally separated on number of errors in the middle range of difficulty. The performance curves resemble those of Figure 5.1.

For the four-letter and five-letter arrays, the curves diverged as the interval increased, but did not again converge, presumably because the full difficulty dimension was not represented. It is speculative to draw inferences about differences in information processing from these results because the findings can apparently be accounted for by the generalized performance deficit of the retarded subjects together with the probably greater true-score variance of scores in the middle range of difficulty.

## Some Erroneous Solutions

In order to draw conclusions about the nature of retarded subjects' deficits, it is unsuitable to select subgroups of atypically poor-scoring nonretarded subjects and atypically high-scoring retarded subjects, matching retarded and nonretarded subjects on accuracy on one task and then comparing them on a second task. This method is unsuitable because it is complicated by the problems of statistical regression. On their scores on the second task, these atypically scoring subgroups will usually regress toward the means of the larger groups from which they were drawn. This reflects the fact that, if scores at the two points have a positive but imperfect correlation, a subject's score on a second task tends to be a function of the mean of his group on that task plus some fraction of the difference between his first score and the group mean on that first score.

Matching of subgroups is a useful design primarily on those unusual tasks on which the population of regarded and nonretarded subjects show little or no difference. On such tasks, the design problem discussed in this chapter does not exist. For example, Thor (1973) compared retarded and nonretarded boys on several tasks of tracking a flashing light by pressing a button each time the light flashed. The two groups did not differ in total errors. Thor's manipulation of his independent variables yielded several different conditions of testing which differed in difficulty. His comparisons of the response of his two groups to these variables was not invalidated by the difference in difficulty of the various testing conditions because the retarded and normal boys did not differ on total accuracy.

Attempts to equate the groups of retarded and nonretarded subjects statistically almost invariably lead to erroneous applications of statistical methods. The most common tool for this purpose has been the analysis of covariance, in which one covaries out the effects of intelligence. Such application of analysis of covariance to pre-existing groups that are disparate on the covariate is fallacious, as discussed by several writers, including Lord (1967). Using an accuracy score, the regression line for nonretarded subjects will typically be higher than the regression line for the retarded subjects. As a result, if one covaries out the effects of one score on a second score for both groups, one is sure to find a remaining deficit for retarded subjects on the second score. There is an identical fallacy in using regression analysis instead of covariance for this purpose. Regression analysis and analysis of covariance are closely related procedures. In regression analysis, one predicts what score a subject should earn on the second task assuming any given score on the first task, and assigns residualized error scores (obtained score minus predicted score) on the second task. The groups are certain to differ on the residualized error scores because of the difference in elevation of the regression lines.

We believe that there is no purely statistical solution to the defects of unmatched tasks in the comparison of retarded and nonretarded groups. The problem should instead be finessed by a matching of the tasks on true-score variance.

## How Tasks Should be Matched

Let us now turn to the problem of just how to go about matching on true-score variance. Since true-score variance is the product of reliability and observed-score variance, true-score variance will be greater when observed-score variance and reliability are greater. Both the observed-score variance and the reliability tend to be greater when the items are more numerous, when the items fall more often in the middle range of difficulty, and when the items tend to measure the same ability. The matching on difficulty should not be just on mean-item difficulty but also on the distribution of item difficulty, that is, on both the variance of item difficulty and on the shape of the distribution of item difficulty. Without equivalent distributions of item difficulty, the tests could become unmatched on variance and on reliability for groups of differing mean-ability level. Items near a ceiling on accuracy for nonretarded subjects alone cannot be meaningfully matched. The matching of tasks will be meaningful only if nonretarded subjects show variance in the easier items and if the tasks are matched on the easy items as well as on the task as a whole. The requirement of variance for nonretarded subjects on the easier items will often require that the nonretarded and retarded subjects be chosen so that they are closer on ability level than are the samples of nonretarded and retarded subjects in some published studies. It would probably be unwise, for example, to choose groups of equal CA with mean IQs of 60 and 100 for comparison on response to two variables that affect ability to handle abstract ideas. Equivalent reliability of two tests can usually be achieved by choosing items so that the tests have about the same distributions of item-scale correlations.

*Choice of Standardization Groups for Matching Tasks.* Nonretarded subjects are the appropriate standardization group. One should not match tasks for combined groups of nonretarded and retarded subjects because the reliabilities would be affected by any true differential deficit due to retardation. The tasks with the greater deficit due to retardation would have the larger true-score variance for retarded and nonretarded subjects combined and, hence, the higher reliability. Matching of tasks on reliability for retarded and nonretarded subjects combined would tend to eliminate this evidence of the retarded subjects' differential deficit in ability. This is because in order to match the two tasks for retarded and non-retarded subjects combined, one would have to choose the less reliable items for the task on which retarded subjects have the greater deficit.

*Matching on Reliability.* Often the most convenient estimate of reliability for matching purposes is Coefficient Alpha (equivalent to Kuder–Richardson Formula 20), which is the mean of all possible split-half reliability values. (See Nunnally, 1967, or Lord & Novick, 1968).

*Insuring that the Same Ability is Tested at Different Difficulty Levels.* The investigator must guard against the possibility that the items at the various levels of difficulty of a task measure different abilities. If different abilities are measured at the various difficulty levels, the reliability estimates obtained for nonretarded subjects alone will not be meaningful for the nonretarded and retarded subjects combined. Also, the tasks would tend to measure different abilities for nonretarded and retarded subjects so that the tasks would no longer be suitable for studying the differential deficit of retarded subjects. The investigator may guard against this possibility in two ways. First, he should scrutinize the items. He might, for example, decide not to use a task calling for definitions of words in which (as in the Stanford–Binet Vocabulary Subtest) the easier items refer more often to concrete events and the more difficult items refer more often to abstract ideas. Second, the investigator might factor analyze each task for normal subjects alone and verify that the same factors are present in easy items as in hard items.

## CONCLUSION

Designs using matched tasks can yield valid conclusions concerning differential deficit of retarded subjects. Without task matching, conclusions about differential deficit of ability will seldom be justified.

## REFERENCES

Baumeister, A. A. (1967). Problems in comparative studies of mental retardates and normals. *American Journal of Mental Deficiency, 71,* 869–875.

Belmont, J. M., & Butterfield, E. C. (1969). The relations of short-term memory to development and intelligence. In L. P. Lipsitt & H. W. Reese (Eds.), *Advances in child development and behavior.* (Vol. 4). New York: Academic Press.

Berkson, G., & Cantor, G. N. (1962). A note on method in comparisons of learning in normals and the mentally retarded. *American Journal of Mental Deficiency, 67,* 475–477.

Ellis, N. R. (1969). A behavioral research strategy in mental retardation: Defense and critique. *American Journal of Mental Deficiency, 73,* 557–566.

Lord, F. M. (1952a). A theory of test scores. *Psychometric Monographs,* (No. 7).

Lord, F. M. (1952b). The relation of the reliability of multiple-choice tests to the distribution of item difficulties. *Psychometrika, 17,* 181–194.

Lord, F. M. (1967). A paradox in the interpretation of group comparisons. *Psychological Bulletin, 68,* 304–305.

Lord, F. M., & Novick, M. R. (1968). *Statistical theories of mental test scores.* Reading, MA: Addison-Wesley.

Mosley, J. L. (1981). Iconic store readout of mildly mentally retarded and nonretarded individuals. *American Journal of Mental Deficiency, 86,* 60–66.

Nunnally, J. C. (1967). *Psychometric theory.* New York: McGraw Hill.

Thor, D. H. (1972). Counting and tracking of sequential visual stimuli by EMR and intellectually average children. *American Journal of Mental Deficiency, 78,* 41–46.

Winters, J. J., Jr. (1972). Proposed analyses of floor and ceiling effects. *American Journal of Mental Deficiency, 77,* 296–300.

Section *II*

# *RESEARCH APPROACHES*

# CHAPTER 6

# The Correlates of Intelligence*

*Earl Hunt*

*The University of Washington*

What are the characteristics of intelligent people? The answer to this apparently simple question depends upon how we interpret it, and upon how we think about intelligence itself.

Intelligence has been defined as ". . . what the intelligence tests test" (Boring, 1923). This is a pragmatic view, we define people to be intelligent if they can answer questions on "intelligence tests." One can then ask what characteristic cognitive behaviors good test-takers display. The question is particularly interesting if the other behaviors include behaviors that are thought to be basic to cognition. An analogy to athletics is useful. "Good athletes" are defined by their performance in a variety of games. Do good athletes have low blood pressure, large biceps, or rapid reaction times? Can one find basic information-processing tasks that play the same role, vis a vis intelligence, that cardiac condition, muscle tone, and quickness play in athletics?

Consider one of the "elementary" skills that might be called upon in displays of verbal intelligence, the ability to make sense out of language. Human languages are based on arbitrary symbol-meaning correspondences. There is no particular reason that the symbol CAT should refer to a small, domesticated feline, but in English, it does. The process by which people connect sights and sounds to semantic concepts is called *lexical access*. Several procedures have been developed to evaluate a person's speed of lexical access for common words. A typical example is the lexical-decision task, in which people are asked to recognize whether or not a string of letters, for example, CAT or CAK, is a word. People who score well on tests involving complex verbal tasks, such as paragraph

---

*I would like to thank Prof. James Pellegrino for the opportunity to discuss the issues presented here with him and with the members of his seminar on "Intelligence." Naturally neither Dr. Pellegrino nor, certainly, the members of the class, necessarily agree with the opinions expressed here.

157

comprehension, tend to make lexical decisions quickly (Hunt, Davidson, & Lansman, 1981). The correlation between lexical-decision performance and conventional verbal-comprehension scores is moderate in normal, well educated adults ($r$ = .3 to .4), but mildly retarded people, who do very poorly on tests of verbal ability, are extremely slow in lexical access (Warren & Hunt, 1981).

Relationships between mental test performance and elementary information-processing ability, such as lexical access, have been called *cognitive correlates* (Pellegrino & Glaser, 1979). The term could be used to refer to any naturally occuring correlation between a measure of cognition and some other physical, mental, or social characteristic. It is fairly easy to establish the existence of a cognitive correlate, but determining what the correlation means is quite another matter. Perhaps the best illustration of a controversy over interpretation is the long, bitter, and generally noninformative debate over the meaning of correlations between test scores and measures of ethnic status. (See Loehlin, Lindzey & Spuhler, 1975, for one of the few balanced descriptions of the controversy.) Other, fortunately less bitter, debates have also occurred. The fact that these arguments flourish suggests to me that too little thought has been given to the conceptual issues involved in interpreting studies of the correlates of intelligence. This chapter is an attempt to present the major conceptual issues that apply to all interpretations of correlations. Empirical studies will be used as illustrations [1], but no attempt will be made to present a comprehensive survey of the literature.

## THE CONCEPTUAL BASIS
## OF CORRELATIONAL STUDIES

In the social and behavioral sciences a distinction is often drawn between *experimental* and *correlational* studies. In correlational studies two or more naturally occuring measures are taken, and inferences are drawn by noticing how the measures covary. To offer an example, the incidence of mental retardation is elevated in the children of women who consume alcohol heavily during pregnancy (Streissguth, Lanesman-Dwyer, Martin, & Smith, 1980). This is called the *fetal alcohol syndrome,* implying that the mother's alcohol consumption is a cause of the child's mental deficiency. The logic of this argument can be attacked. The women who drank heavily were self-selected to be exposed to the drug. None of the studies of fetal alcoholism in humans have (or should have!) used an experimental approach in which alcohol was administered to some pregnant women and not to others, under controlled conditions. It could be that

---

[1] At times illustrations will be cited to make a point about limitations. The studies are not meant to be "bad" examples. Any experiment has its limitations. Within these limitations the studies cited here were generally well designed and executed.

women who are predisposed toward heavy drinking are also predisposed toward having mentally retarded children, irrespective of their alcohol consumption. The same argument could be made with regard to lexical access. It is not at all clear that the ability to recognize common words rapidly is a causative factor in verbal intelligence. Both rapid word recognition and more complex linguistic acts might depend upon common causes, without the complex acts depending on rapid word recognition.

Because "correlation does not imply causation," experimental studies are often considered superior to correlational studies. But there are many legitimate questions that can only be investigated by the correlational methods.[2] Human fetal alcoholism cannot be studied experimentally for ethical reasons. Lexical access cannot be studied experimentally because we know of no way of manipulating an individual's speed of lexical access, so that one person can be made a fast and another a slow recognizer of symbol meanings.[3]

The basic argument of this paper is that correlational studies are interpretable, providing that they are done in the context of a theory. If one is attempting to establish a link between intelligence, as measured by an intelligence test (or, for that matter, in some other way) and some more basic property of a person, then one should have a theory of how the basic property exerts its influence on the processes that we label *intelligence*. In fact, such a theory exists for both the lexical access and fetal alcoholism examples, as will be described subsequently. If a theory predicts a detailed pattern of correlations between observables, and if no other reasonable theory makes the same prediction, then observation of the pattern is strong evidence for the truth of the theory. This is an informal argument for Bayesian inference. It applies equally well to correlational and experimental data.

The argument does depend on having a theory. At this point our fuzzy ideas about what intelligence is become limiting. What do we mean by this term?

We began with the pragmatic view that the intelligence test defines intelligence. More precisely there exists a set of tests, called *intelligence tests* that establish a mental "space" defined by such dimensions as verbal and spatial

---

[2]There is a literature on "pseudo-experimental designs", in which some natural occurrence mimics the conditions that would have been established by an experiment. Perhaps the best example in the intelligence field is the study of the intellectual performance of identical twins who have been adopted by "randomly chosen" foster parents. While circumstance can produce such situations, they seem to be rather rare. It is also often the case that, on inspection, the "natural experiment" may turn out to be less a mimicry of a controlled experiment than one would have wished.

[3]It is possible to arrange situations in which lexical decision making is altered in people, in general. This is beside the point. What is required is some way of altering the mental performance of different people, in different ways, when the people are tested in identical situations.

intelligence. Individuals are thought of as being located at points in this space; a person's intelligence is defined to be the coordinates of the person's location. There is a good reason for taking such a narrow view of intelligence. Test performance predicts (albeit imperfectly) success in a variety of academic and working situations. Prediction could be achieved in two ways. The testing situation might demand those mental skills that are required for success elsewhere. This point has been made forcefully by one of the most prominent test developers, David Wechsler (1975), who proposed that a test be looked upon as a "structured interview" that forces a person to display behaviors that are needed in many problem-solving situations. The logic of the pragmatic approach is depicted in Figure 6.1. It contains one, very large assumption: that any behavior not actually displayed on the test is not part of intelligence.

Does anyone believe this? It seems doubtful that many people would want to equate the concept of intelligence with performance on an intelligence test. But surprisingly, people, including psychologists, often act as if test performance and intelligence are identical. To take an extreme case (and the reference is purposely omitted), a distinguished neuropsychologist once wrote that a certain type of brain injury did not reduce intelligence because the patients in question had postinjury test scores equivalent to scores they had obtained before the injury. Yet the patients in question had to be hospitalized, sometimes for life, due to serious mental incompetence! Surely it is not sensible to say that such people have normal intelligence.

It can be useful to equate test scores with the concept of intelligence as a temporary expedient. Problems occur when the temporary expedient assumes a life of its own.

An alternative view is to look upon *intelligence* as a collective term, used to refer to the possession of useful knowledge and special informative-processing capabilities. This will be called the *cognitive science* view of intelligence (Hunt, 1983). Its logic is shown in Figure 6.2. It states that no one thing can be defined as intelligence, but there are a number of statistically associated skills that, collectively, lead a person to display a characteristic level of mental competence. Performance on an intelligence test is seen as a statistical indicator that a person has (or does not have) critical skills or information, but performance on the test itself does not define intelligence. To return to the neuropsychological example, the cognitive-science view would be that the affected patients had lost vital, information-processing abilities, and that if this was not reflected in their intelligence test scores, then the test was not valid for those individuals because it no longer predicted their cognitive ability.

When the pragmatic view is stated baldly people seldom find it appealing. However, it is useful. It can be used to generate interesting and manageable research questions about what different intelligence tests measure. The utility

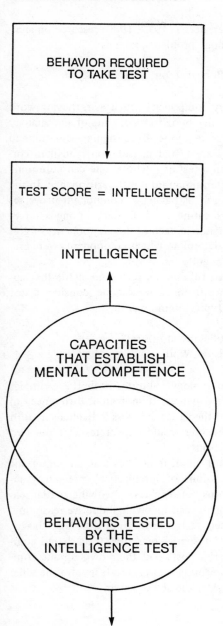

Figure 6.1. The pragmatic view of intelligence. Intelligence as a concept is defined by the ability to execute the tasks used in an intelligence test.

Figure 6.2. The cognitive science view of intelligence. Intelligence as a concept is defined by the possession of a variety of capabilities that, collectively, cause a person to display a characteristic level of mental competence. The intelligence test evaluates some of these capabilities.

of the approach is well illustrated by Sternberg's (1977, 1980) research on analogies test.[4] Sternberg has shown that analogy problems, such as

Dog is to Cat as Wolf is to (Bobcat, Lion, Bear, Skunk)

are solved by executing more elementary components, such as retrieving word meaning, determining relations between the two first elements of the analogy (here Dog, Cat), and then applying these relations. By designing situations in which each of the component processes are tested in isolation, and then correlating component scores with scores on a test as a whole, one can determine which components are most critical in determining total test performance. In the athletic analogy, one might look upon golf as having as component processes determining what club to use, visually locating the ball, determining a target location, and swinging the club. Performance in each of the components of golf could be correlated with golf scores, to determine which components were crucial in determining the score of the average golfer.

Sternberg's approach can be extended to a search for components that appear in several tests with different surface forms. For example, consider a test made up of verbal classification items. A typical item might be

Which item does not belong in this set?
Dog, Fox, Horse, Wolf

Although classification is different from analogy solution, both the examples just given require lexical access to animal names. If individual differences in lexical access account for a major part of the variance across individuals in both classification and analogy problems, then one would expect tests of the two types of items to be correlated for that reason.

The search for common components in different tests is an important endeavor. One evidence for the "dimensions of intelligence" previously referred to is that there are high correlations between tests involving spatial reasoning, or tests involving verbal reasoning, or tests involving inductive reasoning, and markedly lower correlations between tests drawn from different classes. Such a correlational pattern would arise if spatial reasoning tests shared components not shared with verbal tests, verbal tests had their own unique components, and so forth. In some cases discovering that two tests involve the same component may be counterintuitive. Consider the analogy item

---

[4]The example offered is intended to show how one can take the structured interview approach seriously. I do not mean to imply that Sternberg takes this approach as a more general theoretical stance. In fact, one of the best statements of the epiphenomenal nature of intelligence testing is Sternberg's address to the American Psychological Association (Sternberg, 1982).

3 is to 9 as 6 is to (7, 36, 10, 14).

Formally, both the verbal analogy problem given earlier and the numerical analogy problem contain the same components; determining the meaning of terms, and inferring relations by comparing meanings. But is the component of determining the meaning of numbers the same as determining the meaning of words? Probably not. Is "inferring a relation between numbers" the same as "inferring a relation between words?" Possibly. A correlational approach applied to components can lead to a better understanding of "what intelligence is", within the pragmatic view that intelligence is defined by the behavior occurring during intelligence testing.

Viewing an intelligence test score as an epiphenomon rather than as a definition of mental capacity is more in accord with our intuitions than is the pragmatic view. Unfortunately the cognitive-science approach results in a more complex argument for interpreting studies of cognitive correlates. This can be seen by considering the role of vocabulary tests in establishing verbal intelligence.

Verbal intelligence, as defined in most intelligence test batteries, is determined by several tests, including a vocabulary test, tests of the ability to recognize properly formed sentences, and tests of the ability to comprehend information presented in paragraphs. The sentences and paragraphs are written in restricted vocabularies, so that two people could have markedly different vocabulary scores and still have identical scores on sentence and paragraph comprehension. In fact, though, this seldom happens. Vocabulary score is the best single indicator of full scale verbal test scores ($r = .85$, Matarazzo 1972). Why? Sternberg and Powell (1983) have pointed out that a vocabulary test does two things. Most obviously, it identifies people with large and small vocabularies. Since most words are learned without explicit tuition, identifying relative vocabulary size may indirectly identify those people who are good (or poor) at picking up information from verbal contexts. In fact, this is true. If one presents a sentence with an unknown word in it, as in the sentence

"The oam rose from the boiling pot."

people who have high verbal-intelligence scores are more likely to guess the meaning of the unknown word.

Figure 6.3 schematizes the cognitive science view. Consider any intellectual task: taking a test, playing chess, or writing a paper. Performance on the task is assumed to be an achieved "program", loosely analogous to a computer program, that constitutes a model of how a person does the task. The program for a given task will draw upon three sorts of more elementary capacities. These are (a) basic information-processing capacities, such as the lexical access process described earlier; (b) general knowledge about how to solve problems; and (c) task specific knowledge. Different tasks will depend upon specific elementary

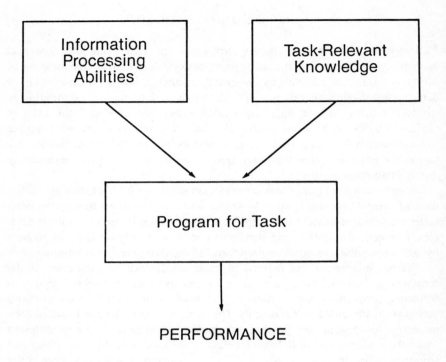

Figure 6.3. The cognitive science approach to thinking. A mental problem is solved by executing a task-specific "program" that requires the possession of relevant knowledge and the ability to execute the primitive information processing action that the program requires.

capacities to different degrees. The purpose of a cognitive-correlates study is to determine whether or not two tasks depend upon the same capacities. Particular interest centers upon those situations in which one of the tasks involved depends almost entirely upon a single elementary process. The lexical identification task described earlier is an example. When such a task is included in a cognitive-correlates study, it can be used as a calibrating measure of a theoretical entity much the way that the reading on a blood pressure "arm cuff" is used to define cardiac efficiency. The interpretability of such a study depends upon the validity of the theory used to select the calibrating task.

Strictly speaking, the cognitive-science approach does not contain a concept of "intelligence." Certainly intelligence tests have no special place in the theory. As intelligence tests are not important in themselves, (in the sense that performance in automobile driving or learning mathematics is important in itself), why bother to study them at all?

Test scores serve as a practical, albeit imperfect, way of identifying individuals whose performance "in life" does differ. By looking at the basic information processing and knowledge-possession correlates of test scores one has a heuristic method for identifying individual differences that are theoretically understandable and that may be important in a wide variety of human endeavors. Identifying these correlates is a first step toward identifying the individual differences that establish relative mental competence, but it is only a first step. The next step is to show how individual differences in basic information processing and individual differences in knowledge interact to produce individual differences in complex cognitive behavior. Studies aimed at this goal may not use intelligence tests at all.

There is another reason for being interested in the cognitive correlates of mental test performance. When different types of mental performance are graded, the scores are almost always positively correlated. Technically, this phenomenon is called *positive manifold*. For instance, although spatial and verbal intelligence are distinct dimensions of ability, there is usually a moderate positive correlation between spatial and verbal tests. One explanation for positive manifold is that it is produced by some underlying, nonbehavioral factor ("general intelligence") that influences a wide variety of cognitive processes. An appeal to general intelligence does not fit well with the cognitive-science approach that emphasizes the components of thinking. The phenomenon of positive manifold still must be explained.

There are two ways in which positive manifold could occur. The strategies for two different tasks may draw upon the same underlying knowledge and/or information-processing capacities. To the extent that this is so, one would expect positive correlations between the tasks. However, there is an important qualification to this conclusion. Correlations can be produced only if there are substantial individual differences in both variables. One can conceive of situations in which a particular information-processing capacity was vital to performance, but there were only small individual differences in the possession of that capacity. This is easily seen in terms of the athletic analogy. The fact that people are bipedal is crucial to an understanding of our motor performance, but the correlation between the "number of legs" and the performance of track-and-field competitors is zero. Because we cannot see mental capacities, cognitive examples are harder to give. They may well exist. For instance, short-term memory is obviously necessary for the comprehension of speech. However, it has been argued that there is so little variation in the short-term memory capacity of average individuals that it does not provide a good predictor of general intellectual capability (Matarazzo, 1972).

This example provides an illustration of the sort of questions that the cognitive science approach can raise. The fact is that in a population of people with normal intelligence short-term memory, *as measured by the digit span procedure used in the Wechsler Adult Intelligence Scale,* is not a terribly accurate predictor of general cognitive performance. Matarazzo (1972) suggested that this was because there is little interindividual variation in short-term memory itself. Klapp, Mashburn, and Lester (1983) have offered evidence showing that the testing procedure itself is not a good measure of short-term memory. In other words, Klapp et al. question the theory of the instrument, while Matarazzo explains the same observation by assuming something about the underlying phenomenon. More generally, the *absence* of an observed correlation can only be ascribed to an underlying cause if one has a good understanding of how the measuring instruments work.

Correlations between performances on complex mental tasks can occur even if the two tasks do not require the same elementary capacities, if people who possess the capacities required for the first task are statistically likely to possess the capacities required by the second. The studies of vocabulary knowledge can be seen in this light. Good performance on a vocabulary test requires knowledge of uncommon words, good performance on a paragraph comprehension test requires the ability to grasp the meaning of passages stated in common words. The two abilities are not the same, but a third variable (here, speculatively, the ability to understand meaning in context) may produce a correlation between the two.

How are the general considerations discussed thus far translated into practice? The next section discusses some of the practical problems of designing a cognitive correlates study, and illustrates them with two examples.

## THE CORRELATES APPROACH
## IN PRACTICE

The reason for studying cognitive correlates is usually to uncover a relation between two theoretical variables, such as "verbal intelligence" and "the ability to memorize information." What is observed, however, is a relation between overt measures, such as a person's score on the Wechsler Adult Intelligence Scale and the number of trials she or he requires to learn arbitrary word–number pairings. In all but a few experiments, the observable relation is of interest only insofar as it permits inferences about the unobservable theoretical relationship. The theoretical relations fall under two headings: (a) relations between observables and the theoretical variables they are intended to measure, and (b) relations between the theoretical variables themselves. This is illustrated in Figure 6.4. While the logic behind this figure may seem simplistic, it is important that it be grasped.[5]

---

[5]Figures 6.4, 6.8 and 6.9 resemble the usual diagrams for "causal modeling", as embodied in the statistical technique known as the Analysis of Covariance Structures (Jöreskog and Sörbom, 1979). The argument presented here is compatible with the logic behind the technique, but is intended to be generalized beyond a particular statistical procedure.

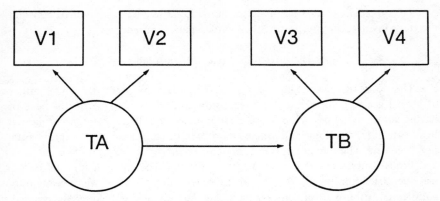

Figure 6.4. The typical study of cognitive correlates is intended to reveal the relation between theoretical variables (TA and TB). These are unobservable in principle, but are imperfectly revealed by observable measures. The data analyzed are the correlations between the observable measures (V1-V4).

In order to study the relation between theoretical variables one must have an explicit model of how they interact to produce observable performance. Consider the lexical-decision task. A possible model for this task is

1. Using the normal rules for English pronunciation, form an auditory representation of the visual stimulus.
2. Interrogate one's memory for words to determine whether the internally generated "sound" is the name of a word.
3. Depending on the outcome of 2., respond "yes" or "no" by pressing the appropriate key on the apparatus.

The processes involved in step 2 are clearly part of verbal intelligence; the processes in step 1 might be (or, more properly, might be part of reading ability), and the processes involved in step 3 would not normally be considered verbal intelligence. (A person with a sprained finger would be slow in executing step 3, but we would hesitate to say that the person's brain was injured.) The time taken to execute each process will be part of the observed reaction time. How are the processes to be measured separately?

The same argument can be made about a measure of "verbal intelligence." A simplified view of verbal processing assumes the following steps

1. Identify incoming symbols as words and fetch their meaning,
2. Connect the meaning of the word just fetched to the overall meaning of the sentence being processed or, if this cannot be done,
3. Hold the meaning of the newly identified word until further information is received that determines the word's meaning in context.

To appreciate why this model is needed, the reader is invited to consider the steps involved in interpreting the "garden path" sentence

The horse raced past the barn fell.

The point of these examples is not to argue for any particular model, either of lexical access or of verbal comprehension, but rather to argue for the need of having some model of each process. Such models are called *measurement models* in statistical terminology, and *process models* in the terminology of experimental psychologists. The two are not precisely equivalent.

Process models state how a task is performed. The model just given for lexical identification is an example. Measurement models state what elementary abilities contribute to an observable score, but do not state how the score is produced. Process models are intuitively more satisfying, because each parameter of a process model (e.g., the time required to search for an item in the lexicon) has an interpretation in terms of a psychological action. Unfortunately, process models often prove difficult to construct or analyze. Two people may approach the same task using different process models.[6] Also, process models may produce parameter estimates that are interpretable, but that have undesireable statistical properties. This is particularly true if a parameter estimate is based on the calculation of a difference between two error-prone scores. Conceptually, this is a nuisance, but practically it may prove an extremely difficult problem to solve. (See Lansman, 1981, for some interesting examples of the difficulty one can encounter using process models in studies of intelligence.)

Measurement models are much simpler to use, because they refer to the "average" contribution of a theoretical process to an observable task. For instance, one could postulate that "on the average", individual differences in visual to auditory conversion account for $x\%$ of the variance in the time required to make lexical identifications, $y\%$ of the individual variations in the lexical access process, and $z\%$ of the individual differences in response processes with $w\%$ left over. Given appropriate experimental designs (Bentler, 1980), these assumptions are testable. The same approach can be used with respect to the dependent variable. Once could construct a model in which short-term memory processes accounted for $a\%$ of the variation in individuals' ability to comprehend sentences, and identification processes accounted for y%. Again, the model would be testable and could be related to a model for lexical identification. The statistical and design issues involved in testing measurement models are much simpler to handle than those involved in analyzing process models. The drawback, though, is that a model that fits the averaged data may not fit the data for any one individual.

---

[6]For example, there is considerable evidence indicating that good readers often bypass the visual to auditory conversion step in reading (McCusker, Hillinger, & Bias, 1981).

Causal models link independent theoretical variables to dependent theoretical variables. The typical causal model assumes that the relationship between variables is linear and identical throughout the range of abilities in the population being studied. Causal models are of interest only in multivariate studies, for any study that deals with only two variables provides no way to distinguish between the observable correlations and different causal models that might have produced it.

Two illustrations of the analysis of correlational studies will be offered, taken from the study of spatial and verbal ability.

*Spatial Ability. Spatial ability* is, loosely, the ability to reason about visual displays. It is believed to be an important skill for many occupations involving mechanical skills, psychomotor co-ordination, and the interpretation of diagrams. Constructing a jig-saw puzzle is a good example of a task requiring high spatial ability. Spatial ability itself is divided into several subabilities. One of these is the ability to recognize relationships that are invariant when an object is rotated in two or three dimensions. This is called spatial relations ability (Egan, 1979). One of the most widely used tests of the ability to deal with spatial relations is the Primary Mental Abilities "Space" (PMA-Space) test (Thurstone, 1965). Figure 6.5 shows the sort of item that appears on the test. The examinee is shown a standard figure and five comparison figures. Each comparison item is constructed either by rotating the standard item in the picture plane or by rotating its mirror image. The examinee's task is to discriminate rotated standard items from rotated mirror images. The test score is the number of items answered correctly in a fixed time period.

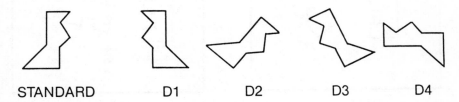

STANDARD　　　　　D1　　　　　D2　　　　　D3　　　　　D4

Figure 6.5. A test item similar to those used on the Primary Mental Abilities "Space" test. (The figure has been drawn for illustrative purposes only.) The left hand figure is a standard figure, the four right hand figures (D1 to D4) are comparison figures. The task is to indicate which of the comparison figures could be duplicated by rotating the standard figure in the picture plane.

Pellegrino and Kail (1982) report a series of studies in which they and their colleagues presented individual pairs of PMA standard and comparison figures and measured the time required to determine whether the two standard and comparison were identical except for orientation. The reason they did this was that a considerable body of other research had shown that comparison tasks such as this contain at least four distinct phases: (a) an encoding stage in which a mental representation is formed from the visual stimulus, (b) a rotation stage in which the two internal figures are somehow moved into identical orientation, (c) a comparison stage in which the aligned mental representations are compared, and (d) a response selection and execution stage (Cooper & Shepard, 1974). Pellegrino and Kail systematically varied the pairs of stimuli in order to obtain measures of people's ability to execute some (not all) of these stages. Figures 6.6 (a) and (b) show comparisons of two PMA figures that are identical except for the degree of rotation required to align figures. Figures 6.6 (c) and (d) show similar comparisons for familiar letter stimuli.

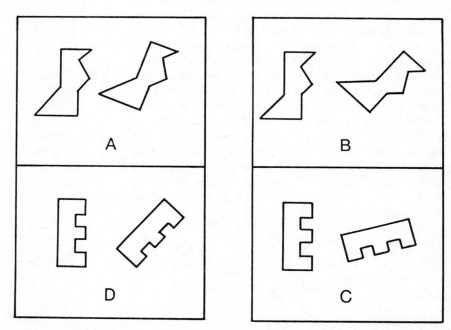

Figure 6.6. "PMA-like" items used in the studies reported by Pellegrino and Kale (1982). The observer is shown two items and asked if one could be produced by rotating the other in the picture plane. The items may require varying degrees of rotation (panels A and C vs. Panels B and D). The figures may be unfamiliar (panels A and B) or familiar letter-like figures (panels C and D).

Figure 6.7 shows how the time required to discriminate standard and mirror image figures changed as a function of angle of rotation. The relation is clearly linear. The slope of the linear function can be interpreted as a measure of the speed of rotation of an internal visual image. The intercept is assumed to reflect the time to form a visual image of the figures, before rotation and the time required to select and make a response. Note that in the Figure 6.7 the functions relating reaction time to angle of orientation are different for the two types of stimuli. Pellegrino and Kail argued that, when dealing with the PMA stimuli, subjects must develop new encoding and code manipulating processes, while well practiced processes can be used when dealing with letters.

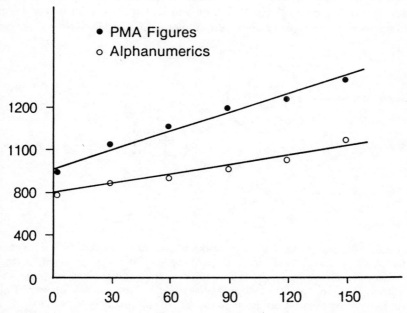

Figure 6.7. The time required to determine whether the items shown in Figure 6.6 are "same" or "different" varies linearly with the angle of rotation required. The function is different for familiar and unfamiliar stimuli, indicating that unfamiliar figures are dealt with more slowly "in the mind's eye." (The figure is redrawn from Pellegrino and Kail's report.)

The usual PMA score (the number of items correct) confounds the processes of encoding, mental rotation, and dealing with unfamiliar stimuli. Pellegrino and Kail (1982) showed that each of these processes make a separate contribution to the total score. Their statistical analysis, which was mildly complex, will not be presented here. What is important is the logic of their design.

Figure 6.8 is a diagram of the thinking behind the Pellegrino and Kail study. They began with a notion of "spatial relations", which was to be defined solely by score on the PMA. The PMA, however, had been chosen on the basis of the results from many studies that showed that it was indeed a marker test for a factor that influences many other psychometric tests. (This is shown by the dotted lines in Figure 6.8.) As independent theoretical variables Pellegrino and

Kail (1982) considered three elementary processes, each of which was defined by a particular experimental measure. The measure for each process was justified by appeal to a previously established process model for the task as a whole. One could conceive of other experimental situations that would draw on the same elementary processes assembled in different task models. If so, it should be possible to substitute or add the new measures (again shown by dotted lines, on the right of Figure 6.8). The Pellegrino and Kail study can be looked upon as a framework to be expanded in future studies using basically the same design.

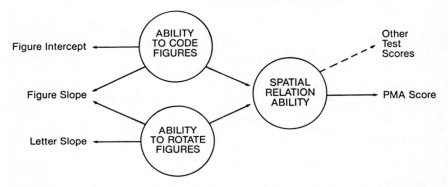

Figure 6.8. The logic of the Pellegrino and Kail studies. The psychometric factor "spatial relation ability" has been defined by several tests, among them the PMA-space test. Encoding ability was defined by the ability to deal with unfamiliar stimuli, rotation ability by the ability to deal with stimuli presented at different angles of orientation. Both contribute to the spatial relation dimension of individual differences.

### Verbal Comprehension

One of the reasons that the spatial-relations trait can be analyzed in terms of process models is that the trait itself is defined by explicit reference to well-defined tests. Verbal comprehension ability is not so easily defined. Loosely, this is the ability to extract meaning from written or spoken passages. Adult verbal comprehension is almost always tested by asking people to read brief passages and answer questions. Although people obviously can do this, it is not as easy to establish a model of comprehension as it is to establish a model for the solution of PMA space problems. On the other hand, a measurement model for comprehension can be defined.

Three classes of processes underlying comprehension can be identified: (a) elementary information processing steps that deal with the meaning of word or sentence units in isolation, (b) integrative processes that deal with the co-ordination of information presented in different parts of a text, and (c) pragmatic processes that deal with the meaning of a message in terms of information already possessed by the recipient. To appreciate the distinction between these processes, consider the brief story

> John was hungry so he went into a restaurant.
> After he had finished the meal he was embarrassed
> • to find that he had left his wallet at home.

In order to understand the story, word meanings must be fetched and sentences must be analyzed. Ambiguous references, for example, the "he" in the second sentence, must be connected to previous referents in the text. Understanding why John was embarrassed requires knowledge of restaurant customs.

Now consider how verbal comprehension is typically assessed: by giving a person something to read and then asking questions about it. This procedure confounds two issues: speed of reading and comprehension of a text that has been read. Intuitively, the processes involved in text integration and applying background knowledge should affect text comprehension. But what about the "lower order" processes of lexical access, parsing, and the recognition of simple, well known relationships? It is known that these processes are related to verbal comprehension in general (cf. the earlier citations to lexical access studies). Do they exert their influence through an influence on reading speed, or do they also influence the comprehension process? This question will be addressed in a constructed example, using some data gathered in a study done by my colleagues at the University of Washington (Palmer, MacLeod, Hunt & Davidson, 1984).

Seventy-five college students took tests of reading speed and separate tests of comprehension of material that had been read. The same students participated in experiments designed to evaluate various, elementary information-processing abilities thought to be important in reading. Only eight of the measures taken by Palmer et al. (1984) will be considered. Four of them were measures of reading:

1. The Nelson and Denny reading speed test. An examinee reads a paragraph for one minute, and then marks the last word read.
2. The Minnesota Reading Speed Test. The examinee reads short paragraphs containing an obviously irrelevant phrase. The phrase is to be crossed out. The score is the number of phrases crossed out in 5 minutes.
3. The Nelson and Denny reading comprehension test. The examinee reads short paragraphs and answers questions about these.
4. The Davis reading comprehension test. The procedure is essentially identical to the Nelson and Denny procedure.

The experimental tasks to be considered were:

5. Word matching. Two words were displayed. Words could be identical, as in the pair (SINK SINK); the same words in a different case, as in the pair (SINK sink); or different, as in the pairs (SINK WINK) or (SINK wink). The task was to indicate whether or not the two words' had the same "name", that is, if the words would be pronounced identically. Homonyms (e.g. DOUGH and DOE) were never presented.
6. Lexical access. The lexical-access task described earlier.
7. Picture–sentence verification. A picture was presented, either a plus above a star or a star above a plus. The picture display was then removed, and a sentence describing the picture was displayed, as in "The plus is above the star." The task was to indicate whether or not the sentence correctly described the picture.
8. Semantic verification. Subjects were shown a sentence asserting a class inclusion relation, for example, "A python is a snake."

The task was to indicate whether or not the inclusion relation was true.
Table 6.1 presents the correlation matrix for these tasks.

### Table 6.1. Correlations Between Verbal Tests and Experimental Tasks[a]

| Task | Test | | | | | | | |
|------|------|------|------|------|------|------|------|------|
|      | 1 | 2 | 3 | 4 | 5 | 6 | 7 | 8 |
| 1 |   | .66 | .53 | .40 | .30 | .27 | .24 | .39 |
| 2 |   |   | .37 | .33 | .18 | .27 | .25 | .32 |
| 3 |   |   |   | .80 | .29 | .30 | .36 | .47 |
| 4 |   |   |   |   | .30 | .33 | .43 | .44 |
| 5 |   |   |   |   |   | .71 | .51 | .78 |
| 6 |   |   |   |   |   |   | .55 | .84 |
| 7 |   |   |   |   |   |   |   | .92 |

The tests are: 1. Nelson-Denny Reading Speed Test; 2. Minnesota Reading Speed Test; 3. Nelson-Denny Reading Comprehension Test; 4. Davis Reading Comprehension Test; 5. Word matching; 6. Lexical access; 7. Picture–sentence verification; and 8. Semantic verification.

[a]Data from Palmer et al., 1984

Different process models clearly apply to the different experimental tasks. However, a "basic skill" ability could be said to exist if one underlying factor accounted for a substantial portion of the variation on all tasks. This is shown by the measurement model on the left of Figure 6.9. The numbers on the arrows leading from the "basic skill" circle to the four tasks were produced by a statistical analysis that estimated the extent to which a common, underlying skill could account for the variance on each of the individual tasks. This number, which is called a *loading,* is an estimate of the correlation between an hypothetical "basic skill" score and the observed score on each of the information processing measures.[7] As can be seen, the loadings are substantial. This suggests that the presumed "basic reading skills" trait does exist.

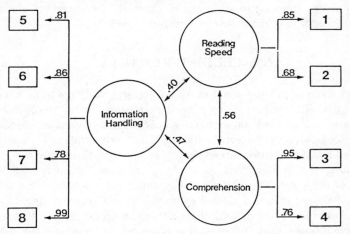

Figure 6.9. The results of a factor analysis of the data in Table 1. Two reading/ verbal comprehension abilities can be identified, reading speed and the ability to comprehend a text that has been read. The two are correlated. Both reading speed and comprehension are correlated with (and presumably depend upon) the ability to do the basic information processing actions involved in lexical access and syntactical and semantic analysis of simple sentences.

The measurement model applied to the reading tests is shown on the right of Figure 6.9. It assumes a "speed" trait, with loadings on the two, reading speed tests, and a "comprehension" trait, with loadings on the two comprehension tests. The speed and correlation traits were correlated ($r = .59$), indicating that people who read rapidly tend to comprehend well, but that the relationship is not perfect. This is a common finding (Perfetti, 1983).

The basic-skills trait was correlated with both the reading speed and reading comprehension traits ($r$ about .45 in each case). The relation between an ability

---

[7]Three factors were extracted from Table 6.1 using the Principal Factors method of analysis. The factors were then rotated to a best fit to a specified target matrix, using the Procrustes technique (Mulaik, 1972). The target matrix specified that the two reading speed measures define one factor, the two comprehension measures another, and the four experimental tasks define a third. Palmer et al. (1984) used the Analysis of Covariance Structures technique (Jöreskog, 1978) and based their analysis on additional variables. The analysis reported here is thus a very considerable summarization of the original results.

to execute elementary reading skills and reading comprehension is not mediated solely through reading speed. We may ask why this is so. (Speculation on the topic would carry us too far afield. See Hunt, in press, for a more complete discussion.) Also, the size of the correlations indicate that a substantial part of reading comprehension is not accounted for either by reading speed or by skill in elementary information processing. This result points the way toward further research. Future studies might well examine the relation between verbal comprehension and measures of integrative and pragmatic processes.

## CONCLUDING REMARKS

It is not possible to put the world into a laboratory. Many scientific questions must be answered by relying, in part, upon correlational data. An observed correlation must be explained: understanding depends upon observing correlations and explaining them by theoretical models. The models themselves may often be suggested by combinations of experimental and correlational studies.

To illustrate this point, let us return to an example introduced at the beginning of this paper, the fetal alcohol syndrome. It was pointed out that the correlation between maternal alcohol consumption and the child's mental status could be explained by two models: that drinking harms the fetus or that women who are predisposed to drink are also predisposed to have retarded children. Explanatory experimental studies argue strongly for the first explanation. Rats who are exposed to alcohol as their brains are developing show substantial neural damage (Diaz & Samson, 1980). Ethanol ingestion by pregnant monkeys induces anoxia in the fetus (Mukherjee & Hodgen, 1982). Such data provide a physiological explanation for a correlation between maternal alcohol ingestion and brain condition. What we do not know, yet, is precisely how the brain condition affects intellectual behavior in humans. We strongly suspect that a causal relation does exist. The physiologists have done their bit; the next step is up to the psychologist.

There will always be gaps in causal reasoning. How far one wants to go in explaining a correlation depends on one's purpose. Studies of cognitive correlates can tell us a great deal about intelligence if these studies are guided by well constructed theory.

## REFERENCES

Bentler, P. M. (1980). Multivariate analysis with latent variables: Causal modeling. *Annual Review of Psychology, 31,* 419–456.
Boring, E. G. (1923). Intelligence as the tests test it. *The New Republic.* (June 6) 35–37.

Cooper, L., & Shepard, R. (1973). Chronometric studies of mental images. In Chase, W. G. (Ed.) *Visual Information Processing*. New York: Academic Press.

Diaz, J., & Samson, H. H. (1980). Impaired brain growth in neonatal rats exposed to alcohol. *Science, 208,* 751-753.

Egan, D. (1979). Testing based on understanding: Implications from studies of spatial ability. *Intelligence, 3,* 1-15.

Hunt, E. (1983). The nature of intelligence. *Science, 219,* 141-146.

Hunt, E. (in press). Verbal ability. In R. J. Sternberg (Ed.), *Human Abilities: An Information Processing Approach*. San Francisco: Freeman.

Hunt, E., Davidson, J. E., & Lansman, M. (1981). Individual differences in long term memory access. *Memory and Cognition, 9,* 599-608.

Jöreskog, K. G. (1978). Structural analysis of covariance and correlation matrices. *Psychometrika, 43,* 443-477.

Klapp, S. T., Marshburn, E. A., & Lester, P. T. (1983). Short-term memory does not involve the "Working memory" of information processing: The demise of a common assumption. *Journal of Experimental Psychology: General 112*(2), 240-264.

Lansman, M. (1981). Ability factors and the speed of verbal processing. In Friedman, M. P., Das, J. P., and O'Connor, N. *Intelligence and Learning*. New York: Plenum Press.

Loehlin, J. C., Lindzey, G., & Spuhler, J. N. (1975). *Race Differences in Intelligence*. San Francisco, CA: Freeman.

McCusker, L. X., Hillinger, M. L., & Bias, R. G. (1981). Phonological recoding and reading. *Psychology Bulletin, 89,* 217-245.

Matarazzo, J. D. (1972). *Wechsler's measurement and appraisal of adult intelligence*. (5th ed.) Baltimore, MD: Williams and Wilkins.

Mukherjee, A. B., & Hodgen, G. D. (1982). Maternal ethanol exposure induces transient impairment of umbilical circulation and fetal hypoxia in monkeys. *Science, 218,* 700-702.

Mulaik, S. A. The foundations of factor analysis. New York: McGraw-Hill, 1972.

Palmer, J. P., MacLeod, C. M., Hunt, E., and Davidson, J. E. (in press). Some relations between information processing and reading. *Journal of Verbal Learning and Verbal Behavior.*

Pellegrino, J. W., & Glaser, R. (1979). Cognitive correlates and components in the analysis of individual differences. *Intelligence, 3,* 187-214.

Pellegrino, J. W., & Kail, J. (1982). Process analysis of spatial aptitude. In Sternberg, R. J. (ed.) *Advances in the Study of Intelligence*. (Vol. 1). Hillsdale, NJ: Erlbaum Associates.

Perfetti, C. A. (1983). Individual differences in verbal processes. In R. F. Dillon and R. R. Schmeck, (Eds.) *Individual differences in cognition*. New York: Academic Press.

Sternberg, R. J. (1984). Intelligence testing without intelligence tests. Address to Division 1, American Psychological Association Meetings. Washington, DC.

Sternberg, R. J., & Powell, J. S. (1983). Comprehending verbal comprehension. *American Psychologist, 8,* 878-893.

Streissguth, A. P., Lanesman-Dwyer, S., Martin, J. C., and Smith, D. W. (1980).

Tetragenic effects of alcohol in human and laboratory animals. *Science, 209*, 1343-1347.

Thurstone, T. G. (1965). *Technical Report: Primary Mental Abilities, 1962 Revision.* Chicago IL: Science Research Associates.

Warren, J., & Hunt, E. (1981). Cognitive processing in children with Prader-Willi Syndrome. In Holme, V. A., Sulzbacher, S. J., & Pipes, P. L. (eds.) Prader-Willi Syndrome. Baltimore, MD: University Park Press.

Wechsler, D. (1975). Intelligence defined and redefined: A relativistic appraisal. *American Psychologist, 30*, 135-139.

# CHAPTER 7

# Componential Analysis: A Recipe*

Robert J. Sternberg

*Yale University*

## INTRODUCTION

Many psychological phenomena are so very complex that no single approach to understanding these phenomena seems capable of doing justice to their complexity. Intelligence would seem to be a prime example of such a phenomenon. No matter how one defines intelligence, its complexity seems to overwhelm the conceptual resources any one approach can bring to bear upon understanding it. Even limited aspects of intelligence seem almost staggering in their complexity. Consider, for example, that aspect of intelligence measured by conventional IQ tests. If almost a century of research on IQ test performance has shown anything, it is that no simple conceptual scheme or methodological approach has been, or perhaps will be, able to understand all the complexities that underlie test performance. The conceptual scheme and methodology one chooses will of course depend in large part upon the kinds of questions one wishes to address.

Two classes of questions that have been particularly salient in the literature on intelligence are ones concerning the origins of subject variation in test performance and ones concerning the origins of item or stimulus variation in such performance. The first question deals with what makes some individuals score higher than others on intelligence tests; the second question deals with what makes some intelligence-test items easier than others. Traditionally, these questions were addressed by different investigators, and by different research paradigms.

The question of individual differences has traditionally been addressed through the use of psychometric methodologies. These methodologies have had

*Preparation of this chapter was supported by Contract N0001483K0013 from the Office of Naval Research and the Army Research Institute to Robert J. Sternberg.

in common their reliance upon correlational techniques, and especially factor analysis, which seeks to discover the latent, psychological sources of observed variation on psychometric tests, including tests of intelligence. Factor analysis starts with a matrix of intercorrelations between all possible pairs of tests in a battery, and ends up with a matrix of correlations between these tests and a set of factors that is postulated to underlie observed, individual differences on the tests. This final matrix thus tells the investigator the extent to which each test measures each factor identified in the analysis. The factors are generally considered to represent latent "mental abilities."

Although the problems associated with the use of traditional factor analysis are of some consequence (see, e.g., Sternberg, 1977b), many investigators believe that factor analysis provides a useful method for exploratory theorizing and data analysis (e.g., Humphreys, 1962; Sternberg, 1977b, 1980c; Thurstone, 1947). Moreover, its usefulness for providing a sort of broad topographical map for the structure of human intelligence seems almost unquestionable (Burt, 1940; Carroll, 1981; Vernon, 1971). If traditional factor analysis has been unilluminating in any respect, at least to date, that respect would seem to be in its ability to reveal the mental processes underlying human intelligence (Eysenck, 1967; Sternberg, 1977b). Not all investigators would agree with this assessment (Carroll, 1981; Guilford, 1967). But I am unaware of any instance in which traditional (i.e., exploratory) factor analysis has succeeded in the direct isolation of the processes underlying intelligent performance, whether it be on tests or on anything else.

An alternative approach to understanding human intelligence has specialized in addressing precisely those questions that the psychometric approach seems least adept at addressing, in particular, those questions regarding the processes people use in task performance. This approach, the cognitive or information-processing approach, uses a variety of methods of task analysis to identify these latent processes. One method, the "thinking-aloud" method, has subjects describe how they are performing a task at the time they are performing it. These protocols are then used as a basis for formulating or testing a theory of mental processing. A second method, computer simulation, is sometimes used in conjunction with the thinking-aloud method. In this method, a computer program is written that is alleged to mimic the processes human subjects use in performing the task or tasks under study. Outputs from program execution are sometimes compared to data from human subjects to evaluate the validity of the computer model. Indeed, just getting the program to run is often considered a major accomplishment, in that it demonstrates the sufficiency (if not the validity) of the model for performing the given task. A third method, mathematical modeling, seeks to simulate task performance by producing a set of equations that, with the proper substitutions for variables, predict human performance on the cognitive tasks in question. All of these methods, then, have in common their attempts to isolate the processes and strategies underlying cognitive-task performance.

Information-processing methodologies, like psychometric methodologies, are not above question or reproach (see, e.g., Sternberg, 1977b). Few people, however, seem to have questioned their usefulness for process analysis. If there is any respect in which they have fallen short, it would seem to be in their utilization for the analysis of individual differences and of the latent structures underlying task performance. Traditionally, information-processing researchers have simply not been terribly interested in individual-differences analysis. And this lack of interest was expressed in papers that analyzed task variation at the same time that they treated subject variation as unwelcome "noise" in the data.

Cronbach (1957), recognizing the complementarity of the substantive questions that correlational and experimental (cognitive) methods had addressed, proposed that attempts be made to unify the two disciplines of scientific psychology: experimental and correlational psychology. After some years of a lull, aggressive attempts have recently been made to do just that. Componential analysis, the subject of this chapter, is one such attempt that seeks to bring together the best of the psychometric and cognitive approaches to understanding human intelligence.

The goal of this chapter is to enable an investigator to perform a componential analysis. To this end, the chapter is pragmatically organized as a "recipe," presenting the reader with the successive steps one uses in performing a componential analysis.

## OVERVIEW OF COMPONENTIAL ANALYSIS

### Step 1: Selecting or Generating a Theory of Relevant Cognition

The first thing one has to do is to decide what it is one wishes to analyze. Such a decision requires a theory of that aspect of cognition for which one wishes to perform the componential analysis. There are any number of criteria on the basis of which one might evaluate either preexisting theories or one's own new theory. I have proposed five criteria that I believe are particularly useful for this purpose.

1. *Completeness.* A complete theory is one that accounts for all processes involved in the area of cognition of interest.
2. *Specificity.* A specific theory describes in detail the workings of each aspect of cognition. A theory can be complete but not specific if it accounts for all processes, representations, structures, and so on, but does not describe the workings of the processes in detail. A theory can also be specific but not complete if it describes in detail a proper subset of processes, structures, and representations involved in the relevant area of cognition.
3. *Generality.* A theory is general if it is applicable across a wide range of problems within the relevant domain of cognition.

4. *Parsimony.* A theory is parsimonious if it can account for performance in the relevant domain of cognition with a relatively small number of parameters and working assumptions. Parsimony is difficult to evaluate, in part, because many theories that appear parsimonious on their surface have hidden assumptions, whereas other theories that appear less parsimonious can be taken more easily at face value. As might be expected, there tends to be a tradeoff between parsimony, on the one hand, and completeness and specificity, on the other. A difficult problem facing theorists is to strike a reasonable balance between them.

5. *Plausibility.* A theory is plausible if it is able to account for experimental (or other) data that provide a test of the theory. Plausibility also involves intuitive judgments about the reasonableness of the theory. If one theory seems less reasonable on its face than another theory, skeptics may require more compelling evidence to convince them of the former theory than to convince them of the latter theory.

## Step 2: Selecting One or More Tasks for Analysis

Tasks can be selected for componential analysis on the basis of their satisfaction of four criteria originally proposed by Sternberg and Tulving (1977) in a different context (see also Sternberg, 1982): quantifiability, reliability, construct validity, and empirical validity.

1. *Quantifiability.* The first criterion, quantifiability, assures the possibility of the "assignment of numerals to objects or events according to rules" (Stevens, 1951, p. 1). Quantification is rarely a problem in research on intellectual abilities. Occasionally, psychologists are content to use subjects' introspective reports or protocols as their final, dependent variable. The protocols, used in and of themselves, fail the test of quantification. If, however, aspects of the protocols are quantified (see, e.g., Newell & Simon, 1972) and thus rendered subject to further analysis, these quantifications can be acceptable dependent variables so long as they meet the other criteria.

2. *Reliability.* The second criterion, reliability, measures true-score variation relative to total-score variation. In other words, it measures the extent to which a given set of data is systematic. Reliability needs to be computed in two different ways, across item types and across subjects. Because the two indices are independent, a high value of one provides no guarantee or even indication of a high value of the other. Each of these two types of reliability can be measured in two ways, at a given time or over time.

3. *Construct validity.* The third criterion, construct validity, assures that the task has been chosen on the basis of some psychological theory. The theory thus dictates the choice of tasks, rather than the other way around. A task that is construct-valid is useful for gaining psychological insights through the lens provided by some theory of cognition.

4. *Empirical validity*. The fourth criterion, empirical validity, assures that the task serves the purpose it is supposed to serve. Thus, whereas construct validity guarantees that the selection of a task is motivated by theory, empirical validity tests the extent to which the theory is empirically supportable. Empirical validation is usually performed by correlating task performance with an external criterion.

These four criteria are related to each other in a number of ways. First, they fall into two natural and orthogonal groupings of two criteria each. The first and second criteria are ones of measurement theory; the third and fourth are ones of substantive psychological theory. The first and third criteria are discrete and dichotomous, being either satisfied or not; the second and fourth criteria are continuous, being satisfied in greater or lesser degree. Second, the criteria fall into a natural ordering. The first two criteria, those of measurement theory, are prerequisite for the second two criteria, those of psychological theory: The tasks must satisfy certain measurement properties before their psychological properties can be assessed. Moreover, the criteria are ordered within these groupings as well as between them. The first criterion within each grouping is prerequisite for the second. Reliability presupposes quantification in that reliability measures the extent to which the measurement obtained by the quantification is consistent. Empirical validity presupposes construct validity in that empirical validity measures the extent to which the measurements dictated by the theory correspond to that theory.

## Step 3: Decomposing Task Performance

Most tasks, indeed, all of the tasks that my collaborators and I have investigated, can be decomposed into subtasks, where a subtask is defined in terms of its involvement of a subset of the information-processing components that are involved in the full task. There are a number of reasons for attempting to isolate information-processing components from subtasks rather than from composite tasks. First, it is often possible to isolate information-processing components from subtasks that cannot be isolated from composite tasks. The smaller the number of information-processing components involved in any single subtask, the greater the likelihood that the individual components will be susceptible to isolation. Second, use of subtasks requires the investigator to specify in which subtask or subtasks each information-processing component is executed and thus requires tighter, more nearly complete specification of the relationship between task structure and the components that act on that structure. Third, use of subtasks increases the number of data points to be accounted for and thus helps to guard against the spurious good fit between model and data that can result when the number of parameters to be estimated becomes large relative to the number of data points to be predicted. Fourth, use of subtasks results in component-free estimates of performance for a series of nested processing intervals. These estimates can be valuable when one wants to test alternative predictions about global stages of information processing. The decomposition of composite tasks into subtasks, then, represents a useful intermediate step in the analysis of the nature of mental abilities. There are a number of different ways of decomposing composite tasks into subtasks. Some of these will be considered below.

## The Precueing Method of Task Decomposition

In the method of precueing, the first step in a componential analysis is to form interval scores from the decomposition of the global task into a series of nested subtasks, as was done by Johnson (1960) in his pioneering method of serial analysis. The method yields *interval scores* for each of the nested subtasks. Each interval score is a score on one of the series of subtasks and measures performance on a subset of the information-processing components required by the total task. Each subtask in the series of subtasks requires successively less information processing, and hence should involve reduced processing time and difficulty. Consider two examples of the use of precueing.

### Analogies

An example of the use of precueing can be found in the decomposition of performance in analogical reasoning (Sternberg, 1977a, 1977b). Consider the analogy, "FOUR SCORE AND SEVEN YEARS AGO": LINCOLN:: "I'M NOT A CROOK": (a) NIXON, (b) CAPONE. In order to decompose the task, one can eliminate from the subject's information processing successive terms of the analogy. Since the analogy has five terms, up to five subtasks can be formed, although there seems to be no good reason for splitting up the two answer options. Consider, then, four subtasks. In each case, we divided presentation trials into two parts. In the first part, the experimenter presents the subject with some amount of precueing to facilitate solution of the analogy. In the second part, that of primary interest, the experimenter presents the full analogy. Solution of the analogy, however, is assumed to require merely a subset of the full set of components (that is, to be a subtask of the full task), because the experimenter assumes that the subject utilized the precueing presented in the first part of the trial to reduce the processing load in the second part of the trial. Indeed, subjects are encouraged to use the precueing information in order to help their processing in the second part of the trial. In the description of task decomposition that follows, it will be assumed that the analogies are presented either tachistoscopically or via a computer terminal.

In the first subtask (which is identical to the full task), the subject is presented with a blank field (null precueing) in the first part of the trial. The subject indicates readiness to proceed, and then the full analogy appears. The subject solves the analogy, and then presses a button indicating a response of (a) or (b). In the second subtask, the subject still needs to perform most of the task in the second part of the trial. The first part of the trial consists merely of precueing with the first term of the analogy. The subject presses a button to indicate that this term has beeen processed, and then the whole analogy appears on the screen. The subject solves it, and then indicates a response. Note that although the full analogy was presented in the second part of the trial, only the last four terms needed to be processed, since the first term had been preprocessed during precueing. The third subtask involves a smaller subset of the task to be performed in the second part of the trial. The first part of the trial consists of presentation of the first two terms of the analogy; the second part consists of full presentation. The fourth subtask involves a very small subset of the full task in the second part of the trial. The first part of the trial consists of a presentation of the first three terms of the analogy; the second part consists of a full presentation but requires processing of only the last two terms.

The task decomposition described above serves to separate components of information processing that would be confounded if only the full task were presented. In order to see why, one must first know something about the proposed theory of analogical reasoning (Sternberg, 1977a, 1977b). According to the theory, a solution of an analogy requires: (a) *encoding* of each term of the analogy; (b) *inference* of the relation between the first two terms of the analogy ("FOUR SCORE AND SEVEN YEARS AGO" is a quotation from LINCOLN); (c) *mapping* of the relation between the first and third terms of the analogy ("FOUR SCORE AND SEVEN YEARS AGO" and "I'M NOT A CROOK" are both quotations); (d) *application* of the relation from the third term to the answer options ("I'M NOT A CROOK" is a quotation from Nixon, not Capone); and (e) *response* (the correct answer is "a"). Optionally, a sixth *justification* process may be used to justify one option as superior when none seems to be exactly correct. Suppose only the full task were presented to subjects. Then, according to certain information-processing models of analogical reasoning (described in detail in Sternberg, 1977b ) under the general theory, (a) encoding and response would be confounded, since response is constant across all analogy types (five analogy terms always need to be encoded); and (b) inference and application would be confounded, because the relation between the third term and the correct option is always the same as that between the first two terms. But precueing permits disentanglement of components by selective dropout of components required for processing. By varying the amount of encoding required for various subtasks, the method of precueing permits separation of encoding from the response constant. And by eliminating the inference components from the third and fourth subtasks (while retaining the application component), it becomes possible to distinguish inference from application. Recall that in these two subtasks the first two terms of the analogy were presented during precueing, so that inference could be completed before the full analogy was presented.

The precueing method obviously assumes additivity across subtasks. Two methods of testing additivity have been proposed (Sternberg, 1977b), although they can only be briefly noted here. The first requires testing of interval scores for simplicial structure (correlations descending as they become more distant from the main diagonal of a correlation matrix). The second involves comparison of parameter estimates for the uncued condition alone with those for all the conditions combined. Ideally, this comparison would be done between subjects (just in case the very use of precueing affects performance even on items receiving only null precueing); in practice, the comparison may end up being within-subject (with the same subjects receiving each experimental treatment). The data from three experiments on analogical reasoning showed reasonable conformity to the assumption of additivity. More importantly, even when the assumption of additivity was violated to some degree, the method of precueing proved to be robust, yielding sensible and informative data nevertheless. The method was quite successful in its application to analogy problems. The best model under the theory of analogical reasoning accounted for 92%, 86%, and 80% of the variance in the latency data for experiments using People Piece (schematic pictures of people varying on four binary dimensions: height, color, sex, and weight), verbal, and geometric analogies (Sternberg, 1977b).

## Linear Syllogisms

The method of precueing has also been applied in two experiments on linear syllogisms, or three-term series problems (Sternberg, 1980b). In the first experiment, subjects were presented with problems such as "John is taller than Pete. Pete is taller than Bill. Who is tallest? John, Pete, Bill." Order of names was counterbalanced. Trials again occurred in two parts. In the first part, subjects received either a blank field or the two premises of the problem. (A third condition, involving presentation of only the first premise, might have been used but was not.) In the second part, subjects received the whole problem. In each trial, subjects indicated when they were ready to receive the whole item, and then indicated as their response one of the three terms of the problem. A possible limitation of this manner of presentation is that it seems to force serial-ordered processing, whereas when left to their own devices, subjects might process the problems differently, for example, by reading the question first. A second experiment was therefore done.

In the second experiment, the same type of problem was used, except that the question was presented first: "Who is tallest? John is taller than Pete. Pete is taller than Bill. John, Pete, Bill." Again, order of names was counterbalanced. There were three precueing conditions. In the first, a blank field was presented during the first part of the trial. In the second, only the question was presented during the first part of the trial. In the third, the question and the premises were presented during the first part of the trial, so that in the second part of the trial the subjects needed to discover only the ordering of the answer options. The full problem was always presented in the second part of the trial.

The methodology was again quite successful. The best model, my own mixed model (Sternberg, 1980b), accounted for 98% of the variance in the latency data from the first experiment, and 97% of the variance in the latency data from the second experiment. In these experiments (unlike in the analogy experiments), model fits were substantially lower in the conditions comprising the full problems only: 81% and 74%. Worth noting, however, is that the reliabilities of these subsets of the latency data were only .86 and .82, meaning that even here most of the reliable variance was accounted for. The higher fits of the models to data with precueing were due to disentanglement of encoding from response. When only full problems are presented, it is impossible to separate premise encoding time from response time, as both are constant over problem types: There are always two premises and one response. Separation of the encoding component substantially increased the variance in the latency data, and hence the values of $R^2$.

## Other Problem Types

The method of precueing has also been applied in the presentation of classification and series-completion problems (Sternberg & Gardner, 1983). In the classification problems, subjects were presented with two groups of two items each, and a target item. The subjects had to indicate in which group the target belonged. For example, one group might be (a) ROBIN, SPARROW, and the other, (b) HADDOCK, FLOUNDER. If the target were BLUEJAY, the correct answer would be (a). Precueing was accomplished by presenting either a blank field in the first part of the trial, or just the two groups of items without the target. Further precueing might have been accomplished by presenting just one group of items in the first part of the trial, although this was not done in this particular experiment.

In the series-completion problems, subjects were presented with a linear ordering that they had to complete, for example, INFANT, CHILD, ADOLESCENT, (a) ADULT, (b) TEENAGER. Precueing was accomplished by presenting either a blank field or just the first three terms of the item in the first part of the trial. Again, more fine-grained precueing might have been done, but wasn't.

Precueing in these experiments, as in the analogies and linear syllogisms experiment, was quite successful. Models provided good fits to the latency data for schematic-picture, verbal, and geometric items. Details can be found in Sternberg and Gardner (1983).

*Evaluation of method.* The method of precueing has both positive and negative aspects. On the positive side: (a) it permits disentanglement of components that otherwise would be confounded; (b) by doing so, it permits comparison of models that otherwise would be indistinguishable; (c) it increases the number of data points to be modeled, thereby helping to guard against the spurious good fit that can result when relatively large numbers of parameters are estimated for relatively small numbers of observations; (d) it requires the investigator to specify in what interval(s) of processing each mental operation takes place, thereby forcing the investigator to explicate the model in considerable detail; and (e) it provides scores for performance in a series of nested processing intervals, rather than merely for the total task. On the negative side: (a) the method requires at least a semblance of additivity across subtasks; (b) it requires use of tachistoscopic or computer equipment to present each trial; (c) it requires individual testing; and (d) it is not suitable for young children because of its complexity. In the uses to which the method has been put so far, the advantages of precueing have more than offset its limitations.

## Method of Partial Tasks

In the method of partial tasks, complete items are presented involving either a full set of hypothesized components or just some subset of these components. The method differs from the method of precueing in that trials are not split into two parts. Decomposition is effected with unitary trials. The partial and full tasks, however, are assumed to be additively related, as in the method of precueing. Consider two examples of the use of this method.

### Linear Syllogisms

The method of partial tasks has been used in four experiments on linear syllogisms (Sternberg, 1980a, 1980b). The full task consisted of the standard linear syllogism (three-term series problem) as described earlier. The partial task consists of two-term series problems, for example, "John is taller than Pete. Who is tallest?" (The ungrammatical superlative was used in the question to preserve uniformity with the three-term series problems.) The mixed model of linear syllogistic reasoning specified component processes involved in both the two- and three-term series problems, specifying the processes involved in the former as a subset of the processes involved in the latter. The values of $R^2$ were .97, .97, and .97 with all items considered, and .84, .88, and .84 with only three-term series problems considered. Note that these values are quite similar to those obtained under the method of precueing. Values of parameters were also generally similar.

### Categorical Syllogisms

The method of partial tasks has also been applied in the investigation of categorical syllogisms (Sternberg & Turner, 1981). The full task was a standard categorical syllogism, with premises like "All B are C. Some A are B." The subject was presented with a conclusion, such as "All A are C," and had to indicate whether this conclusion was definitely true, possibly true, or never true of the premises. The partial task involved presentation of only a single premise, such as "Some A are B." The subject again had to decide whether a conclusion, such as "All A are B," was definitely, possibly, or never true of the (in this case, single) premise.

Whereas the primary dependent variable of interest in the previously de-scribed experiments was solution latency, the primary dependent variable in this experiment was response choice. The preferred model of syllogistic reasoning, the transitive-chain model, accounted for 96% of the variance in the response-choice data from the full task, and 96% of the variance in the response-choice data from the partial task. Fits were not computed for the combined data, as in this particular experiment we happened to be interested in the full task as an "encoding plus combination task" and in the partial task as an "encoding only" task. These data indicate not only that the method of partial tasks can be applied successfully to categorical syllogisms, but that it can be applied to response-choice as well as to latency data.

*Evaluation of Method.* This method seems to share all of the advantages of the method of precueing, but only one of its disadvantages, namely, the as-sumption of additivity, in this case between the partial and the full task. The method of partial tasks therefore seems to be the preferred method when one has the option of using either of the two methods. Two additional points need to be considered. First, additivity may be obtained across precueing conditions but not from partial to full tasks, or vice versa. Thus, some amount of pilot testing may be needed to determine which method is more likely to yield addi-tivity across conditions. Second, some tasks are decomposable by either method, but others may be decomposable only by one or the other method. I have found the method of precueing applicable to more tasks than the method of partial tasks, although the differential applicability may be a function of the particular tasks I have investigated. In any case, the decision of which method to use can be made only after a careful consideration of task demands and decomposability. In some cases, the investigator may choose to use both methods, as in Stern-berg (1980b).

## Method of Stem-Splitting

The method of stem-splitting involves items requiring the same number of information-processing components, but different numbers of executions of the various components. It combines features of the method of precueing with those of the method of partial tasks.

### Analogies

So far, the method has been applied only to verbal analogies. Using the method of stem-splitting, we presented verbal analogies in three different formats (Stern-berg & Nigro, 1980):

1. RED : BLOOD :: WHITE : (a) COLOR, (b) SNOW
2. RED : BLOOD :: (a) WHITE : SNOW, (b) BROWN : COLOR
3. RED : (a) BLOOD :: WHITE : SNOW, (b) BRICK :: BROWN : COLOR

The number of answer options was allowed to vary from two to four for individual items. Consider how the different item types involve different numbers of executions of the same components. The first item requires encoding of five terms, inference of one relation, mapping of one relation, application of two relations, and one response. The second item requires encoding of six terms, inference of one relation, mapping of two relations, application of two relations, and one response. The third item requires encoding of seven terms, inference of two relations, mapping of two relations, application of two relations, and one response. (In each case, exhaustive processing of the item is assumed.) Varying the number of answer options also creates further variance in the numbers of operations required.

This method has been used with children as young as at the third-grade level and as old as at the college level. The data from the experiment were quite encouraging, both for the tested theory and the method. Multiple correlations *(R)* between predicted and observed data points were .85, .88, .89, and .92 for the preferred models in grades 3, 6, 9, and college, respectively.

*Evaluation of Method.* This method has barely been tried, and so I am not in a position to evaluate it fully. On the positive side: (a) it could be (although it has not yet been) used for group testing in conjunction with booklets of the kind described in the next section; (b) it requires no special equipment to administer items; (c) it is feasible with young children; and (d) it seems to create a certain added interest to the problems for the subjects. On the negative side: (a) the success of the method has not yet been adequately tested; (b) the generality of the method to problems other than analogies has not yet been shown; and (c) the method seems more likely than the preceding ones to generate special strategies that are inapplicable to standard (complete) tasks.

## Method of Systematically Varied Booklets

In previous methods, the unit of presentation was the single item. In this method, the unit of presentation is the booklet. In previous methods, subjects were given as long as they needed to complete each individual item. In this method, subjects are given a fixed amount of time to complete as many items as they can within a given booklet. The number of items in the booklet should exceed the number of items that subjects can reasonably be expected to complete in the given time period. The key to the method is that all items in the booklet should be homogenous with respect to the theory or theories being tested. Although the same items are not repeated, each item serves as a replication with respect to the sources of difficulty specified by the theory. Although items within a given booklet are homogeneous, items are heterogeneous across booklets. In this method, specifications of the items within a booklet are varied in the same way that specifications of single items are varied in the preceding methods.

## *Analogies*

The method of systematically varied booklets has been employed only with two types of schematic-picture analogies (Sternberg & Rifkin, 1979). In the two experiments done so far, the method has been used successfully with children as young as the second-grade level and as old as college age. Subjects at each grade level were given 64 seconds in which to solve the 16 analogies contained in each booklet. Independent variables were numbers of schematic features changed between the first and second analogy terms, first and third analogy terms, and the first and second analogy answer options. Items within a given booklet were identical in each of these respects. Three dependent variables were derived from the raw data. The first was latency for correctly answered items, obtained by dividing 64 by the number of items correctly completed. This measure takes into account both quality and quantity of performance. The second dependent variable was latency for all answered items, obtained by dividing 64 by the number of items completed, whether they were completed correctly or incorrectly. This measure takes into account only quantity of performance. The third dependent variable was error rate, obtained by dividing the number of items answered incorrectly by the number of items answered at all. This measure takes into account only quality of performance.

In a first experiment, model fits ($R^2$) for the best model were .91, .95, .90, and .94 for latencies of correct reponses at grades 2, 4, 6, and college respectively; they were .87, .94, .93, and .94 for latencies of all responses at each grade level; and they were .26, .86, .52, and .65 for error rates at each level. The fits for errors, although lower than for the latencies, were almost at the same levels as the reliabilities of each of the sets of data, indicating that only slightly better fits could possibly have been obtained. Model fits in a second experiment were slightly lower than in the first experiment, but so were the reliabilities of the data.

*Evaluation of method.* The method of systematically varied booklets has three distinct advantages and two distinct disadvantages. Its advantages are that (a) it is practical even with very young children; (b) it requires no special equipment for test administration; and (c) it is adopted for group testing. Its disadvantages are that (a) it is not possible to obtain a pure measure of time spent only on items answered correctly (or incorrectly), because times are recorded only for booklets, not for individual items; and (b) the method is not particularly well suited to disentangling components. In some of the models tested, for example, encoding and response, and inference and application, were confounded.

# Method of Complete Tasks (Standard Method of Presentation)

The method of complete tasks is simply the standard method of presenting only the composite item. It is suited to items in which no confoundings of components occur. Consider two examples of the use of the method.

### Categorical Syllogisms

The method of complete tasks was used in the presentation of categorical syllogisms (Guyote & Sternberg, 1981). In a first experiment, subjects were presented with syllogistic premises, such as "All B are C. All A are B," plus a set of four possible conclusions (called A, E, I, and O in the literature on syllogistic reasoning), "All A are C. No A are C. Some A are C. Some A are not C," plus the further conclusion, "None of the above." Subjects had to choose the preferred conclusion from among the five. In a second experiment, concrete rather than abstract terms were used. Premises were either factual (No cottages are skyscrapers), counterfactual (No milk cartons are containers), or anomalous (No headphones are planets). In a third experiment, the quantifiers "most" and "few" were used instead of "some." In a fourth experiment, premises were presented in the form "All A are B. X is an A" and subjects were asked simply to judge whether a conclusion such as "X is a B" was valid or invalid. Our transitive-chain model outperformed the other models of response choice to which it was compared, yielding values of $R^2 = .97$ for abstract content, .91 for concrete factual content, .92 for concrete counterfactual content, .89 for concrete anomalous content, .94 when "most" and "few" were substituted for "some," and .97 for the simpler syllogisms requiring only a valid-invalid judgment. Latency models were also fit to some of the data, with excellent results.

### Conditional Syllogisms

The method of complete tasks was also used in testing the transitive-chain model on conditional syllogisms of the form "If A then B. A. Therefore, B." The subject's task was to evaluate the conclusion as either valid or invalid. The model accounted for 95% of the variance in the response-choice data.

*Evaluation of Method.* The main advantages of this method are that it is the simplest of the methods described, and it does not require any assumptions about additivity across conditions of decomposition. The main disadvantage of the method is that in many, if not most tasks, information-processing components will be confounded. These confoundings can lead to serious consequences, as discussed in Sternberg (1977b). The method is the method of choice only when it is possible to disentangle all component processes of interest.

## Step 4: Quantification of Componential Model

Once scores have been obtained for the various subtasks (if any) involved in task performance across conditions, it is necessary to quantify the information-processing model (i.e., the model expressed as a flow chart or in other information-processing terms). The exact method of quantification will depend upon the task being studied and the method used to decompose the task. I will therefore first state some general principles of quantification, and then give a single example of a quantification—analogies. Other examples of quantifications can be found in others of my writings (e.g., Guyote & Sternberg, 1981, for categorical and conditional syllogisms; Schustack & Sternberg, 1981, for causal inferences; Sternberg, 1980b, for linear syllogisms; Tourangeau & Sternberg, 1981, for metaphors).

Generally, quantification is done so as to use multiple regression as a means of predicting a dependent variable from a series of independent variables. The dependent variable will usually be reaction time, error rate, or probability of a given response or response set. Independent variables will usually be the numbers of times each of a given set of information-processing components is performed. Thus, one predicts latency, error rate, or response probability, from numbers of times each of the operations in the model are performed.

Latency parameters (raw regression weights) represent the durations of the various components. Response time is usually hypothesized to equal the sum of the amounts of time spent on each component operation. Hence, a simple linear model can predict response time to be the sum across the different component operations of the numbers of times each component operation is performed (as an independent variable) multiplied by the duration of that component operation (as an estimated parameter).

Proportion of response errors is hypothesized to equal the (appropriately scaled) sum of the difficulties encountered in executing each component operation. A simple linear model predicts proportion of errors to be the sum across the different component operations of the number of times each component operation is performed (as an independent variable) multiplied by the difficulty of that component operation (as an estimated parameter). This additive combination rule is based upon the assumption that each subject has a limit on processing capacity (or space; see Osherson, 1974). Each execution of an operation uses up capacity. Until the limit is exceeded, performance is flawless except for constant sources of error (such as motor confusion, carelessness, momentary distractions, etc.). Once the limit is exceeded, however, performance is at a chance level. For a discussion of other kinds of error models, see Mulholland, Pellegrino, and Glaser (1980).

In the response-time models (with solution latency as dependent variable), all component operations must contribute significantly to solution latency, because by definition each execution of an operation consumes some amount of time. In the response-error models (error rate as dependent variable), however, all component operations need not contribute significantly to proportion of errors. The reason for this is that some operations may be so easy that no matter how many times they are executed, they contribute only trivially to prediction of errors.

## An Example of a Quantification: Analogies

In the analogy experiments of Sternberg (1977a, 1977b), mathematical modeling was done by linear multiple regression. Parameters of the model were estimated as unstandardized regression coefficients.

Consider the basic equations for predicting analogy solution times in the Sternberg (1977a, 1977b) experiments described earlier. In these experiments, subjects received precueing with either 0, 1, 2, or 3 cues, and were then asked to solve the full item as rapidly as possible. The equations shown here are for the simplest model, the so-called Model I, in which all operations are assumed to be executed exhaustively. Other models introduce further degrees of complication, and other publications should be consulted for details of their quantification (Sternberg, 1977a, 1977b; Sternberg & Gardner, 1983).

$$RT_0 = 4a + fx + gy + fz + c$$
$$RT_1 = 3a + fx + gy + fz + c$$
$$RT_2 = 2a + gy + fz + c$$
$$RT_3 = a + fz + c$$

In these equations, $RT_i$ refers to reaction time for a given number of precues, $i$. Among the parameters, $a$ refers to exhaustive encoding time; $x$ refers to exhaustive inference time; $y$ refers to exhaustive mapping time; $z$ refers to exhaustive application time; and $c$ refers to constant response time. Among the independent variables, the number of encodings to be done in each condition are given numerically (4, 3, 2, 1); $f$ refers to the number of attributes to be inferred or applied (in the exhaustive model, they are confounded); $g$ refers to the number of attributes to be mapped.

All parameters of each model enter into analogy processing in the 0-cue condition. The subjects must encode all four terms of the analogy, as well as perform the inference, mapping, application, and response processes. The 1-cue condition differs only slightly. The first term was presented during precueing and is assumed to have been encoded at that time. Hence, the 1-cue condition requires the encoding of just three analogy terms rather than all four. In the 2-cue condition, the A and B terms of the analogy were precued, and it is assumed that inference occurred during precueing. Hence, the inference parameter $(x)$ drops out, and there is again one less term to encode. In the 3-cue condition, the A and C terms were precued, and hence it is assumed that mapping as well as inference occurred during precueing. The mapping parameter $(y)$ therefore drops out, and there is again one less term to encode. In general, the successive cueing conditions are characterized by the successive dropout of model parameters.

Parameter dropouts also resulted from null transformations in which no changes occurred from A to B and/or from A to C. These dropouts occurred in degenerate analogies (0 A to B and 0 A to C attribute changes) and in semidegenerate analogies (0 A to B or 0 A to C attribute changes, but not both 0).

Indeed, these degenerate and semidegenerate analogies were originally included to provide a zero baseline for parameter estimation. For example, in the 0-cue condition, the inference and application parameters drop out when no changes occur from A to B, and the mapping parameter drops out when no changes occur from A to C. The same type of selective dropout occurs in all four cueing conditions.

The models make separate attribute-comparison time or error "charges" only for non-null value transformations. This type of "difference parameter" was used throughout these and other experiments, and has been used by many others as well (e.g., Clark & Chase, 1972). Value identities are not separately charged. Subjects are assumed to be preset to recognize null transformations ("sames"), and the parameter is assumed to represent amount of time or difficulty involved in alteration of the initial state.

Where needed, the optional justification parameter was estimated as a function of the product of the distance from the keyed-answer option to the ideal option times the number of previous attribute-comparison operations to be checked, both as determined by ratings provided by subjects otherwise uninvolved in the experiments. The idea is that the further the keyed option is from the ideal one, the more likely is checking to be necessary. If the keyed and ideal options are identical, then the value of the justification parameter will be zero, and hence it will be irrelevant to the analogy solution. If, however, not even the best presented option corresponds to the ideal option, then justification is required. This parameter was used only in the forced-choice geometric analogies.

This description does not contain all of the details included in the models, nor is it intended to be used to reproduce the data in the experiments. Instead, it is intended to be illustrative of the kinds of procedures used in quantification of a particular task.

## Step 5: Model Testing: Internal Validation

Once the model is formulated, it is necessary to test it, either by multiple regression or by other means. There are any number of tests that may be used. I have found the following tests useful in internally validating a componential model:

1. $R^2$ *for Model.* This descriptive statistic gives the overall squared correlation between predicted and observed data, and thus represents the proportion of variance in the data that the model is able to account for. It is a measure of relative goodness of fit.
2. *RMSD for Model.* The root-mean-square deviation (RMSD) statistic gives the overall root-mean-square deviation of observed from predicted data. It is a measure of absolute badness-of-fit. Because it is an "absolute" measure, its value will be affected by the variance of the observed and predicted data.

3. $F_{Regression}$ *for Model.* This statistic is the basis for deciding whether to reject the null hypothesis of no-fit of the model to the data. Higher values are associated with better fits of the model to the data. Because the inferential statistic takes into account the number of parameters in the model, I have found the statistic useful in deciding among alternative models with differing numbers of parameters.

4. $F_{Residual}$ *for Model.* This statistic is the basis for deciding whether to reject the null hypothesis of no discrepancy between the proposed model and the data. Lower values are associated with better fits of the model to the data. It is important to compute this statistic or an analogue, in that a model may account for a large proportion of variance in the data, and yet be capable of being rejected relative to the "true" model.

5. *Relative Values of Statistics 1-4 for Alternative Models.* It is highly desirable to compare the fit of a given model to alternative models. The fact that a given model fits a set of data very well may merely reflect the ease with which that data set can be fit. In some cases, even relatively implausible models may result in good fits. Testing plausible alternative models guards against fits that are good but nevertheless trivial.

6. $F_{Regression}$ *for Individual Parameter Estimates.* Significance of the overall regression $F$ does not imply that each parameter contributes significantly to the model. Thus, individual parameters should be tested for significance in order to assure their nontrivial contribution to the model.

7. $\Delta R^2$ *for Individual Parameter Estimates.* The $\Delta R^2$ statistic indicates the contribution of each parameter when that parameter is added to all others in the model. When independent variables in the model are intercorrelated, this descriptive statistic gives information different from that obtained in the step above. A parameter may be statistically significant, and yet contribute only a very small proportion of variance when added to all of the others.

8. *Interpretability of Parameter Estimates.* Parameters may pass the two tests described above, and yet have nonsensical values. The values may be nonsensical because they are negative (for real-time operations!), or because their values, although positive, are wildly implausible.

9. *Examination of Residuals of Observed from Predicted Data Points.* Residuals of observed from predicted data points should be assessed in order to determine the specific places in which the model does and does not predict the data adequately. The residuals will usually later be useful in reformulating the model.

10. *Substantive Plausibility of the Model.* This criterion is a substantive rather than a statistical one. The model may "fit" statistically, and yet make little or no psychological sense. The model should therefore be considered for its substantive plausibility.

11. *Heuristic Value of the Model.* This criterion is again substantive rather

than statistical. One should ask whether the model is at the right level of analysis for the questions being asked, whether it will be useful for the purposes to which it later will be put, and whether it is likely to generalize to other tasks and task domains.

12. *Consideration of Model for Individual-subject as well as Group-average Data.* The analyses described above can be applied to both group-average and individual data. It is important to test the proposed model on individual-subject as well as group-average data. There are at least two reasons for this. First, averaging of data can occasionally generate artifacts whereby the fit of the model to the group data does not accurately reflect its fit to individual subjects. Second, there may be individual differences in strategies used by subjects that can be discerned only through individual-subject model fitting. One wishes to know what individual subjects do, as well as what subjects do "on the average." I have found in at least several cases that what individual subjects do does not correspond in every case to the strategy indicated by the best group-average model (e.g., Sternberg & Ketron, 1982; Sternberg & Weil, 1980).

## Step 6: Model Testing: External Validation

External validation requires testing the parameters of the proposed model against external criteria. Such validation actually serves at least two distinct purposes.

First, it provides an additional source of verification for the model. Often, one will make differential predictions regarding correlations of individual parameter estimates with external criteria. The external validation can serve to test these predictions and thus the validity of the model. Consider, for example, my research on linear syllogisms. Some of the components in the mixed model were predicted to operate upon a linguistic representation for information, and others to operate upon a spatial representation for information (Sternberg, 1980b). It was important to show that the parameters theorized to operate upon a linguistic representation showed higher correlations with verbal than with spatial ability tests; similarly, it was important to show that the parameters theorized to operate upon a spatial representation showed higher correlations with spatial than with verbal ability tests. These predicted patterns were generally confirmed.

Second, it provides a test of generality for the proposed model. If interesting external criteria cannot be found that show significant and substantial correlations with the individual parameter estimates for the proposed model, then it is unclear that the model, or perhaps the task, is of much interest. For example, for parameters of analogical reasoning to be of theoretical interest, they should be shown to correlate with scores on a variety of inductive reasoning tests but not with scores on perceptual-speed tests. This differential pattern of correlations was in fact shown (Sternberg, 1977b).

The above examples may serve to point out that two kinds of external

validation need to be performed. The first, convergent validation, assures that
parameters do, in fact, correlate with external measures with which they are
supposed to correlate; the second, discriminant validation, assures that parameters do not, in fact, correlate with external measures with which they are not
supposed to correlate, but with which they might be plausibly correlated according to alternative theories. Some investigators have performed only convergent
but not discriminant validation (e.g., Shaver, Pierson, & Land, 1974), with what
seem like auspicious results. The problem, though, is that obtained correlations
may be due to the general factor in intellectual performance, rather than to the
particular operations specified as of interest in the theory. Thus, convergent
validation without discriminant validation is usually of little use.

Although I have emphasized correlations of parameters with external measures, it is an unfortunate fact of life that oftentimes parameter estimates for
individual subjects will not be as reliable as one would like. In these cases, and
even in cases where the estimates are fairly reliable, it is desirable to correlate
total task scores as well as subtask scores with the external measures. Although
such correlations may reflect various mixtures of operations in the tasks and
subtasks, they are likely to be more stable than the correlations obtained for the
parameter estimates, simply because of the higher reliability of the composite
scores and because of the fact that obtaining correlations for these scores is not
dependent upon the correctness of one's theory, as it is for component scores.

## Step 7: Reformulation of Componential Model

In practice, most first-pass (and even subsequent) models, whether componential or otherwise, are not correctly formulated. It will often be necessary to
reformulate one's model on the basis of a given data set, and then to cross-
validate the revised model on subsequent sets of data. It is worth underscoring
that cross-validation is essential. With enough fiddling, almost any data set can
be fit by some model. What is hard is showing that the model fits data sets other
than the one that was used in its formulation. The steps described above provide
a wealth of data to use in revising one's model. The investigator should use the
data to the best advantage in reformulating the model. Once the reformulation
is complete, the model is ready to be tested again on new data.

## Step 8: Generalization of Componential Model

Once a given task has been adequately understood in componential terms, it is
important to show that the proposed model is not task-specific. If the model is,
in fact, task-specific, then it is unlikely to be of much psychological interest. My
own strategy has been to extend componential models from a single task, task
format, and task content first to multiple task formats and contents, and later
to other tasks. For example, the componential model of analogical reasoning was

originally tested on true-false People Piece analogies, then extended to true-false verbal analogies, then extended to forced-choice geometric analogies, and finally generalized to other tasks, including classifications and series completions, both of which were theorized to involve the same inductive components as are required for analogical reasoning (and for each other). This process of generalization is needed in order to establish the priority of the information-processing theory, rather than of the task analysis, per se. Inevitably, one can start only with the analysis of one or a small number of tasks. But eventually, one must extend one's analysis to multiple tasks, with the choice of tasks being guided by the theory that generated the first task that was studied.

# CONCLUSIONS

I have described in this article a set of procedures—collectively referred to as *componential analysis*—that can be used in the formulation and testing of theories of cognitive processing. A componential analysis generally involves decomposition of a task into subtasks, and then the internal and external validation of one or more componential models of task performance.

Several advantages accrue to the decomposition of a global task into subtasks. Scores from subtasks (a) allow separation of components that otherwise would have been confounded, (b) enable comparison of models that otherwise would have been indistinguishable, (c) increase degrees of freedom for the residual in prediction, (d) require precise specification of the temporal ordering and location of components, (e) prevent distortion of results from external validation, and (f) provide component-free estimates of performance for nested processing intervals.

Further advantages accrue from the use of component scores representing subjects' performances on each of the information-processing components used in task performance. Component scores (a) estimate scores by inferentially powerful, componential models, (b) interpret performance in terms of mental processes, (c) pinpoint individual sources of particular strength and weakness for diagnosis and training, and can (d) derive estimates of measurement error from data for individual subjects.

Finally, use of reference ability scores that are correlated with subtask and component scores (a) allows identification of correlates of individual differences in performance for each component, (b) prevents overvaluation of task-specific components, and (c) potentially provide for both convergent and discriminant validation of a componential model.

In sum, then, componential procedures have been shown to be applicable to a large number of cognitive domains, and have shown themselves to be valuable in understanding human cognitive performance.

# REFERENCES

Burt, C. (1940). *The factors of the mind.* London, England: University of London Press.

Carroll, J. B. (1981). Ability and task difficulty in cognitive psychology. *Educational Researcher, 10,* 11-21.

Clark, H. H., & Chase, W. (1972). On the process of comparing sentences against pictures. *Cognitive Psychology, 3,* 472-517.

Cronbach, L. J. (1957). The two disciplines of scientific psychology. *American Psychologist, 12,* 671-684.

Eysenck, H. J. (1967). Intelligence assessment: a theoretical and experimental approach. *British Journal of Educational Psychology, 37,* 81-98.

Guilford, J. P. (1967). *The nature of human intelligence.* New York: McGraw-Hill.

Guyote, M. J., & Sternberg, R. J. (1981). A transitive-chain theory of syllogistic reasoning. *Cognitive Psychology, 13,* 461-525.

Humphreys, L. G. (1962). The organization of human abilities. *American Psychologist, 17,* 475-83.

Johnson, D. M. (1960). Serial analysis of thinking. In *Annals of the New York Academy of Sciences,* New York: New York Academy of Sciences, *91.*

Mulholland T., Pellegrino, J., & Glaser, R. (1980). Components of geometric analogy solution. *Cognitive Psychology, 12,* 252-284.

Newell, A., & Simon, H. A. (1972). *Human problem solving.* Englewood Cliffs, NJ: Prentice-Hall.

Osherson, D. N. (1974). *Logical abilities in children. Logical inference: Underlying operations* (Vol. 2). Potomac, MD: Erlbaum.

Schustack, M. W., & Sternberg, R. J. (1981). Evaluation of evidence in causal inference. *Journal of Experimental Psychology: General, 110,* 101-120.

Shaver, P., Pierson, L., & Lang, S. (1974). Converging evidence for the functional significance of imagery in problem solving. *Cognition, 3,* 359-375.

Sternberg, R. J. (1977a). Component processes in analogical reasoning. *Psychological Review, 84,* 353-378.

Sternberg, R. J. (1977b). *Intelligence, information processing, and analogical reasoning: The componential analysis of human abilities.* Hillsdale, NJ: Erlbaum.

Sternberg, R. J. (1980a). The development of linear syllogistic reasoning. *Journal of Experimental Child Psychology, 29,* 340-356.

Sternberg, R. J. (1980b). A proposed resolution of curious conflicts in the literature on linear syllogisms. In R. Nickerson (Ed.), *Attention and Performance VIII.* Hillsdale, NJ: Erlbaum.

Sternberg, R. J. (1980c). Sketch of a componential subtheory of human intelligence. *Behavioral and Brain Sciences, 3,* 573-584.

Sternberg, R. J. (1982). Reasoning, problem solving, and intelligence. In R. J. Sternberg (Ed.), *Handbook of human intelligence.* New York: Cambridge University Press.

Sternberg, R. J., & Gardner, M. K. (1983). Unities in inductive reasoning. *Journal of Experimental Psychology: General, 112,* 80-116.

Sternberg, R. J., & Ketron, J. L. (1982). Selection and implementation of strategies in reasoning by analogy. *Journal of Educational Psychology, 74,* 399-413.

Sternberg, R. J., Ketron, J. L., & Powell, J. S. (1982). Componential approaches to the training of intelligent performance. In D. K. Detterman & R. J. Sternberg (Eds.), *How and how much can intelligence be increased?* Norwood, NJ: Ablex.

Sternberg, R. J., & Nigro, G. (1980). Developmental patterns in the solution of verbal analogies. *Child Development, 51,* 27-38.

Sternberg, R. J., & Rifkin, B. (1979). The development of analogical reasoning processes. *Journal of Experimental Child Psychology, 27,* 195-232.

Sternberg, R. J., & Tulving, E. (1977). The measurement of subjective organization in free recall. *Psychological Bulletin, 84,* 353-378.

Sternberg, R. J., & Turner, M. E. (1981). Components of syllogistic reasoning. *Acta Psychologica, 47,* 245-265.

Sternberg, R. J., & Weil, E. M. (1980). An aptitude-strategy interaction in linear syllogistic reasoning. *Journal of Educational Psychology, 72,* 226-234.

Stevens, S. S. (1951). Mathematics, measurement and psychophysics. In S. S. Stevens (Ed.), *Handbook of experimental psychology.* New York: Wiley.

Thurstone, L. L. (1947). *Multiple factor analysis.* Chicago, IL: University of Chicago Press.

Tourangeau, R., & Sternberg, R. J. (1981). Aptness in metaphor. *Cognitive Psychology, 13,* 27-55.

Vernon, P. E. (1971). *The structure of human abilities.* London, England: Methuen.

# CHAPTER 8

# Instructional Methods of Studying the Ontogeny of Human Intelligence*

## Earl C. Butterfield
### University of Washington

## INTRODUCTION

There are too many ways to study the ontogeny of human intelligence and each way is too complex to treat more than one comprehensibly in a single chapter. Accordingly, I will concentrate here on an approach that seems to me to have been most fruitful in recent years. It is called the instructional approach to developmental cognitive psychology. Other treatises on the instructional approach can be found in Belmont and Butterfield (1977), Borkowski and Cavanaugh (1979), Brown and Campione (1978), and Butterfield, Siladi, and Belmont (1980).

The central feature of the method is the use of instructions to simulate the normal acquisition of intellective skills. An investigator seeks to teach young children ways of thinking that they do not yet use but which are used by older children or adults. The empirical goal is to raise the level of the young children's intellectual performance to the level of the older children or adults. The theoretical goal is to simulate in young children the intellectual processes of older people. Therefore, the user of the method must do more than attain the empirical goal of improving young children's intellectual performance. The user must raise young children's performance by teaching them to use the same intellectual processes that older people use. Experience has shown that it is relatively easy to achieve the empirical goal of teaching children how to perform on any of several intellective problems as well as older children or even

*The ideas expressed in this paper were developed during my long collaboration with John Belmont, to whom I am deeply indebted. The preparation of this paper was supported by USPHS grant HD-16241.

as well as adults (Butterfield & Ferretti, in press). It is much harder to establish that the theoretical goal has been met.

The challenge and pitfalls of the instructional approach lie in the fashioning of procedures to determine whether instructions that induce young children to perform as well as older children or adults do so by inducing young children to use the same processes as the older children or adults. The purpose of such procedures is to rule out the possibility that performance has been raised by the teaching of tricks that do not resemble the processes used by intellectually more advanced individuals when they solve the problems on which the children are instructed.

Two approaches have been used to determine whether an experiment meets the theoretical goal of simulating older persons' intellectual processes by instructing younger children. They are the control-groups approach and the process-measurement approach. In the control-groups approach, older as well as younger people are studied, and some of each are instructed while others are not. Whether the instructions induce younger children to use the same intellectual processes as uninstructed older people is judged by the effects of the instructions on the performance of both younger and older people. If the instructions raise the younger people's performance to the level of the uninstructed older people, and if the instructed and uninstructed older people perform equally, the inference is drawn that the instructions induced the use of the processes that the older people were using without instruction. In the process-measurement approach, measures of intellectual processes, as opposed to measures of performance, are used to determine whether instructing younger people induced them to use the same processes as uninstructed older people. Each approach has both strengths and weaknesses, which has led to the proposal that the two should be used in combination (Butterfield, Siladi, & Belmont, 1980). Before considering the merits of this proposal, I will illustrate and discuss the two approaches separately.

## THE CONTROL-GROUPS APPROACH

The full logic of the control-group approach calls for a minimum of two kinds of subjects and three kinds of conditions. The two kinds of subjects should differ in their intellectual levels, either because of their ages or for other reasons. Thus, an instructional experiment of the control-group variety might compare younger and older people, retarded and nonretarded people, brain damaged and undamaged people, and so on. Regardless of the basis for assigning subjects to different intellectual levels, subjects at each level should receive three kinds of conditions. An uninstructed condition should be included to establish how well people at each level perform when they use whatever processes they choose. An instructional condition should be used to simulate the intellectual processes thought to be employed by people of the higher intellectual level. Another instructional condition should be used to simulate the intellectual processes thought to be employed by people of the lower intellectual level. In other words, the full logic of the instructional method requires simulation of the thought processes of both more and less intelligent people.

Table 8.1. Illustration of Three Patterns of Results from a
Hypothetical Experiment Using the Full Logic of the
Control Groups' Approach to Instructional Research

| Intellectual Level | Uninstructed | High Simulation | Low Simulation |
|---|---|---|---|
| *PATTERN 1: AFFIRMATION OF HYPOTHESIS ABOUT INTELLECTUAL DEVELOPMENT* | | | |
| High | 75% | 75% | 25% |
| Low | 25% | 75% | 25% |
| *PATTERN 2: AFFIRMATION OF HYPOTHESIS ABOUT NONDEVELOPMENTAL PROCESS* | | | |
| High | 25% | 90% | 60% |
| Low | 10% | 40% | 10% |
| *PATTERN 2: INDICATION THAT INSTRUCTIONS SIMULATE DEVELOPMENT IMPERFECTLY* | | | |
| High | 75% | 75% | 60% |
| Low | 25% | 40% | 25% |

The simplest design for an instructional experiment that meets the full logic of the control groups approach is a 2 × 3 factorial, with different people in each of the six cells of the design. Table 8.1 depicts such a design three times, each time with a different pattern of results. It shows that the design has three groups of people at each of two intellectual levels. One group at each level is uninstructed about how to solve the criterion problem, which is selected because its solution depends upon intellectual processes. One group at each intellectual level receives instructions designed to promote use of the processes that the groups with higher intellectual levels are believed to be using to solve the problem when they are not instructed. Another group at each intellectual level receives instructions designed to promote use of the processes that the groups with lower intellectual levels are believed to be using to solve the problem when they are not instructed.

If the instructions satisfactorily simulate the processes used by both the higher and the lower groups, then the results of the experiment should resemble the pattern shown in the top panel of Table 8.1. The two uninstructed groups should differ reliably from one another, a confirmation that solving the criterion problem requires intellectual processes that the high and low group use differentially. Under Pattern 1 of Table 8.1, this is indicated by a larger score (75% vs. 25%) in the uninstructed condition for the group with a high intellectual level than for the group with a low intellectual level. Following instruction designed to simulate the processes used by the group with the high intellectual level, both the high and low group should perform like the uninstructed high group. The high group should not change following instructions that simulate how the high group is thinking, but the low group should improve to the level of the high group following such instructions. This is indicated under Pattern 1 of Table 8.1 by identical entries of 75% in the column headed "High Simulation." The low group should not change following instructions that simulate how the low group is thinking, but the high group's performance should fall to the level of the low group. This is indicated under Pattern 1 of Table 8.1 by identical entries of 25% in the column headed "Low Simulation."

The entries in Table 8.1 are percentages in order to indicate that an instructional experiment using the control-groups approach must avoid scale attenuation. The highest levels of performance observed must lie below the measurement ceiling. This is indicated in Table 8.1 by the fact that the highest level of performance lies below 100%. The lowest levels of performance observed must lie above the measurement floor. Thus, the lowest level of performance in Table 8.1 lies above 0%. When an experiment like that depicted in Table 8.1 results in data that are uninfluenced by scale attenuation, and when the results are like those under Pattern 1 in Table 8.1, the logic of the experiment calls for the inference that the instructional conditions employed simulate the processes underlying uninstructed performance differences between the groups studied. Such a pattern of results, when unfettered by floor and ceiling effects, indicates that the instructions employed embody a fully adequate theory of intellectual differences between the groups studied.

The sort of results shown under Pattern 2 of Table 8.1 allow a different inference about the processes underlying intellectual performance. Pattern 2 depicts the situation in which instruction designed to simulate how more intelligent people think improves the performance of both high and low groups, and instruction designed to simulate how less intelligent people think degrades the performance of both high and low groups. Neither sort of instruction diminishes the performance difference between the groups. The critical difference between Pattern 1 and Pattern 2 is that in Pattern 1 the high and low simulation instructions both eliminate the differences between the groups and neither instruction changes the group whose processing it was intended to simulate, while in Pattern 2 neither instruction reduces the difference between the groups and both the high and the low simulation instruction change both groups equally. Therefore, Pattern 1 justifies the inference that the instructions embody a theory that accounts for the differences between the groups, while Pattern 2 justifies the inference that the instructions embody a theory of a process that influences performance but does nothing to explain the differences between groups. Pattern 2 cannot be the result of scale attenuation, because the high simulation instructions improved the performance of the high group (from 75% to 90%) and the low simulation instructions degraded the performance of the low group (from 25% to 10%).

Pattern 3 in Table 8.1 allows yet another inference. It shows the situation in which an instructional experiment partially eliminates the uninstructed differences between high and low intellectual groups. At the same time, the high simulation instructions leave the performance of the high intellectual group unchanged, and the low simulation instructions leave the performance of the low intellectual group unchanged. Provided that scale attenuation effects can be ruled out as the reason for the unchanged performance of the high group under high instructions and the low group under low instructions, this pattern of results allows the inference that the instructions embody a partial theory of the differences between the high and low groups. The equality of the uninstructed and high simulation conditions for the high intellectual group indicates that the instructions are not changing the thinking of the high group. The equality of the uninstructed and low simulation conditions for the low intellectual group indicates that the low simulation instructions are not changing the thinking of the low simulation group. Therefore, both sorts of instruction must embody some elements of a theory about how the two groups are thinking. Since neither instruction completely eliminated the difference between the low and high groups, neither instruction must embody a complete theory of how the two groups are thinking. This pattern of results indicates that the instructional researcher has made progress but still has a way to go before he understands the development of the intellectual performance under study.

Belmont and Butterfield (1971) reported an experiment whose results are very similar to those of Pattern 3 in Table 8.1. Their dependent measure was performance on a memory problem for which there is good reason to believe that rehearsal improves performance (Glanzer & Cunitz, 1966; Ellis & Hope, 1968; Belmont & Butterfield, 1969; Moss & Sharac, 1970). Their subjects were mentally retarded and normal children, for whom Belmont and Butterfield produced observational evidence of differences in rehearsal. To test the hypothesis that the observed rehearsal differences accounted for differences between their subjects in memory performance, Belmont and Butterfield instructed some retarded and some nonretarded subjects about how to rehearse. Belmont and Butterfield instructed other retarded and nonretarded subjects to approach the memory tasks in a way that was incompatible with rehearsal. The rehearsal instruction improved the performance of the retarded subjects, but it did not raise it to the level of nonretarded subjects, who were uninfluenced by the rehearsal instruction. The instruction designed to interfere with rehearsal decreased the performance of normal subjects, but it did not lower their performance to the level of retarded subjects, who were uninfluenced by the interfering condition. The logic of the control-group approach to cognitive instruction justifies the inference that rehearsal processes account for some of the difference between normal and retarded children's memory performance. By exclusion, other processes must be sought to account for the remainder of the difference. In fact, other process differences were sought and found (Butterfield, Wambold, & Belmont, 1973). They have to do with retrieval processes and with the coordination of retrieval and rehearsal processes, which is a metacognitive difference between normal and retarded children (Butterfield et al., 1973).

In summary, experiments that realize the full logic of instructional experimentation can produce at least three results. They can produce results that seem to fully validate a theory of intellectual development. They can produce results that seem to validate a theory of processes that influence intellectual performance but do not account for intellectual development. They can produce results that seem to indicate that a theory of intellectual development is partially valid but needs to be more complete. Under what circumstances can these apparent results be incorrect?

Scale attenuation is a main source of incorrect inferences from instructional experiments. Consider that Pattern 3 in Table 8.1 is identical to Pattern 2, except that in Pattern 2 the high intellectual group benefitted from the high simulation instructions and the low group was hurt by the low simulation instructions. Neither of these effects are present in Pattern 3. The absence of such effects can be the direct result of scale attenuation, but inferences from patterns with and without the effects are markedly different. Pattern 2 indicates no progress toward explaining intellectual development, while Pattern 3 indicates substantial progress. Fortunately, scale attenuation can be evaluated by examination of the data from an instructional experiment. Thus, in the experiment by Belmont and Butterfield (1971) it was evident that scale attenuation was not the reason that retarded people were not hurt by the instructions designed to prevent rehearsal, because the distribution of scores for retarded people in this condition was not skewed toward the measurement floor.

The more invidious source of incorrect inferences from instructional experiments using the control group design arises from the possibility of changing processing without changing performance. Since the control-groups approach makes no explicit allowance for direct comparison of processes employed under the various conditions, the high simulation instructions can change the processing of the high simulation group without changing its performance. Also, the low simulation instructions can change the processing of the low intellectual group, while leaving the accuracy of that group unchanged. Under either or both of these circumstances, one would incorrectly infer that the instructions employed embodied a valid theory of intellectual development, when instead the instructions embodied a trick that just happened to produce levels of performance comparable to that of either or both the low or high intellectual groups. An antidote for this possibility is to employ process measurements, which is the alternative approach to determining whether an instructional experiment has attained its theoretical goal of equating performance by inducing people of certain intellectual levels to use processes like those of people at other intellectual levels.

## THE PROCESS-MEASUREMENT APPROACH

The process-measurement approach requires a group of people with a low intellectual level and a group with a high intellectual level. As with the control-groups approach, the groups may be chosen because they differ in age, intelligence quotient, central nervous system integrity, or any other factor associated with different intellectual levels. The two groups are first assessed under uninstructed conditions to determine that they differ in criterion performance and determine that they are using different processes to solve the criterion problem. Then, the group with the lower intellectual level is instructed to use the processes employed by the group with the higher intellectual level, and the group with the higher intellectual level is instructed to use the processes employed by the group with the lower intellectual level. Finally, the two groups are assessed again with both process and performance measures, and these posttest measures are compared to the pretest measures. The comparisons focus on the extent to which the posttest measures of the high group resemble the pretest measures of the low group and the extent to which the posttest measures of the low group resemble the pretest measures of the high group. When these cross group comparisons indicate that the instructions precisely reversed the pattern of performance and process measurements, the inference is drawn that the instructions embody a theory of intellectual development.

The simplest design for an instructional experiment that meets the full logic of the process-measurement approach uses two groups, both of which are given a pretest, instruction, and a posttest. Table 8.2 depicts such a design three times, each time with a different pattern of results. It shows that the design has one group of people at each of two intellectual levels. Both groups are given a pretest to assess their level of performance and their mode of processing the criterion problem, which is selected because its solution depends upon known and measureable intellectual processes. Following the pretest, the group at the low intellectual level is given instructions designed to induce use of the processes that the pretest measures showed were used by the subjects at the high intellectual level. The group at the high intellectual level is given instructions designed to induce use of the processes that the pretest measures showed were used by the subjects at the low intellectual level. Then, both groups are given a posttest to assess both their performance levels and the processes they use to solve the criterion problem.

**Table 8.2. Illustration of Three Patterns of Results from a
Hypothetical Experiment Using the Full Logic of the
Process Measurement Approach to Instructional Research**

| Measure of | Low Intellectual Level (Given High Simulation) | | High Intellectual Level (Given Low Simulation) | |
|---|---|---|---|---|
| | Pretest | Posttest | Pretest | Posttest |
| *PATTERN 1: AFFIRMATION OF HYPOTHESIS ABOUT INTELLECTUAL DEVELOPMENT* | | | | |
| Process | A | A+B+C | A+B+C | A |
| Performance | 25% | 75% | 75% | 25% |
| *PATTERN 2: INDICATION OF INADEQUATE INSTRUCTIONS* | | | | |
| Process | A | A+B | A+B+C | A+C |
| Performance | 25% | 40% | 75% | 60% |
| *PATTERN 3: INDICATE THAT INSTRUCTIONS SIMULATE DEVELOPMENT IMPERFECTLY* | | | | |
| Process | A | A+B+C | A+B+C | A |
| Performance | 25% | 40% | 75% | 60% |

If the instructions satisfactorily simulate the processes used by both the high and low groups, then the results of the experiment should resemble the pattern shown in the top panel of Table 8.2. Pattern 1 in Table 8.2 shows that the high and low groups differ reliably from one another on both the process and performance pretest measures, with the high group performing more accurately (75% vs. 25%) and using more processes (A + B + C vs. A alone). The implication is that the additional processing (B + C) resulted in the more accurate performance and accounts for the intellectual difference between the high and low groups. On the posttest following instruction in the use of the high group's pretest processes, the low group performs as accurately as the high group did on the pretest, and the low group uses the same processes as the high group did on the pretest. Conversely, following instruction in the use of the low group's pretest processes, the high group performs as inaccurately as the low group did on the pretest, and the high group uses the same processes as the low group did on the pretest.

In the process-measurement approach, similarity of process measures between groups before and after instruction plays the same role in meeting the theoretical purpose of an instructional experiment as identical performance between instructed and uninstructed groups does in the control-groups approach. In the control-groups approach, when the performance of the high group given the high simulation instruction equals that of the high group no instruction (see

Pattern 1 in Table 8.1), the inference is that the high instructions simulated the processes employed by the high group that received no instruction. The assumption is that if the high instructions did not simulate the processes used by the high group, the instruction would change the performance of the high group. Analogous logic holds for the uninstructed low group and the low group given low simulation instruction. As noted above, the logic is unsound when different processes produce comparable levels of performance. In the process-measurement approach, identical performance and measured processing for the uninstructed high group and the instructed low group warrants the inference that the high instructions simulated the processing of the high group. Analogous logic holds for the uninstructed high group and the low group given high simulation instruction in the process-measurement approach. The assumption is that when performance and process come as a result of instruction to be like those of a different uninstructed group, the instructions have induced the use of the processes employed by the uninstructed group.

The sort of results shown under Pattern 2 of Table 8.2 indicate that the instructions did not simulate the processes at which they were aimed. Following instruction, the process measures show that the low group used only processes A and B, while the purpose of the instructions was to induce the use of process C as well. Similarly, following instruction, the high group used both processes A and C, while the instruction was intended to induce them to use A alone. The role of the process measurements in this case is to pinpoint aspects of the instructions that need to be changed before the investigator can claim to have provided a good test of whether he understands the processes underlying performance differences between the high and low uninstructed groups. When a set of instructions does not induce use of the desired processes, one cannot claim to have tested the relevance of those processes to performance difference between intellectually different groups. The possibility of this finding is one of the advantages of the process-measurement approach over the control-groups approach. In the control-groups approach, one can know that the instructions do not promote the sought-after performance levels, but the reason is not clear. The reason might be that the instructions simulate the processes, but the processes do not account for intellectual differences, or it might be that the instructions do not induce use of the processes. Pattern 2 in Table 8.2 results when a set of instructions do not simulate the processes intended, and its occurrence calls for revision of the instructions.

Pattern 3 in Table 8.2 results when instructions simulate the intended processes, but the processes do not fully account for the differences between high and low intellectual groups.

Butterfield et al. (1973) reported three experiments that illustrate the logic of the process-measurement approach to cognitive instruction by teaching mentally retarded people to use memory processes characteristic of nonretarded adults. The performance measure employed was accuracy on a position-probe-recall task. After studying a list of letters, each of which was presented by itself in a different position in a serial display, a subject was shown one of the letters from the list and required to indicate the position at which it had appeared. The process measures were study times following the presentation of each letter and response times measured from the presentation of a probe letter until the subject indicated the position at which he thought it was presented during study. In the first experiment, mentally retarded people were taught to use rehearsal and attention processes like those used by nonretarded adults. The study-time measures indicated that the instruction was successful, but the performance measures indicated that the retarded people remained less accurate than uninstructed adults. That is, the pattern of results resembled those of Pattern 3 in Table 8.2. Accordingly, Butterfield et al. performed a second experiment in which retarded people were taught both how to rehearse and to use retrieval mechanisms like those employed by nonretarded adults. Study-time and response-time process measures indicated that the instructions succeeded in inducing use of both rehearsal and retrieval mechanisms, but the retarded people did not order the retrieval mechanisms in the way nonretarded adults do. The performance of the retarded children remained below that of nonretarded adults. Again, the pattern of results was like that of Pattern 3 in Table 8.2. In a third experiment, Butterfield et al. taught retarded children to rehearse, to use adult retrieval mechanisms, and to sequence the retrieval mechanisms in the order used by nonretarded adults. Study-time and response-latency measures confirmed that the instruction had induced retarded children to process as nonretarded adults do. Performance measures indicated that the retarded children performed insignificantly more accurately than uninstructed nonretarded adults. This pattern of findings is like that of Pattern 1 in Table 8.2, indicating that the instructions given to retarded children simulated the processing used by nonretarded adults. The logic of the process-measurement approach to cognitive instruction allows the inference that the instruction used in the third experiment by Butterfield et al. (1973) embodies a full theory of the intellectual differences between retarded children and nonretarded adults as they are manifest in a probe-recall problem. Because Butterfield et al. did not instruct nonretarded adults to process as retarded children, their experiment does not illustrate the full logic of the process-measurement approach to cognitive instruction.

In summary, experiments that realize the full logic of the process-measurement approach to instructional experimentation can produce at least three results. They can produce results that seem to fully validate a theory of intellectual development. They can produce results that indicate how a set of instructions fails to simulate the processing which in theory should produce performance differences between intellectually different groups. They can produce results that seem to indicate that a theory of intellectual development is partially valid but needs to be more complete. Under what circumstances can these apparent results be incorrect, and when is the approach not applicable?

As with the control-groups approach, scale attenuation on performance measures can be a main source of incorrect inferences from instructional experiments. Scale attenuation on process measures can also result in uninterpretable data. The discussion of attenuation in the preceding section on the control-groups approach applies equally to the process-measurement approach.

A more serious limit on the process-measurement approach stems from the requirement that the investigator measure all of the processes that are thought to differentiate intellectual groups. The control-groups approach requires only that the processes be embodied in instructions. The process-measurement approach requires that the processes be measureable, and that the measurements be taken while the subjects are solving criterion problems. These requirements rule out the approach for intellectual problems that have been studied only inferentially. That is, prior to undertaking an instructional study using the process-measurement approach, analytic research must have been done, and this research must have fashioned techniques for measuring the processes that contribute to differential levels of performance. Such research has been done for a variety of intellectual problems, but it has not been done for many others. For a fuller discussion of the sorts of problems that have been analysed and of the sorts of research that should precede instructional work, the reader is referred to Butterfield and Dickerson (1976), Butterfield, Siladi, and Belmont (1980), and Butterfield and Ferretti (in press). Butterfield and Dickerson (1976) and Butterfield et al. (1980) also describe the use of convergent-validation techniques that can increase confidence that a control-groups experiment has met its theoretical goal, even when process measurement cannot be made.

## COMBINING THE CONTROL GROUPS
## AND PROCESS MEASUREMENT APPROACHES

The chief limit on the control-groups approach is that it provides only indirect performance checks on whether its instructions have simulated processes that might be responsible for intellectual differences. This limit can be remedied some of the time by supplementing the control-groups approach with process measurements. When that can be done, it should be (Butterfield et al., 1980). When it cannot be done, the investigator can either use the controls-groups approach, with or without preliminary studies to establish convergent validation (Butterfield et al., 1980) or the investigator can turn his or her attention to task analytic work that will develop process measurements. While this is the longer approach, it seems the more desirable, since the power of the instructional approach is most fully realized when the investigator collects the fullest and most direct evidence about the extent to which instructions simulate processes that differentiate intellectual groups. Under these conditions, the instructional approach amounts to a fully experimental test of developmental cognitive theory. To the best of my knowledge, no other approach allows fully experimental tests of developmental theory.


## ILLUSTRATIVE APPLICATIONS OF THE
## INSTRUCTIONAL APPROACH TO STUDYING THE
## ONTOGENY OF HUMAN INTELLIGENCE

The instructional approach has been used widely to study the ontogeny of human intelligence. Belmont and Butterfield (1977) found 114 articles in the developmental literature that either used or discussed instructional research for purposes of clarifying the ontogeny of cognition. The range of intellective problems to which the approach has been applied is impressive, including practically all of tasks used by Piagetians to study concrete and formal operations (cf., Brainerd & Allen, 1971; Kuhn, 1974) and all studies of production and mediation deficiencies (cf., Flavell, 1970; Butterfield, Siladi, & Belmont, 1980). Several comprehensive reviews summarize other kinds of cognition to which the instructional approach has been applied (cf., Belmont & Butterfield, 1977; Borkowski & Cavanaugh, 1970). Here, I will limit myself to two pieces of instructional research that have not previously been treated in reviews of instructional research. They illustrate strengths and problems of the approach.


### Verbal Elaboration in the Development of Recall

Rohwer (1973) summarized the use of cognitive instruction, which he called *prompting,* to study the development of elaborative processes for forming associations between pairs of words or pictures that were to be recalled together. His developmental hypothesis was that older people more readily generate meaningful elaborative networks that serve to make either of two nouns or pictures elicit recollection of the other. Among the studies he reported as tests of this hypothesis was one by Rohwer and Bean (Rohwer, 1973) in which 11-year-olds and 16-year-olds studied 36 pairs of words under either of three conditions. In an uninstructed condition, children were simply asked to learn the pairs of words. In a high simulation condition, which Rohwer and Bean called the *augmented prompt condition,* the pairs were presented in a sentence and the subjects were told to repeat the sentences during the interval prior to the presentation of the next pair. In a low simulation condition, which Rohwer and Bean called an *antagonistic condition,* children were told to repeat the noun pair during the interval prior to the presentation of the next pair. All 36 pairs were presented once, followed by a test trial, and then the 36 pairs were presented again, followed by a second test trial. The dependent variable was the mean number of pairs recalled on the two test trials. The percentages corresponding to these scores are presented in Table 8.3.

**Table 8.3. Percent Correct Recall under Differential Instructional Conditions for Two Experients on Verbal Elaboration**

| Age | Uninstructed | High Simulation | Low Simulation |
|---|---|---|---|
| | ROHWER AND BEAN[a] | | |
| 11 years old | 31% | 53% | 31% |
| 16 years old | 67% | 61% | 31% |
| | Minimal | Augmented | Antagonistic |
| | ROHWER AND GUY[b] | | |
| 11 years old | 23% | 40% | 9% |
| 16 years old | 55% | 51% | 49% |

[a]Adapted from Figure 2 in Rohwer (1973).
[b]Adapted from Table V in Rohwer (1973).

The top panel of Table 8.3 shows the results obtained by Rohwer and Bean (Rohwer, 1973). Their study follows the logic of the control-groups approach to instructional research, and the pattern of results is very similar to the one that confirms a developmental hypothesis about intellectual development (cf., Pattern 1 in Table 8.1). Sixteen-year olds performed much better than 11-year-olds in the uninstructed condition. Under the high simulation condition, both age groups performed comparably to the uninstructed 16-year olds. Under the low simulation condition, both age groups performed comparably to the uninstructed 11-year-olds. There is no reason in the procedures employed or the results obtained to doubt that sentence elaboration of the sort used in the high simulation condition is used by uninstructed 16-year-olds and not by uninstructed 11-year-olds. However, there is reason to wonder in the results of a replication conducted by Rohwer and Guy and reported by Rohwer (1973).

The only difference between the experiment conducted by Rohwer and Guy (Rohwer, 1973) and that conducted by Rohwer and Bean (Rohwer, 1973) is that Rohwer and Guy used 50 pairs of nouns instead of 36 pairs. The results obtained by Rohwer and Guy are shown in the lower half of Table 8.3. Comparing the upper and lower halves of Table 8.3 shows a profound failure of the two experiments to agree with one another, except in the uninstructed condition. In the uninstructed condition, the 16-year-olds performed appreciably better than the 11-year-olds, as in the experiment by Rohwer and Bean. The somewhat lower overall percentage recalled in the experiment by Rohwer and Guy can be attributed most directly to their use of 50 rather than 36 noun pairs. In the high simulation condition, 11-year-olds did not approach the accuracy of 16-year-olds, even though 11-year-olds did do better in the high simulation condition than in the uninstructed condition. Evidently, sentence elaboration did not completely account for the difference between 11- and 16-year-olds in the study by Rohwer and Guy, as it seemed to in the study by Rohwer and Bean. More damagingly, the low simulation condition did not influence the 16-year-olds, but it reduced the accuracy of the 11-year-olds.

The pattern of results obtained by Rohwer and Guy not only fails to replicate Rohwer and Bean, it is internally inconsistent. The failure of the low simulation to reduce accuracy of the 16-year-olds suggests that they were not relying on elaboration. But if they were not relying on elaboration, then the high simulation condition should have helped them. Moreover, if the 16-year-olds were not relying on elaboration, then there is no explanation for why their recall was greater than that of 11-year-olds in the uninstructed condition. The difference between the uninstructed and high simulation conditions for the 11-year-olds, as well as their inferiority to the 16-year-olds in the uninstructed condition, suggests that the uninstructed 11-year-olds were not relying on elaboration. Even though the high simulation did not raise the 11-year-olds' performance all the way to that of 16-year-olds, it did raise it part way, indicating again that the uninstructed 11-year-olds were not using elaboration. Therefore, it is internally inconsistent that the low simulation condition reduced the performance of the 11-year-olds. This is especially inconsistent, since the low simulation condition did not reduce the performance of the 16-year-olds.

When two instructional experiments disagree, or when an instructional experiment is internally inconsistent, investigators have a very difficult time making interpretative sense of the findings, unless they have collected process measures. Neither Rohwer and Bean (Rohwer, 1973) nor Rohwer and Guy (Rohwer, 1973) collected process measures. Consequently, their results simply conflict, and there is no way to decide why. While it is not clear what sorts of process measures they might have collected (instructions to think aloud while studying the pairs or post experimental reports about the use of elaboration?), had they collected some, they would have had a chance to answer questions such as the following: *Were the 16-year-olds in the uninstructed conditions of the two experiments comparable in their use of elaboration?* If the 16-year-olds studied by Rohwer and Bean employed elaboration to achieve their relatively high levels of performance, but Rohwer and Guy's used some other approach (rote rehearsal?), then the discrepancies between the two studies would be more sensible and the theory of what develops could be extended to processes other than elaboration. *Were the high and low simulation instructions equally effective in inducing their desired modes of processing in the two experiments and across ages within the experiment of Rohwer and Guy?* If the 16-year-olds in the low simulation condition of the experiment by Rohwer and Guy somehow avoided using the mechanisms taught in that condition, then the obtained pattern of results would be more interpretable. A failure of an instructional condition to have its desired effects on processing invalidates it as a test of the effects of changing the processing in the desired ways, but without process measures, one cannot know whether a failure of an instructional condition to influence performance is a technical problem or an important contradiction of hypothesis guiding the formulation of the instructions. *Did the 16-year olds in the uninstructed and high simulation conditions use elaboration equally?* An assumption of the control-groups approach to instructional experimentation is that when their performance levels are equal the older subjects use the same processes in the un-instructed condition as in the high simulation condition. Especially in the study by Rohwer and Guy, there is a possibility that the similar performance levels of these two groups resulted from different sorts of processing. Without process measures, it is impossible to do more than speculate about this possibility.

The chief advantage of process measures is that they allow answers to questions such as the ones raised in the foregoing paragraph. In so doing, they markedly reduce the reliance an investigator must place on untested speculation. Process measures markedly increase an investigator's bases for interpreting his findings and improving his theory. It is doubtful that Rohwer and his associates will ever be able to untangle the inferential knots created by the failure of these two studies to replicate, unless they supplement future instructional research with process measurements.

## Metacognitive Determinants of Transfer

Instruction can be used to diagnose production deficiencies. When it is known that older people use a particular process or strategy, and that younger people do not, a developmentalist cannot avoid asking why. Do younger children not use the same processes as older ones because the processes would not work for younger children? If the answer to this question is "yes", the younger children have a mediation deficiency. Do they not know that the processes would work as well for them as for older people? If the answer to this question is "yes", the younger children have a production deficiency. To answer these questions, one can instruct children to use the processes employed by older people, and if the instruction induces use of the processes and raises performance, the inference is that the uninstructed poorer performance of the younger children results from a production deficiency. Knowing this, a developmentalist cannot fail to ask why younger children are production deficient. There is as yet no definitive answer to this question, but there is a general hypothesis. The hypothesis is that children are deficient at the metacognitive level.

Of the several specific versions of the general metacognitive hypothesis, one says that children do not understand the importance of monitoring the rela-tionship between their cognitive processing and the performance that results from it. This hypothesis has been advanced as an explanation for a common outcome of instructional experiments, which is that instruction frequently raises young children's performance to the level of older children's and adults' on the problem used during instruction, but not on transfer problems whose solution depends upon the instructed processes. The hypothesis is that if children monitored the difference in performance achieved when they did and when they did not use an instructed process that produces relatively high levels of performance, they would use that process on a transfer test as well as on the problems used to convey the instruction. Ringel and Springer (1980) performed an instructional experiment to test this hypothesis.

Ringel and Springer studied 6-, 8-, and 10-year-olds, all of whom were asked to sort a set of 20 pictures into categories and then to recall the names of the pictures. All children were given a pretest during which they received no instructions about the kinds of categories into which to sort the pictures. Children at each age were then divided into three groups that were matched within ages on the number of pictures recalled during the pretest. One of the three groups at each age was given two more sets of 20 pictures without any instruction. Thus, there was an uninstructed group at each age. One group of children at each age was instructed to sort a second set of 20 pictures into semantically distinct categories as a means of preparing for their second recall test. These groups were then given a third set of 20 pictures as a test of whether they transferred the semantic sorting strategy. Thus, one group at each age was given an instruction designed to improve their recall, but these groups were given no instruction designed to enhance their chances of transferring the sorting strategy. The third group at each age received instruction in semantic sorting, and they were given feedback about the effects of the sorting strategy on their recall of the second list of 20 pictures. This feedback was intended to overcome a hypothesized metacognitive deficit of the younger children. It was hypothesized that the younger children would not spontaneously monitor the effects of using the instructed sorting strategy. Therefore, Ringel and Springer (1980) provided feedback designed to highlight its effectiveness. This third group of subjects at each age was then given a third set of 20 pictures as a test of whether they transferred the sorting strategy taught on the second group of pictures, about which feedback was given.

The experiment by Ringel and Springer (1980) has a considerably more complex design than any other instructional experiment described in this chapter. This illustrates the flexibility of the approach and the complexity of the questions it can address. The results of the experiment are shown in Table 8.4, and they raise several interesting questions about the approach.

The pretest data from all three conditions and all of the data from the uninstructed condition show a small but reliable effect of age on uninstructed recall. Recall accuracy increased with age. The difference between the 6- and 8-year-olds was larger than the difference between the 8- and 10-year-olds, but even the difference between the 6- and 10-year-olds was only 13%, which is fewer than 3 of 36 pictures. Within the instructional approach, small performance differences between the age groups compared are a sign of probable diffi-

culty. The reason is that small performance differences usually result from
substantial overlap in the processes employed by the different age groups. The
presence of substantial overlap means that if any age group benefits from high
simulation instruction, all groups will. If all groups benefit, then the purpose
of explaining uninstructed differences among the age groups cannot be met.
This problem can be avoided by using process measures to select groups that
are using different processes, but Ringel and Springer (1980) did not do this.

**Table 8.4. Percent Correct Recall under Different Instructional and
Feedback Conditions (Adapted from Ringel & Springer, 1980)**

|  | Pretest | Acquisition Posttest | Transfer Posttest |
|---|---|---|---|
| *6-YEAR-OLDS* | | | |
| Uninstructed | 47% | 54% | 43% |
| High Simulation | 46% | 69% | 65% |
| High Simulation + Feedback | 43% | 54% | 54% |
| *8-YEAR-OLDS* | | | |
| Uninstructed | 59% | 55% | 51% |
| High Simulation | 56% | 65% | 60% |
| High Simulation + Feedback | 54% | 79% | 71% |
| *10-YEAR-OLDS* | | | |
| Uninstructed | 57% | 61% | 53% |
| High Simulation | 63% | 76% | 70% |
| High Simulation + Feedback | 62% | 81% | 73% |

Table 8.4 shows that all subject groups did benefit from the sorting instruction. Moreover, all groups benefitted substantially. The inference is that semantic sorting did not simulate even approximately the processes used by the older
groups. This can also be seen in process measures that Ringel and Springer
(1980) did collect. They classified the sorts made by children as semantic or
nonsemantic. During the pretest, only one of 90 children sorted semantically.
On the second list of pictures, following semantic sorting instructions, 88 of 90
children sorted semantically. Clearly, the instructed processes could not have
accounted for the uninstructed age differences, because there were no uninstructed differences among the age groups in the processes instructed. Whether
this matters for the purpose of studying transfer is an interesting question.

In order to study transfer, one must first train or teach people something that might transfer. To have a good chance of observing transfer, the teaching should create a large difference between instructed performance and uninstructed performance, so that if transfer is not complete, performance has a chance of remaining above the uninstructed level. In this respect, Ringel and Springer's (1980) semantic sorting instructions were successful. Depending upon one's conception of the determinants of transfer, having large instructional effects is or is not enough to insure a good test of whether a particular manipulation promotes transfer. It can be argued that skills which fit the cognitive capabilities of children are more likely to be transferred. A definitive test of whether skills fit cognitive capabilities is whether children use those skills without instruction. Ringel and Springer (1980) provided evidence that children between 6 and 10 years do not use semantic sorting unless they are instructed to do so. Therefore, if their feedback condition failed to create transfer, the reason might be that the instructed strategy did not well fit children's cognitive machinery. This interpretive possibility could have been eliminated by selecting a criterion problem on which children show clear processing differences that result in large performance differences among the age groups when they are uninstructed. Then, the training whose transfer was to be studied would be designed to induce use of the processes employed by the older children. The cost of this procedure would be that the oldest children could not participate in the transfer phase of the experiment, because instruction would not improve their performance. The benefit would be that a failure to observe enhanced transfer could not be attributed to a mismatch of children's cognitive machinery and the instructed processes whose transfer was sought.

Table 8.4 shows what Ringel and Springer (1980) observed about the effects of feedback upon transfer. Several features of the data indicate that their results allow no clear interpretation of the metacognitive hypothesis they undertook to test. Nevertheless, since the design of their experiment was well suited to their experimental purpose, their findings highlight the pitfalls of the instructional approach.

One of the most well established principles of memory research is that level of delayed recall depends upon level of immediate recall (Underwood, 1975; Belmont, 1966). Ringel and Springer's (1980) transfer test is a delayed recall test in which the thing to be recalled is the strategy taught rather than the material learned during sorting of the second list of 36 words. Accordingly, to fairly compare their different groups' levels of recall during the transfer test, Ringel and Springer should have insured comparable recall for the second list. They did not. Six-year olds recalled substantially less during the second recall test than did 8-year olds who were given feedback and than did all instructed 10-year olds. The 8-year olds who were instructed but not given feedback recalled less than the 8-year olds who were given feedback. This is an inexplicable difference, since feedback was given after recall. Since theirs was an instructional experiment, and since Ringel and Springer (1980) were not concerned to teach younger children to process like older ones, there is no reason not to have employed a criterion procedure according to which all trained groups were brought to the same level of performance before testing for transfer. The instructional approach is ideally suited to such equating of groups, and in the vast majority of experiments such equation increases both the power of the experiment and its interpretability. For Ringel and Springer's (1980) experiment, the interpretative question is with whether differences observed on the transfer test were due to differences in the levels of performance created by training or to the degree of carryover from the training.

If the metacognitive hypothesis about feedback is correct, then training in how to sort with feedback should have created more transfer than training in how to sort without feedback, at least for the younger children. Table 8.4 shows that this was not the case for 6-year-olds nor 10-year-olds, since at these ages the two trained groups recalled comparably on the transfer test. For the 8-year-olds, training plus feedback was associated with greater recall on the transfer test than training without feedback, but the magnitude of this difference is no greater than the magnitude of the difference immediately following training. Therefore, one can attribute this difference to differential training of the sorting strategy as readily as to differential transfer.

Ringel and Springer (1980) suggested that 10-year-olds showed no difference between the two training conditions because they spontaneously employed the metacognitive strategy of monitoring the relationship between sorting and accuracy. That is, they hypothesized that 10-year-olds should not have benefitted from feedback because they were assessing the effectiveness of sorting for themselves. This inference is an example of the logic of the control-groups approach to instructional research, which it was argued earlier can be strengthened by the use of process measures taken during criterion performance. Ringel and Springer (1980) took no concurrent process measures, but they did perform postexperimental interviews which they interpreted as evidence that 10-year-olds knew the importance of monitoring the results of the processes they employed. It would have markedly strengthened Ringel and Springer's (1980) case if they had collected concurrent data to show that 10-year olds actually did monitor the effects of their processing, since there are many indications in the literature that children's reports of what they know do not relate to what they actually do in particular circumstances.

If 10-year olds did not benefit from feedback because they did not need it to assess the utility of the sorting strategy, then only younger subjects should have shown a difference between instruction alone and instruction with feedback. Six-year-olds showed no such difference, and the difference shown by 8-year-olds cannot be attributed to transfer rather than to the extent to which they benefitted from training in how to sort semantically.

For the reasons given above, the experiment by Ringel and Springer (1980) provides no evidence for or against their metacognitive hypothesis. Had the criterion problem been one in which uninstructed children showed large performance differences, had the training been carried to a criterion, and had concurrent process measures been employed, this experiment would have been an excellent example of the use of cognitive instruction to test an hypothesis about metacognitive development. It is to be hoped that as the instructional approach is refined, more investigators will realize its full potential.

# REFERENCES

Belmont, J. M. (1966). Long-term memory in mental retardation. In N. R. Ellis (Ed.), *International review of research in mental retardation* (Vol. 1). New York: Academic Press.

Belmont, J. M., & Butterfield, E. C. (1969). The relations of short-term memory to development and intelligence. In L. Lipsitt & H. Reese (Eds.), *Advances in child development and behavior,* (Vol. 4). New York: Academic Press.

Belmont, J. M., & Butterfield, E. C. (1971). Learning strategies as determinants of memory deficiencies. *Cognitive Psychology, 2,* 411–420.

Belmont, J. M., & Butterfield, E. C. (1977). The instructional approach to developmental cognitive research. In R. Kail and J. Hagen (Eds.), *Perspectives on the development of memory and cognition.* Hillsdale, NJ: Erlbaum.

Borkowski, J. G., & Cavanaugh, J. C. (1979). Maintenance and generalization of skills and strategies by the retarded. In N. R. Ellis (Ed.), *Handbook of mental deficiency, psychological theory and research,* (2nd ed.). Hillsdale, NJ: Erlbaum.

Brainerd, C. J., & Allen, T. W. (1971). Experimental inductions of the conservation of "first-order" quantitative invariants. *Psychological Bulletin, 75,* 128–144.

Brown, A. L., & Campione, J. C. (1978). Permissible inferences from the outcome of training studies in cognitive development research. In W. S. Hall, & M. Cole (Eds.), *Quarterly Newsletter of the Institute for Comparative Human Development, 2,* 46–53.

Butterfield, E. C., & Dickerson, D. J. (1976). Cognitive theory and mental development. In N. R. Ellis (Ed.), *International review of research in mental retardation* (Vol. 8). New York: Academic Press.

Butterfield, E. C., & Ferretti, R. P. (in press). Some extensions of the instructional approach to the study of cognitive development and a sufficient condition for transfer of training. In P. H. Brooks, C. McCauley, & R. Sperber (Eds.), *Learning and cognition in the mentally retarded.* Baltimore, MD: University Park Press.

Butterfield, E. C., Siladi, D., & Belmont, J. M. (1980). Validating theories of intelligence. In H. W. Reese & L. P. Lipsitt (Eds.), *Advances in child development and behavior,* (Vol. 15). New York: Academic Press.

Butterfield, E. C., Wambold, C., & Belmont, J. M. (1973). On the theory and practice of improving short-term memory. *American Journal of Mental Deficiency, 77,* 654–669.

Ellis, N. R., & Hope, R. (1968). Memory processes and the serial position curve. *Journal of Experimental Psychology*, 77, 613-619.

Flavell, J. H. (1970). Developmental studies of mediated memory. In H. Reese & L. Lipsitt (Eds.), *Advances in child development and behavior* (Vol. 5). New York: Academic Press.

Glazner, M., & Cunitz, A. R. (1966). Two storage mechanisms in free recall. *Journal of Verbal Learning and Verbal Behavior*, 5, 351-360.

Kuhn, D. (1974). Inducing development experimentally: Comments on a research paradigm. *Developmental Psychology*, 10, 590-600.

Moss, S. M., & Sharac, J. A. (1970). Accuracy and latency in short-term memory: Evidence for a dual retrieval process. *Journal of Experimental Psychology*, 84, 40-46.

Ringel, B. A., & Springer, C. J. (1980). On knowing how well one is remembering: The persistence of strategy use during transfer. *Journal of Experimental Child Psychology*, 29, 322-333.

Rohwer, W. D. (1973). Elaboration and learning in childhood and adolescence. In H. W. Reese (Ed.), *Advances in child development and behavior*, (Vol. 8). New York: Academic Press.

Underwood, B. J. (1975). Individual differences as a crucible in theory construction. *American Psychologist*, 30, 128-134.

CHAPTER *9*

# A New Look at Infant Intelligence*

*Joseph F. Fagan III*

*Case Western Reserve University*

## INTRODUCTION

For the past 50 years attempts have been made to predict levels of intellectual functioning during childhood from various indices of infant sensori-motor development (e.g. Anderson, 1939; Bayley, 1933). Tests such as the Gesell Developmental Schedules (Gesell & Amatruda, 1954), the Cattell Infant Intelligence Scale (Cattell, [1940] 1960), the Griffiths Scale of Mental Development (Griffiths, 1954), the Bayley Scales of Infant Development (Bayley, 1969), the Neonatal Behavior Assessment Scale (Brazelton, 1973), and the Graham-Rosenblith Behavioral Examination of the Neonate (Rosenblith & Graham, 1961) have been administered to infants expected to function in the normal range of intelligence as well as to infants suspected to be at risk for later intellectual deficit. The basic result has been that infant "mental" tests based on sensori-motor functioning have proven to be ineffective in predicting later intelligence (e.g. McCall, Hogarty & Hurlburt, 1972). Fagan and Singer (in press), for example, in reviewing studies of the predictive validity of infant mental tests such as the Bayley Scales note that correlations obtained between tests given during the 3- to 7-month period and standard intelligence tests at 3 years or beyond average about .11 for normal samples and about .18 for high risk and clinical samples.

The most common theoretical explanation for the lack of relationship between infant sensori-motor performance and later intellectual status has been that the growth of intelligence is a discontinuous process (e.g. Kopp & McCall,

---

*The preparation of this chapter was supported, in part, by Major Research Project Grant HD-11089 from the National Institute of Child Health and Human Development.

223

1980; Lewis, 1973). According to the discontinuity notion, the kind of intelligence measured on later intelligence tests does not exist during infancy. Thus, infant sensori-motor test performance does not relate to later intellectual performance because the infant's intelligent activity is not the same kind of intelligent activity as the child's. Another way to view the discontinuity position is that the predictive shortcomings of infant tests have been interpreted as a fundamental change in the nature of intelligence with development.

I feel that there is an alternative to the discontinuity explanation for the low correlation between early sensori-motor functioning and later intellectual performance. My explanation is based on the fact that standard tests of infant "intelligence" measure the development of simple sensory and motor skills. Tests of sensory functioning or motor proficiency are not related to differences in intelligence later in life. Why then should such tests be expected to be early indicators of intelligence? I assume, that to predict later intelligence, the task is to sample infant behaviors which tap processes known to be related to later intelligence. On later intelligence tests children are asked, for example, to abstract or identify similarities and differences among stimuli, to retain new information, to categorize stimuli, and to retrieve useful information. To the extent that is possible to ask an infant to exhibit such processes as discrimination, abstraction or identification, retention, and categorization it should be possible to develop a valid test of infant intelligence. In fact, the purpose of the present chapter is to show how developments in the measurement and study of cognitive functioning during infancy have recently led to the demonstration of continuity in intellectual functioning from infancy to childhood.

The chapter begins with a summary of methods employed to study visual recognition memory during infancy. A survey is then made of the major results derived from such methods. In that survey we will see that infants are able to exhibit such processes as discrimination, retention, abstraction, and categorization. A final section on major issues and potential extensions of the findings on infant cognition will begin with a survey of studies in which evidence emerges for the validity of tests of infant recognition memory for predicting later intelligence. The final section concludes with a discussion of some theoretical and practical consequences that flow from these initial discoveries of continuity in intelligence from infancy to childhood.

## METHODS

The study of early cognitive functioning has been based largely on the observation of the infant's visual behavior. Specifically, visual perception is usually defined by the infant's tendency to devote more fixation to some stimuli than to others. The infant's tendency to respond differentially in the presence of novel and previously seen targets defines recognition memory.

Historically, the study of infant visual perception began with the visual-interest or preferential-looking test originated by Fantz (1956). The test assumes that if an infant looks more at one stimulus than at another he must be able to differentiate between the two targets. Differential visual fixation, operationally defined, is when one of a pair of targets elicits significantly more than 50% of the infant's total fixation time. The procedure for determining an infant's visual fixation is illustrated in Figure 9.1. The infant is placed in front of a "stage" which holds targets. An observer, looking through a peephole centered between the targets observes the corneal reflection of the targets over the pupils of the infant's eyes. The length of fixation paid to each stimulus is recorded. Inter-observer agreement as to length of fixation is quite high ( > .95) even for tests made during the first days of life (Miranda, 1970). The test is inexpensive and simple to use either in a laboratory setting or in the infant's home.

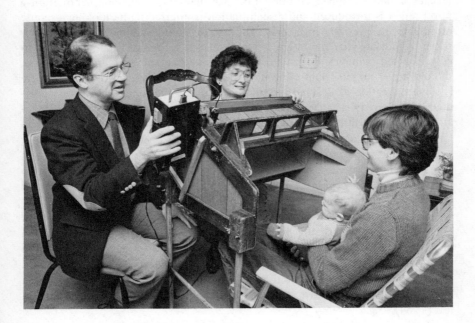

Figure 9.1. Visual Preference Testing

The study of the origins of visual cognition was given great impetus when investigators began to take advantage of certain naturally occuring visual prefer-ences to solve the problem posed by the fact that infants sometimes prefer to fixate one target as much as another. Such lack of differential fixation may im-ply either lack of discrimination or the equal attention values of stimuli that are actually discriminable. The solution to the problem of equal visual fixation was to rely on a known visual preference to increase the salience of one of the members of a target pair. Thus, one means researchers used to test the infant's ability to discriminate between two targets evoking equal attention was to pair the targets following exposure to one of them. It is a well documented finding that, after exposure to a target, infants will prefer to view a novel stimulus when the opportunity to do so is presented. Preference for novel over previously exposed targets shows that the two targets are discriminable, and also indicates that the infant can recognize or identify one of the targets as familiar.

Based on the visual-interest test, two specific paradigms have been developed to test the infant's recognition memory. In one procedure the same stimulus is presented for a number of trials. Typically, the infant's response to the repeatedly exposed target declines or "habituates" over trials. Some investigators insure that response decline over trials has taken place by testing until the infant reaches a predetermined criterion for "habituation". Following habituation a novel target is introduced and dishabituation is inferred if the looking response returns to its previous high level. The habituation/dishabituation sequence is taken to indicate that the infant has stored some information about the repeatedly exposed stimulus. Following the initial decline and recovery of response, the old target may be reintroduced. If the infant's response again declines, there is some indication of delayed recognition. The habituation/dishabituation paradigm came into use as a measure of infant recognition memory following demonstrations of its utility by Caron and Caron (1968), Lewis, Fadel, Bartels and Campbell (1966), and by Pancratz and Cohen (1970).

A second paradigm developed to test infant visual-recognition memory, also based on the visual-interest test, is to expose the infant to a target for a certain period of time (e.g., 2 minutes). Following this "familiarization" or study period the infant is presented with the recently exposed and novel targets simultaneously. Infants typically devote the greater part of their visual fixation to the novel target when tested with this paired-comparison approach. Delayed recognition memory is tested by varying the time that elapses between the end of the study period and the presentation of the test pairing. Early tests of memory in which a novel and a previously exposed target were paired were carried out by Fagan (1970), Fantz (1964, Fantz and Nevis (1967), and Saayman, Ames, and Moffett (1964).

Both the habituation/dishabituation and paired-comparison paradigms measure the infant's visual interest by differential looking. A third paradigm developed to test infant recognition memory measures visual interest by the infant's rate of sucking where sucking is employed as an instrumental response by the infant to produce visual stimulation. In the high amplitude sucking paradigm used to test visual recognition (Siqueland & Delucia, 1969), a visual stimulus is brought into focus as a contingent reinforcement for high amplitude sucking. As the infant habituates to the repeated target, sucking declines. After the infant reaches some criterion of habituation, a new target is made contingent on high amplitude sucking. If the sucking response returns to its previous high amplitude in the presence of the novel target, recognition is inferred.

In summary, paradigms have been developed to observe the infant's visual behavior in the presence of novel and previously exposed targets. Attentiveness preferences in such a context have been used to infer discrimination between two targets: identification of targets as familiar or novel, and retention of such identifications over time. In the next section we will see how investigators have employed the infant's preference for visual novelty to explore early cognitive development.


# IMPORTANT FINDINGS

In the present section, the purpose is to show that the infant is able to act intelligently. Intelligent action on the part of the infant means that the infant displays processes which are also employed by the child and the adult to solve problems on intelligence tests. Specifically, we begin by considering evidence for the infant's ability to remember and by noting some of the parameters governing early memory. The fact that infants display many of phenomena found in studies of adult memory is pointed out. Proof of the infant's ability to abstract invariant relations, that is, to categorize visual information, is then considered. The common methodological thread among studies of memory, abstraction and categorization during infancy is that evidence for each is based on observation of the infant's behavior in the presence of a novel and a previously exposed stimulus.


## Memory

Infants, from birth, are able to recognize which of two targets they have seen before, provided that they have been allowed a fairly long period to study the to-be-remembered target and that the novel and previously exposed targets vary along many dimensions. Werner and Siqueland (1978), for example, employed the high amplitude sucking paradigm to test infants at 6 days of age who had been born 5 weeks prior to term. Following at least 5 minutes of study, the neonates in Werner and Siqueland's experiment were able to differentiate between novel and previously exposed checkerboards which varied in size and number of pattern elements as well as in hue and brightness.

With increasing age, infants are able to distinguish on a recognition test between pairs of stimuli with fewer and fewer between-target differences. Examples of stimulus pairings that can be discriminated on a recognition test at 3, 4, and 5 months are illustrated in Figure 9.2. Thus, at 3 months, the infant can remember which of two widely discrepant black and white targets he has

Figure 9.2. Target Pairings on Recognition Tests

seen before (top row of Figure 9.2). At 4 months targets differing only in the
manner in which the same elements are arranged (middle row) can be distinguished. By 5 months the infant can recognize which of two face photos he has
seen before (bottom row).

In addition to displaying finer differentiations among stimuli over age, the
older infant needs relatively little time to study a target before being able to

recognize it as familiar. How much study time the infant needs for later recognition depends on the nature of the novel and previously exposed targets to the discriminated. Fagan (1974) asked 5-month-old infants to distinguish on a recognition test among pairs of abstract stimuli varying along a number of dimensions, abstract targets varying only in pattern arrangement, and photos of faces. Examples of those pairings are pictured in Figure 9.2. Amount of study time necessary to elicit a novelty preference on recognition testing varied over tasks. As little as 4 seconds of prior study time was needed to differentiate a novel from a previously seen target when the targets varied widely (top row). Novelty preferences were not in evidence for pairs of targets differing solely on patterning (middle row) unless 17 seconds had been spent studying the to-be-familiar target. Distinctions among faces (bottom row) required at least 20 seconds of prior study. Variations in the amount of prior study needed to solve each task corresponded to age-related differences in ease of discrimination with tasks requiring little study also being the tasks solved at an earlier age. Since the Fagan (1974) study, the efficacy of brief study times for infant recognition and the interaction of study time with target discriminability have been reported by a number of investigators (Cornell, 1979; Fagan, 1977a; Lasky, 1980; Lasky and Spiro, 1980; Rose, 1980; 1981).

With increasing age, the infant is able to retain previously seen information for long periods of time and such retention is not easily disrupted. A study by Fagan (1973) found that infants 5 to 6 months of age recognized, after 2 days, which member of a pair of abstract targets they had originally studied even when the targets varied only in patterning. A second experiment in the Fagan (1973) study demonstrated delayed recognition for photos of faces at intervals of 3 hours, 1, 2, 7, and 14 days on the part of 5-month old infants. The main findings of the 1973 study by Fagan have been confirmed in subsequent investigations by Cornell (1979), Martin (1975), Strauss and Cohen (1980), and Topinka and Steinberg (1978). With regard to disruption of infant memory, a series of experiments by Fagan (1973, 1977b) demonstrated that 5-month-old infants were well able to remember which face photo they had seen before even though the infants had been subjected to possible retroactive interference from other face photos. Findings similar to Fagan's (1973, 1977b) with regard to the infant's generally high resistance to interference have been reported by Bornstein (1976), Cohen, Deloache and Pearl (1977), and by McCall, Kennedy, and Dodds (1977).

Thus far, we have noted that infants, from birth, are able to differentiate among highly discriminable targets on an immediate-recognition test following lengthy study of the to-be-remembered stimulus. Successively finer distinctions are made with increasing maturational level. The infant, at least from 5 months, requires relatively little study of a target for subsequent recognition. Also by 5 months, the infant's recognition memory is long lasting and is not easily disrupted. Thus, important phenomena found in studies of adult memory have their origins in the first 6 months of life. In general, the recognition memory of infants, like adults, varies with length of study time allowed prior to recognition testing, with the nature of the distinctions to be made between novel and previously exposed targets; and memory, when evidenced, is usually long-lasting and is not easily disrupted. Additionally, more specific memory phencmena common to infants and adults, which we will now consider, include the effects of encoding and retrieval context on memory, the form of the serial position effect, and variations in performance due to distribution of practice.

Students of adult memory have long been aware that manipulation of the context in which an item is encoded or the context in which it is retrieved has powerful effects on later recognition or recall (e.g., Craik & Lockhart, 1972; Craik & Tulving, 1975; Hyde & Jenkins, 1969; Thomson & Tulving, 1970; and Tulving & Osler, 1968). The manipulation of encoding or retrieval contexts also has effects on the recognition-memory performance of infants. As to the effects of encoding context on retention, it has been found that certain conditions of study are more apt to result in the infant's recognition of a target than are others. Specifically, recognition may be facilitated by allowing the infant to study a related target as well as the to-be-remembered target prior to recognition testing. Fagan (1978), for example, found that the 7-month-old infant's recognition memory for a man's face (when that man was to be differentiated from another man) was improved by allowing the infant prior study of various poses of the to-be-remembered man. An additional experiment in the Fagan (1978) study found that the provision of related instances of a target during study facilitates not only facial recognition but the recognition of abstract patterns as well. Aside from the Fagan (1978) study, instances of facilitation of infants' recognition of form, patterning, or facial characteristics due to manipulation of study context are contained in reports by Olson (1979), Nelson, Morse, and Leavitt (1979), and Ruff (1978), respectively.

More recently, Rolfe and Day (1981) and Ruff (1981) have found that the degree of similarity in context between conditions of encoding and retrieval also has a strong effect on infants' recognition memory. In each study, 6-month-old infants were allowed to look at and/or handle objects during study. Subsequent recognition tests for half the infants either duplicated study conditions (e.g., bimodal test following bimodal study) or did not duplicate study conditions (e.g., biomodal study followed by unimodel test). In each experiment, recognition memory was either superior or evident only in those conditions in which the context remained the same from study to test.

Context effects are not the only phenomena common to studies of infant and adult memory. Recent studies by Cornell (1980; 1982), for example, have shown that two well established phenomena in the adult literature—the distribution effect (distributed study superior to massed study for later recognition) and the serial-position effect (primacy and recency effects plus labile recency effect over delay)—are present at 6 months. The reason for citing each of these instances of memory phenomena common to infants and adults is to make the argument that, since adults and infants respond in the same manner following

particular manipulations, it seems reasonable to suppose that common mechanisms, invariant over age, underlie those behaviors. In effect, what I am
suggesting is that the fact that phenomena found in adult memory may be
duplicated during infancy raises the possibility that there is a set of memory
processes fundamental to humans which are continuous over age. By logical
extension, if memory is also an important process for determining performance
on later intelligence tests, then continuity, over age, in intelligence would be
expected.

## Abstraction

The ability to detect similarities among otherwise diverse stimuli would seem to
be a basic intellectual process. Such abstraction is necessary if two or more
objects are to be treated as equivalent, a behavior which serves as an operational
definition of categorization (Mervis & Rosch, 1981). The solution of various
tasks such as defining similarities and differences, solving analogies, and so forth,
on standard intelligence tests requires the ability to abstract common features.
Consider the perceptual-learning history of a child required to point to the
correct picture when asked to identify the word *bus* on the Peabody Picture
Vocabulary Test. At some time in the past, that child must have noted particular
attributes (e.g., size, shape, function) common to the subset of vehicles we know
as buses. He must also have noted features distinguishing those objects from
other objects (e.g., cars) in that set. In addition, features and relations among
features invariant across objects would have to be perceived. The detection of
an invariant pattern would be necessary so that the object (bus) would be identified as such regardless of distinguishable but nondefining transformations, that
is, the bus must still be seen as a bus despite changes in perspective (front, back,
side, etc.). Detection of invariants would also be necessary for the child to realize that various representations could signify the same object, that is, an actual
bus, a picture of a bus, and a line drawing of a bus would be treated as similar.
Information across modalities signifying the same object would be abstracted as
well, so that the sight, sound and feel of a bus would be noted together. Finally,
abstraction of the features common to buses would lead to the formation of a
mental representation such as a prototype which could ultimately be associated
with and evoked by the word *bus*. The purpose of the present section is to show
that the study of responsiveness to novelty has made it possible to demonstrate
that the infant is capable of abstraction. Specifically, that the infant separates
attributes, notes invariants in form over transformations in perspective, sees
similarities across different representations, is capable of transferring information across modalities, and can form prototypes.

The ability to combine attributes, when necessary, and to distinguish
among them, when necessary, is basic to the formation of categories. An important developmental question is whether or not infants perceive particular

combinations of attributes (e.g., form and color) as separable. On a recognition memory task, for example, the infant faced with a novel, red square and a previously seen, green square may solve the problem by separating color from form and by picking the correct color cue (i.e., "red"). Alternately, the infant could solve the problem by compounding the attributes of form and color and by picking the "red square". Whether the infant sees form and color as separable dimensions may be determined by controlling conditions so that attention to a compound dimension can be separated from attention to component dimensions. A test of attention to component or separable dimensions reported by Fagan (1977a) was to familiarize the infant to a form–color compound, and then to present a pair of targets with a familiar and a novel cue along one dimension and the same two novel cues along the other. In the Fagan (1977a) study, for example, the infant might be shown a red diamond during study and then tested on the paring red square versus green square. A reliable preference for the novel color cue (green) would indicate that color had provided a component solution and that form and color were separable dimensions. In the Fagan (1977a) study, infants at 5 months proved capable of attending to both form and color as separable dimensions. More recent work by Mundy (1982), employing the same experimental design as Fagan (1977a), has indicated that form and color may not be separable dimensions for the 3-month old infant. At exactly what early age particular dimensions are first treated as separable is a question for further study. The point, however, is that questions about the separability of attributes may be approached in the first few months of life through the study of visual-recognition memory.

Many experiments have demonstrated that infants are able to detect the pattern or form of a stimulus despite changes in its orientation. McGurk (1972), using an habituation/dishabituation procedure, showed that 6-month old infants recognize the form of a simple stick figure despite discriminable changes in its orientation. Employing a paired-comparison approach, Cornell (1975) and Fagan (1979) tested infants 4- to 5-months-old and verified McGurk's finding that infants faced with abstract figures can detect invariance in patterning over changes in orientation. The infant's ability to recognize invariant patterning is also true for facial representation. A study by Fagan (1976) using photos of faces in various poses showed that 7-month old infants recognized a man as familiar on recognition testing even though that man had appeared in a different pose during study (Fagan, 1976, Experiment 3) and even though such a change in pose could be easily discriminated (Fagan, 1976, Experiment 2). Additional demonstrations of the infant's ability to recognize invariant aspects of faces such as sex or affective expression have been provided by Caron, Caron, and Myers (1982), Cohen and Strauss (1979), Fagan (1976), and by Nelson, Morse, and Leavitt (1979).

Tests of visual recognition have also found that infants are able to transfer information from one representation to another. For example, infants, by 5-

months old, are able to recognize information common to an object and to a picture of that object. Five-month old infants will respond to photographs of dolls (Deloache, Strauss, & Maynard, 1979) or to photographs of people (Dirks & Gibson, 1977) as familiar after having been allowed to study the actual doll or person. Indeed, the fact that infants from 5- to 7-months old make subtle discriminations on recognition tests among face photographs (see review by Fagan, 1979) proves the general point that infants can generalize or transfer the information abstracted from months of viewing three-dimensional, chromatic, moving, real faces to two-dimensional, achromatic, still representations such as photos.

Infants are also able to associate the sight of an object with its sound or feel. Taking advantage of the fact that infants, at 4 months, prefer to view a scene accompanied by an appropriate sound rather than a scene associated with an inappropriate sound (Spelke, 1976), Bahrick, Walker & Neisser (1981) provided a striking example of the infant's ability to associate sight and sound. Bahrick, Walker, and Neisser allowed 4-month old infants to view two films superimposed on the same screen. During study, a soundtrack appropriate for one of the films was played. When the infants were later allowed to view the two films separately, they preferred to look at the "novel" film—the one for which the sound track had been inappropriate. Presumably, during study, listening to the sound track had biased the infants to visually attend to the film naturally associated with that sound, hence the ultimate preference for the novel film on test. In addition to associating sights and sounds, infants, by the end of the first year, can associate haptic and visual information. For example, infants can visually recognize what they have been previously allowed to handle but not to see (Gottfried, Rose, & Bridger, 1977; 1978; Rose, Gottfried, & Bridger, 1978).

Finally, infants are able to abstract the common features from a set of related objects to form a prototypic mental representation. Specifically, experiments by Hussaim and Cohen (1980), by Sherman (1981) and by Strauss (1979; 1981) have shown that infants, by 10 months, after being shown a series of related, schematic faces will recognize a prototype of that face as familiar.

In summary, we have seen that the ability to abstract invariants begins in infancy. Specifically, infants are able to identify previously seen targets on a recognition test even though such changes are discriminable. In other words, infants are able to treat two or more distinguishable objects as equivalent, a behavior which Mervis and Rosch (1981) cite as their operational definition of categorization. Additional examples might be given of the kinds of invariant information that infants abstract, but such detail would go beyond the scope of the present chapter. The point is simply that tests of visual recognition tell us that the infant has the ability to abstract invariant features, to transfer information, and, in effect, to categorize the visual world. If processes of abstraction represent intelligent activity later in life, it is justifiable to assume that their exercise early in life represents intelligent activity on the part of the infant.

## MAJOR ISSUES

The manner in which infants distribute their attention to novel and previously exposed stimuli reveals the operation of processes employed by older children and adults in solving intelligence tests. The fact that infants appear to behave in such an "intelligent" manner raises three major issues: empirical, theoretical, and practical. The major empirical issue is whether or not individual differences among infants in responsiveness to novelty are predictive of later intelligence. We begin the present section by summarizing recent evidence which suggests that an individual's performance on tests of early visual recognition memory is related to that individual's performance on a later test of intelligence. These empirical demonstrations of continuity between early visual-recognition memory and later intelligence raise the major theoretical question of the basis for such continuity, a question to which we shall devote our attention. One major practical issue is whether it is feasible to construct a test of infant intelligence based on visual-recognition memory. We conclude the present section by noting that such a test has recently been constructed and by pointing out some of the uses of a valid test of infant intelligence.

### The Empirical Issue of Validity

It would appear that variations in recognition memory during infancy are related to later intelligence. Concurrent validity for the extent of an infant's visual preference for a novel target as a measure of intelligence is provided by studies where groups of infants expected to differ in intelligence later in life have been compared for their ability to recognize a previously seen stimulus. The possibility that individual differences in visual-recognition memory during infancy might be linked to later differences in intelligence was first tested in a longitudinal study by Fantz and Nevis in 1967. In the Fantz and Nevis study, offspring of highly intelligent parents were compared with offspring of parents of average intelligence. The sample as a whole showed a preference for novelty beginning at about 2- to 3-months-old, but the preference developed earlier in age on the part of the offspring of the highly intelligent parents. Since 1967, many investigators have compared groups of infants expected or suspected to differ in intelligence later in life for their recognition memory ability. With few exceptions (Cohen, 1981, Fagan, Fantz and Miranda, 1971), groups of infants expected to differ in intelligence later in life also differ in their ability to recognize a familiar visual target. Such a conclusion is true for offspring of highly intelligent parents as compared to offspring to parents of average intelligence as were studied by Fantz and Nevis (1967), for comparisons of normal with Down-syndrome infants (Cohen, 1981; Miranda & Fantz, 1974), and when term and preterm infants are compared (Caron & Caron, 1981; Rose, 1980; Rose, Gottfried & Bridger, 1979; Sigman & Parmalee, 1974).

In addition to studies providing concurrent validity, published reports are available in which the relationship between tests of infant visual-recognition memory and later intelligence have been explored for individuals. Specifically, studies by Fagan (1981), Fagan and McGrath (1981), Fagan and Singer (1983), Lewis and Brooks-Gunn (1981), and by Yarrow, Klein, Lomonaco and Morgan (1975) include tests of predictive validity for 12 samples of children. Table 9.1 lists the correlations between visual-recognition tests given during infancy and later intelligence for the samples of children tested. The table also includes the number of children in each sample, the number of novelty problems (items) upon which their memory scores were based, and the average age for the children on earlier and later tests.

**Table 9.1. Correlations Between Visual Recognition Tests Given During Infancy and Later Tests of Intelligence**

| Sample | N | N of items | Age (weeks) | Age (years) | Correlation |
|--------|-----|-----------|-------------|-------------|-------------|
| 1 | 57 | 1.0 | 12 | 2.0 | .40 |
| 2 | 22 | 2.0 | 12 | 2.0 | .52 |
| 3 | 39 | 1.0 | 24 | 3.0 | .35 |
| 4 | 16 | 3.0 | 29 | 3.0 | .38 |
| 5 | 52 | 3.0 | 29 | 3.0 | .44 |
| 6 | 19 | 3.0 | 29 | 3.0 | .51 |
| 7 | 35 | 3.0 | 29 | 3.8 | .41 |
| 8 | 19 | 2.0 | 22 | 4.3 | .33 |
| 9 | 12 | 3.5 | 14 | 6.5 | .50 |
| 10 | 20 | 5.0 | 18 | 6.5 | .66 |
| 11 | 25 | 3.0 | 29 | 6.8 | .36 |
| 12 | 19 | 3.0 | 22 | 7.5 | .46 |

For each of the 12 samples a significant association exists between early recognition memory and later intelligence. Preferences for visual novelty during infancy yield moderate predictive validity coefficients ranging from .33 to .66 across the 12 samples with a mean of .44 ($SD$=.09). Moreover, the general finding that early novelty preferences are related to later intelligence appears to be quite robust, occuring as it does despite many subject and procedural variations from study to study. Thus, with regard to subject variables, the associations between early novelty preferences and later IQ hold for blacks (Samples 3, 4, 6) as well as whites (Samples 1, 2, 5, and 7 through 12) and, within samples, for males as well as females. Also, the associations hold for initial tests made between 3 and 7 months and for intelligence measured at 2 to 7 years. Procedural variations make little difference as to outcome. Differential paradigms for measuring recognition memory such as the habituation/dishabituation procedure (Samples 1 and 2) and the paired-comparison method (all other samples) yield similar results. Correlations between novelty preferences during infancy and later IQ are obtained for a variety of early recognition test materials such as abstract patterns (Samples 1, 2, 8, 9, 10, 11, 12), objects (Sample 3) or photos of faces (Samples 4, 5, 6, 7). Finally, with the exception of Samples 4, 5, and 6, the experiments in which the children had originally participated as infants had not been designed as tests of individual differences. For example, standard test administration, typical of studies aimed at measuring individual differences, was obviated by the requirements of good experimentation to make random novel and familiar targets over subjects. Despite the attenuation caused by such inappropriate (though inadvertent) experimental design, significant correlations were obtained between infants' novelty preferences and later intelligence.

Assessment of the scope of the average correlation of .44 between infants' novelty preferences and later IQ found over the 12 samples should also be based on the fact that all of the correlations listed in Table 9.1 very likely underestimate the predictive validity of infant recognition memory tests. Attenuation of each of the 12 correlations was due to two factors. The first source of attenuation was the restricted range of intelligence within which predictions were made. For example, IQ scores across 8 of the 12 samples listed in Table 9.1 (Samples 4, 5, and 7 through 12) ranged from 90 to 130 with a mean of 108 and a standard deviation of 10. In future studies, one would expect higher validity coefficients for infant memory tests of intelligence if wider ranges of intellectual functioning are tapped. But the major source of attenuation of predictive validity for each sample was the low reliability of the tests of infant memory employed across studies. The low reliability of infant memory scores was due to the small number of visual-novelty preferences (from one to five tests of preference) upon which the memory scores were based from sample to sample. Fagan and McGrath (1981) and Fagan (1981), for example, who account for 6 of the coefficients listed in Table 9.1, report a median estimated reliability of .42 for infant memory tests composed of an average of 3.5 novelty preferences. Assuming a reliability of .90 for the intelligence tests given at later ages and a value of .42 for early memory tests, we may calculate the validity coefficient to be expected if the early and later tests had perfect reliability. The average validity coefficient "corrected for attenuation" is .72. The corrected correlation of .72 should not, of course, be substituted for the obtained average validity of .44. The fact that the correlation rises substantially when "corrected" simply means that it would be reasonable to assume that future tests of the relation between infant memory and later IQ based on more pairings of previously exposed and novel targets should yield higher predictive validity coefficients than those obtained so far.

In summary, substantial concurrent and predictive validity exists for the assumption that tests of visual recognition memory administered during infancy reflect intelligent activity on the part of the infant and for the idea that such intelligence is continuous over age.

## Theoretical Issues

The chief theoretical issue raised by the demonstration of continuity in intelligence from infancy to childhood is the question of the basis for such continuity. My assumption is that the basis of continuity lies in similarities in the processes underlying early recognition memory tasks and later intelligence. According to this view, intelligence may be seen as a small set of basic processes for the acquisition of knowledge, processes which are largely innate, dependent on neural integrity, and continuous with age. For example, the ability to detect similarities across varying contexts is involved in the choice of a novel over a previously seen target, in the consistent application of a verbal label to two stimuli which share a common feature, and in the detection of an analogy. Other processes, in addition to simple similarity detection, are also involved in the recognition of a previously seen target, the acquisition of vocabulary, and the solving of analogies. The point is that the theoretical task in the search for continuity is to discover common processes which may mediate performance across different problems from one age to the next. The goal would be to construct models and to conduct appropriate tests so that earlier and later tasks might be reduced to their constituent component processes. Once such componential analyses have been carried out, the final step would be to note those components which are invariant over tasks.

I would like to suggest that the effort to explain continuity in intelligence on the basis of the existence of a small set of basic processes may be linked to current work by cognitive psychologists such as Detterman (1982), Humphreys (1979), Jensen (1979), Sternberg (1981) and others who are seeking to explicate the nature of the general factor in intelligence ("g"). Humphreys (1979, p. 115), for example, in discussing interpretations of "g", defines intelligence as "the resultant of the processes of acquiring, storing in memory, retrieving, combining, comparing, and using in new contexts information and conceptual skills." Detterman (1982, p. 105), after noting the empirical definition of "g" as a common source of variance across tasks, calls for an "attempt to devise a set of independent parameters that accounts for the common source of variance" and goes on to point out that such an attempt "will certainly be a tedious task." In the present discussion I am suggesting that there exists a small set of processes for knowledge acquisition which provide the basis for continuity in intellectual functioning during development and which underlie "g". In other words, I am hypothesizing that the search for the basis of intellectual continuity over age is formally the same as the search for the basis of "g" and that findings and explanations in each sphere of endeavor will be of mutual benefit.

The discovery that intelligence is continuous from infancy also has implications for the question of the contribution of genetic endowment and environmental circumstance to intellectual functioning. In general, tests of infant intelligence based on recognition memory should allow a more accurate determination of the relative influence of genetics and environment on intelligence from infancy to adulthood. Estimates of genetic and environmental influences on infant intelligence are currently based on tests of sensori-motor functioning, tests which are not predictive of later intelligence. Plomin (Chapter 12) concludes that hereditary influence on intelligence is negligible during infancy. But one may justifiably question any estimate of the extent of hereditary influence on infant intelligence based on the application of statistical techniques to invalid measures of infant intelligence. The role that genetic influence plays in determining infant intelligence will only be understood when the techniques of behavior genetics for assessing the relative contribution of heredity and environment are applied on valid tests of infant intelligence.

Tests of infant visual recognition should also allow us to discover periods in development when specific environmental effects on intelligence become operable. For example, specific medical problems in the neonatal period such as asphyxia, anoxia, hypoxia, Respiratory Distress Syndrome, hyperbilirubinemia, neonatal seizures, intracranial hemorrhage, profound acidosis, hypoglycemia, hyponatrenia, and hypocalcemia can be evaluated for their influence on infant intelligence. Demographic factors of race, sex, birth order, and socioeconomic status can also be assessed for their influence on early and later intelligence. An example of the study of the influence of such factors on early and later intelligence comes from the results of Fagan (1981), a study noted earlier (Samples 4 and 5 in Table 9.1). In the Fagan (1981) report, a sample of 52 white infants and a sample of 16 black infants who resided in the same suburban, middle class neighborhoods, were tested for novelty preferences at 7 months of age. At 3 years these 68 children were given tests of intelligence. Preferences for novelty at 7 months were not influenced by sex, race, birth order, or parental education. Many of the factors not associated with the infant's early recognition memory, however, were related to the child's later intelligence. Specifically, children with earlier birth orders had higher IQs than children of later birth orders. Mothers with higher education had children with better IQ scores, and IQ scores for whites were greater than those for blacks. The implication of such findings, subject to further test, is that infant intelligence is relatively independent of any influence associated with the general environmental circumstances peculiar to a child's sex, race, birth-order, or socioeconomic status.

In summary, the demonstation that variations in recognition memory during infancy predict later intelligence raises the theoretical question of the basis for such continuity, a question which may be linked to current efforts to explicate the nature of the general factor in intelligence. Moreover, a valid test of infant intelligence may aid the determination of the relative influence of heredity and environment on intelligence and may allow us to determine specific periods in development when particular environmental circumstances begin to influence intellectual activity.

## Practical Issues

Given that sufficient evidence exists to link early recognition memory with later intelligence, the practical issue is how to construct a valid test of infant intelligence based on visual-recognition functioning. In fact, a major goal of my research since 1977 has been to develop an infant intelligence test based on tests of visual recognition. Details of the test, as developed thus far, are given in Fagan (1982) and Fagan and Singer (1983). Briefly, the test is based on the infant's ability to recognize visual stimuli as measured by paired-comparison tests of the infant's differential visual fixation to novel over previously exposed targets. The basic component of the test is a "novelty problem". Each novelty problem consists of a pairing of two stimuli immediately following exposure to one of the two stimuli. My assumption was that the most advantageous approach to standard assessment of early recognition memory was to allow each infant a particular amount of study fixation, the same amount for each infant, and then to test for recognition by pairing a novel and previously seen target. Following this procedure with a variety of tasks allowed each infant a composite novelty preference score derived from many items.

Some 1,400 infants were seen in order to discover which combinations of standard study times (i.e., all infants were allowed the same study time on a particular problem) and stimulus pairings would lead, at each of 4 ages, to a set of 3 novelty problems that could easily be administered during a single session and which individually, could be solved (i.e., preferences for novelty greater than chance for each problem). The result was a 12-problem test which included 3 pairs of abstract, black and white patterns administered as novelty problems at 16 weeks; 2 sets of face photos, and 2 pairs of abstract patterns constituting 4 novelty problems at 22 weeks; and 3 novelty problems composed of pairs of face photos at 29 weeks. Norms for the 12-item test were developed by conducting a longitudinal study employing a sample of 92 infants with recognition tests administered at 52, 56, 62, and 69 weeks of conceptional age (e.g., an infant born at 37 weeks of gestation would be given the test developed for 12 week old infants at 15 weeks postnatal age, the 16 week test at 19 weeks of age, etc.) The normative sample included blacks as well as whites and infants from environments representing a wide-socioeconomic range.

In summary, my current work has led to the development of a standard, multi-item visual recognition test of infant cognition which may be administered between 3 and 7 months of age. Ultimately, my psychometric goal is to determine the predictive validity of the various items comprising the test of infant intelligence. Hopefully, such item analysis will allow the combination of those items with the highest predictive validity into a final infant test which will be brief, highly reliable, most valid, and easily administered.

A number of practical uses may be found for a valid test of infant intelligence. The primary use would be to separate normal from abnormal individuals within groups of infants suspected to be at risk for a slower rate of intellectual development due to various prenatal or perinatal factors. In fact, we have employed the 12-problem, visual-memory test of infant intelligence to assess the early cognitive functioning of groups of infants suspected to be at risk for later cognitive deficit. Some of these were premature. Some were the offspring of diabetic mothers. Others had experienced growth failure either in utero or subsequent to birth. Some had shown positive signs of damage to the central nervous system (e.g., seizures, chronic bouts of apnea). As a group, such at-risk infants showed lower absolute novelty preferences than normal infants on the 12-item test. This disparity in novelty preferences between normal and at-risk samples was statistically reliable. At the same time, normal infants and infants at risk for later cognitive deficit found the same novelty problems to be relatively difficult or easy. Therefore, the differences between at-risk and normal samples in overall recognition-memory functioning were not due to differences on a few selected novelty problems, indicating that the 12-item test, as developed, is not "biased" in a statistical sense. In short, we have found it feasible to apply the 12-problem test of visual memory to various at risk samples with the hope of predicting which types of initial risk conditions in general (i.e., prematurity, being the offspring of a diabetic mother, etc.) may lead to better or poorer outcomes and to identify which infants in each condition will be particularly affected.

A second important use of a valid test of infant intelligence would be to provide an early assessment of the effects of intervention. Pediatricians, for example, are concerned with the lapse in time that occurs in the evaluation of treatment procedures for infants in neonatal intensive care units. As Fitzhardinge (1980, p. 1) puts it, the major problem is "the unavoidable gap in the time between treatment of a neonate and the reliable assessment of his or her neurological and intellectual status. The obvious and severe complications can be diagnosed by one or two years of age, but less severe forms of impairment are difficult to assess with accuracy even after a year or two of schooling. Changes in perinatal care, though, proceed at a much more rapid rate." Hopefully a test of infant intelligence based on visual recognition will fill this "unavoidable gap in time" between treatment and the assessment of that treatment for its effects on intelligence. Educational psychologists could employ a valid test of infant intelligence to provide baseline estimates of early cognitive functioning for experimental and control groups in tests of remedial programs. Clinical psychologists might use the results of a valid test of infant intelligence to encourage parents to treat as normal those infants who score well on tests of visual memory but who, because of small size or unusual motor development, might appear to be abnormal.

The final use of a valid test of infant intelligence to be mentioned here is its extension to various populations for whom conventional tests of intelligence are inappropriate. Such a program of alternative testing has begun with profoundly retarded children (Shepherd & Fagan, 1981) and with severely handicapped 18-month-olds (Mundy, Siebert, Hogan & Fagan, 1983).

## SUMMARY

Conventional tests of infant intelligence based on individual differences in sensori-motor development have failed to predict later intelligence. One interpretation of such failure of prediction is that intelligence is inherently discontinuous. Another interpretation is that tests of sensori-motor functioning are not related to intelligence per se. If intelligence is to be predicted from infancy, the task is to tap the same cognitive processes at early and at later points in development. Tests of the infant's ability to recognize a previously seen target involve cognitive processes similar to those processes employed to solve later tests of intelligence. The assumption that variations in early visual-recognition memory are both current and predictive indicators of intelligence has empirical support. The recognition memory abilities of normal infants have been found to be superior to those of infants considered to be at risk for later intellectual deficit. Evidence for the predictive validity of infant recognition memory tests emerges from longitudinal studies in which a significant relationship between the extent of infant's visual preferences for novel targets and later performance on standard tests of intelligence has been confirmed.

Inquiry into the theoretical basis of continuity in intelligence from infancy to childhood will both aid and profit from current attempts by cognitive psychologists to explain the nature of the general factor in intelligence. Moreover, the demonstration of continuity in intelligence has implications for the study of genetic and environmental effects on intelligence. Practically, the development of a standard test of infant intelligence based on individual differences in visual-recognition memory has proven to be feasible. The new test of infant intelligence, based on memory, may be used to diagnose developmental deficit, to provide baseline and outcome estimates for intervention studies, and may be extended to assess nonverbal, handicapped children.

# REFERENCES

Anderson, J. E. (1939). The limitations of infant and preschool tests in the measurement of intelligence. *Journal of Psychology, 8,* 351–379.

Bahrick, L. E., Walker, A. S., & Neisser, U. (1981). Selective looking by infants. *Cognitive Psychology, 13,* 377–390.

Bayley, N. (1933). Mental growth during the first three years: A developmental study of 61 children by repeated tests. *Genetic Psychology Monographs, 14,* 1–92.

Bayley, N. (1969). *The Bayley Scales of Infant Development,* New York: Psychological Corporation.

Bornstein, M. H. (1976). Infants' recognition memory for hue. *Developmental Psychology, 12,* 185–191.

Brazelton, T. (1973). *Neonatal Behavioral Assessment Scale.* Philadelphia, PA: Lippincott.

Caron, R. F., & Caron, A. J. (1968). The effects of repeated exposure and stimulus complexity on visual fixation in infants. *Psychonomic Science, 10,* 207–208.

Caron, A. J., & Caron, R. F. (1981). Processing of relational information as an index of infant risk. In S. L. Friedman and M. Sigman (Eds.), *Preterm Birth and Psychological Development.* New York: Academic Press.

Caron, R. F., Caron, A. J., & Myers, R. S. (1982). Abstraction of invariant face expressions in infancy. *Child Development, 53,* 1008–1015.

Cattell, P. (1960). *The Measurement of Intelligence in Infants and Young Children.* New York: Science Press, 1940. Reprinted by the Psychological Corporation.

Cohen, L. B. (1981). Lags in the cognitive competence of prematurely born infants. In S. L. Friedman & M. Sigman (Eds.), *Preterm Birth and Psychological Development.* New York: Academic Press.

Cohen, L. B., Deloache, J. S., & Pearl, R. A. (1977). An examination of interference effects in infants' memory for faces. *Child Development, 48,* 88–96.

Cohen, L. B., & Strauss, M. S. (1979). Concept acquisition in the human infant. *Child Development, 50,* 419–424.

Cornell, E. H. (1975). Infants' visual attention to pattern arrangement and orientation. *Child Development, 46,* 229–232.

Cornell, E. H. (1979). Infants' recognition memory, forgetting, and savings. *Journal of Experimental Child Psychology, 28,* 359–374.

Cornell, E. H. (1980). Distributed study facilitates infants' delayed recognition memory. *Memory and Cognition, 8,* 539–542.

Cornell, E. H. & Bergstrom, L. I. (1982, March). Serial position effects in infants' recognition memory. Paper presented at the Third International Conference on Infant Studies. Austin, TX.

Craik, F. I. M. & Lockhart, R. S. (1972). Levels of processing: A framework for memory research. *Journal of Verbal Learning and Verbal Behavior, 11,* 671–684.

Craik, F. I. M., & Tulving, E. (1975). Depths of processing and the retention of words in episodic memory. *Journal of Experimental Psychology, 104,* 268–294.

Deloache, J. S., Strauss, M. S., & Maynard, J. (1979). Picture perception in infancy. *Infant Behavior and Development, 2*, 77-89.

Detterman, D. K. (1982). Does "g" exist? *Intelligence, 6*, 99-108.

Dirks, J., & Gibson, E. J. (1977). Infants' perception of similarity between live people and their photographs. *Child Development, 48*, 124-130.

Fagan, J. F. (1970). Memory in the infant. *Journal of Experimental Child Psychology, 9*, 217-226.

Fagan, J. F. (1973). Infants' delayed recognition memory and forgetting. *Journal of Experimental Child Psychology, 16*, 424-450.

Fagan, J. F. (1974). Infant recognition memory: The effects of length of familiarization and type of discrimination task. *Child Development, 45*, 351-356.

Fagan, J. F. (1976). Infants' recognition memory of invariant features of faces. *Child Development, 47*, 627-638.

Fagan, J. F. (1977a). An attention model of infant recognition. *Child Development, 48*, 345-359.

Fagan, J. F. (1977b). Infant recognition memory: Studies in forgetting. *Child Development, 48*, 68-78.

Fagan, J. F. (1978). Facilitation of infants' recognition memory. *Child Development, 49*, 1066-1075.

Fagan, J. F. (1979). The origins of facial pattern recognition. In M. Bornstein, & W. Kessen (Eds.), *Psychological Development from Infancy*. Hillsdale, NJ: Lawrence Erlbaum Associates.

Fagan, J. F. (1981, April 4). Infant memory and the prediction of intelligence. Paper presented at Society for Research in Child Development Meeting, Boston, MA.

Fagan, J. F. (1982, March). A visual recognition test of infant intelligence. Paper presented at the International Conference on Infant Studies, Austin, TX.

Fagan, J. F., Fantz, R. L., & Miranda, S. B. (1971, April 4). Infants' attention to novel stimuli as a function of postnatal and conceptional age. Paper presented at Society for Research in Child Development Meeting, Minneapolis, MN.

Fagan, J. F., & McGrath, S. K. (1981). Infant recognition memory and later intelligence. *Intelligence, 5*, 121-130.

Fagan, J. F., & Singer, L. T. (1983). Infant recognition memory as a measure of intelligence. In L. P. Lipsitt (Ed.), *Advances in Infancy Research*, (Vol. 2), Norwood, NJ: Ablex.

Fantz, R. L. (1956). A method for studying early visual development. *Perceptual and Motor Skills, 6*, 13-15.

Fantz, R. L. (1964). Visual experience in infants: Decreased attention to familiar patterns relative to novel ones. *Science, 146*, 668-670.

Fantz, R. L., & Nevis, S. (1967). The predictive value of changes in visual preference in early infancy. In J. Hellmuth (Ed.), *The Exceptional Infant*, (Vol. 1). Seattle, WA: Special Child Publications.

Fitzhardinge, P. (1980). Current outcome: ICU populations. In A. W. Brann & J. J. Volpe (Eds.), *Neonatal Neurological Assessment and Outcome, Report of the 77th Ross Conference on Pediatric Research*. Columbus, OH: Ross Laboratories.

Gesell, A., & Amatruda, C. S. (1954). *Developmental Diagnosis.* New York: Paul B. Holber, Inc.

Gottfried, A. W., Rose, S. A., & Bridger, W. H. (1977). Cross-modal transfer in human infants. *Child Development, 48,* 118-123.

Gottfried, A. W., Rose, S. A., & Bridger, W. H. (1978). Effects of visual, haptic, and manipulatory experiences on infants' visual recognition memory of objects. *Developmental Psychology, 14,* 305-312.

Griffiths, R. (1954). *The Abilities of Babies.* New York: McGraw-Hill.

Humphreys, L. G. (1979). The construct of general intelligence. *Intelligence, 3,* 105-120.

Hussaim, J. S., & Cohen, L. B. (1980). Infant learning of ill-defined categories. Paper presented at the International Conference on Infant Studies, New Haven, CT.

Hyde, T. S., & Jenkins, J. J. (1969). Differential effects of incidental tasks on the organization of recall of a list of highly associated words. *Journal of Experimental Psychology, 82,* 472-481.

Jensen, A. R. (1979). g: Outmoded theory or unconquered frontier? *Creative Science and Technology, 2,* 16-29.

Kopp, C. B., & McCall, R. B. (1980). Stability and instability in mental performance among normal, at-risk, and handicapped infants and children. In P. B. Baltes & O. G. Grim, Jr. (Eds.), *Life-span Development and Behavior,* (Vol. 4), New York: Academic Press.

Lasky, R. E. (1980). Length of familiarization and preference for novel and familiar stimuli. *Infant Behavior and Development, 3,* 15-28.

Lasky, R. E. & Spiro, D. (1980). The processing of tachistoscopically presented visual stimuli by five-month-old infants. *Child Development, 51,* 1292-1294.

Lewis, M. (1973). Infant intelligence tests: Their use and misuse, *Human Development, 16,* 108-118.

Lewis, M., & Brooks-Gunn, J. (1981). Visual attention at three months as a predictor of cognitive functioning at two years of age. *Intelligence, 5,* 131-140.

Lewis, M., Fadel, D., Bartels, B., & Campbell, H. (1966). Infant attention: The effect of familiar and novel visual stimuli as a function of age. Paper presented at Eastern Psychological Association, New York.

Martin, R. M. (1975). Effects of familiar and complex stimuli on infant attention. *Developmental Psychology, 11,* 1978-185.

McCall, R. B., Hogarty, P. S., & Hurlburt, N. (1972). Transitions in infant sensori-motor development and the prediction of childhood IQ. *American Psychologist, 27,* 728-748.

McCall, R. B., Kennedy, C. B., & Dodds, C. (1977). The interfering effects of distracting stimuli on the infant's memory. *Child Development, 48,* 79-87.

McGurk, H. (1972). Infant discrimination of orientation. *Journal of Experimental Child Psychology, 14,* 151-164.

Mervis, C. B., & Rosch, E. (1981). Categorization of natural objects. In *Annual Review of Psychology, 32,* 89-115.

Miranda, S. B. (1970). Response to novel visual stimuli by Down Syndrome and normal infants. Proceedings of the 78th Annual Convention of the American Psychological Association, 6, 275–276.

Miranda, S. B., & Fantz, R. L. (1974). Recognition memory in Down's syndrome and normal infants. Child Development, 45, 651–660.

Mundy, P. C. (1982, March). Encoding processes in infant recognition. Paper presented at the Third International Conference on Infant Studies, Austin, TX.

Mundy, P. C., Siebert, J. M., Hogan, A. E., & Fagan, J. F. (1983). Novelty Responding and Behavioral Development in Young, Developmentally Delayed Children. Intelligence.

Nelson, C. A., Morse, P. A., & Leavitt, L. A. (1979). Recognition of facial expressions by seven-month-old infants. Child Development, 50, 1239–1242.

Olson, G. M. (1979). Infant recognition memory for briefly presented visual stimuli. Infant Behavior and Development, 2, 123–134.

Pancratz, C. N., & Cohen, L. B. (1970). Recovery of habituation in infants. Journal of Experimental Child Psychology, 9, 208–216.

Rolfe, S. A., & Day, R. H. (1981). Effects of the similarity and dissimilarity between familiarization and test objects on recognition memory in infants following unimodal and bimodal familiarization. Child Development, 52, 1308–1312.

Rose, S. A. (1980). Enhancing visual recognition memory in preterm infants. Developmental Psychology, 16, 85–92.

Rose, S. A. (1981). Developmental changes in infants' retention of visual stimuli. Child Development, 52, 227–233.

Rose, S. A., Gottfried, A. W., & Bridger, W. H. (1978). Cross-modal transfer in infants: Relationship to prematurity and socioeconomic background. Developmental Psychology, 14, 643–652.

Rose, S. A., Gottfried, A. W., & Bridger, W. H. (1979). Effects of haptic cues on visual recognition memory in full-term and preterm infants. Infant Behavior and Development, 2, 55–67.

Rosenblith, J., & Graham, F. K. (1961). Behavioral Examination of the Neonate as Modified by Rosenblith from Graham. Brown Duplicating Service, Providence, RI.

Ruff, H. A. (1978). Infant recognition of the invariant form of objects. Child Development, 49, 293–306.

Ruff, H. A. (1981). Effects of context on infants' responses to novel objects. Developmental Psychology, 17, 87–89.

Saayman, G., Ames, E., & Moffett, A. (1964). Response to novelty as an indicator of visual discrimination in the human infant. Journal of Experimental Child Psychology, 1, 189–198.

Shepherd, P. A., & Fagan, J. F. (1981). Visual pattern detection and recognition memory in children with profound mental retardation. In N. R. Ellis (Ed.), International Review of Research in Mental Retardation, New York: Academic Press.

Sherman, T. (1981). Categorization skills in infants. Paper presented at the meetings of the Society for Research in Child Development, Boston, MA.

Sigman, M., & Parmalee, A. H. (1974). Visual preferences of four-month-old premature and full-term infants. *Child Development, 45,* 959–965.

Siqueland, E. R., & Delucia, C. A. (1969). Visual reinforcement of non-nutritive
sucking in human infants. *Science, 165,* 1144–1146.

Spelke, E. (1976). Infants' intermodal perception of events. *Cognitive Psychology, 8,* 553–560.

Sternberg, R. (1981). Intelligence and nonentrenchment. *Journal of Educational
Psychology, 73,* 1–16.

Strauss, M. S. (1979). Abstraction of prototypical information by adults and 10-
month-old infants. *Journal of Experimental Psychology: Human Language
and Memory, 5,* 618–632.

Strauss, M. S. (1981). Infant memory of prototypical information. Paper presented at the meetings of the Society for Research in Child Development,
Boston, MA.

Strauss, M. S., & Cohen, L. B. (1980, April). Infant immediate and delayed
memory for perceptual dimensions. Paper presented at the International
Conference on Infant Studies, New Haven, CT.

Thomson, D. M., & Tulving, E. (1970). Associative encoding and retrieval:
Weak and strong cues. *Journal of Experimental Psychology, 86,* 255–262.

Topinka, C. V., & Steinberg, B. (1978, March). Visual recognition memory in
3½ and 7½ month-old infants. Paper presented at the International Conference on Infant Studies, Providence, RI.

Tulving, E., & Osler, S. (1968). Effectiveness of retrieval cues in memory for
words. *Journal of Experimental Psychology, 77,* 593–601.

Werner, J. S., & Siqueland, E. R. (1978). Visual recognition memory in the preterm infant. *Infant Behavior and Development, 1,* 79–94.

Yarrow, L. J., Klein, R. P., Lomoncao, S., & Morgan, G. A. (1975). Cognitive
and motivational development in early childhood. In B. X. Friedlander,
G. M. Sterritt, and G. E. Kirk (Eds.). *Exceptional Infant,* (Vol. 3), New
York: Brunner/Mazel.

CHAPTER *10*

# Preschool Compensatory Education and the Modifiability of Intelligence: A Critical Review

*Craig T. Ramey, Donna M. Bryant, and Tanya M. Suarez*

*Frank Porter Graham Child Development Center*
*University of North Carolina at Chapel Hill*

## INTRODUCTION

During the past quarter century the United States government has committed itself to assisting the development of socially disadvantaged families to an unprecedented degree. The forms of that assistance have been many and varied including civil rights legislation, urban renewal programs, nutritional and health care services, and intensive educational efforts. A theoretically controversial set of endeavors has come to be known as compensatory education. Frequently developed for preschool-aged children and/or their families, these programs have attempted, ultimately, to modify the course of early development so as to better prepare socially disadvantaged children for public school. This approach to "breaking the cycle of poverty" has been taken because it has been established repeatedly that the children who perform most poorly scholastically and intellectually tend to come disproportionately from lower socioeconomic families (e.g., Heber, Dever & Conry, 1968; Knobloch & Pasamanick, 1953; Kushlick & Blunden, 1974; Ramey, Stedman, Borders-Patterson & Mengel, 1978).

Compensatory education was chosen as one of the social strategies to boost performance of disadvantaged children because of its common sense and theoretical relationship to social competence. Compensatory education programs have been primarily controversial, because they have frequently evaluated their efforts with IQ tests. IQ tests are controversial mainly because of the continuing debate concerning the roles that genetic influences and environmental factors play in determining performance on tests of intelligence (see for example,

Herrnstein, 1982; Jensen, 1969). However, IQ tests are the only developmental measures common to all of the compensatory education studies, and are therefore the one measure that allows direct comparison of outcome across studies.

In this chapter we will review briefly the theoretical background of early compensatory education, summarize the programmatic features and intellectual results from exemplary educational experiments, and make recommendations for future research and program development.

## THEORETICAL AND HISTORICAL BACKGROUND FOR COMPENSATORY EDUCATION

### The Role of Early Experience

A pervasive model for intellectual development has been apparent in American psychology for the past quarter century. Kessen (1979, p. 819) has dubbed this model "the doctrine of primacy of early experience." The child's experiences during the opening years of life have been widely regarded as critical determinants of later social and intellectual functioning. Yarrow (1961) has observed that: "The significance of early infant experience for later development has been reiterated so frequently and so persistently that the general validity of this assertion is now almost unchallenged" (p. 459). Kagan (1979) concurs, arguing that a central premise of the modern conceptualization of human development is the belief that psychological structures created by early experience are stable throughout the lifespan. Although the doctrine of the primacy of early experience has recently been challenged (Clarke & Clarke, 1976; Kagan, Kearsley, & Zelazo, 1978; Ramey & Baker-Ward, 1982), large claims concerning the critical importance of the child's earliest experiences continue to be made (e.g., Klaus & Kennell, 1976).

The idea that the individual's early experiences are of particular consequence for later development is an old one, yet the significance of early experience has been advanced only intermittently in the history of Western thought. Other concepts have more frequently provided the dominant models of human development. In the 19th century, predeterminism was advanced by Galton and other proponents of the primacy of heredity in development. Predeterminism, unlike the earlier notion of preformationism, acknowledged maturational changes in form as well as size, but held that these changes were relatively encapsulated and consequently unaffected by early experiences (Gottlieb, 1971). In the first half of the 20th century, this view induced two empirical traditions that denied the contribution of early experience to later development: the study of instincts as unlearned patterns of behavior, and the investigation of behavioral development as controlled only by the child's rate of maturation (Hunt, 1979).

The early experience paradigm replaced the concept of predeterminism in development with that of probabilistic epigenesis. While predeterminism assumes that the maturational process is relatively unaffected by experience, probabilistic epigenesis emphasizes the importance of sensory stimulation and movement for subsequent development (Gottlieb, 1971). The early experience paradigm further held that the presence or absence of stimulation or other experiences at some critical period in development could shape the individual's ontogeny.

How did the doctrine of the primacy of early experience come to be so thoroughly entrenched in American psychology in such a relatively short period of time?

## The Scientific Bases of the Early Experience Paradigm

Evidence from three major streams of investigations flowed together in establishing the doctrine of the primacy of early experience. Freud's theory of psychosexual development (e.g., 1905) focused attention on childhood experiences and contributed significantly to the popular acceptance of the concept that early experience is a major determinant of adult behavior. Ethology also contributed to the establishment of the early experience paradigm. The phenomena of imprinting (Lorenz, 1937) were interpreted as representing a unique predisposition for learning, present for only a brief critical period. The third scientific stream provided a neuropsychological theory for the existence of critical periods in intellectual as well as social development (Hebb, 1949). Subsequent investigations with animals revealed that variations in early experiences affected both the organization and the biological bases of subsequent behavior (e.g., Thompson & Heron, 1954).

As the early experience paradigm flowered, its roots branched from the Freudian idea that early experience is important for later social and sexual behavior to the belief that it is also critical for later intellectual and instrumental competencies. Further, the conceptualization of the impact of early experience was broadened and deepened. Initially, early experience was seen to predispose an individual toward a certain personality structure and a consequent propensity to respond to certain situations in predictable ways. Later, the extension of the concept of critical periods to humans conceptualized early experience as imparting stable and irreversible neurological consequences that could set a ceiling for later problem-solving behavior. Although the empirical support for this notion was both scant and limited to investigations with laboratory animals, this interpretation of the effects of early experience formed the basis for much of the work done in the area of intellectual development and particularly in compensatory education for the past two and a half decades. Educators and psychologists began to believe that intelligence could be improved through the provision of specific and positive early experiences.

The educational implications of this empirical background were assimilated in the works of J. McVicker Hunt and Benjamin Bloom. Hunt's "concept of the match" (1961), an application of Piaget's dialectic model of development, assigned a greater role in intellectual development to the characteristics of the environment than to the hereditary make-up of the individual. Successful developmental outcomes were seen as the cumulative result of the child's successive interactions with increasingly complex stimuli. Hence, adequate development depended upon the child's receiving the appropriate stimulation at the appropriate point in development. Although Hunt's statement did not postulate critical periods in development, it implied that early experiences were particularly important.

In *Stability and Change in Human Characteristics,* Bloom (1964) made two major points that provided a major impetus for preschool intervention. First, he posited that intellectual growth occurred most rapidly in the first four or five years of life, and tapered off by the time the child had entered grade school. Second, Bloom argued that the first five years of life was a critical period for intellectual development. Intellectual development was characterized by plasticity only during the early years. Consequently, the first few years provided the only opportunity for facilitating intellectual development by enriching the child's environment.

### Extra-scientific Bases of the Early Experience Paradigm

The political zeitgeist of the 1960s was also an important influence on the public acceptance of the early experience paradigm in relation to compensatory education. Public attention was directed in the early 1960s to widespread poverty and social injustice in the United States (see Richmond, 1974). In an effort to eradicate poverty while preserving the structure of the American economic system, economic deprivation was construed as cultural deprivation. The early experience paradigm was embraced by policy makers. The environmentalist viewpoint and the emphasis on intellectual attainment in the compensatory education movement harmonized with the American ethos (Kessen, 1979).

Pragmatic concerns facilitated the immediate implementation of Project Head Start, the center of the compensatory education movement and the social policy embodiment of the early experience paradigm (Zigler & Anderson, 1979). As a service for children with a common-sense appeal, it enabled administrators to meet mandates to achieve program administration by the poor without resistance from local governments, thereby assisting the creation of the controversial Community Action Programs.

A strong emphasis on the importance of early experience in determining intellectual development involves the corollary that positive changes in the child's environment could result in increases in measured intelligence. This corollary formed the rationale for the compensatory education movement as well as for other educational innovations. The early experience paradigm purported to identify the causes of psychosocial retardation, and to specify the means by which it could be eradicated. According to the early experience paradigm, intellectual deficiencies arose from the inadequacy of the poor child's environment. These deficiencies and the resulting "cycle of poverty" could be ameliorated by providing poor children with compensatory education during the preschool years, the paradigm-specified critical period for intellectual development.

Over the past two and a half decades the field of compensatory education has generated a large body of data on intellectual plasticity during early childhood. Child and family education has been used as a mechanism to improve the development of children from socially disadvantaged families. The various projects that have been completed or that are still in progress can be construed as social experiments to alter the course of development in young children. The programs have frequently had several major goals, including (a) improving academic readiness and performance, (b) improving child health and nutrition, and (c) improving the quality of family life. Although these broad goals have frequently been discussed by the designers and creators of these educationally oriented projects, it is the realm of intellectual development and academic achievement that has received the most systematic and sustained research attention. As a matter of fact, the field of compensatory education contains the majority of experimental studies relevant to the modifiability of intellectual development in young children. It is the purpose of the next section to review the conceptual models that have explicitly or implicitly guided research in compensatory education.

## A Transactional Model of Intellectual Development

Current theories of human intellectual development such as Piaget's emphasize the dynamic interplay between the biology of an individual and the environmental forces that are encountered. Neither biology nor experience alone is sufficient to account for the process of development. For example, biological factors such as prematurity affect the way the infant initially behaves, but the quality of the environment to which the child is exposed will codetermine the subsequent development level (Parmalee, 1977).

In their influential review of perinatal risk and developmental outcome, Sameroff and Chandler (1975) noted evidence of the biology–environment interplay for a variety of risk conditions and proposed what they called a general "transactional model" of development. In such a model, the child's initial biological characteristics, including genotype, are not fully expressed at the time of conception. However, as time progresses, the genotype and environmental experiences exert a continuing influence on the child's phenotype, or observed status. For any point in time, the child's phenotype is the sum of the interactions of genotype with experiences and the environment. Furthermore, phenotypic characteristics at any point in time influence subsequent transactions with the environment.

## Educational Implications of the Transactional Model

In order to apply the transactional model to the education of young children, it is necessary to conceptualize how knowledge, social values, and culture are believed to be transmitted from generation to generation. It is a process in which the child is affected not only by the family system but also by the broader network in which the family operates—the family's financial resources and constraints, cultural milieu, sources of stress, and sources of support.

Based on the nature of systems and networks theory, as described by Lazlo, (1972); Miller, (1978); Ramey, MacPhee, and Yeates (1982), and Sarason, Carroll, Maton, Cohen and Lorentz (1977), seven major assumptions that implicitly undergird compensatory education efforts have been noted by Ramey, Trohanis and Hostler (1982). These seven assumptions are as follows:

1. Development generally proceeds toward regularized functioning, and hence, predictability.
2. A pattern that is replicated has been reinforced.
3. A family system is an adaptation to the broader network of which it is a part.
4. The functioning of a family system can be modified, whereas the network in which it operates is more resistant to change.
5. A family, like other systems, proceeds toward increased sufficiency and interdependence of functioning.
6. A family system can most easily be changed when it is in transition, for example, during early development.
7. For the developing child, the impact of proximal events declines through time and distal events increase in importance until both are sufficiently influential to be codeterminants of actions.

From the seven assumptions, it is possible to deduce a general model for the education of children that is represented schematically in Figure 10.1. In this model the infant initially enters into a family system that has certain expectations based upon the attitudes, knowledge and prior experiences of family members—factors influenced by the broader sociocultural environment. The initial status of the infant and the expectations of the caregivers codetermine specific social transactions, which vary with the skills of those involved and the opportunities that exist for their occurrence. These skills and opportunities are affected by stresses on the family and the supports that exist to deal with these stresses.

The social transactions between infants and caregivers are the initial filters through which the infant's world is experienced and are hypothetically causally related to alterations in the infant's social, cognitive, motor, temperamental, and sensory status. Through time, significant others, such as peers and other extra-familial persons, come to exercise an increasingly important role in the infant's and young child's development. The altered status of the infant and revised

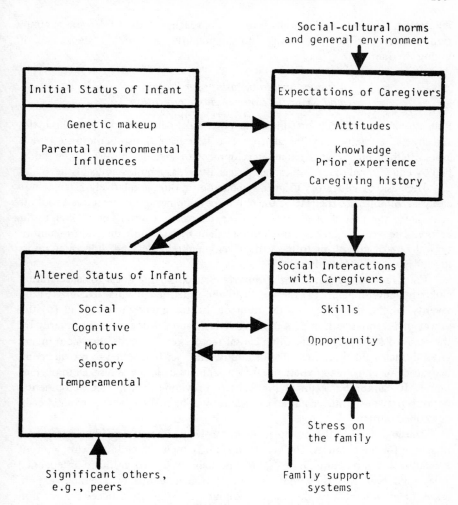

Note: From *Finding and Educating High-Risk and Handicapped Infants,* by C. T. Ramey and P. L. Trohanis, 1982. Copyright 1982 by LINC Resources, Inc. Reprinted by permission.

Figure 10.1

expectations of the caregivers codetermine new interactions, and the transactional process continues.

Within this context, early education can be implemented by working directly with the child, or indirectly by counseling the family or instructing the parents in alternative interactional styles. The comparative value of various approaches to early education then becomes a matter of systematic experimentation. The rationale for the various approaches derives from the assumptions concerning the functioning and adaptability of family systems and of young children.

*Transactional Implications for Preventive*
*and Remedial Compensatory Education*

Educational intervention presumes the potential malleability of the child, the caregiver, the family, and the environment. It is an optimistic enterprise. However, whether and to what extent development of specific abilities can be modified by educational practices is an empirical as well as a philosophical issue.

The task of educators using a remediation model is relatively clear, if not easily accomplished. The rate of the child's development must be altered so that, at least for the period of intervention, it proceeds at a faster course than it did before. The explicit goal of intervention might be to return the child to a more typical rate of growth or to have the developmentally delayed child catch up to that of more typical children.

Four factors are particularly important when setting goals for accelerating children's development: (a) the length of the time the delay has existed, (b) the severity of the delay, (c) the duration of the treatment interval, and (d) the power of the intervention procedure. The last factor is determined primarily by the state of knowledge concerning causal factors regulating development in any given domain and the knowledge or ability that can be applied to provide compensatory or enhancing experiences. Developmental timing is also an important factor. It cannot be assumed that merely providing at a later developmental period a previously missed earlier experience will be sufficient to allay an already developed deficit.

The logic, if not the practice, of preventive compensatory education is simpler than for remediation. The goal is to identify high-risk children who, without educational intervention, have a high probability of a significant intellectual delay, and then to ensure that they get sufficient exposure to crucial experiences to provide at least the minimal amount of stimulation necessary for normal growth and development.

In the remainder of this chapter we will review existing data from preventive and remedial compensatory education programs and discuss them in light of the issues which we have raised thus far in the chapter.

## THE RESEARCH STUDIES

### Caveats and Qualifications

Although a very large number of service and demonstration projects have been conducted in the past 20 years, relatively few studies have met basic criteria to be considered true experiments. The most frequent flaw from the point of view of research design has been the failure to adequately insure the initial equivalence of educationally treated and control groups. The most traditional and simplest experimental method in social and behavioral science to insure initial equivalence is to assign individuals at random to groups which are then treated differently. Given a sufficient number of cases in each group, sampling theory allows one to interpret subsequent mean differences between groups as plausibly due to the educational procedures used. In the absence of initial equivalence of groups, subsequent group differences are not scientifically interpretable in any straightforward manner.

In this chapter we have restricted our attention to studies which the various authors described as true experiments. By so restricting our choice of projects we hope to arrive at generalizations of effects which are at most conservative estimates of the current scientifically defensible knowledge-base.

The 18 studies which met our criteria to be reviewed in this chapter are presented in Table 10.1, along with the references we used in researching their subject characteristics, intervention description, research design, and IQ results. In many cases, more than one primary source was used to obtain this information, and in some cases, the different sources reported slightly different information, for example in numbers of subjects or the process of group assignment. In these cases we used our best judgement as to which numbers to report here and cited the specific source of the information in the tables that follow.

### Table 10.1. Eighteen Compensatory Education Research Studies*

---

*Infancy Programs*

---

*CENTER-BASED, CHILD AND PARENT FOCUSED*

1. Milwaukee Project
   (Garber, 1982; Garber & Heber, 1981; Heber & Garber, 1971)
2. Project CARE
   (Ramey, Bryant, Sparling, & Wasik, 1983; Ramey, Sparling & Wasik, 1981)
3. Carolina Abecedarian Project
   (Ramey & Bryant, 1983; Ramey, MacPhee, & Yeates, 1982; Ramey, Yeates, & Short, 1983)
4. Field's Center—Home Visit Comparison
   (Field, 1980, 1982)

*CENTER-BASED, PARENT FOCUSED*

5. Birmingham Parent-Child Development Center (PCDC)
   (Andrews, Blumenthal, Johnson, Kahn, Ferguson, Lasater, Malone, & Wallace, 1982)
6. Houston Parent-Child Development Center (PCDC)
   (Andrews et al., 1982)
7. New Orleans Parent-Child Development Center (PCDC)
   (Andrews et al., 1982)

*continued*

**Table 10.1.  Eighteen Compensatory Education Research Studies\* (continued)**

---

*Infancy Programs*

---

*HOME VISIT, PARENT FOCUSED*

8.  Mobile Unit for Child Health
    (Gutelius, Kirsch, MacDonald, Brooks, McErlean & Newcomb, 1972;
    Gutelius et al., 1977)

9.  Florida Parent Education Project
    (Gordon & Guinagh, 1974; Gordon & Guinagh, 1978; Guinagh & Gordon,
    1976; Olmsted, Rubin, True, & Revicki, 1980)

10. Ypsilanti–Carnegie Infant Education Project
    (Epstein & Weikart, 1979; Lambie, Bond, & Weikart, 1974)

11. Family-Oriented Home Visiting
    (Gray & Ruttle, 1980)

12. Field's Home Visit Study
    (Field, Widmayer, Stringer, & Ignatoff, 1980; Field, 1982)

---

*Early Childhood (Preschool) Programs*

---

*CENTER-BASED, CHILD AND/OR PARENT FOCUSED*

13. Perry Preschool Project
    (Schweinhart & Weikart, 1980)

14. Early Training Project
    (Klaus & Gray, 1968; Gray & Klaus, 1970; Gray, Ramsey, & Klaus, 1982)

15. Academic Preschool
    (Bereiter & Englemann, 1966)

16. Curriculum Comparison Study
    (Miller & Dyer, 1975)

17. Five Preschool Comparisons
    (Karnes, Hodgins, Teska, & Kirk, 1969)

---

*Kindergarten Program*

---

*CENTER-BASED, CHILD FOCUSED*

18. Dual Kindergarten
    (Bereiter & Washington, 1969)

---

\*Use Table 10.1 to check references for studies discussed in this chapter.

The programs have been grouped in Table 10.1 under the following three developmental periods corresponding to when the child entered the program: (a) Infancy, (b) Early childhood, or (c) Kindergarten. The projects that began in infancy have been further classified as to whether they were (a) center-based with a child-and-parent focus, (b) center-based but primarily parent-focused, or (c) home-based and primarily parent-focused. Within each of these headings, programs are arranged in order of their apparent intensity of education as judged by the number of hours per month that projects sought to have contact with parents and/or children. The Early Childhood Programs have also been ordered in intensity of contact from those that had the most hours or years of contact to those that had the least. Throughout this chapter the studies will be grouped in the same order.

It is important to note that experiments in compensatory education have been conducted solely with children from socially, educationally, and economically disadvantaged families. This has been the case because such children are at elevated risk for lower scores on standardized tests of intelligence and academic achievement (see, for example, Broman, Nichols & Kennedy, 1975; Knobloch & Pasamanick, 1953; Ramey, Stedman, Borders-Patterson, & Mengel, 1978). Therefore, it has been hypothesized that systematic educational programs might be especially advantageous to this vulnerable segment of the population—especially as our society becomes increasingly more technological.

Figure 10.2 contains timelines depicting the years during which each of the 18 projects conducted their intervention program(s)—symbolized by double solid lines—and years in which systematic follow-up data have been reported—symbolized by dashed lines. Several points about this timeline are noteworthy. First, the projects varied in the years of their inception from the early 1960s to the late 1970s. Thus, these projects were conducted during an historical period of rapid development of many social action programs aimed at reducing the impact of poverty. Thus, there is the question of whether the "natural ecology" of the environments in which these projects were conducted were comparable. It is reasonable to assume that those programs which began later, began in social climates characterized as being relatively richer in resources than earlier projects. If this is so, then the performance of control-group children might be expected, on average, to be somewhat higher in the later projects than in the earlier ones—all other factors being equal. That is, to the extent that President Johnson's Great Society Programs were successfully developed and implemented, the effect on poor families would be expected to be positive.

A second noteworthy feature of the timeline is that most of the individual projects lasted for a relatively brief historical period—about 3 to 5 years—and that there has been less systematic follow-up by investigators than might have been anticipated. Of course, the recent monograph by Lazar, Darlington, Murray, Royce, and Snipper (1982), which has reported follow-up on some of the projects to be discussed here, has made a major contribution which helps to counter this generalization. Nevertheless, the amount of information about the adjustment of families to the larger society and particularly about the adjustment of children to school is relatively thin. Gray, Ramsey, and Klaus's recent book (1982) concerning the life courses of children from the Early Training Project is also a refreshing counter-trend to this broad generalization.

Third, most of the projects are no longer actively involved in compensatory education. The exceptions to this trend are the Carolina Abecedarian Project

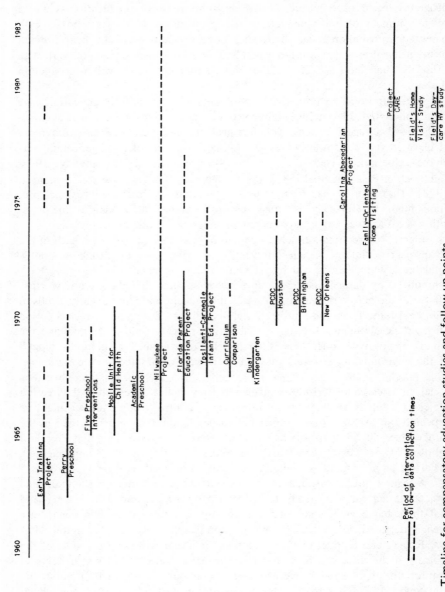

Figure 10.2. Timeline for compensatory education studies and follow-up points

258

and Project CARE—both being conducted at the Frank Porter Graham Child Development Center at the University of North Carolina at Chapel Hill.

In order to understand these 18 studies and their findings in relation to the malleability of intelligence, it is important to look consistently at key characteristics. The selected studies are therefore described in discussions of: (a) characteristics of the subjects; (b) research design; (c) characteristics of the intervention; and (d) IQ results.

## Characteristics of the Subjects

Table 10.2 contains a brief description of each project including children's age at entry, race of participants, type of community in which the project was conducted and salient family characteristics as reported by the investigators.

With the exception of the Mobile Unit for Child Health Project in which subjects were selected before birth, all of the studies were begun when the children were between birth and 5 years of age. As Table 10.2 and the subsequent descriptive tables depict, two-thirds of the studies began when the children were infants. A particularly noticeable characteristic of these studies was that most of the children who participated were black and lived in urban settings in the Eastern half of the United States. While urban black families were particularly targeted for assistance in the 1960s and 1970s due to social and economic injustices, it should be noted that, as a result, what we know about the effects of early compensatory education comes from studies which concentrated heavily on a subgroup of the socially disadvantaged population. The notable exception to this is the Houston PCDC which targeted intervention to low SES Mexican-American children and their families.

The children came from families of low economic and educational status and lived in homes having, on the average, five to seven people in them. Within this general description, however, there were dramatic differences in the families. For example, in some studies, children lived with single parents (e.g., Field's Center-Home Visit Comparison [Field, Widmayer, Stringer, & Ignatoff, 1980]) while in others (e.g., Houston Parent Child Development Center—PCDC [Andrews, Blumenthal, Johnson, Kahn, Ferguson, Lasater, Malone, & Wallace, 1982]) almost all lived with both parents. Some were children of teenage mothers while most were not. In most of the studies, some of the families lived in public housing or received some form of public assistance. The percentage of these families varied considerably among the studies, however. While these 18 studies are comparable in the composition of their samples (low socioeconomic status and mostly black families), other family characteristics which might be related to outcome have not been systematically varied and may not be directly comparable across projects.

**Table 10.2. Characteristics of the Subjects**

| Name of Study | Child's Age at Entry | Race | Type of Community | Family Characteristics |
|---|---|---|---|---|
| *Infancy Programs* | | | | |
| *I. CENTER-BASED, CHILD AND PARENT FOCUSED* | | | | |
| Milwaukee Project | 3-6 months | Black | Urban (Milwaukee, WI) | From economically depressed census tract in innercity; mothers' IQ < 75 |
| Project CARE | 3 months | 95% B 5% W | Small Town (Chapel Hill, NC) | Family's average income = $6,500; mother's and father's education = 11 yrs.; average IQ of mothers = 87; about 25% 2-parent families |
| Carolina Abecedarian Project | 3 months | Black | Small town (Chapel Hill, NC) | Average earned income = $1,455; mother's education = 10 yrs.; average IQ of mothers = 85; 25% two-parent families |
| Field's Center-Home Visit Comparison | Birth | Black | Urban (Miami, FL) | Teen mothers ≤ 19 yrs. old; full-term babies |
| *II. CENTER-BASED, PARENT-FOCUSED* | | | | |
| Birmingham PCDC | 3-5 months | Black | Urban (Birmingham, AL) | Approximately $4,000 yearly income; mother's education = 11 yrs.; average number people in home = 5; about 50% fathers head of household; most lived in public housing; less than 50% received welfare. |
| Houston PCDC | 1 year | Mexican -Amer- ican | Urban (Houston, TX) | Average income = $6,000; most owned or rented a house; mother's education = 7.5 yrs.; 90% fathers present; more than 5 people in home; 1/3 of mothers spoke only Spanish. |

| | | | | |
|---|---|---|---|---|
| New Orleans PCDC | 2 months | Black | Urban (New Orleans, LA) | Average income = $4,000; about 1/3 lived in public housing; mothers education = 10–11 years; approximately 5 people in home; approximately 50% fathers head of household. |

### III. HOME VISIT, PARENT-FOCUSED

| | | | | |
|---|---|---|---|---|
| Mobile Unit for Child Health | at 7 months of pregnancy | Black | Urban (Washington, DC) | Teenage unmarried mothers living in low income area; most income from unskilled labor; only 3 families receiving public assistance at entry; mother's scores > 20 on Peabody; for most, grandmother was head of household. |
| Florida Parent Education Project | 3 months | 80% B 20% W | Urban, small town and rural (Gainesville, FL, and surrounding 12 counties) | Families below poverty level as defined by hospital criteria. |
| Ypsilanti-Carnegie Infant Education Project | 3, 7, or 11 months | Black and white | Urban (Ypsilanti, MI) | Few parents employed; mother's and father's education = 10 yrs., approximately 6 people in home. |
| Family-Oriented Home Visiting | 17–24 months with sibling aged 2–5 | 50% B 50% W | Urban (Nashville, TN)[a] | Average income < $4,137; mother's education = 10 years; 72% 2-parent families; mother had to be nonworking or working at night (so that visits could be made). |
| Field's Home Visit Study | Birth (preterm babies) | Black | Urban (Miami, FL) | Lowest SES; teenage, unmarried mothers; mother's education = 10 yrs.; most lived with their mother who was often the primary caregiver. |

continued

**Table 10.2. Characteristics of the Subjects (continued)**

| Name of Study | Child's Age at Entry | Race | Type of Community | Family Characteristics |
|---|---|---|---|---|
| | | | *Early Childhood Programs* | |
| | | | *I. CENTER-BASED, CHILD AND/OR PARENT FOCUSED* | |
| Perry Preschool Project | 1st cohort = 4 years 2nd-5th cohorts = 3 years | Black | Urban (Ypsilanti, MI) | 70% had at least one parent employed; mother's education = 9.7, father's education = 8.8; 53% 2-parent families; approximately 7 people in home. |
| Early Training Project | 3 or 4 years | Black | Small towns (Tennessee) | Average income < $3,000; unskilled or semiskilled occupations; mother's education ≤ 8 yrs.; 67% 2-parent families; approximately 6-7 people in home. |
| Academic Preschool | 4 years | Mostly Black | Urban (Champaign, IL) | 30-40% were receiving some form of welfare; parents usually unskilled or semi-skilled laborers. |
| Curriculum Comparison | 4 years | Mostly Black | Urban (Louisville, KY) | Average income = $3,440; 30-50% received welfare; mother's and father's education = 11 yrs.; 39% 2-parent families, approximately 5-7 people in home. |
| Five-Preschool Comparisons | 4 years | 67% B 33% W | Urban (Champaign, IL) | Families from economically depressed neighborhoods of the city. |
| | | | *Kindergarten Program* | |
| Dual Kindergarten | 5 years | 75% B 25% W | Urban (Champaign, IL) | NR[b] |

[a]Personal communication
[b]NR = Not reported

262

## Research Design

Table 10.3 contains a brief description of each of the 18 projects' sampling plan, intervention research design, the IQ-assessment instruments and standardization norms, the number of child participants, and data on sample attrition.

From Table 10.3 it will be noticed that most of the projects recruited a pool of potential subjects and then randomly assigned children and/or families to a single treatment condition or to an educationally nontreated, control condition. However, several noteworthy exceptions to this relatively simple procedure occurred regarding assignment. Specifically, the Milwaukee Project assigned children to experimental or control groups by monthly cohorts instead of randomly assigning each individual. The Florida Parent Education Project used a combination of random assignment of individuals and assignment of geographic areas to various treatment conditions or to a control group. Five studies—the Ypsilanti-Carnegie Infant Education Project, the Perry Preschool, the Academic Preschool, the Curriculum Comparison, and the Five Preschool Comparisons— used stratified, random-sample assignment to groups. This procedure is standard; however, some of the studies also made nonrandom "adjustments" in the groups to balance for race or sex. When assignment procedures vary from truly random, our interpretation of results should be cautious.

Several projects had more than one experimental condition: Project CARE compared daycare-and-home visits to home visits only to controls; Field also compared center-and-home visits to home visits only to controls; the Florida Parent Education Project compared the timing and duration of six combinations of home-visits and/or playgroups to a control group; the Early Training Project compared 3 years of summer school and home visits to a 2-year program to controls; the Curriculum Comparison Project compared four types of prekindergarten programs including Bereiter-Englemann, Montessori, Ameliorative and Traditional but had no randomly assigned control group; and the Five Preschool Comparisons also compared prekindergarten programs but had no randomly assigned control group.

With respect to intellectual assessment instruments, the most commonly used measure was the Stanford–Binet (Terman & Merrill, 1973) during early childhood. During the infancy period various projects, as noted, used the Gesell (Gesell & Amatruda, 1947), the Griffiths (Griffiths, 1964) and/or the Denver (Frankenberg & Dodds, 1968), although the Bayley (Bayley, 1969) was the most widely used test. The extent to which the scores from these various infant tests are similar, especially for these samples of socially disadvantaged, primarily black samples is, at present, not known. Another potential discrepancy between the intellectual results of the projects is the norms used in the scoring of the Stanford–Binet—1960 or 1972. Most of the projects that were completed after 1972 continued to use 1960 norms, apparently for continuity in testing procedures. This difference should be noted, particularly when interpreting the results of the Milwaukee Project, the Birmingham, Houston and New Orleans PCDCs, the Mo-

Table 10.3. Research Design

| Name of Study | Sampling Plan | Intervention Design | IQ Assessments | Numbers | | Attrition |
|---|---|---|---|---|---|---|
| | | | | Entry | End | |
| | | *Infancy Programs* | | | | |
| | | *I. CENTER-BASED, CHILD AND PARENT-FOCUSED* | | | | |
| Milwaukee Project | Families assigned by alternate monthly cohorts to E or C group | E = parent training and daycare<br>C = testing only | Gesell, 10–22 months; Stanford-Binet (1960 norms), 2-6 years; WISCs, 7-10 years | E 20<br>C 20 | 17<br>18 | E=15%<br>C=10% |
| Project CARE | Families ranked by mother IQ and High-Risk Index, then randomly assigned to 1 of 3 groups | E1 = daycare + home visits and infant formula<br>E2 = home visits and infant formula<br>C = infant formula | Bayleys through 2 years, Stanford-Binets (1972 norms) at 2 and 3 yrs., McCarthy at 2½ | E1 16<br>E2 27<br>C 23 | 14<br>25<br>22 | E1=12%<br>E2= 7%<br>C = 4% |
| Carolina Abecedarian Project | Families ranked by mother IQ and High-Risk Index, then randomly assigned to E or C group | E = daycare, social work services and infant formula<br>C = social work services and infant formula | Bayleys, 3–18 months; Stanford-Binet (1972 norms), 2, 3, 4 & 5 yrs., McCarthy, 2½, 3½, 4½; WPPSI at 5 yrs. | E 57<br>C 54 | 49<br>47 | E=14%<br>C=13%<br>through age 5 |
| Field's Center-Home Visit Comparison | Mother's randomly assigned to E1, E2, or C group | E1 = daycare and parent training<br>E2 = home visits<br>C = testing only | Denver at 4 months; Bayleys at 8 and 12 months | E1 20<br>E2 20<br>C 20 | NR[a]<br>NR<br>NR | NR |

264

## II. CENTER-BASED, PARENT-FOCUSED

| | | | | | | |
|---|---|---|---|---|---|---|
| Birmingham PCDC | Randomly assigned to E or C after agreeing to participate in either group | E = daycare, parent training and work experience in daycare; C = small stipend for testing | Bayleys at 4, 10 and 20 months, Stanford-Binet (1960 norms) at 36 and 48 months | E 162; C 89 | 71; 65 | E=56%; C=27% |
| Houston PCDC | Eligible families randomly assigned to E or C, then invited to participate in the assigned group | E = home visits, day care and family services; C = testing only | Bayleys at 12 and 24 months, Stanford-Binet (1960 norms) at 36 months | E 97; C 119 | 44; 58 | E=55%; C=51% |
| New Orleans PCDC | Recruited mothers randomly assigned to E or C groups | E = daycare, parent training and family services; C = offered health services and stipend for testing | Bayleys at 7, 13, 19 and 25 months. Stanford-Binet (1960 norms) at 36 and 48 months | E 67; C 59 | NR; NR | E=50%; C=25% |

## III. HOME VISIT, PARENT-FOCUSED

| | | | | | | |
|---|---|---|---|---|---|---|
| Mobile Unit for Child Health | Mothers were recruited during pregnancy and randomly assigned to E or C before child's birth | E = medical services and infant stimulation services at home; C = referred to other available health services | Bayleys through 2 yrs., Stanford-Binet (1960 norms) at 3 yrs. | E 47; C 48 | 44; 45 | E= 6%; C= 6% |

*continued*

**Table 10.3. Research Design (continued)**

| Name of Study | Sampling Plan | Intervention Design | IQ Assessments | Numbers Entry | End | Attrition |
|---|---|---|---|---|---|---|
| Florida Parent Education Project | Families randomly assigned to various E groups or C group; later, more were randomly assigned to the E=HLC or C group. Assignment was made by area of town or county. | E = 1 of 6 Home visit and/or playgroup combinations of 1, 2 or 3 yrs. duration. C = testing only | Griffiths at 1 year; Bayley at 2 yrs.; Stanford-Binet (1960 norms); at 3-6 yrs.; WISC-R at 10 yrs. | 3 yrs. NR<br>2 yrs. NR<br>1 yr. NR<br>C NR<br>Total 309 | 24<br>35<br>83<br>50<br>192 | 37% overall |
| Ypsilanti-Carnegie Infant Education Project | Stratified random sample by age of entry | E = home visits<br>C = testing only | Bayleys from 3–37 months; Stanford–Binet (1960 norms) at 6 and 7 yrs. | E NR<br>C NR | 22<br>22 | Total=26% Significantly more whites than blacks dropped out |
| Family-Oriented Home Visiting | 3 waves recruited and randomly assigned to E or C groups. | E = home visits<br>C = 4 social visits, photographs of children, and noneducational presents | Bayley at pretest (17-24 months) and Stanford-Binets (1972 norms) at post-tests (26-52 months) | E 27<br>C 20 | 20<br>17 | E=26%<br>C=15% |
| Field's Home Visit Study | Mothers agreed to participate, then randomly assigned to E or C group | E = home visits<br>C = testing only | Denver at 4 months; Bayley at 8 and 12 months | E 30<br>C 30 | 27<br>25 | E=10%<br>C=17% |

*Early Childhood Programs*

## I. CENTER-BASED, CHILD AND/OR PARENT FOCUSED

| | | | | | | | |
|---|---|---|---|---|---|---|---|
| Perry Preschool Project | Recruited children with IQs between 70–85; stratified random sample by IQ with adjustments made for SES, sex, siblings and mother's ability to participate in the E group. | E = 2 yrs. preschool C = testing only | Stanford–Binet (1960 norms) yearly from 3–10; WISC at 14 | E<br>C | 61<br>67 | 58<br>65 | E=5%<br>C=3% |
| Early Training Project | Children were randomly assigned to E1, E2, or C conditions. | E = 3 yrs. of summer school and home visits; E 2 = 2 yrs. of summer school and home visits; C = occasional gifts, picnics, and twice weekly play periods in the last summer. | Stanford–Binet (1960 norms) administered to all children before and after each summer program, at 1st and 2nd grade entry, and at 2nd and 4th grade exit; WISC at 17 | E1<br>E2<br>C1 | 22<br>21<br>18 | 19<br>19<br>18 | E=12%<br>C= 0% |
| Academic Preschool | Stratified sample (by IQ) with adjustments for race and sex | E = 2 yrs. of Academic Preschool; C = 1 yr. of traditional preschool & 1 yr. of public school kindergarten | Stanford–Binet (1960 norms) 1st yr. fall and spring; 2nd yr. spring only | E<br>C | 15<br>28 | 12<br>NR | E=20%<br>C=NR |

*continued*

**Table 10.3. Research Design (continued)**

| Name of Study | Sampling Plan | Intervention Design | IQ Assessments | Numbers Entry | End | Attrition |
|---|---|---|---|---|---|---|
| Curriculum Comparison[b] | Stratified random assignment (by sex) to E or non-E classes within each of 4 schools. | E = 1 of 4 types of prekindergarten program | Stanford–Binet (1960 norms) before and after preschool, at end of kindergarten, 1st and 2nd grades | E 214 | 213[c] | E < 1% |
| Five Preschool Comparisons[d] | Stratified sample (by IQ); children assigned to class units; adjustments made for race & sex, each class then randomly assigned to a treatment | E = 1 of 5 types of preschool | Stanford–Binets (1960 norms) before and after preschool | Tr 30<br>Am 30<br>DV NR<br>CI NR<br>Mo NR | 25<br>24<br>23<br>16<br>13 | Tr=17%<br>Am=20%<br>DV=NR<br>CI=NR<br>Mo=NR |
| *Kindergarten Program* | | | | | | |
| Dual Kindergarten | Children selected from Head Start programs and randomly assigned to E or C groups | E = public school kindergarten in a.m.; Bereiter-Engelmann program in p.m. C = public school kindergarten | Stanford–Binet (1960 norms) pre and post kindergarten | E 10<br>C 10 | 10<br>9 | E= 0%<br>C=10% |

*Note.* E and C are used to refer to the experimental and control groups.

[a]NR = Not Reported.

[b]Non-E children were not tested. This study included a non-random comparison group of children from Head Start waiting lists who received no preschool. Results from this group are not discussed here.

[c]Additional data from Lazar & Darlington, 1982.

[d]At school entry, all Ss were placed non-randomly into a public kindergarten or Bereiter-Engleman class. These results are not discussed here.

268

bile Unit for Child Health, the Florida Parent Education Project, the Ypsilanti-Carnegie Infant Education Project, the Perry Preschool Project, the Early Training Project, the Academic Preschool Curriculum Comparison, the Five Preschool Comparison, and the Dual Kindergarten, all of which used the 1960 Stanford-Binet Norms. Using the 1972 norms were Project CARE, the Carolina Abecedarian Project, and the Family-Oriented Home Visiting Project. Although the difference in norms will not affect the magnitude of group differences within projects, it will affect comparability across projects of mean performances in both experimental and control groups. The use of 1972 norms results, in general, in about a 10 point lower IQ than identically performing children who are scored using 1960 norms (Bryant, Burchinal, & Ramey, 1983).

It should also be noted that most of the projects have a relatively small number of children per experimental or control condition (typically 20-30) and that there was a wide range of attrition across projects—ranging from 0% for control subjects in the Early Training Project to 55% of experimental group children in the Houston PCDC. Because initial sample sizes were small, the potential for systematic bias in the results of projects due to selective attrition cannot be dismissed lightly even though statistical comparisons may not be significant. Given the low statistical power for such small samples, fairly large differences between those participants who dropped and those who continued participation could be apparent but not statistically significant. However, even if attrition can be presumed to be random (i.e., not selective across or within groups), it may be particularly important to examine the overall differential attrition rates to determine the probable future appeal of programs with varying formats or other programmatic characteristics.

## Characteristics of the Intervention

Although it is very difficult, and undoubtedly an injustice to the complexity of the educational programs, we have attempted a capsule description of the characteristics of the intervention process for each of the 18 programs. Table 10.4 summarizes (a) the site of the educational intervention (usually either the family's home or a child development center), (b) the targets of the intervention (usually either the child, the mother, or both), (c) the duration of the educational treatment, (d) the intensity of the treatment or treatments within projects, and (e) a brief description of typical activities as reported by the projects. In Table 10.4 we have followed the convention established in Table 10.2 of ordering projects by intensity within developmental periods.

Typically, a center or school was the intervention site for the studies ranked most intense within their age of intervention category. This is probably so because it is easier and perhaps more cost-effective for a child or parent to spend several hours in a daycare center than it is for a home visitor or teacher to spend several hours in one child's home. Most home visit programs consisted of 90 minutes of intervention conducted once a week or less often. The most in-

**Table 10.4. Characteristics of the Intervention**

| Name of Study | Intervention Site | Primary Target(s) | Duration | Intensity | Activities |
|---|---|---|---|---|---|
| | | | *Infancy Programs* | | |
| | | | *I. CENTER-BASED, CHILD AND PARENT-FOCUSED* | | |
| Milwaukee Project | Home and Center | Child and mother | Home=4 months Center = 6 yrs. for child; 2 years for mother | Many hours of HVs[a] in 1st 4 months, then full-day daycare year-round | Children in educational program having a cognitive-language orientation in a structured environment using prescriptive teaching techniques. Vocational and social education program for mothers including job training and remedial education. |
| Project CARE | Center and home | Child and mother in center group; mother in home group | To date, 3 yrs.; project continues | Full-day daycare, year-round + biweekly HVs | Children in educational daycare program with focus on language and cognitive development and adaptive social behavior. All medical care provided. HVs to both E groups with focus on responsive parenting, learning activities, behavior management, and problem solving. |
| Carolina Abecedarian Project | Center | Child | To date, 5 yrs.; project continues | Full-day daycare, year-round | Children in educational daycare program with focus on language and cognitive development and adaptive social behavior. All medical care provided. |
| Field's Center-Home Visit Comparison | Center or home | Mother and child for Center group; mother for home group | 12 months | Center= 20 hours / week; home = 1/2 hour HV biweekly | Curriculum items modelled by HV; activities designed from the Denver and Bayley test items. Parent training in child development and in job skills via CETA employment. |

## II. CENTER-BASED, PARENT-FOCUSED

| | | | | |
|---|---|---|---|---|
| Birmingham PCDC | Center | Mother and child | 31–33 months | to 11 months= 12 hours/week 12–17 months= 20 hours/week 18–36 months= 40 hours/week | To 11 months = Training in parenting and child development; mothers cared for own child with assistance from center staff. 12–17 months = 4 halfdays as understudies to teaching mothers; 1 halfday training in child development and family topics. 18-30 months = 4 mornings as teaching mothers, remaining time in training, taking care of own child, class preparation and social groups. |
| Houston PCDC | Year 1- home Year 2- center | Mother, child and family | 24 months | Yr. 1=1½ hour HVs for 30 weeks + 4 family workshops; Yr. 2-3 hour sessions for 4 days/week for 8 months + nightly meetings | Year 1 = HV topics in child development, parenting, home as learning environment, parent–child activities. Family workshops for problem solving and communication skills. Year 2 = Training in home management, child development and parenting; videotape and discussions of parent-child interactions. English classes offered weekly. |
| New Orleans PCDC | Center | Mother and child | 34 months | 3 hours 2 times per week | One weekly session to counsel on child development with 1-hour discussion group and 2-hour parent-child laboratory experience. One weekly session focused on adult and family life. |

*continued*

**Table 10.4. Characteristics of the Intervention (continued)**

| Name of Study | Intervention Site | Primary Target(s) | Duration | Intensity | Activities |
|---|---|---|---|---|---|
| | | | *III. HOME VISIT, PARENT-FOCUSED* | | |
| Mobile Unit for Child Health | Home and Mobile Health Unit | Mother and Child | 3 yrs. | At least 20 medical and 24 infant stim. 1-hour HVs over 3 years | Prenatal counseling; well-baby care; infant stimulation activities with emphasis on language; educational toy given to family often. 1st cohort received training on child development and family problems. |
| Florida Parent Education Project | Home | Mother for 1st 2 years, mother and child in last year | 3 yrs. for 1 group, 2 yrs. for 3 groups, and 1 yr. for 3 groups | Weekly 1-hour HVs for 3 years + playgroup for 2 hours twice a week in third year | HVs used infant stimulation activities with child and mother to help mother become more effective teacher of her child. Home Learning Center (HLC) in 3rd year, supervised by experienced parents was a backyard playgroup for socialization skills. |
| Ypsilanti-Carnegie Infant Education Project | Home | Mother and child | 16 months | Weekly 60-90 minute HV | Focus on mothers as teachers of their children. Piagetian-based formal set of infant activities to support objectives for mothers; emphasis on fine and gross motor skills. |
| Family-Oriented Home Visiting | Home | Mother | 9 months | 30 weekly 60-90 minute HV | Activities were based on DARCEE principles and materials for mothers of toddlers. Intervention tailored to each family, but emphasized teaching style, competence, language, and behavior management. Used inexpensive homemade materials. |

| | | | | | |
|---|---|---|---|---|---|
| Field's Home Visit Study | Home | Mother | 12 months | Biweekly ½-hour HVs | Curriculum items modelled by HV; activities designed from the Denver and Bayley test items. Goals to educate mothers on developmental milestones and to facilitate mother-child interaction. |

*Early Childhood Programs*

*I. CENTER-BASED CHILD AND/OR PARENT FOCUSED*

| | | | | | |
|---|---|---|---|---|---|
| Perry Preschool Project | School and home | Center-child; Home=child and mother | 1st cohort= 30 weeks; cohorts 2-5=60 weeks | Center= 12½ hours/week; Home =weekly 1½ hour HV | High/Scope Cognitively Oriented Curriculum used; Piagetian-based; emphasis on concrete experience and expression in language. |
| Early Training Project | School and home | Summer=child; Winter-child and mother | E1=3 summers and 3 winters; E2=2 summers and 2 winters | Summer program=4 hours daily for 10 weeks; winter program =weekly 1-hour HVs for 9 months | Curriculum focused on perceptual and language development and acquisition of basic concepts. Tried to improve achievement motivation, persistence, and delay of gratification. Used common preschool toys and materials; the HV program tried to involve the parent in the child's education. |
| Academic Preschool | School | Child | 2 school terms | 2 hours/day | Direct instruction (Bereiter-Englemann curriculum) was provided in relation to 15 learning objectives; focus was on rapid attainment of basic academic concepts. |

*continued*

**Table 10.4. Characteristics of the Intervention (continued)**

| Name of Study | Intervention Site | Primary Target(s) | Duration | Intensity | Activities |
|---|---|---|---|---|---|
| Curriculum Comparison | School | Child | 9 month school term | 6½ hours /day | Adopted the curriculum and activities of 4 previously developed programs: 1) Bereiter-Engelmann (4 classes); 2) DARCEE (4 classes); 3) Montessori (2 classes); and 4) Traditional Preschool (4 classes) |
| Five Preschool Comparisons | School | Child | 7-8 months | 2 hours and 15 minutes/ day | Used the curriculum and activities of 4 previously developed programs: 1) Traditional (2 classes); 2) Ameliorative (2 classes); 3) Bereiter-Englemann (2 classes); 4) Community-Integrated (1 class); and 5) Montessori (1 class) |
| | | | *KINDERGARTEN PROGRAM* | | |
| Dual Kindergarten | School | Child | 9 month school term | 2-3 hours/ day | Both Es and Cs received public school kindergarten program. E's also received a Bereiter-Englemann direct verbal instruction class; focus on rapid attainment of basic academic concepts. |

[a]HV = home visit

tense infancy and early childhood programs included center training as well as home visiting, thus attempting to alter the child's developmental course by changing the child directly and by changing parents' behavior and/or attitudes. Some of the most intense programs (e.g. the Milwaukee Project) also taught job skills, which if successful, would affect an even broader range of the child's environment.

The duration of the most intense studies lasted from birth until public school entry. Other studies intervened for a year or two during infancy, during early childhood, or for the one year preceding public school entry. A comparison of some of these studies based on age at intervention might pinpoint more definitively just how early the "early experiences" have to occur in order to have an effect, either short-term or long-term, on intellectual development.

All studies included, as part of their treatment, specific educational activities designed to teach the infant or child certain concepts or skills. Depending on the mechanism targeted, these activities were either taught directly to the child (e.g., Abecedarian Project) or were taught to the mother so that she could teach her child (e.g. Florida Parent Education Program). These activities were many and varied—gross motor activities, perceptual development, language, adaptive social behavior, and Piagetian-based activities. Three of the preschool programs and the Dual Kindergarten program used the Bereiter–Englemann curriculum (or Direct Verbal or DISTAR as it is now called) in comparison to control groups or to groups who received other forms of preschool education.

Many projects included curricula for parents in order to encourage greater parent involvement in the child's intellectual, emotional, and social development. The Milwaukee Project, Project CARE, the PCDCs, and the Mobile Unit project included parent training in areas such as problem solving, family life, and communication. Field's Center-Home Visit Companion and the Milwaukee Project also included job training as part of the experimental treatment.

The activities conducted as part of the interventions were so diverse that it is difficult to make a general summary statement about treatments. Some treatments were described in a few pages or less, and some treatments used curricula that have been published and widely circulated. Most treatments were reported to be based on clearly defined theoretical models, yet the intervention was not specified in enough detail to determine that. It is clear that, even if we determine that some compensatory education programs have significant effects on IQ, little research to date addresses the question of which components of the programs are most effective.

## IQ Results

The data base for the discussion to follow is composed of the mean IQ measures of experimental (E) and control (C) groups, where appropriate, in each of the 18 intervention studies. These scores are presented in Table 10.5. Unless indicated otherwise, the early scores (4–25 months) are from the Bayley Mental Develop-

Table 10.5. Summary of IQ Results from Eighteen Compensatory Education Studies

| | 4-7 mos. | 10-13 mos. | 18-19 mos. | 22-25 mos. | 27-33 mos. | 35-37 mos. | 38-43 mos. | 4 yrs. | Grade: K / 5 yr. | 1st / 6 yr. | 2nd / 7 yr. | 3rd / 8 yr. | 4th / 9 yr. | 5th / 10 yr. | Later Follow-Up |
|---|---|---|---|---|---|---|---|---|---|---|---|---|---|---|---|
| **MILWAUKEE PROJECT** | | | | | | | | | | | | | | | |
| E | 117g | 119* | 118*g | 125*s | 124* | 126* | 125* | 126* | 118* | 119* | 103*w | 103*w | 103*w | 104*w | |
| C | 113 | 108 | 101 | 96 | 94 | 94 | 95 | 96 | 93 | 87 | 81 | 83 | 84 | 86 | |
| **PROJECT CARE** | | | | | | | | | | | | | | | |
| E1 (Daycare + HV) | 109 | 119* | 119* | 114* | 108*m | 105* | | | | | | | | | |
| E2 (HV only) | 107 | 108 | 94 | 89 | 90 | 89 | | | | | | | | | |
| C | 105 | 108 | 103 | 97 | 100 | 93 | | | | | | | | | |
| **ABECEDARIAN PROJECT** | | | | | | | | | | | | | | | |
| E | 107 | 111* | 107* | 96*s | 102*m | 101* | | 102* | 101*p | | | | | | |
| C | 101 | 105 | 90 | 85 | 93 | 84 | | 89 | 94 | | | | | | |
| **FIELD'S CENTER HV COMPARISON** | | | | | | | | | | | | | | | |
| E1 (Center) | 35d | 119* | | | | | | | | | | | | | |
| E2 (HV) | NR | 108 | | | | | | | | | | | | | |
| C | 36 | 106 | | | | | | | | | | | | | |
| **BIRMINGHAM PCDC** | | | | | | | | | | | | | | | |
| E | 113* | 111 | | 97* | | 98* | | 100* | | | | | | | |
| C | 106 | 107 | | 89 | | 91 | | 95 | | | | | | | |
| **HOUSTON PCDC** | | | | | | | | | | | | | | | |
| E | | 103 | | 99* | | 108 | | | | | | | | | |
| C | | 102 | | 91 | | 104 | | | | | | | | | |
| **NEW ORLEANS PCDC** | | | | | | | | | | | | | | | |
| E | 121 | 111 | 97 | 101 | | 105* | | 109* | | | | | | | |
| C | 123 | 107 | 99 | 100 | | 99 | | 97 | | | | | | | |

276

## MOBILE UNIT FOR CHILD HEALTH

| | | | | | | | | |
|---|---|---|---|---|---|---|---|---|
| E | 106 | 108* | 100* | 99* | | | | |
| C | 103 | 102 | 91 | 91 | | | | |

## FLORIDA PARENT EDUCATION PROGRAM

| | | | | | | | | |
|---|---|---|---|---|---|---|---|---|
| E1 (3 years) | | 85 | | 99* | 98* | 98* | 97* | 89w |
| E2 (2 years) | | 83 | | 95 | 96* | 94 | 95 | 87 |
| E3 (1 year) | | 90 | | 94 | 95* | 94 | 95 | 81 |
| A11 E groups combined[1] | 111*r | 85 | | 95 | 94* | 94* | 94* | 88* |
| C | 107 | 91 | | 91 | 88 | 89 | 88 | 78 |

## YPSILANTI-CARNEGIE INFANT EDUCATION PROGRAM

| | | | | | | | | |
|---|---|---|---|---|---|---|---|---|
| E | 96 | 104 | 110 | 106 | 104 | 111 | 106 | |
| C | 92 | 98 | 106 | 102 | 101 | 111 | 106 | |

*Note.* Results at the various ages are from the following tests, unless indicated otherwise: 4-25 months; Bayley Mental Development Index; 27 mo.-10 yrs., Stanford-Binet; 13-17 years, Wechsler Intelligence Scale for Children.

* Significant at the .05 level or better.

— Underlined E group scores indicate PRE or POST-intervention results; non-underlined scores are tests given during intervention.

-- Dotted lines indicate that the PRE-test was given 8 weeks, after intervention began.

[d] Denver Developmental Screening Test

[g] Gesell Developmental Schedules (DQ)

[1] Figures used after age 2 are from Lazar & Darlington, 1982

[m] McCarthy Scales of Children's Abilities

[P] WPPSI (Wechsler Preschool and Primary Scale of Intelligence)

[q] Scores at entry (16-24 mo.), at end of intervention (27-33 mo.) and at follow-ups (37-43 mo. & 53 mo.)

[r] Griffiths Mental Development Scales

[s] Stanford-Binet Intelligence Test

[w] WISC (Wechsler Intelligence Scale for Children) or WISC-R

continued

## Table 10.5. Summary of IQ Results from Eighteen Compensatory Education Studies (continued)

| | 4-7 mos. | 10-13 mos. | 18-19 mos. | 22-25 mos. | 27-33 mos. | 35-37 mos. | 38-43 mos. | Grade: K 4 yrs. | 5 yr. | 1st 6 yr. | 2nd 7 yr. | 3rd 8 yr. | 4th 9 yr. | 5th 10 yr. | Later Follow-Up |
|---|---|---|---|---|---|---|---|---|---|---|---|---|---|---|---|
| **FAMILY-ORIENTED HOME VISIT PROGRAM[q]** | | | | | | | | | | | | | | | |
| E | | | 99 | | 89 | | 93* | 93 | | | | | | | |
| C | | | 94 | | 83 | | 85 | 87 | | | | | | | |
| **FIELD'S HV STUDY** | | | | | | | | | | | | | | | |
| E | 35*d | 115* | | | | | | | | | | | | | |
| C | 31 | 105 | | | | | | | | | | | | | |
| **PERRY PRESCHOOL** | | | | | | | | | | | | | | | |
| E | | | | | | 79 | | 96* | 95* | 91* | 92* | 88 | 88 | 85 | 81^w (age 14) |
| C | | | | | | 78 | | 83 | 84 | 86 | 87 | 87 | 87 | 84 | 81 |
| **EARLY TRAINING PROJECT** | | | | | | | | | | | | | | | |
| E | | | | | | 90 | | 95 | 97* | 96* | 99* | 94* | | 88 | 79^w (age 17) |
| C | | | | | | 85 | | 90 | 88 | 83 | 91 | 88 | | 85 | 76 |
| **ACADEMIC PRESCHOOL** | | | | | | | | | | | | | | | |
| E | | | | | | | | 95 | 112* | 121* | | | | | |
| C | | | | | | | | 95 | 102 | 100 | | | | | |
| **FOUR PRESCHOOL PROGRAMS** | | | | | | | | | | | | | | | |
| Bereiter-Englemann | | | | | | | 93 | 98 | 94 | 90 | 87 | | | | |
| DARCEE | | | | | | | 96 | 97 | 94 | 94 | 91 | | | | |
| Montessori | | | | | | | 92 | 97 | 95 | 95 | 93 | | | | |
| Traditional | | | | | | | 90 | 96 | 94 | 93 | 90 | | | | |
| All E groups combined[1] | | | | | | | 93 | 97* | 94 | 92 | 90 | | | | 85 (age 13) |

## FIVE PRESCHOOL INTERVENTIONS

| | | |
|---|---|---|
| Traditional | 94 | 102 |
| Ameliorative | 96 | 110 |
| Bereiter-Engelmann | 95 | 108 |
| Community-Integrated | 93 | 98 |
| Montessori | 93 | 99 |

### DUAL KINDERGARTEN

| | | |
|---|---|---|
| E | 86 | 100 |
| C | 89 | 97 |

*Note.* Results at the various ages are from the following tests, unless indicated otherwise: 4-25 months; Bayley Mental Development Index; 27 mo.-10 yrs., Stanford-Binet; 13-17 years, Wechsler Intelligence Scale for Children.

\* Significant at the .05 level or better.

__ Underlined E group scores indicate PRE or POST-intervention results; non-underlined scores are tests given during intervention.

-- Dotted lines indicate that the PRE-test was given 8 weeks, after intervention began.

d Denver Developmental Screening Test

g Gesell Developmental Schedules (DQ)

1 Figures used after age 2 are from Lazar & Darlington, 1982

m McCarthy Scales of Children's Abilities

PWPPSI (Wechsler Preschool and Primary Scale of Intelligence)

q Scores at entry (16-24 mo.), at end of intervention (27-33 mo.) and at follow-ups (37-43 mo. & 53 mo.)

r Griffiths Mental Development Scales

s Stanford–Binet Intelligence Test

w WISC (Wechsler Intelligence Scale for Children) or WISC-R

279

ment Index (MDI) and the later scores are from the Stanford-Binet. Pre- and post-intervention means are indicated with underlined E scores. Scores from tests given during the intervention are not underlined. Statistically significant E-C group differences are indicated by asterisks (*).

The Ypsilanti-Carnegie Infant Education Program, the Family-Oriented Home Visit Program, and Field's Center-Home Visit Comparison originally included other experimental groups, which, due to attrition or other problems, were not included in the data analyses of the original studies. We have also eliminated those groups from our discussion. The Florida Parent Education Program and the Miller and Dyer Comparison of Four Preschool Programs each included several treatment groups. For these two studies, we have elected to include in Table 10.5 a row of scores that describe the mean IQ scores of all E groups combined. These scores are from the monograph by the Consortium for Longitudinal Studies (Lazar et al., 1982).

Our discussion of results will be divided into four sections: results from infant intervention studies through age 2; results from a subset of the infant interventions that lasted through age 3; early childhood IQ results from the preschool interventions for 3–5-year-olds; and results from one study that began intervention at age 5.

*Infancy Results.* Eleven of the 18 studies intervened during infancy. Table 10.6 presents a summary of their results. A comparison of the 9 studies that gave Bayley tests at 12 months indicates that the mean MDI scores of both experimental and control groups were unusually high for low-SES populations presumed to be at elevated risk for lower development (E mean = 111; C mean = 104). The scores of the experimental groups were always greater than the scores of the control groups. In 6 of the 9 studies the differences were statistically significant; however, in 2 of those 6 studies (both of Field's studies) the curriculum was based on the test items, so those differences are to be expected. Of the remaining four studies, Project CARE showed an 11-point E-C difference at 12 months, and the Abecedarian and Mobile Unit projects each showed a 6-point difference. The Florida Project also showed a significant 4-point difference on the Griffiths test, presumably because of the large number of subjects participating. With the exception of Project CARE, then, none of the 11 infancy intervention projects showed a striking advantage for the treated groups by 12 months, perhaps because the scores of the control groups were still at or above average. Biological or maturational factors may play primary importance in the development of intelligence in the infancy period, a developmental process that will occur if the infant is given at least minimal levels of sustenance and stimulation (McCall, 1981).

Of the 11 studies that intervened during infancy, 9 reported 2-year scores. Seven projects used Bayley tests and the Milwaukee and Abecedarian projects

Table 10.6. Early Infancy Studies Ranked by E–C Difference at 2 Years

| | E–C Differences | | Experimental Scores | | | Control Scores | | |
|---|---|---|---|---|---|---|---|---|
| | 12 months | 24 months | 12 months | 24 months | Change | 12 months | 24 months | Change |
| Milwaukee Project | 4 | 29 | 117[g] | 125*[s] | +8 | 113 | 96 | −17 |
| Project CARE | 11 | 17 | 119* | 114* | −5 | 108 | 97 | −11 |
| Abecedarian | 6 | 9 | 111* | 96*[s] | −15 | 105 | 85 | −20 |
| Mobile Unit | 6 | 9 | 108* | 100* | −8 | 102 | 91 | −11 |
| PCDC-Birmingham | 4 | 8 | 111 | 97* | −14 | 107 | 89 | −18 |
| PCDC-Houston | 1 | 8 | 103 | 99* | −4 | 102 | 91 | −11 |
| Ypsilanti-Carnegie | 6 | 4 | 104 | 106 | +2 | 98 | 102 | +4 |
| PCDC-New Orleans | 4 | 1 | 111 | 101 | −10 | 107 | 100 | −7 |
| Field's Center-HV Study | 13 | | 119* | | | 106 | | |
| Field's Teen HV Study | 10 | | 115* | | | 105 | | |
| Florida Parent Education | 4 | −6 | 111*[r] | 85 | −26 | 107 | 91 | −16 |
| Mean Bayley MDI | | | 111.2 (N=9) | 100.3 (N=7) | | 104.4 (N=9) | 94.4 (N=7) | |

Note. All tests are Bayleys except where indicated otherwise:
[g]Gesell at 10 months
[s]Stanford-Binet at 2 years
[r]Griffiths at 12 months
* Difference between E and C group significant at the .05 level or better

281

gave the Stanford-Binet. A comparison of the 2-year Bayley MDI scores indicates that E scores were greater than C scores for all studies (E mean = 100; C mean = 94) except for the Florida Parent Education Program. The Abecedarian and Milwaukee E-group Stanford-Binets were also significantly greater than the C-group scores (E mean = 111; C mean = 91). In all, 6 of the 9 studies reported that the E-C differences were statistically significant, indicating that the effects of the interventions on IQ did seem to be measurable by 2 years of age.

Why were these differences significant? Were the E scores improving or were the C scores decreasing? In 5 of the 6 studies that tested with the Bayley at both 12 and 24 months, the E *and* C scores dropped over that time. The average C drop was 12 points and the average E drop was 8 points. Thus, the early intervention did not improve Bayley scores for the E groups, but it prevented a decline as large as that which occurred in the untreated control groups.

The Ypsilanti-Carnegie Infant Education Project was the only study that showed Bayley gains for both groups, 2 points for the Es and 4 points for the Cs. The Milwaukee Project, which reported the largest E-C difference at 2 years (29 IQ points), was the only study to show an E group increase (8 points) and a C group decrease (17 points). However, subjects received the Gesell at 10 months and the Stanford-Binet at 24 months, making it difficult to evaluate these change scores.

It is interesting to note that the range of 24-month C scores was 85–102, and that in only 2 of the studies were the scores below 90—85 in the Abecedarian Project (which used the Stanford-Binet at age 2) and 89 in the Birmingham PCDC study. In general, the C scores were within the normal range, although most were somewhat lower than the standardization mean of 100. They were not, however, in the range that would have been labelled mild mental retardation, regardless of the criteria used.

The two projects which showed the largest E-C differences at 2 years—the Milwaukee Project (29 points) and Project CARE (17 points)—also had the highest absolute E scores at 2 years (125 and 114, respectively). Both projects provided full-day, year-round daycare for E children as well as support services for the family, such as family education through center training and home visits. The Milwaukee Project also provided job training and placements for the E mothers. These most intense studies yielded the most dramatic results at 2 years. It should be noted, however, that the Milwaukee Project used the 1960 standardization norms of the Stanford-Binet, resulting in scores that are about 10 points higher than if the 1972 norms had been used, while in Project CARE the later norms were used.

Four other projects showed statistically significant intervention effects at 2 years, although less dramatic than the Milwaukee or CARE projects. The Abecedarian Project, the Mobile Unit for Child Health, and the Birmingham and Houston PCDC studies all showed significant 8- or 9-point E-C differences and absolute 2-year E scores ranging from 96 to 100. The Abecedarian Project was a full-day, year-round, daycare intervention with fewer family support services than the Milwaukee or CARE projects. In type of treatment, though, it was most closely related to the most intense studies, yet in the 2-year outcome it was more similar to the parent-focused studies. Perhaps this was because the 1972 version of the Stanford-Binet was the test used at 2 years, whereas all other studies used the Bayley or the 1960 version of the Stanford-Binet. A 10-point increase in Abecedarian E and C scores would have put it in the results range (for both E and C groups) of the most intense intervention studies. Instead, its results fall in the moderate range.

The other three projects which showed moderate, but statistically significant, intervention effects at 2 years were parent-focused studies. Two of these studies were PCDC interventions at Birmingham and Houston, which included extensive center training for parents. The third project, the Mobile Unit for Child Health, was also a parent home visit program which included the provision of medical care, nutritional supplements and educational activities for the infants. These moderately intense programs showed significant intervention effects with E-group IQ scores averaging about 100.

The remaining infancy interventions were all home visit programs, the least intense treatments reviewed in this chapter. None resulted in statistically significant 2-year outcomes. The E-group Bayley scores of the Ypsilanti-Carnegie Infant Education Program and the New Orleans PCDC averaged around 100, but the C-group scores averaged around 100 as well. If these samples of children were at risk for developmental delay, it was not evidenced in the 2-year C scores, nor were the E scores significantly higher as a result of treatment. Gordon's Florida Parent Education Program also showed no treatment effect by age 2, and all E groups combined actually scored lower than the C group. The conclusion from these studies seems to be that weekly parent-focused home visits alone are not enough intervention to significantly alter the child's intellectual status by age 2.

Taken all together, the 2-year results from the 11 infancy interventions support an intensity hypothesis. Home visits alone have not been shown to alter IQ by age 2. Home visits with medical and educational intervention or parent-focused center training have moderate effects on IQ. Providing daycare plus other family services causes the most improvement in intellectual development. It is unclear which category of intensity encompasses the results from the provision of daycare alone.

*Results from Interventions Through Age 3.* With the exception of the two Field's studies, all of the infant intervention studies discussed in the previous section continued intervention and data collection through age 3. In addition, Gray's Family-oriented Home Visit Program, which started when the children were 16-24 months old, also collected follow-up scores around age 3 (actually

38–43 months). Table 10.7 presents a comparison of the 3-year results of these 10 studies with a rank-ordering based on magnitude of E–C differences in Stanford-Binet scores.

Table 10.7. Early Childhood Results at Age 3

|  | E–C Difference | Stanford-Binet Scores | | Norms Used |
|---|---|---|---|---|
|  |  | E | C |  |
| Milwaukee Project | 32 | 126[a] | 94 | 1960 |
| Abecedarian Project | 17 | 101[a] | 84 | 1972 |
| Project CARE | 12 | 105[a] | 93 | 1972 |
| Mobile Unit | 8 | 99[a] | 91 | 1960 |
| Family-Oriented HV | 8 | 93[a] | 85 | 1972 |
| PCDC-Birmingham | 7 | 98[a] | 91 | 1960 |
| PCDC-New Orleans | 6 | 105[a] | 99 | 1960 |
| PCDC-Houston | 4 | 108 | 104 | 1960 |
| Florida Parent Education | 4 | 95 | 91 | 1960 |
| Ypsilanti–Carnegie | 3 | 104 | 101 | 1960 |

[a]Difference between the E and C group significant at the .05 level or better.

When the 10 studies are compared based on the magnitude of treatment effect, the order is very similar to age-2 results, and they seem to cluster into four groups. The Milwaukee Project, one of the three most intense treatments, showed the largest E–C difference (32 points) and forms a category of its own. The other two, full-day, daycare projects, Abecedarian and CARE, showed E–C differences of about one standard deviation (17 and 12 points, respectively) and form a second cluster. These three most intense studies, taken together, produced the strongest treatment effects.

The third cluster of studies includes four programs which had significant group differences, but differences of 6, 7, or 8 IQ points, approximately one-half standard deviation. Two of these were PCDC center-based, parent-focused interventions. The other two were home-visit, parent-focused studies. In our presumed hierarchy of intensity, the Mobile Unit for Child Health seemed more intense and lasted for twice as long as the Family-oriented Home Visiting Program, yet both had effects of 8 points. These latter two studies used different Stanford–Binet norms, which should not have affected difference scores, although it may have affected absolute scores. The Family-oriented Home Visiting Program was the least intense of the 7 studies which showed significant treatment effects. It was also the project with the lowest mean E-group IQ, 93 points.

The fourth cluster of studies with results through age 3 includes the three projects with no significant E–C group differences. They are the Houston PCDC program, the Florida Parent Education Program, and the Ypsilanti-Carnegie Infant Education Program. In 2 of these 3 studies (Houston and Ypsilanti) both the E and C groups had mean Stanford–Binet scores greater than 100. In the Florida Parent Education Project experimental subjects who had participated in all three years of intervention were performing significantly higher than controls, however, when all E groups were combined (including 1- and 2-year treatment groups) the difference was not significant.

On the basis of the mean IQ of the experimental group children, the 10 studies form two groups—the Milwaukee Project (E mean = 126) and all the other studies (E mean = 101, range 93-108). Given the range of intensities represented by the other 9 studies, none of the E groups approach the high level of performance of the Milwaukee subjects. It is important to bear in mind that the Milwaukee Project used 1960 Stanford–Binet norms, but even taking this into account, their performance still surpasses all the others, including the two, full-day, year-round daycare projects—Abecedarian and CARE. The job training skills and experiences provided for the mothers by the Milwaukee Project in the first two years may have been a significant intervention above and beyond daycare and parenting skills; or some other aspect of their program, perhaps undocumented, may have been responsible for the large group difference and high E scores.

Among the other studies the intensity hypothesis, which was supported by the rankings of E–C differences, is less clearly supported by the absolute scores of the experimental children. For example, one of the least intense studies, the Houston PCDC (E mean = 108), had higher E scores than one of the most intense studies, Project CARE (E mean = 105) although the differences between the 1960 Binet scores in the Houston Program and the 1972 norms in Project CARE may account for this apparent anomaly. A 3-year program of home visits and play groups, the Florida Parent Education Program (E mean = 95) had only slightly higher scores than a 9-month home visit program, Family-oriented Home Visiting (E mean = 93).

All but one study that had significant treatment effects at age 2 continued to show significant E–C differences at age 3 (all but Houston PCDC). In addition the New Orleans PCDC and the Family-oriented Home Visiting Program showed significant effects for the first time at age 3. Patterns that were established earlier still seem to be present at age 3, although there were more changes in the E scores from 2 to 3 years of age than there were in the C scores. These changes are difficult to evaluate because most studies changed tests from the 2-year assessment to the 3-year assessment.

*Preschool Results.* The data base for discussion of IQ changes in the preschool years (ages 3-5) is composed of fewer studies than were available for the infancy period or the period through age 3. Three studies used random assignment to E or C groups and intervened for 1 to 3 years beginning at age 3 or 4

(Perry Preschool, Early Training Project, and Academic Preschool). Two studies intervened during the last preschool year (beginning at about age 4), but had no randomly assigned control group (Miller and Dyer's Four Preschool Programs and Karnes's Five Preschool Interventions). Both studies, however, used random assignment to the various experimental groups. Two studies that began intervention in infancy continued treatment through the preschool years (Milwaukee Project and Abecedarian Project) and another is still in progress (Project CARE). Two studies ceased intervention at age 3, but continued to test children during the preschool years (Florida Parent Education Program and Ypsilanti-Carnegie Infant Education Program). Results from these studies are presented in Table 10.8. In some studies the IQ tests were given before and after the preschool rather than on the child's birthday, so the ages are approximately 3, 4, or 5 years.

### Table 10.8. Preschool Results

| Age in years | Experimental | | | | Control | | | |
|---|---|---|---|---|---|---|---|---|
| | 3 | 4 | 5 | Change | 3 | 4 | 5 | Change |
| Perry Preschool | 79 | | 95[a] | +16 | 78 | | 84 | +6 |
| Early Training Project | 90 | | 97[a] | +7 | 95 | | 88 | -7 |
| Academic Preschool | | 95 | 112[a] | +17 | | 95 | 102 | +7 |
| Four Preschool Programs | 93 | 97 | | +4 | no randomly assigned controls | | | |
| Five Preschool Programs | | 94 | 103 | +9 | no controls | | | |
| Milwaukee Project | 126[a] | | 118[a] | -8 | 94 | | 93 | -1 |
| Abecedarian Project | 101[a] | | 101[a,b] | 0 | 84 | | 94 | +10 |
| Florida Parent Education | 95 | | 94[a] | -1 | 91 | | 89 | -2 |
| Ypsilanti-Carnegie | 104 | | 111 | +7 | 101 | | 111 | +10 |

[a]Difference between the E and C group significant at the .05 level or better.

[b]The Wechsler Preschool and Primary Scale of Intelligence (WPPSI) was given at age 5.

Two studies showed a remarkable improvement in IQ scores of the E-group after intervention. Experimental children in the Academic Preschool improved 17 points, and experimental children in the Perry Preschool improved 16 points. Perry Preschool children were initially selected based on IQ scores less than 85, whereas Academic Preschool children were selected from a disadvantaged population but had an average IQ of 95 upon entry. Scores of the control-group children in both of these studies also improved about 6 or 7 points. Both of these studies involved at least one full school term of intervention and succeeded in producing significant E–C differences.

The Early Training Project intervened most intensely during 10-week, summer sessions with home visits during the year. This study also produced significant E-C differences by 5 years, and differences of about the same magnitude as the Perry Preschool. In absolute gains, the Es in the Early Training Project gained only 7 IQ points over 2 years of intervention, but, because the Cs decreased 7 points over the same time period, the outcome at age 5 looked very similar to the Perry Preschool.

The Miller and Dyer and the Karnes preschool comparison studies have no randomly assigned control groups, so the only comparisons that can be made are between various types of interventions. None of the Miller and Dyer treatments seemed to effect IQ to a significant degree, and the range of scores, both for pretests and posttests, was very small. None of the treatment groups had pretest scores less than 90 nor did any have posttest scores greater than 100. Presumably these disadvantaged children had not had any other intervention before age 3, yet their IQ scores, although below average, were not very far below average.

The same was true for the children in the Karnes preschool comparison. None of the E groups' average entry IQ was less than 93 at age 4. The Ameliorative and the Bereiter-Engelmann interventions seemed to produce the most IQ change at the end of the school term, but the group differences were not statistically significant.

Results from the two studies that continued intervention up to school entry, the Milwaukee and Abecedarian Projects, showed significant E-C differences at age 5. The Milwaukee E children still averaged far above the mean (Stanford–Binet IQ=118) and the Abecedarian E children scored right at the mean (WPPSI IQ = 101). The intensity differences between these 2 studies have been discussed previously and may be the reason for the difference in the absolute E scores. The tests used by the 2 studies were also different.

The Florida Parent Education Project continued testing although did not continue intervention past age 3. The IQs of the E children were significantly higher than those of the C children at ages 4 and 5. Since age 3, the scores of the control children had fallen a few points, to 88 or 89. The controls in the Florida Education Project illustrate that the 3–5 year old range is the age at which the C children in some of the projects, but not all, begin falling to the levels that might be considered mild mental retardation and which might target them for special education classes in elementary school. However, the Ypsilanti-Carnegie study, which also continued testing beyond the end of intervention, was one which showed no IQ differences in preschool and showed no relative disadvantage for the children in the untreated control group. As a matter of fact, both E and C groups averaged 111 on the Stanford-Binet, well above average. These subjects were perhaps less disadvantaged than the Florida sample, yet for a disadvantaged sample, they scored quite high.

Overall, the preschool results seem to show that continuing interventions continued to have effects on intelligence, and that programs that began at age

3 or 4 also were able to raise IQ levels significantly. No studies experimentally addressed the issue of timing of the intervention, but the Perry Preschool and the Early Training Project, which began at age 3, and the Academic Preschool, which began at age 4, were all able to produce significant IQ gains by age 5 in the children who received the experimental treatment.

*Kindergarten Results.* The Dual Kindergarten program was conducted by Washington and Osborn as part of a preschool research program of Bereiter, Englemann, and colleagues in the mid-1960s (Bereiter & Washington, 1969). Of all the compensatory education programs we reviewed, it was the only study using random assignment which began intervention at age 5. Other prekindergarten or kindergarten-type programs conducted intervention during that age, but they had begun their intervention earlier.

The Dual Kindergarten was a small-scale comparison of the effects on disadvantaged children of half-day kindergarten alone compared to half-day kindergarten plus another half-day of instruction using direct verbal teaching methods. Before the intervention began, both E and C groups scored in the high-80s on the Stanford–Binet. After a school year of intervention the group that received both kindergarten and the direct verbal program scored only slightly higher than the group that received only kindergarten. The results of the Dual Kindergarten imply that one year of public school kindergarten alone is sufficient to improve IQ scores by 6–10 points, and that the addition of a half-day with the Bereiter-Englemann curriculum did not result in significant improvements in intellectual development.

## CONCLUSIONS FROM EMPIRICAL STUDIES

Our review of 18 compensatory education programs first summarized the sociopolitical context in which the studies were conducted, then the subjects, design, and intervention of the studies themselves, and concluded with a close look at the IQ results of each of the studies. After nearly a quarter of a century of research within the compensatory early education paradigm, we have learned several major lessons that can form the basis for future research and program development relative to enhancing intellectual performance.

First, we have learned that experimentally adequate research designs can be implemented in a longitudinal fashion with socially disadvantaged families. Although this is primarily a logistical point, it is a basic and necessary step to test strong hypotheses concerning intellectual malleability in young children. Therefore, for research purposes, quasi-experimental designs, with their likely confounded variables, can no longer be considered as adequate or desirable.

Second, we have learned that a variety of child-centered and/or family-focused programs are reasonably attractive service systems as evidenced by sustained child and/or family participation. Again, this is primarily a logistical point, one necessary for adequate tests of intellectual malleability with socially disadvantaged families.

Third, the preponderance of evidence seems to suggest that programs which are of high intensity (defined by amount and breadth of contact with children and/or families) are likely to bear a direct and positive relationship to the degree of intellectual benefit derived by children participating in such programs.

Fourth, we have learned that intellectual benefits can be derived by children when compensatory education is begun at various points during the preschool years. Although the data are not perfectly clear on this issue, it appears that significant benefits can be obtained whether programs are begun in infancy, early childhood or during the kindergarten years. Such results cast further doubt on the critical period hypothesis discussed earlier. In addition, the results from programs that began intervention essentially at birth cause one to question whether sufficient risk exists during the first year of life (for most disadvantaged infants) to warrant educational efforts during the first 12 months.

Fifth, we have learned that of the various curriculum comparisons conducted to date that it is not likely that variations across currently well developed educational methods and practices are strongly implicated in differential intellectual enhancement and development. This is not to imply that variations in systematic curricula *cannot* be important but only that, within the range of alternatives explored thus far (traditional nursery school, concentrated didactic teaching, Montessori's methods etc.) these variations on a theme seem not to be particularly potent.

Sixth, we have learned that the function of systematic early education is not primarily to enhance early intellectual development to superior levels of performance but rather to prevent or slow the declines from average performance. The results from the Milwaukee Project and possibly from the Academic Preschool Project are exceptions to this generalization.

Seventh, we suspect that the high attrition rates in projects requiring extraordinary participation by disadvantaged mothers on a frequent and sustained basis may indicate that this change mechanism is not perceived by families as particularly desirable.

Eighth, we have learned through an examination of control group intellectual performance that, during the preschool years, relatively few children score below the level that would officially earn them the diagnostic label of mentally retarded. However, it is unclear why this is the case. Three major plausible explanations for this fact occur to us. First, the use of 1960 Stanford–Binet norms by even fairly recent projects may overestimate the relative performance of these groups. Second, the location of most of these projects near universities, perhaps with an accompanying increased availability of social, medical and other services, may not have allowed the recruitment of those individuals most at risk for retarded development. Alternatively, the social action programs of the Great Society are now more widely available and the debilitating social conditions present in the first half of this century may have been, to some degree, ameliorated, thus buffering the impact of what would otherwise have been the natural ecology. Third, the developmental course of nonorganically caused mental retardation may not be fully expressed during the preschool years so that a longer developmental perspective may be needed to show the full detrimental impact of poverty on intellectual achievement.

## RELATIONSHIP OF COMPENSATORY EDUCATION IQ RESULTS TO THE EARLY EXPERIENCE PARADIGM

We discussed in the beginning of this chapter how the early experience paradigm and the implicit transactional orientation were guiding forces in the creation of the preschool compensatory education movement. Having reviewed the results of these innovative programs we would like to return our attention to the implications that we derive relative to those paradigms.

In the broadest sense the IQ results provide support for the idea that early experience is quite important for more optimal development during the preschool years for children from socially disadvantaged families. That support takes the form of data which strongly imply that without some sort of systematic educational experience a significant portion of children from socially disadvantaged families are not likely to approach their full intellectual potential. On the other hand, if systematic education is provided, intellectual levels can be boosted by modest to quite dramatic amounts, depending primarily upon the intensity of the educational treatments. Unfortunately for policy makers, however, the news appears to be that we are unlikely to find that inexpensive programs will have the magnitude of effects that were once hoped for. However, for students of human behavior there is a silver lining in that political cloud. If mild interventions are not likely to produce strongly positive effects on intellectual modifiability, then relatively brief and mildly deleterious environments are also not likely to leave permanent intellectual scars. In short, the young child appears to be responsive to sustained alternations in the quality of the environment whether the approach is one of prevention or remediation—at least during the preschool period. However, the demonstrated malleability during various phases of the preschool years does call into question strong forms of the critical period hypothesis—at least for variations in timing within this relatively brief developmental period.

Although the importance, if not the criticalness of early experience, generically, has been supported by the IQ results, we are still somewhat in the dark about which specific aspects of early experience are causally linked to specific aspects of intellectual development. Given the results from the curriculum comparison studies it appears that systematic variations within what Scarr and Weinberg (1978) have called "humane environments" may be functionally equivalent for intellectual development—at least when it is measured somewhat summatively and, therefore, globally as has been done with IQ tests. These might well be a direct parallel between cumulative risk as described by Rutter (1981) and cumulative competence, or intellectual adaptability has shown that individual risk factors specifically are not as highly related to deleterious outcomes as are the number of risk factors present for a given child or family. Similarly, there may be many paths to intellectual competence depending on the number of strengths or supportive or protective factors in the child's environment.[1]

With respect to the transactional hypothesis as presented schematically in Figure 10.1, the compensatory education experiments afford some indirect if not direct support. The notion that the infants' intellectual development can be altered by modifying the propensities of caregivers through systematic education has plausibility even though the magnitude of the impact is modest and below that which has been shown by working directly with the child. However, the theoretically important point seems to be that intellectual development can potentially be influenced by systematic efforts aimed at a variety of modes in the social interactional system of infants and their caregivers.

## RECOMMENDATIONS FOR FUTURE RESEARCH

Even though a large data base as been constructed concerning the malleability of intellectual development through compensatory education, there are still large gaps in our knowledge. These gaps are perceived clearly, however, precisely because of the contributions that have been made by the studies just reviewed. Nevertheless, the gaps do exist and are worthy of additional research. Therefore, we conclude with the following recommendations.

First, additional research needs to be conducted with more representative samples of the full spectrum of socially disadvantaged families. For example, the Houston PCDC which studied Mexican-American families provided results that are somewhat anomolous with those projects which concentrated primarily on black families. Thus, we need to know more about various cultural subgroups, including disadvantaged Indians, whites, and Spanish-speaking minorities. We also need more studies conducted in the Western part of the United States as well as more studies with rural, disadvantaged populations.

Second, global measures of IQ such as derived from the Stanford–Binet test need to be supplemented by assessments of the components of intelligence. We

---

[1] For a fuller discussion of this issue of risk and vulnerability among the poor, the interested reader is referred to a recent paper by Ramey and MacPhee (in press).

are in need of greater specificity of the most vulnerable cognitive processes so that those might be targeted more efficiently for therapeutic or preventive educational programs.

Third, more research attention needs to be focused on determining differential patterns of intellectual response to various compensatory education approaches. We need more information about which children profit the most or the least from various interventions, so that compensatory education programs and predisposing characteristics of children and/or families might be more efficiently and effectively matched.

Fourth, greater effort needs to be expended on studying the mechanisms targeted for change, and how those mechanisms relate to intellectual outcomes in children. At present the studies which have been reviewed are encouraging with respect to the malleability of intelligence, but the psychological mechanisms whereby these results have been produced are poorly understood.

Fifth, greater understanding of the issues of developmental timing and program intensity are called for from a practical as well as a theoretical perspective. We need to know more about how early, and for how long, interventions must be conducted to have a meaningful influence on intelligence. To this end, longer term follow-up of individuals who have participated in compensatory education needs to be conducted. However, we should be wary of expecting "permanent" positive effects of compensatory education if it is delivered during periods of rapid development. Currently no major theory of intellectual development predicts permanence of alterations unless there is a substantial alteration of the basic environmental conditions that indicate intellectual risk. In short, because intellectual development is a dialectical process co-determined by characteristics of an individual at a given point in time and the environmental characteristics to which that individual is sequentially exposed, permanence could be predicted only for steady-state intellectual functioning in a relatively stable environment. In other words "permanence" can be predicted only if no further development is to occur. Such a concept is, of course, antithetical to the very premise of education generally and to compensatory education specifically. Instead, what is needed is a greater specification of what intellectual abilities develop, how they are transformed across developmental periods, and what environmental or educational processes enhance or retard that development.

Finally, from the point of view of public policy, we need to realize that intellectual development is an important, but limited, goal of compensatory education and that future research needs to expand its scope to include assessments of other modes of functioning as well.

## REFERENCES

Andrews, S. R., Blumenthal, J. B., Johnson, D. L., Kahn, A. J., Ferguson, C. J., Lasater, T. M., Malone, P. E., & Wallace, D. B. (1982). The skills of mothering: A study of Parent Child Development Centers. *Monographs of the Society for Research in Child Development, 47*(6, Serial No. 198).

Bayley, N. (1969). *Manual for the Bayley Scales of Infant Development.* New York: The Psychological Corporation.

Bereiter, C., & Engelmann, S. (1966). *The effectiveness of direct verbal instruction on IQ performance and achievement in reading and arithmetic.* Champaign, IL: Academic Preschool.

Bereiter, C., & Washington, E. D. (1969). *Research and development program on preschool disadvantaged children, Final Report to DHEW.* Champaign, IL: Academic Preschool.

Bloom, B. S. (1964). *Stability and change in human characteristics.* New York: John Wiley & Sons.

Broman, S. H., Nichols, P. L., & Kennedy, A. (1975). *Preschool IQ: Prenatal and early developmental correlates.* Hillsdale, NJ: Lawrence Earlbaum Associates.

Bryant, D. M., Burchinal, M. B., & Ramey, C. T. (1983). *A comparison of Stanford-Binet and Bayley MDI results at age 2.* Manuscript in preparation.

Clarke, A. M., & Clarke, A. D. B. (1976). *Early experience: Myth and evidence.* London, England: Open Books.

Epstein, A. S., & Weikart, D. B. (1979). *The Ypsilanti–Carnegie Infant Education Project: Longitudinal follow-up.* Ypsilanti, MI: High/Scope Educational Research Foundation.

Field, T. (1980). *Progress report on home and center-based intervention for teenage mothers and their offspring.* Washington, DC: Administration for Children, Youth, and Families.

Field, T. M. (1982). Infants born at risk: Early compensatory experiences. In L. Bond & J. Joffe (Eds.), *Facilitating infant and early childhood development.* Burlington, VT: University of Vermont Press.

Field, T., Widmayer, S., Stringer, S., & Ignatoff, E. (1980). Teenage, lower class black mothers and their preterm infants: An intervention and developmental follow-up. *Child Development, 51,* 426–436.

Frankenberg, W., & Dodds, J. (1968). *Denver Developmental Screening Test.* Denver, CO: University of Colorado Medical Center.

Freud, S. (1905). *Drei Abhandlungen zur Sexualtheorie.* Vienna, Austria: Deuticke. (Translated as *Three essays on the theory of sexuality,* 1962.)

Garber, H. (1982, August). *Preventing mild mental retardation: Decimating a complex.* Paper presented at the IASSMD Symposium, Toronto, Ontario, Canada.

Garber, H., & Heber, R. (1981). The efficacy of early intervention with family rehabilitation. In M. Begab, H. C. Haywood, & H. L. Garber (Eds.), *Psychosocial influences in retarded performance.* Baltimore, MD: University Park Press.

Gesell, A., & Amatruda, C. S. (1947). *Developmental diagnosis* (2nd ed.). New York: Hoeber.

Gordon, I. J., & Guinagh, B. J. (1978). *A home learning center approach to early stimulation* (Final report to the National Institute of Mental Health). Gainesville, FL: Institute for Development of Human Resources, University of Florida, 1974. Published in *JSAS Catalog of Selected Documents in Psychology, 8* (6) (Ms. No. 1634).

Gordon, I. J., & Guinagh, B. J. (1978, March). *Middle school performance as a function of early stimulation.* (Final report to the Administration of Children, Youth and Families, Project No. NIH-HEW-OCD-90-C-908). Gainesville, FL: University of Florida, Institute for Development of Human Resources; and Chapel Hill, NC: University of North Carolina, School of Education.

Gottlieb, G. (1971). *Development of species identification in birds.* Chicago, IL: University of Chicago Press.

Gray, S. W., & Klaus, R. A. (1970). The early training project: A seventh year report. *Child Development, 41,* 909–924.

Gray, S. W., Ramsey, B. K., & Klaus, R. A. (1982). *From 3 to 20: The Early Training Project.* Baltimore, MD: University Park Press.

Gray, S., & Ruttle, K. (1980). The Family-oriented home visiting program: A longitudinal study. *Genetic Psychology Monographs, 102,* 299–316.

Griffiths, R. (1964). *The abilities of babies.* London, England: University of London Press.

Guinagh, B. J., & Gordon, I. J. (1976). *School performance as a function of early stimulation.* (Final report to OCD, Grant # NIH-HEW-09-C-638). Gainesville, FL: University of Florida.

Gutelius, M. F., Kirsch, A. D., MacDonald, S., Brooks, M. R., & McErlean, T. (1977). Controlled study of child health supervision: Behavioral results. *Pediatrics, 60,* 294–304.

Gutelius, M. F., Kirsch, A. D., MacDonald, S., Brooks, M. R., McErlean, T., & Newcomb, C. (1972). Promising results from a cognitive stimulation program in infancy. *Clinical Pediatrics, 11,* 585–593.

Hebb, D. O. (1949). *The organization of behavior.* New York: Wiley.

Heber, R. F., Dever, R. B., & Conry, J. (1968). The influence of environmental and genetic variables on intellectual development. In H. Prehm, L. A. Hamerlynck, & J. E. Crosson (Eds.), *Behavioral research in mental retardation.* Eugene, OR: University of Oregon.

Heber, R., & Garber, H. (1971, October). *Rehabilitation of families at risk for mental retardation. A progress report.* Madison, WI: Rehabilitation Research and Training Center in Mental Retardation.

Herrnstein, R. J. (1982). IQ testing and the media. *The Atlantic, 250*(2), 68–74.

Hunt, J. McV. (1961). *Intelligence and experience.* New York: The Ronald Press Co.

Hunt, J. McV. (1979). Psychological development: Early experience. *Annual Review of Psychology, 30,* 103–143.

Jensen, A. R. (1969). How much can we boost IQ and scholastic achievement? *Harvard Educational Review, 39,* 1–123.

Kagan, J. (1979). Structure and process in the human infant: The ontogeny of mental representation. In M. H. Bernstein & W. Kessen (Eds.), *Psychological development from infancy: Image to intention.* Hillsdale, NJ: Lawrence Erlbaum Assoc.

Kagan, J., Kearsley, R., & Zelazo, P. (1978). *Infancy: Its place in human development.* Cambridge, MA: Harvard University Press.

Karnes, M. B., Hodgins, A. S., Tesda, J. A., & Kirk, S. A. (1969). *Investigations of classroom and at-home interventions: Research and development pro-*

*gram on preschool disadvantaged children.* Final Report. Urbana, IL: University of Illinois.

Kessen, W. (1979). The American child and other cultural inventions. *American Psychologist, 34,* 815–820.

Klaus, M. H., & Kennell, J. H. (1976). Parent-to-infant attachment. In V. C. Vaughan III & R. B. Brazelton (Eds.), *The family—Can it be saved?* Chicago, IL: Yearbook Medical Publishers, Inc.

Knobloch, H., & Pasamanick, B. (1953). Further observation on the behavioral development of Negro children. *Journey of Genetic Psychology, 83,* 137–157.

Kushlick, A., & Blunden, R. (1974). The epidemiology of mental subnormality. In A. M. Clarke, & A. D. B. Clarke (Eds.), *Mental deficiency: The changing outlook.* New York: The Free Press.

Lambie, D. Z., Bond, J. T., & Weikart, D. B. (1974). *Home teaching with mothers and infants: The Ypsilanti–Carnegie Infant Education Project—An experiment.* Ypsilanti, MI: High/Scope Educational Research Foundation.

Lazar, I., Darlington, R., Murray, H., Royce, J., & Snipper, A. (1982). Lasting effects of early education: A report from the Consortium for Longitudinal Studies. *Monographs of the Society for Research in Child Development, 47*(2–3, Serial No. 195).

Laszlo, E. (1972). *Introduction to systems philosophy: Toward a new paradigm of contemporary thought.* New York: Harper & Row.

Lorenz, K. (1937). The companion in the bird's world. *Auk, 54,* 245–273.

McCall, R. B. (1981). Nature-nurture and the two realms of development: A proposed integration with respect to mental development. *Child Development, 52,* 1–12.

Miller, J. G. (1978). *Living systems.* New York: McGraw-Hill.

Miller, L. B., & Dyer, J. L. (1975). Four preschool programs: Their dimensions and effects. *Monographs of the Society for Research in Child Development, 40*(5–6, Serial No. 162).

Olmsted, P. P., Rubin, R. I., True, J. H., & Revicki, D. A. (1980). *Parent education, the contributions of Ira J. Gordon.* Washington, DC: Association for Childhood Education International.

Parmalee, A. H., Jr. (1977). Planning intervention for infants at high risk identified by developmental evaluation. In P. Mittler (Ed.), *Research to practice in mental retardation: Volume I Care and intervention.* Baltimore, MD: University Park Press.

Ramey, C. T., & Baker-Ward, L. (1982). Psychosocial retardation and the early experience paradigm. In D. Bricker (Ed.), *Handicapped and at-risk infants.* Baltimore, MD: University Park Press, 269–289.

Ramey, C. T., & Bryant, D. M. (1983, August). *Enhancing the development of the socially disadvantaged child with programs of varying intensity.* Paper presented at the American Psychological Association meeting, Los Angeles, CA.

Ramey, C. T., Bryant, D. M., Sparling, J. J., & Wasik, B. H. (1983, May). *Educational intervention to prevent mild mental retardation.* Paper presented at the 2nd International Workshop on the "At Risk" Infant, Jerusalem, Israel.

Ramey, C. T., & MacPhee, D. (in press). Developmental retardation among the poor: A systems theory perspective on risk and prevention. In D. C. Farran & J. D. McKinney (Eds.), *Risk in intellectual and psychosocial development.* New York: Academic Press.

Ramey, C. T., MacPhee, D., & Yeates, K. O. (1982). Preventing developmental retardation: A general systems model. In L. A. Bond, & J. M. Joffe (Eds.), *Facilitating infant and early childhood development.* Hanover, NH: University Press of New England.

Ramey, C. T., Sparling, J. J., & Wasik, B. H. (1981). Creating social environments to facilitate language development. In R. Scheifelbush & D. Bricker (Eds.), *Early language intervention.* Baltimore, MD: University Park Press.

Ramey, C. T., Stedman, D. J., Borders-Patterson, A., & Mengel, W. (1978). Predicting school failure from information available at birth. *American Journal of Mental Deficiency, 82,* 525-534.

Ramey, C. T., Trohanis, P. L., & Hostler, S. L. (1982). An introduction. In C. T. Ramey & P. L. Trohanis (Eds.), *Finding and educating high-risk and handicapped infants.* Baltimore, MD: University Park Press.

Ramey, C. T., Yeates, K. O., & Short, E. J. (in press). A systems theory perspective on the plasticity of intellect.

Richmond, J. B. (1974). The state of the child: Is the glass half-empty or half-full? *American Journal of Orthopsychiatry, 44,* 488-490.

Rutter, M. (1981). Stress, coping, and development: Some issues and questions. *Journal of Child Psychology and Psychiatry, 22,* 323-356.

Sameroff, A. J., & Chandler, M. J. (1975). Reproductive risk and the continuum of caretaking casualty. In F. D. Horowitz (Ed.), *Review of child development research* (Vol. 4). Chicago, IL: University of Chicago Press.

Sarason, S., Carroll, C., Maton, K., Cohen, S., & Lorentz, E. (1977). *Human services resource networks.* San Francisco, CA: Jossey Bass.

Scarr, S., & Weinberg, R. A. (1978). The influence of "family background" on intellectual attainment. *American Sociological Review, 43,* 674-692.

Schweinhart, L. J., & Weikart, D. B. (1980). *Young children grow up: The effects of the Perry Preschool Program on youths through age 15.* Ypsilanti, MI: High/Scope Educational Research Foundation.

Terman, L. M., & Merrill, M. A. (1973). *The Stanford-Binet Intelligence Scale.* New York: Houghton Mifflin Co.

Thompson, W. R., & Heron, W. (1954). The effects of early restriction in activity in dogs. *Journal of Comparative and Physiological Psychology, 47,* 77-82.

Yarrow, L. J. (1961). Maternal deprivation: Toward an empirical and conceptual re-evaluation. *Psychological Bulletin, 58,* 459-490.

Zigler, E., & Anderson, K. (1979). An idea whose time had come. In E. Zigler & J. Valentine (Eds.), *Project Head Start.* New York: Free Press.

CHAPTER *11*

# Behavioral Genetics*

Robert Plomin

*Institute for Behavioral Genetics,
University of Colorado, Boulder*

## INTRODUCTION

A volume on the topic of research methodologies employed to study intelligence would not be complete without a discussion of behavioral genetics. Behavioral genetic approaches permit assessment of the relative importance of both nature and nurture in the development of mental ability, the oldest continuously researched question in the behavioral sciences. In 1924, the first twin study and the first adoption study were reported, and both focused on mental ability. Since then, IQ tests have been administered to more than 4,000 individuals in adoptive relationships, to more than 4,500 twin pairs, and to more than 24,000 family members in pursuit of an answer to this question. If anything, the pace of research on the topic has picked up in recent years: Nearly as much data have been reported in the past 5 years as in the previous 50 years combined. This historical continuity and the magnitude of resources devoted to this issue reflect an abiding interest.

The goal of the present chapter is to review behavioral genetic methodologies, especially new approaches, at a conceptual level with references providing further details. Examples of findings relevant to intelligence are used throughout. Single-gene and chromosomal studies are mentioned briefly, although the majority of the review focuses on quantitative, behavioral genetic approaches, which consider multifactorial genetic and environmental influences and which

*The preparation of this review was supported in part by grants from the National Science Foundation (BNS82-00310), from NICHD (HD-10333), and from the Spencer Foundation; it was written while the author was the recipient of a Research Scientist Development Award (AA-00041). I gratefully acknowledge suggestions made by J. C. DeFries and A. R. Jensen in their review of an earlier version of this chapter. I thank Rebecca G. Miles for her expert editorial advice.

provide the bulk of the evidence for substantial genetic involvement in variability in intelligence. Throughout the chapter, the point will be made that behavioral genetic methodologies are just as useful for studying environmental influences as they are for studying genetic influences.

## SINGLE-GENE STUDIES

Single-gene effects which show typical Mendelian segregation ratios have been related to mental retardation. Most of this research involves the identification of metabolic defects that are related to retardation and show pedigree patterns of inheritance consistent with a single-gene hypothesis (see Plomin, DeFries, & McClearn, 1980). Over 100 single-gene effects have been identified, although most of them are quite rare (McKusick, 1978). The best known of these effects is called PKU, phenylketonuria, in which severe retardation results from a defective enzyme, phenylalanine hydroxylase, unless a diet low in phenylalanine is administered from birth until 5 years of age. Because the allele responsible for the defective enzyme is recessive, it must be inherited in a double dose (homozygosis) in order for the syndrome to develop. This happens in about 1 out of 20,000 live births. Bessman, Williamson, and Koch (1978) found that two-thirds of the PKU individuals' siblings in their study who were least able to convert phenylalanine to tyrosine (presumably carriers) had an average IQ score 10 points lower than that of other siblings who were better able to synthesize tyrosine. The frequency of carriers is sufficiently high (greater than 1%) that this single gene can explain a small portion of the genetic variance in IQ scores.

Another approach to studying single-gene influences on cognitive abilities that display gender differences is to look for patterns of inheritance consistent with linkage on the X-chromosome (such as less resemblance between fathers and sons than for other parent-offspring combinations). For example, the possibility that a major recessive allele influencing spatial ability is located on the X-chromosome (thus explaining higher scores for males than females) has aroused a great deal of interest. However, several large studies have not replicated earlier reports of X-linkage for spatial ability (for example, see Corley, DeFries, Kuse, & Vandenberg, 1980). A useful method for evaluating X-linkage is hierarchical multiple-regression analysis (see DeFries, Johnson, Kuse, McClearn, Polovina, Vandenberg, & Wilson, 1979). This method is highly flexible and powerful in testing other differential expectations for familial correlations such as changes in familial resemblance during development or genotype-environment interaction; both applications are described later in this chapter.

An exciting new area of research in mental retardation involves what is known as the *fragile X* (Lubs, 1983). For unknown reasons, certain points on the X-chromosome of some individuals are subject to breakage when the chromosomes are prepared in a specific manner using exacting tissue-culture methods. These breakage points serve as markers that relate to X-linked mental retardation.

It is thought that fragile X may explain most of the excess of mental retardation in males who also display macro-orchidism (Turner & Opitz, 1980). Fragile X may also account for some lowering of IQ in females with a single fragile X-chromosome. Because females are mosaic for the X-chromosome (that is, the paternal X-chromosome is expressed in some cells and the maternal X is expressed in others), it has been suggested that the proportion of heterozygote females' cells that display the fragile X may correlate with IQ.

Human behavioral genetics has not yet profited from the stunning advances made in molecular genetics during the past few years (e.g., Housman & Gusella, 1980). These advances have led to new genetic tools such as nucleotide base sequencing, precise restriction enzymes, radioactively labeled hybridization probes, and recombinant DNA libraries. Although these techniques hold the promise of directly assessing genetic variability among individuals and relating such genetic variations to observed individual differences in cognitive abilities, my guess is that studies of large samples of individuals using these tools and relating them to intelligence are decades away.

Some steps in the direction of understanding the pathways from single genes to behavior have been taken by means of Benzer's (1973) "genetic dissection of behavior," which involves the screening of behavioral mutants. These investigations have usually studied bacteria and fruit flies, so it comes as no surprise that the implications of this research for understanding genetic influences on IQ are as yet limited to a few general principles, although attempts to study learning phenomena have been made (e.g., Dudai, Jan, Byers, Quinn, & Benzer, 1976). One of these principles is that many genes are likely to be involved in normal behavior: At least 40 genes are responsible for normal swimming in bacteria, and over 100 genes are involved in the structure of the eye of fruit flies. Any one of these genes can alter behavior. Similarly in humans, any one of many genes can disrupt cognitive development, but the normal range of behavioral variation is more likely to be orchestrated by a system of many genes, each with small effect, as well as by environmental influences. For that reason, this chapter will focus on polygenic approaches.

## CHROMOSOMAL ANALYSES

In addition to studying the relationship between single genes and intelligence, it is possible to study the effect of a missing or extra chromosome or part of a chromosome. Chromosomal anomalies are worth considering because about 1 in 200 births involves chromosomal abnormalities and many of these affect IQ. Down syndrome (trisomy of one of the small chromosomes) remains the single most important cause of retardation, accounting for as many as 10% of institutionalized retarded individuals.

During the past 5 years, new karyotyping techniques have resulted in a quadrupling of the number of identifying bands on human chromosomes and the discovery of many minor chromosomal anomalies. Although no study has systematically related such minor chromosomal abnormalities to IQ, a general rule of thumb is that the decrement in IQ is related to the amount of extra or missing "active" DNA—which is reasonable if many genes affect IQ.

## QUANTITATIVE BEHAVIORAL GENETIC ANALYSES

Because cognitive ability is so complex, it is unlikely that specific single-gene or chromosomal effects will be found to explain more than a small portion of the observed variability in this trait. It is quantitative genetic approaches, considering the effects of many genes as well as the influence of the environment, that have been most rewarding in the study of intelligence. The basic methods of quantitative genetics have been around since at least the 1920s and will be mentioned only briefly here. (For details, see Plomin et al., 1980.)

### Methods Using Nonhuman Animals

Animal research methods may contribute to the study of human cognition; for example, they may prove useful for testing neurological theories, especially as animal researchers become more interested in cognitive behavior. These methods include family studies, strain comparisons, and selective breeding studies. Family comparisons confound genetic and environmental influences, but they do provide evidence for the *sine qua non* of genetic effects: familial resemblance. Moreover, in animal studies, classical Mendelian crosses can be easily conducted, and certain useful types of offspring, such as paternal half-siblings, can be easily produced.

Strain studies compare variance among and within genetically different inbred strains produced by at least 20 generations of brother–sister mating. The inbreeding process makes each animal in a strain virtually a clone of all other members of the strain. Genetically influenced characters should show average differences between inbred strains, whereas differences within strains provide estimates of environmental influence. Because it has been demonstrated that genetic effects are ubiquitous in animal behavior, 2-strain comparisons are no longer very interesting. More powerful methodologies, particularly the diallel method of complete intercrossing in which several inbred strains and all possible F1 hybrid cross are compared simultaneously, are *de rigueur* because they yield substantially more information than do comparisons of only two strains. Over 100 inbred strains of mice are available. Heterogeneous stocks, deliberately outbred animals derived from crosses of inbred strains, are also useful because they incorporate much of the genetic variability of the species. A new methodology, the recombinant inbred strain method, is the most powerful tool available for isolating major-gene effects by deriving several inbred strains from the F2 generation produced by a cross between two inbred strains.

Selection studies provide the clearest evidence for genetic influence: If a trait is heritable, you can select for it, as animal breeders have long known. Selective breeding also yields animal models that are useful in other research programs. For example, at the Institute for Behavioral Genetics, selective breeding of mice for alcohol sensitivity as measured by "sleep time" following a hypnotic dose has resulted in low and high lines that do not overlap in their sleep-time response (McClearn & Kakihana, 1981). These animals have been widely used in an intensive search for the neuropharmacological source of the difference between the selected lines (Collins, 1981). Selection studies can produce lines selected for adaptive functions, as in Tolman's (1924) and Tryon's (in Tyler, 1969) attempts to select for maze learning in rats, and then search for the physiological underpinnings of the genetic effect. Alternatively, we can select for certain biological traits and then observe behavioral correlates—for example, selection for neurotransmitter properties thought to be important in learning followed by exploration of behavioral concomitants.

## Human Methodologies

Of course inbred-strain comparisons and selection studies are not possible with humans. Although it is common to decry the lack of control in studying human beings, there is a silver lining to this cloud: Researchers are forced to work with genetic and environmental variability as it exists outside the laboratory, the "real world" conditions to which we are trying to generalize our results. For this reason, the results of human behavioral-genetic studies are much more generalizable to the human species as a whole than the results of nonhuman animal studies are to other members of their species.

Both human and nonhuman studies are based on the quantitative genetic model that began with Sir Ronald Fisher's 1918 treatise on *The Correlation between Relatives on the Supposition of Mendelian Inheritance.* Fisher unified Mendelian and non-Mendelian approaches by putting the finishing statistical touches on a multifactorial model which shows that the additive effects of many genetic loci, each operating in a Mendelian fashion and contributing a small amount of variance, yield smooth normal distributions rather than the characteristic bimodal curves seen for pure Mendelian characteristics. For characters of interest to behavioral scientists, it is safe to assume a multifactorial model in which many genetic factors and many environmental factors contribute to observed variance. There is no known case of a complex behavior for which a significant amount of variance is determined by a single gene. As mentioned earlier, more than 100 single-gene mutations have been found that have a deleterious effect on IQ, but their incidence is relatively rare; thus, even though such mutations have a tremendous impact on the IQ of afflicted individuals, they cannot account for appreciable IQ variance in the population. Moreover, the term "quantitative genetics" (or "biometrical genetics," as it is called in Great Britain) is a misnomer in that it implies a search only for *genetic* influence. As will be seen later in this chapter, quantitative genetic methodologies are just as useful in elucidating the effects of environmental variables.

Thus, the application of quantitative genetic methodologies represents a reasonable first step in the quest for understanding of the etiology of individual differences in intelligence. The basic empirical tools of human quantitative genetics include family, twin, and adoption studies. At the most elementary level, these methods can be seen as natural experiments testing a hypothesis of genetic influence. If heredity is important for IQ, then relatives must be similar. First-degree relatives should be more similar than second-degree relatives. Of course, family environment could also account for such patterns of similarity among relatives; however, familial resemblance is not necessarily predicted by an environmental hypothesis, whereas it is an essential indicator of genetic influence. The classical twin study compares two groups that differ drastically in terms of their genetic similarity: identical (monozygotic, MZ) twins, who are identical genetically; and same-sex fraternal (dizygotic, DZ) twins, who, like other sibling pairs, share 50% of their segregating genes, on the average. If intelligence is not influenced by heredity, then the 2-fold greater genetic similarity of MZ twins as compared to DZ twins would not affect the within-pair similarity for IQ scores. If heredity affects IQ, we would expect identical twins to be more similar than fraternal twins.

The adoption method disentangles the genetic and environmental effects that are intertwined in nonadaptive families by studying resemblances between genetically related individuals who do not share family environment (for example, biological parents and their adopted-away children), as well as those between individuals who share family environment but are not genetically related (for example, adoptive parents and their adopted children). This powerful design is described in terms of path diagrams in Figures 11.1 and 11.2. At the simplest level, path diagrams illustrate designs: In this case, Figure 11.1 indicates that nonadoptive parents share both heredity and family environment

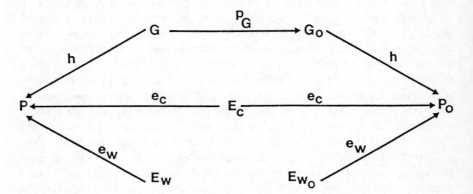

Figure 11.1. Path diagram of the correlation between parents (P) and offspring ($P_o$) in a nonadoptive family. See text for explanation. (From DeFries, Plomin, Vandenberg, & Kuse, 1981.)

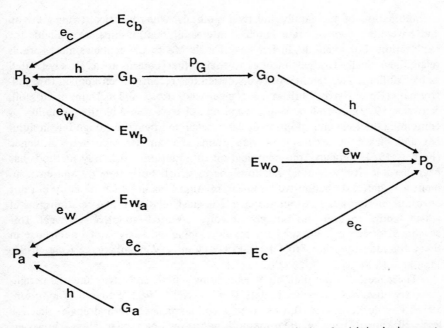

Figure 11.2. Path diagram of the parent–child correlation for biological parents $(P_b)$ and their adopted-away offspring $(P_o)$ and for adoptive parents $(P_a)$ and their adopted children $(P_o)$. See text for explanation. (From DeFries, Plomin, Vandenberg, & Kuse, 1981.)

with their children; Figure 11.2 describes how the adoption design separates these influences. As discussed in the next section, path analysis, originally developed by Sewall Wright (1931) to solve problems of quantitative genetic inheritance (using IQ data as an example), is useful for deriving expectations in structural modeling approaches (Li, 1975). For example, the simple path diagram in Figure 11.1 yields an expectation that the parent–offspring correlation in non-adoptive homes is equivalent to $h^2 P_G + e_c^2$, where $h^2$ is narrow-sense heritability, $P_G$ is a genetic path coefficient that equals 0.5 when there is no assortative mating, and $e_c^2$ is family environment influences shared by parents and their children. In contrast, as shown in Figure 11.2, the expected parent-offspring correlation for biological parents and their adopted-away offspring is $h^2 P_G$; for the adoptive parent/adopted children correlation, the expectation is $e_c^2$ in the absence of selective placement.

In the past two decades, the trend in human quantitative genetic research has been to combine family, twin, and adoption designs to incorporate additional comparisons into quantitative genetic analyses. The newly developed structural modeling approaches discussed in the next section are particularly useful for this purpose. One popular design that was first considered only a decade ago is a combination of the family and twin methods. When identical twins grow up and have their own separate families, interesting relationships are available for exploration. For example, in families of male MZ twins, nephews/nieces are as related genetically to their uncle as to their father; cousins are as closely related as half-siblings. This families-of-twins design has recently been applied to cognitive data (Rose, Harris, Christian, & Nance, 1979; Rose, Miller, Dumont-Driscoll, & Evans, 1979). Considerable interest also has been aroused by the possibility of combining the twin and adoption designs. Separated twins, although few in number and biased in selection, provide dramatic examples of genetic influence (Farber, 1981). Finally, the combination of adoption and family methods has been used to study familial relationships in which both heredity and environment are shared (nonadoptive families), relationships in which heredity but not environment is shared (adopted-apart biological relatives), and relationships in which family environment but not heredity is shared (adoptive relatives). This combined design is being used for the developmental analysis of intelligence in the Colorado Adoption Project (DeFries, Plomin, Vandenberg, & Kuse, 1981; Plomin & DeFries, 1983, 1984).

These methods and their use in estimating genetic and environmental parameters are discussed in several texts (e.g., Cattell, 1982; Fuller & Thompson, 1978; Plomin et al., 1980); this chapter will emphasize methodologies that are less well known. Each of these methods has its own particular failings; however, the convergence of evidence in the area of IQ is impressive, as shown in Table 11.1 (also, see Bouchard & McGue, 1981), although dissent remains (see, for example, Eysenck & Kamin, 1981). The data converge on the conclusion, remarkable as it seems, that fully half of the variance in IQ scores is due to genetic differences among individuals. Of course, this means that half of the variance is also due to nongenetic sources of variance. Still, to my knowledge, there is no finding in the behavioral sciences that begins to approach the magnitude of this result. For example, the much touted relationship between family size/birth order and IQ accounts for less than 2% of the variance of IQ. In other words, if all you know about someone is their family size and birth order, you would not have any useful information for predicting their IQ. However, if you knew the IQ of one of their first-degree relatives, you could make a modestly accurate prediction of their IQ (a correlation of about 0.30), and the accuracy of prediction could be substantially increased by knowing the IQs of several first-degree relatives.

The recent data presented in Table 11.1 permit a comparison of the widely cited older IQ data with data reported during the past 5 years. It is noteworthy that the newer data point to less heritable influence on IQ than is indicated by the older data. This finding is consistent across twin studies and studies of nontwin siblings, as well as parent-offspring comparisons in family and adoption studies. The cause or causes of the differences between the older and newer data are not understood. Because heritability is a population parameter, it is possible

Table 11.1. Correlation Coefficients for Old and New IQ Data[a]

| | Old Data | | New Data | |
|---|---|---|---|---|
| | Correlation | Number of Pairs | Correlation | Number of Pairs |
| *Genetically identical:* | | | | |
| Same individual tested twice | . . . | . . . | 0.87 | 456 |
| Identical twins reared together | 0.87 | 1,082 | 0.86 | 1,300 |
| Identical twins reared apart | 0.75 | 107 | . . . | . . . |
| *Genetically related (first-degree):* | | | | |
| Fraternal twins reared together: | | | | |
| Same sex | 0.53 | 2,052 | 0.62 | 864 |
| Opposite sex | 0.53 | (total) | 0.62 | 358 |
| Nontwin siblings reared together | 0.49 | 8,228 | 0.34 | 776 |
| Nontwin siblings reared apart | 0.40 | 125 | . . . | . . . |
| Parent–child living together | 0.50 | 371 | 0.35 | 3,973 |
| Parent–child separated by adoption | 0.45 | 63 | 0.31 | 345 |
| *Genetically unrelated:* | | | | |
| Unrelated children reared together | 0.23 | 195 | 0.25 | 601 |
| Adoptive parent–adopted child | 0.20 | not reported | 0.15 | 1,594 |
| Unrelated persons reared apart | –0.01 | 15,086 | . . . | . . . |

[a]After Plomin and DeFries (1980).

that they may be attributable to environmental or genetic changes in the population. However, methodological variations in restriction of range, age adjustment, and test administration may also account for some of the observed differences (Caruso, 1983).

The remainder of this section will include more detailed discussion of new methods in behavioral genetic research: structural models, multivariate genetic-environmental analyses, developmental analyses, assessments of genotype-environment interaction and correlation, and the decomposition of environmental variance into shared and nonshared components.

## Structural Models

Although family, twin, and adoption data on IQ appear to indicate the presence of substantial genetic influence upon IQ, it is necessary to acknowledge the various assumptions that underlie each method. For all of these methods, we have implicit causal models of the effects of assortative mating (the tendency for like to mate with like), which increases familial correlations for first-degree relatives (but not for identical twins). We also make assumptions about additive genetic variance (that component of genetic variance that "breeds true"): Parents and offspring share only half of the additive genetic variance; siblings share some nonadditive, as well as half of the additive, genetic variance; and identical twins completely share all sources of genetic variance, regardless of whether it is additive or nonadditive. In addition, there are implicit models specific to each method. For example, we make assumptions about the comparability of twin and nontwin environments and of the environments of identical and fraternal twins. In adoption studies, we make assumptions about selective placement, which can inflate both genetic and environmental estimates.

Rather than considering each "experiment" separately, behavioral geneticists have moved in the direction of analyzing the combined data from several experiments. Structural models (also called biometrical models, causal models, or path models), even though modeling is sometimes better referred to as muddling, are superior to the piece-by-piece approach in several ways: They permit analysis of all data simultaneously, they make assumptions explicit, they permit tests of the relative fit of the model, and they allow tests of different (for example, simpler) models. Modeling basically involves fitting a series of overdetermined simultaneous equations in order to estimate genetic and environmental parameters that best fit observed familial correlations. Path analysis is typically used in the formulation of such equations. Maximum-likelihood solutions have now supplanted weighted least-square methods for the analysis of simultaneous equations, although it should be mentioned that both approaches yield similar parameter estimates (Rao, Morton, Elston, & Yee, 1977).

The mathematical procedures for solving an extensive series of simultaneous equations are complicated. However, we should not stand too much in awe of these methods. Loehlin, in an excellent introduction to the topic as it relates to IQ data, puts it in perspective:

> One strategy is to divide and conquer. A series of independent experiments is carried out that purport to estimate the same parameter. One might, for example, estimate the heritability of a given trait from a comparison of identical and fraternal twins, then from a parent-child regression, then from a comparison of natural and adoptive siblings, and so on. If all these estimates agree (and the models employed are mutually compatible), excellent: one has substantial confidence that one is on the right track. And if they don't, the particular pattern of disagreement may help suggest what is wrong. . . .
>
> A strategy of this kind has much to commend it. It is straight-forward and relatively easy to apply and to understand, and conforms (more or less) to the historical development of human behavior genetics as different investigators carried out their twin and adoption and family studies in more-or-less comparable populations in America and Europe. But there is a second strategy that has recently come into some vogue, which involves the simultaneous consideration of data from twins, adoptees, and so on . . . In

short, in consolidating the three experiments into one by following the second major strategy we gain two major advantages: a single solution that best fits all the data, and a statistical test of how well that solution fits, or how it compares with another. (Loehlin, 1979, pp. 308–310)

Applications of structural models to IQ data have led to strikingly different results in different studies, although they all agree that genetic influence is significant (Loehlin, 1978). For example, genotype-environment correlation appears prominent in analyses by Jencks (1972) but not in analyses conducted by researchers at the University of Birmingham (Jinks & Eaves, 1974). The Birmingham group found evidence for substantial nonadditive genetic variance, whereas the Hawaii group did not (Rao, Morton, & Yee, 1974; 1976). In comparing these approaches, Loehlin (1978, p. 417) noted that minor discrepancies in the data sets and differences in analytic methods were not critical; what was important was differences in assumptions concerning genetic dominance, assortative mating, and twin environments. Loehlin concludes:

> This analysis would seem to point to two morals. One is that it is easy to make mistakes in specifying causal models of how heredity and environment affect traits. . . . The second moral, and I believe the more important one, is that conclusions depend on assumptions, and that therefore when making somewhat arbitrary assumptions (e.g., no selective placement, no dominance, no G x E covariance) in order to solve a complex model, the theorist is well advised not only to offer some justification for the choice he makes but also to offer the reader some information about what the consequences would be if he were to make it differently. . . . This should not be construed as implying that such modal building is pointless. On the contrary, it is in my view extremely valuable. It is only when assumptions are embedded into explicit models that one can see what the consequences of these assumptions *are* (as opposed to what the theorist thinks they might be). (Loehlin, 1978, p. 430)

In well studied areas such as intelligence, causal modeling is becoming more and more common in behavioral genetic research. As described above, the advantages are clear, although Loehlin's cautions certainly should be considered. In addition, we must keep in mind that the results of such analyses can only be used to reject certain models as untenable; as in tests of any scientific hypothesis, they do not prove that a particular model is correct. Also, it is important not to stray too far from the data: Correlations or variance/covariance matrices should be presented so that researchers can evaluate the overall pattern of the basic results and apply different models to the data.

## Multivariate Genetic-Environmental Analysis

Behavioral genetic studies have traditionally been univariate, analyzing the variance of characters considered one at a time. However, quantitative genetic methods can be readily extended to analyses of covariance among characters;

the same principles apply, and the same quantitatvie methodologies are applicable (e.g., Plomin & DeFries, 1979). The usefulness of this approach for investigating the domain of intelligence has been demonstrated by behavioral-genetic researchers who have increasingly turned to the study of specific cognitive abilities in addition to general cognitive ability, or IQ. They have found that, by and large, specific cognitive abilities show about the same amount of genetic influence as does IQ. Whether or not various abilities are equally heritable is subject to current debate. There is some evidence that verbal and spatial factors tend to show greater genetic influence than do memory and perceptual speed factors, but these differences are neither large nor very consistent from study to study (DeFries, Vandenberg, & McClearn, 1976). However, it is extremely unlikely that completely different genes affect each specific cognitive ability. Just as we have studied the phenotypic (observed) factor structure of cognitive abilities, we can also study genetic and environmental factor structures that provide the foundation for the factor structure that is observed.

Figure 11.3 depicts the bivariate case. The phenotypic correlation between two characters can be mediated genetically or nongenetically. The genetic contribution in the path diagram is $h_x h_y r_G$. The genetic correlation, $r_G$, is the correlation between genetic deviations that affect character X and genetic differences that affect character Y. Even if genes do not much influence either character, the genetic correlation can be high. Even if heritabilities for traits X and Y are high, the genetic correlation between them can be low. The genetic contribution to the phenotypic correlation between two traits is the genetic correlation weighted by the square roots of the heritabilities of the two traits. It should be noted that this is merely a more general extension of the typical univariate model, $h_x h_x r_G = h_x^2$, which gives the genetic contribution to phenotypic variance for trait X. Similarly, the environmental contribution to the phenotypic correlation between two characters is the environmental correlation weighted by the square roots of values that represent environmental influences on the two traits. Thus, the phenotypic correlation between characters X and Y can be expressed as

$$r_P = h_x h_y r_G + e_x e_y r_E$$

If two traits show no phenotypic correlation, it is most likely that neither the same genes nor the same environmental factors affect both characters. The only other possible explanation for this result would be that the signs of the genetic and environmental correlations differ so that the two contributions to the phenotypic correlation counterbalance each other.

This bivariate example can be extended to the multivariate case by considering matrices of such bivariate genetic components and environmental components. Multivariate genetic–environmental analysis can be used to ask whether the same genes influence several cognitive abilities, as the Spearman "g" hy-

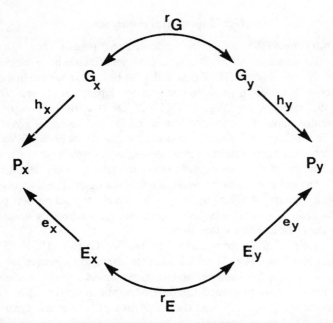

Figure 11.3. Path model of the phenotypic correlation between two characters ($P_x$ and $P_y$). The phenotypic correlation ($r_{P_xP_y}$) is composed of a genetic contribution ($h_xh_yr_G$) and an environmental contribution ($e_xe_yr_E$).

pothesis might predict (Jensen, 1980a), or if these abilities are genetically unrelated. Similarly, are there major environmental factors that have broad systematic influences across a wide range of specific cognitive abilities, or do different environmental influences affect different abilities? These are weighty questions, and preliminary findings so far indicate that the answer in each case is in the middle—genetic and environmental influences salient to specific cognitive abilities are neither very broad nor completely idiosyncratic in their effects. Rather, there are several sets of genetic factors and environmental factors, and these roughly correspond to the phenotypic factor structure of the abilities. In the case of scholastic abilities, however, analyses suggest that the same set of genes affects the major areas of academic achievement and that the environmental influences are similarly structured (Plomin & DeFries, 1979).

Analyses of genetic and environmental correlations will be useful in other research on intelligence such as investigations of the etiology of the relationship between reaction time measures and IQ (Jensen, 1982), explorations of the genetic and environmental structures underlying componential models of intelligence (Sternberg, 1977), and studies of the causes of change and continuity in development, which is the topic of the next section.

## Developmental Analyses

Genes are not running at full throttle at conception; "genetic" does not necessarily imply stable or static. Although quantitative genetics has been conceptualized in terms of structural genes (DNA that codes for peptides), we are just beginning to learn about the role of genes in creating developmental change. The simple operon model emphasizing "regulator genes" has recently been supplanted by new knowledge about the dynamic nature of DNA. "Jumping genes," "exon shuffling" in "split genes," and the multiple combinatorial possibilities provided by the hierarchical organization of multigene systems are sources of tremendous genetic variability at the molecular level (Hunkapillar, Huang, Hood, & Campbell, 1982). The old static view of genes as beads strung on a string has given way to a dynamic picture of DNA, making it reasonable to assume that genes that affect a character at one time in development are not necessarily the same genes that affect the character at another time.

At the turn of the century, twin studies by Galton (1875), Thorndike (1905), and Merriman (1924) asked whether there are changes in similarity between twins during development and generally found a negative answer to the question when they are examined the developmental transition from childhood to adolescence. We now know that the proportion of genetic and environmental influences on IQ changes from infancy to early childhood. Genetic influence is negligible in infancy, then rises rapidly to levels characteristic of adolescent and adult populations by the early school years (Plomin & DeFries, 1981). Methods for analyzing developmental changes in the relative influences of genes and environment using cross-sectional data are available, and studies in which these methods have been used suggest that the mix of genetic and environmental influences on specific cognitive abilities does not change much during the early school years (Ho, Foch, & Plomin, 1980).

Even more informative than cross-sectional analyses of changes in the relative influences of genes and environment is the longitudinal analysis of genetic and environmental contributions to change and continuity in development. One approach has been used in the analysis of longitudinal data from the Louisville Twin Study (Wilson, 1978, 1983). Age-to-age changes (spurts and lags) and overall profile levels of MZ and DZ twins are analyzed using repeated-measures analysis of variance. MZ correlations generally exceed DZ correlations for both age-to-age change and overall level, which suggests some heritable basis for these developmental phenomena, although both phenomena are complex functions of genetic influence at each age and genetic and phenotypic correlations among the ages.

Another approach to longitudinal analysis involves a simple extension of the multivariate genetic–environmental analysis discussed in the previous section. As seen in Figure 11.4, we merely need to consider measurements obtained at two times rather than measurements of two different characters. Thus, phenotypic stability $(r_{P_1 P_2})$ can be mediated genetically $(h_1 h_2 r_G)$ and environmentally $(e_1 e_2 r_E)$. More specifically, phenotypic stability emerges as a result of the genetic correlation between two ages weighted by the square root of heritability at each age. The genetic correlation describes the extent to which the genetic systems that affect a character at two ages overlap. Similarly, the environmental correlation denotes the extent to which environmental factors that affect a character at one age also affect the character at another age. An absence of stability indicates that the genetic and environmental factors that affect the character do not correlate across age (unless the unlikely counterbalancing of genetic and environmental components of different signs occurs).

Although no analyses of this type have been conducted, a reasonable speculation is that both genetic and environmental factors that affect IQ in the early school years are highly correlated with the genetic and environmental factors that affect adult IQ (Plomin & DeFries, 1981). Moreover, application of a path analytic model to data from the Colorado Adoption Project suggests that, al-

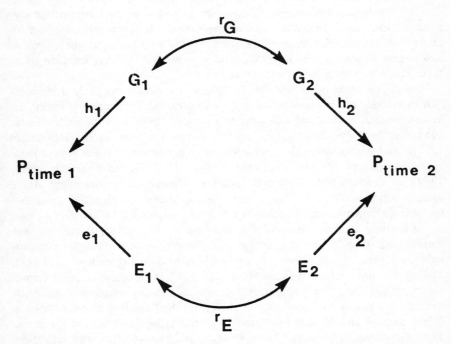

Figure 11.4. Path model of the phenotypic correlation (stability) between measurements obtained at two ages. The phenotypic correlation between ages 1 and 2 $(r_{P_1 P_2})$ is composed of a genetic contribution $(h_1 h_2 r_G)$ and an environmental contribution $(e_1 e_2 r_E)$.

though hereditary influence on mental ability in infancy is weak, the genetic factors that do affect performance on infant sensorimotor tests are highly correlated with those that affect IQ differences among adults (Baker, DeFries, & Fulker, 1983).

## Genotype-Environment Interaction and Correlation

An interesting yet relatively unexplored analytic area is the interface between genes and environment. Genotype-environment interaction refers to the differential response of individuals of differing genotypes to an environmental influence, or, conversely, the differential effectiveness of an environmental influence on individuals of different genotypes. For example, a particular educational practice might be more effective with "genetically brighter" children (i.e., children who inherit abilities and propensities to do and learn what is necessary to obtain high scores on IQ tests). In contrast, genotype-environment correlation refers to the differential exposure of individuals to environments. For example, "genetically brighter" children may receive opportunities that are not given to other children. Although the line that divides genotype-environment interaction and correlation at a conceptual level is a bit fuzzy, the distinction is clear when we stipulate an environmental measure and then ask whether genotypes interact or correlate with that measure.

Genotype-environment interaction has been studied extensively using nonhuman animals and is often found to have important effects upon behavior. In human studies, analyses of adoption data are capable of isolating such effects, but preliminary investigations of possible genotype-environment interactions for IQ have not been encouraging, although the environmental measures used have been quite limited (Plomin, DeFries, & Loehlin, 1977; Plomin & DeFries, 1983, 1984). It is alluring to think that certain environmental factors might affect some genotypes differently from others. Research aimed at identifying possible aptitude-treatment interactions has not been very successful, however.

Adoption data are also useful in isolating specific genotype-environment correlations. Three types of genotype-environment correlation have been proposed, and methods for assessing them have been discussed (Plomin et al., 1977). The passive type, which is most often considered in quantitative genetic analyses, emerges from the usual situation in which family members share both heredity and family environment. For example, bright children are likely to have bright parents and siblings who provide a stimulating environment for them. The other types of genotype-environment correlation, reactive and active, are likely to be even more important. The reactive type involves a differential response to children that is correlated with their genetic propensities; for example, a teacher provides more stimulation for a brighter child. The active type of genotype-environment correlation occurs when individuals actively seek out environments correlated with their genetic propensities. For example, brighter children seek and find more problems to solve in their transactions with their surroundings. A general theory of development fashioned around these types of genotype-environment correlation essentially posits a shift from the passive to the reactive and active varieties during childhood (Scarr & McCartney, 1983).

Neither genotype-environment interaction nor correlation greatly affects quantitative genetic estimates of the relative effects of heredity and environment upon the behaviors under investigation. Nevertheless, the most valuable contribution of quantitative genetics is that it offers tools to explore the interface between heredity and environment by assessing genotype-environment interactions and correlations. Such analyses are likely to lead to a greater understanding of environmental influences upon intelligence.

## Decomposition of Environmental Variance into Shared and Nonshared Components

A final example of quantitative genetic analyses involves just the environmental component of variance. For first-degree relatives, roughly half of the genetic variance is shared, making family members similar to one another; the other half, which is not shared, leads to differences among members of a family (depending on assortative mating and nonadditive genetic variance). Environmental variance, on the other hand, could be completely shared by family members; it could be completely not shared; or there could be any combination of shared and not shared variance. Nonetheless, our environmental hypotheses typically make the implicit assumption that relevant environmental influences are of the shared (also called common, or $E_2$) variety. For example, we study the effect of parents' reading to their children on IQ *across* families; that is, we study one parent and one child per family. We assume that the family is the salient unit and that other children in the family would receive roughly the same environmental input.

However, it has been exciting to discover that, at least for personality and psychopathology, nearly all the environmental variance is of the nonshared (within-family, $E_1$) variety. That is, whatever the sources of environmental influence might be, they are not shared by members of the same family. For intelligence, there is some shared environmental influence, although perhaps much less than we have thought. Twin studies exaggerate shared environmental influence because twins share substantially more (perhaps twice as much) environmental influence than do nontwin siblings (Plomin & DeFries, 1980). Twin studies have suggested that most of the reliable environmental variance that affects IQ is of the shared variety. A direct estimate of the importance of shared familial environment is the correlation for unrelated children reared together which is, on the average, about .25. This means that about 25% of the total IQ variance, or about half of the environmental variance, is due to shared family environment. However, it has not been previously appreciated that most of these studies involved young children. A tremendously important finding emerged from the only adoption study of postadolescent siblings. Scarr and Weinberg (1978) found a correlation of -.03 for 84 pairs of postadolescent children living together in adoptive families. This finding, which desperately needs replication, suggests that shared family environment, while important prior to adolescence when children are living at home, fades to negligible importance after adolescence. Thus, for IQ, as well as for personality and psychopathology, nonshared environmental influences may have a greater effect than do those that are shared.

Rowe and Plomin (1981) discuss these findings and suggest categories of nonshared environmental variation: accidental events, sibling interaction, family structure, differential parental treatment, and extra-familial factors (such as peer influences). These are systematic sources of nonshared environmental variation. One logical problem is that if such systematic influences are important, why don't they also produce differences between families? For example, if children in a family differ from one another because a parent loves one of them more than the other, then why wouldn't differences in parental love from one family to another also make children different? In other words, it is difficult to propose systematic sources of nonshared environmental variation that are not likely to produce shared environmental variation as well. The problem is that the data are telling us that shared environmental variation is not important. There is a way out of this conundrum. Although shared and nonshared sources of variance may be related, we know too little to say that there is in fact any relationship between these two varieties of environmental influence. For example, average levels of parental love may not be an important source of sibling resemblance— all that children know is *their* parents' love for them, but any differences in parental love shown towards two children in a family may make a big difference in the children's adjustment. Of course, another possibility is to shrug our shoulders and say that nonshared environmental influence involves idiosyncratic, unpredictable events. I submit that it is too early to jump to that gloomy conclusion.

Rowe and Plomin (1981) also suggest methods that can be used to study each category of nonshared environmental influence. For example, because differences within pairs of identical twins can be caused only by environmental factors of the nonshared variety, identical twins may be studied to isolate sources of nonshared environmental influence. Other siblings, of course, could differ for genetic as well as environmental reasons. A problem with this approach is that MZ twins are so similar that differences within pairs may be disproportionate due to errors of measurement, thus making it difficult to find correlates of within-pair differences. Another method is to look for environmental correlates of differences within pairs of genetically unrelated children in adoptive families, for which the genetic correlation within pairs is zero in the absence of selective placement. Differences within pairs could be of genetic origin, of course, but genetic influence can be ascertained by comparisons with data from genetically related siblings. A very different approach has been suggested by McCall (1983), who suggests that environmental factors that contribute to within-individual changes over time might also contribute to environmental differences within families.

Rowe and Plomin (1981) offer the following suggestions:

Future research should pursue the environment where most variation lies: within families. To advance the study of environmental influences on behavior, we advocate that more than one child be studied per family. In addition, behavioral genetic designs may be useful in understanding the role of $E_1$ influences, for example, by studying the causes of differences within pairs of MZ twins. In the past, researchers may have shied away from these methods either because they believed them to be useful only for detecting hereditary influences or because heredity was assumed to have a minimal impact on development. From the preceding review, we conclude that genetic influences, rather than being ignored, should be examined and, more important, controlled when the quarry is environmental contributions. (p. 530)

# DENOUEMENT

There are not many behavioral geneticists. The Behavior Genetics Association, for example, has only about 400 members. There are only a handful of universities where behavioral genetics is taught at the graduate level. However, there are signs that behavioral genetics is entering the mainstream of psychology, and one goal of this chapter is to hasten that process by demonstrating that behavioral genetic methodologies can do a lot more than estimate the relative importance of genetic and environmental influences. Some recent examples have been described: structural models, multivariate genetic-environmental analyses, developmental analyses, assessments of genotype-environment interaction and correlation, and the decomposition of environmental variance. One message that has been emphasized in this discussion is that quantitative behavioral genetics provides powerful tools for the analysis of environmental influence. In addition to the methods described in this chapter, behavioral genetics offers other ways of exploring environmental effects upon behavior. For example, the co-twin control method can be used to study the effects of environmental interventions by using an identical co-twin as a control (Plomin & Willerman, 1975). A similar use for siblings as covariate controls has been proposed by Jensen (1980b), who also discusses other applications of sibling designs. Another novel approach to the study of the environment is the use of behavioral genetic methodologies to investigate the etiology and effects of perceived environment (Rowe, 1981). An obvious but important behavioral-genetic method is to study environmental influences free of hereditary confound by assessing environmental relationships in adoptive families, in which the family environment but not heredity is shared by family members. The influence of heredity in putative environmental relationships can be evaluated by comparing environmental effects observed in adoptive families to those found in nonadoptive homes (Plomin & DeFries, 1983). Our major limitation in the application of behavioral genetic strategies to the study of environmental influences is the dearth of instruments to measure the environment (Wachs & Gruen, 1982).

Although it might seem difficult to obtain samples useful for behavioral-genetic analyses, it has been my experience that it is easier to gather a sample of twins or adoptees than it is to recruit samples of singletons (with the exception of the ever-present and captive college sophomore). Twins and adoptees are "special" and immediately understand why they are needed for research. One of every 85 births is a twin birth (Plomin et al., 1980), and it is said that 1% of the children in the United States have been adopted by families who are not biological relatives (Mech, 1973). Moreover, there are clubs and registers that can be used to assist in recruiting a sample (see Nance, 1978). For example, mothers of twins clubs exist in all major cities of the United States to serve two purposes: to support mothers of twins in their difficult task of rearing their children, and to assist in research (Maxey, 1978). Older twins can be located through school directories. Similarly, associations of adoptive parents are common (nearly all adoptive parents nowadays tell their children that they are adopted), and progressive adoption agencies are sometimes willing to send information about research projects to adoptive parents and solicit their participation. Although abortion, contraception, and "black market" adoptions have drastically reduced the availability of newborn adoptees since the early 1970s, the fact that many children were adopted in the 1950s and 1960s makes it relatively easy to study adoptive families whose children are now adolescents or adults.

I believe that behavioral genetic methodologies have much to offer any researcher interested in individual differences in intelligence. For example, with a twin design, one could study any variable of interest, treating the twins as individuals (and getting a bonus of two children per family). After completing the primary analyses, the researcher could then add another important dimension to the results by conducting a classical twin analysis of the data. Moreover, other methodologies described in this chapter, such as multivariate genetic-environmental analyses, could also be applied to the data. Adding a behavioral genetic perspective to any research design takes an important first step in the direction of understanding the etiology of individual differences.

# REFERENCES

Baker, L. A., DeFries, J. C., & Fulker, D. W. (1983). Longitudinal stability of cognitive ability in the Colorado Adoption Project. *Child Development, 54,* 290–297.

Benzer, S. (1973). Genetic dissection of behavior. *Scientific American, 229*, 24-37.

Bessman, S. P., Williamson, M. L., & Koch, R. (1978). Diet, genetics, and mental retardation interaction between phenylketonuric heterozygous mother and fetus to produce nonspecific diminution of IQ: Evidence in support of the justification hypothesis. *Proceedings of the National Academy of Sciences, 78*, 1562-1566.

Bouchard, T. J., Jr., & McGue, M. (1981). Familial studies of intelligence: A review. *Science, 212*, 1055-1059.

Caruso, D. R. (1983). Sample differences in genetics and intelligence data: Sibling and parent offspring studies. *Behavior Genetics, 13*, 453-458.

Cattell, R. B. (1982). *The inheritance of personality and ability*. London, England: Academic Press.

Collins, A. C. (1981). A review of research using long-sleep and short-sleep mice. In McClearn, G. E., Deitrich, R. A., & Erwin, V. G. (Eds.), *Development of animal models as pharmacogenetic tools* (DHHS Publication No. (ADM) 81-1133). Washington, DC: U.S. Government Printing Office.

Corley, R. P., DeFries, J. C., Kuse, A. R., & Vandenberg, S. G. (1980). Familial resemblance for the Identical Blocks Test of spatial ability: No evidence for X linkage. *Behavior Genetics, 10*, 211-215.

DeFries, J. C., Johnson, R. C., Kuse, A. R., McClearn, G. E., Polovina, J., Vandenberg, S. G., & Wilson, J. R. (1979). Familial resemblance for specific cognitive abilities. *Behavior Genetics, 9*, 23-43.

DeFries, J. C., Plomin, R., Vandenberg, S. G., & Kuse, A. R. (1981). Parent-offspring resemblance for cognitive abilities in the Colorado Adoption Project: Biological, adoptive, and control parents and one-year-old children. *Intelligence, 5*, 245-277.

DeFries, J. C., Vandenberg, S. G., & McClearn, G. E. (1976). The genetics of specific cognitive abilities. *Annual Review of Genetics, 10*, 179-207.

Dudai, Y., Jan, Y. N., Byers, D., Quinn, W. G., & Benzer, S. (1976). Dunce, a mutant of *Drosophila* deficient in learning. *Proceedings of the National Academy of Sciences, 73*, 1684-1688.

Eysenck, H. J., & Kamin, L. (1981). *The intelligence controversy*. New York: Wiley-Interscience.

Farber, S. L. (1981). *Identical twins reared apart: A reanalysis*. New York: Basic Books.

Fisher, R. A. (1918). The correlation between relatives on the supposition of Mendelian inheritance. *Transactions of the Royal Society of Edinburgh, 52*, 399-433.

Fuller, J. L., & Thompson, W. R. (1978). *Foundations of behavior genetics*. St. Louis, MO: C. V. Mosby.

Galton, F. (1875). The history of twins as a criterion of the relative powers of nature and nurture. *Journal of the Anthropological Institute, 6*, 391-406.

Ho, H-Z., Foch, T. T., & Plomin, R. (1980). Developmental stability of the relative influence of genes and environment on specific cognitive abilities during childhood. *Developmental Psychology, 16*, 340-346.

Housman, D., & Gusella, J. (1980). Use of recombinant DNA techniques for linkage studies in genetically based neurological disorders. In Gershon, E. S.,

Matthysse, S., Breakefield, X. O., & Ciaranello, R. D. (Eds.), *Genetic research strategies for psychobiology and psychiatry.* Pacific Grove, CA: Boxwood Press.

Hunkapiller, T., Huang, H., Hood, L., & Campbell, J. H. (1982). The impact of modern genetics on evolutionary theory. In Milkman, R. (Ed.), *Perspectives on evolution.* Sunderland, MA: Sinauer Associates.

Jencks, C. (1972). *Inequality: A reassessment of the effect of family and schooling in America.* New York: Basic Books.

Jensen, A. R. (1980a). *Bias in mental testing.* New York: Free Press.

Jensen, A. R. (1980b). Uses of sibling data in educational and psychological research. *American Educational Research Journal, 17,* 153–170.

Jensen, A. R. (1982). Reaction time and psychometric g. In Eysenck, H. J. (Ed.), *A model for intelligence.* Berlin, West Germany: Springer-Verlag.

Jinks, J. L., & Eaves, L. J. (1974). IQ and inequality. *Nature, 248,* 287–289.

Li, C. C. (1975). *Path analysis—a primer.* Pacific Grove, CA: Boxwood Press.

Loehlin, J. C. (1978). Heredity-environment analyses of Jencks's IQ correlations. *Behavior Genetics, 8,* 415–436.

Loehlin, J. C. (1979). Combining data from different groups in human behavior genetics. In Royce, J. R. (Ed.), *Theoretical advances in behavior genetics.* The Netherlands: Sijthoff and Noordhoff International.

Lubs, H. A. (1983). X-linked mental retardation and the marker X. In A. E. H. Henry, & D. L. Rimoin (Eds.) *Principles and practice of medical genetics, Vol. I.* New York: Churchill Livingstone.

Maxey, J. E. (1978). The interaction of researchers and M.O.T.C. In Nance, W. E. (Ed.), *Progress in clinical and biological research,* (Vol. 24B), *Twin research: Part B. Biology and epidemiology.* New York: Alan R. Liss.

McCall, R. B. (1983). Environmental effects on intelligence: The forgotten realm of developmental variation within individuals. *Child Development, 54,* 408–415.

McClearn, G. E., & Kakihana, R. (1981). Selective breeding for ethanol sensitivity: Short-sleep and long-sleep mice. In McClearn, G. E., Deitrich, R. A., & Erwin, V. G. (Eds.), *Development of animal models as pharmacogenetic tools* (DHHS Publication No. (ADM) 81-1133). Washington, DC: U.S. Government Printing Office.

McKusick, V. A. (1978). *Mendelian inheritance in man* (4th ed.). Baltimore, MD: The Johns Hopkins University Press.

Mech, V. (1973). Adoption: A policy perspective. In Caldwell, B. M., & Ricciuti, H. N. (Eds.), *Review of child development research,* (Vol. III): *Child development and social policy.* Chicago, IL: University of Chicago Press.

Merriman, C. (1924). The intellectual resemblance of twins. *Psychological Monographs, 33,* 1–58.

Nance, W. E. (1978). (Ed.). *Progress in clinical and biological research,* (Vol. 24B), *Twin research: Part B. Biology and epidemiology.* New York: Alan R. Liss.

Plomin, R., & DeFries, J. C. (1979). Multivariate behavioral genetic analysis of twin data on scholastic abilities. *Behavior Genetics, 9,* 505–517.

Plomin, R., & DeFries, J. C. (1980). Genetics and intelligence: Recent data. *Intelligence, 4,* 15–24.

Plomin, R., & DeFries, J. C. (1981). Multivariate behavioral genetics and development: Twin studies. In Gedda, L., Parisi, P., & Nance, W. E. (Eds.), *Progress in clinical and biological research*, (Vol. 69B), *Twin research 3: Part B. Intelligence, personality, and development.* New York: Alan R. Liss.

Plomin, R., & DeFries, J. C. (1983). The Colorado Adoption Project. *Child Development, 54,* 276-289.

Plomin, R., & DeFries, J. C. (in press). The origins of individual differences in infancy: The Colorado Adoption Project. New York: Academic Press.

Plomin, R., DeFries, J. C., & McClearn, G. E. (1980). *Behavioral genetics: A primer.* San Francisco, CA: W. H. Freeman.

Plomin, R., & Willerman, L. (1975). A cotwin control study and a twin study of reflection-impulsivity in children. *Journal of Educational Psychology, 67,* 537-543.

Plomin, R., DeFries, J. C., & Loehlin, J. C. (1977). Genotype-environment interaction and correlation in the analysis of human behavior. *Psychological Bulletin, 84,* 309-322.

Rao, D. C., Morton, N. E., Elston, R. C., & Yee, S. (1977). Causal analysis of academic performance. *Behavior Genetics, 7,* 147-159.

Rao, D. C., Morton, N. E., & Yee, S. (1974). Analysis of family resemblance. II. A linear model for familial correlation. *American Journal of Human Genetics, 26,* 331-359.

Rao, D. C., Morton, N. E., & Yee, S. (1976). Resolution of cultural and biological inheritance by path analysis. *American Journal of Human Genetics, 28,* 228-242.

Rose, R. J., Harris, E. L., Christian, J. C., & Nance, W. E. (1979). Genetic variance in nonverbal intelligence: Data from the kinships of identical twins. *Science, 205,* 1153-1155.

Rose, R. J., Miller, J. Z., Dumont-Driscoll, M., & Evans, M. M. (1979). Twin-family studies of perceptual speed ability. *Behavior Genetics, 9,* 71-86.

Rowe, D. C. (1981). Environmental and genetic influences on dimensions of perceived parenting: A twin study. *Developmental Psychology, 17,* 203-208.

Rowe, D. C., & Plomin, R. (1981). The importance of nonshared ($E_1$) environmental influences in behavioral development. *Developmental Psychology, 17,* 517-531.

Scarr, S., & McCartney, K. (1983). How people make their own environments: A theory of genotype → environment effects. *Child Development, 54,* 424-435.

Scarr, S., & Weinberg, R. A. (1978). The influence of "family background" on intellectual attainment. *American Sociological Review, 43,* 674-692.

Sternberg, R. (1977). *Intelligence, information processing, and analogical reasoning: The componential analysis of human abilities.* Hillsdale, NJ: Lawrence Erlbaum Associates.

Thorndike, E. L. (1905). Measurement of twins. *Archives of Philosophy, Psychology, and Scientific Methods, 1,* 1-64.

Tolman, E. C. (1924). The inheritance of maze-learning ability in rats. *Journal of Comparative Psychology, 4,* 1-18.

Turner, G., & Opitz, J. M. (1980). Editorial comment: X-linked mental retardation. *American Journal of Medical Genetics, 7,* 407–415.

Tyler, P. A. (1969). A quantitative genetic analysis of runway learning in mice.
Unpublished doctoral dissertation, University of Colorado.

Wachs, T., & Gruen, G. (1982). *Early experience and human development.*
New York: Plenum.

Wilson, R. S. (1978). Synchronies in mental development: An epigenetic perspective. *Science, 202,* 939–948.

Wilson, R. S. (1983). The Louisville Twin Study: Developmental synchronies in
behavior. *Child Development, 54,* 298–316.

Wright, S. (1931). Statistical methods in biology. *Journal of the American Statistical Association, 26,* 155–163.

# Author Index

*Italics* indicate bibliographic citations.

## A

Ahmavaara, Y., 81, *94*
Aitken, M., 117, *137*
Algina, J., 66, 69, *94, 97*
Allen, T. W., 213, *221*
Althauser, R. P., 91, *94*
Alwin, D. F., 82, *94*
Amatruda, C. S., 223, *244, 293*
Ames, E., 226, *245*
Anastasi, A., 80, *94*, 105, *136*
Andersen, E. B., 115, 117, 118, 124, *137*
Anderson, J. E., 223, *242*
Anderson, K., 250, *296*
Anderson, T. W., 66, 75, *94*
Andrews, S. R., 255, 259, *292*

## B

Bahrick, L. E., 233, *242*
Baker, L. A., 312, *316*
Baker-Ward, L., 248, *295*
Baltes, P. B., 92, *94*
Bargmann, R. E., 72, *94*
Bartels, B., 226, *244*
Baumeister, A. A., 141, *152*
Bayley, N., 223, *242, 263, 293*
Bechtoldt, H. P., 79, 80, *94*
Belmont, J. M., 141, *152,* 202, 203, 206,
    207, 210, 211, 212, 213, 219, *221*
Bent, D. H., 27, *57*
Bentler, P. M., 71, 72, 75, 91, *94*, 168, *176*
Benzer, S., 299, *317*

Bereiter, C., 256, 288, *292*
Bergman, L. R., 81, 93, *97*
Bergstrom, L. I., *242*
Berkson, G., 141, *153*
Bessman, S. P., 298, *317*
Bias, R. G., 168*n, 177*
Binet, A., 104, 106, *137*
Bloom, B. S., 249, 250, *293*
Bloxom, B., 81, *94*
Blumenthal, J. B., 255, 259, *292*
Blunden, R., 247, *295*
Bock, R. D., 72, *94,* 117, *137*
Bond, J. T., 256, *295*
Bonett, D. G., 75, *94*
Borders-Patterson, A., 247, 257, *296*
Boring, E. G., 157, *176*
Borkowski, J. G., 202, 213, *221*
Bornstein, M. H., 229, *242*
Bouchard, T. J., Jr., 304, *317*
Brainerd, C. J., 213, *221*
Brazelton, T., 223, *242*
Bridger, W. H., 233, 235, *244, 245*
Broman, S. H., 257, *293*
Brooks, M. R., 256, *294*
Brooks-Gunn, J., 235, *244*
Brown, A. L., 202, *221*
Brown, W., 106, *137*
Bryant, D. M., 255, 269, *293, 295*
Budoff, M., 27, *56*
Burchinal, M. B., 269, *293*

# Subject Index